Walt Disney World for Couples

1999–2000

Rick and Gayle Perlmutter

PRIMA PUBLISHING

To our mothers,
who taught us how to enjoy life.
And to our children,
who we hope learned it from us.

We'd like to thank the following people for their help in making our book what it is: Jennie Hess, Beth Patkoske, Rebecca Grinnals, Laura Mancine, Dan Higgins, Karen Haynes, Laura Christian, Troy Knight, Deanne Gabel, Jackie Olazabel, Rochelle LaMontagne, Mamoud Dhonany, Linda Rubino, Doug Smith, Jim Browder, Kris Clinton, Quentin Schofield, Amy Hebert, Denise Villanueva, Clark Corey, Robert Sais, Deborah Robinson, Dee Ruckert, Valerie Fetzner, Amy Foley, Kristin Weymeyer, Lisa Burrows, Eileen Costigan, Chris Frakes, Clyde Min, Treva Marshall, Sybaris Del Hoyo, Tori Rogers, Rebecca Michaels, Wayne Wincey, and the patient folks at WDW Central Reservations.

ISBN 07615-1633-6
ISSN 1091-5850

98 99 00 01 HH 10 9 8 7 6 5 4 3 2 1

Printed in the United States of America

Maps by Rick Perlmutter

The prices herein reflect 1999 figures. Rates for resorts, prices for meals, and ticket costs are all subject to change by Walt Disney World.

This book is not affiliated with, sponsored by, or licensed by Walt Disney World.

How to Order

Single copies may be ordered from Prima Publishing, P.O. Box 1260, Rocklin, CA 95677; telephone (916) 632-4400. Quantity discounts are also available. On your letterhead, include information concerning the intended use of the books and the number of books you wish to purchase.

Visit us online at www.primapublishing.com

Contents

PART 3

The Ultimate Romance at Walt Disney World

What This Guidebook Is All About

Forget everything you know about Walt Disney World. There's more to it than just the world's greatest theme parks. Much more. Luxury resorts, world-class wining and dining, golf, tennis, hot tubs, beaches, spas, and a brand-new world of dazzling nightlife all combine to make Walt Disney World the ultimate adult playground. Add a healthy dose of Florida sunshine and you get one of the world's most unique and exciting vacation destinations.

Whether you are a couple going to Walt Disney World to celebrate your honeymoon (it's the number one honeymoon destination in the world), your anniversary, or simply to celebrate being in love, this is the guidebook for you. If you are a couple with children looking for a vacation that means both family fun *and* romantic times together, then this is the *only* guidebook for you. And if you still think Disney World is just a place for children, then let this book be your wake-up call. It's not just for kids anymore!

The Romance of Walt Disney World

"What's the most romantic thing about Walt Disney World?"

This is the question that we are asked most often. We used to reply by describing one of our favorite romantic adventures: a private fireworks cruise, a stroll on the beach at sunset, an intimate dinner at a fine restaurant, a midnight soak in a hot tub, or an afternoon at the spa. There were other adventures too, but we never quite felt that any one of them captured what was so romantic about a Disney World holiday.

Like all great vacations, the romance really begins with *where* we are staying, and it is this that makes the Disney experience so sublime. Not merely "places to stay," the luxurious Walt Disney World resorts are concoctions designed to transport you to a fantasy world. Each resort tells a story, and a stay there will immerse you in that tale. There is the turn-of-the-century opulence of the Grand Floridian, the South Seas adventure of the Polynesian, the Beach Club's early American holiday at the shore, the romance of Old New Orleans, or the high-timber quest of the Wilderness Lodge. There are others, too, and their experiences are unique, interesting, and fun. Our answer to the above question is now simple and sure: What's the most romantic thing about Walt Disney World? It's the resorts.

But there's more to Walt Disney World than just the resorts. Much more. For us, a trip to Disney means live jazz after a fine dinner, a boat ride at sunset, a stroll along the World Showcase, a picnic lunch in a wildlife sanctuary, all the excitement of a parade, the enchantment of the Studios Animation Tour, and the thrills of Splash Mountain. For incurable romantics such as ourselves, Disney is the perfect place to make an exit from the real world and its demands. It is the last word in resorts and, for couples, a real land of enchantment.

There's so much to do at Walt Disney World that to go there without a plan would be like going to Europe with nothing more than plane tickets. If we could give you only one bit of advice, it would be to learn about what is available and then carefully decide what parts of Disney you want to include in your vacation.

What Kind of Disney Vacation Do You Want?

There's so many different things to do at Walt Disney World that the first question you should be asking yourselves is "What kind of vacation do we want?" Disney World's offerings are nearly limitless. Of course, there's the obvious theme park vacation. But you can also make yours a relaxing one by staying in one of the luxurious Disney resorts, enjoying the pool, the fine dining and pampering, and simply dropping by the parks each day for a few hours of excitement. Or you can make yours a nightlife holiday. Focus yourselves on all the magic and excitement of the new Downtown Disney and its theaters, nightclubs, fine dining, great shopping, and entertainment. Are you sports lovers? Make your Disney holiday a sports special. Golf, tennis, boating, horseback riding, fishing: Disney has all this and more. And if watching sports is your thing, there's Disney's Wide World of Sports, winter home to the Atlanta Braves and training site for the Harlem Globetrotters. There's always a sporting event going on here, from championship tennis to the NFL Experience.

Looking for a romantic getaway? If you have never imagined that Walt Disney World is romantic at all, then we have a surprise for you. "Hidden" inside the Walt Disney World that everyone else visits is an unforgettably romantic place, one that is the perfect destination for lovers. This is the Disney that we have come to know and enjoy. It's a place we go to relax, delight in each other's company, and have fun together. And quite honestly, there's no place like it.

What We Can Do for You

This book will help you with virtually every phase of your Disney vacation. Since where you will be staying will be one of the most important elements of your time together, we have created the most complete guide to the Walt Disney World resorts ever written. And it now includes our experiences aboard the *Disney Magic,* Disney's brand-new cruise ship.

We will help you select the resort that best suits your needs and guide you through every phase of planning your special time at Disney, to make your vacation an easy one. We'll tell you how to find the level of comfort, convenience, and luxury that suits you both.

And since you don't have a gold mine in your backyard, we'll show you how to get as much for your money as possible. If by chance you do have a gold mine in your backyard or if you are planning that once-in-a-lifetime event, we will give you the whole lowdown on the very best Disney has to offer. And how suite it can get! We will show you how to plan the ultimate Disney experience. For the last word on anniversaries, weddings, or honeymoons, Disney is *the* place. In our guide to Disney's Fairy Tale Weddings, we'll show you the options available for a unique, unforgettable Disney wedding. We will also describe some of the weddings that have been staged at Disney, from the small and intimate to the lavish and extravagant.

Wondering if you should opt for a package or make all of your own plans? We'll give you enough information to make this decision with confidence. Traveling with the kids? No problem. You can still have a wonderfully romantic time. We will tell you everything you need to know about doing things as a family and how to get away on your own for those special times together. From family-sized accommodations to unforgettable children's activities, we'll make your family romance trip a special and memorable one.

And once you have arrived, we will help you avoid the pitfalls common to Disney visitors. We'll help you find your own rhythm that will keep the two of you feeling comfortable, pampered, and relaxed: three of the ingredients essential to romance.

For your dining adventures, we have gone beyond anything done before. We will provide you with first-hand information about the World's many wonderful dining establishments. We have seen, done, and eaten it all, and if you are looking for the rarest of steaks, the freshest of fish, or simply the best cup of coffee, we'll let you in on all of our secrets.

For your Disney adventures, you'll get some real insider information, the kind of stuff that you can get only by spending a lot of time looking for it, which is exactly what we have done. From the Animal Kingdom to waterskiing, from Star Tours to wine flights, from high tea to fireworks cruises, we promise not to leave a Disney stone unturned. Looking for that something special? An exotic dinner, a stroll along a quiet beach at sunset, or a quiet cafe for lunch? If you expect Walt Disney World to be more than just some great rides, then take a good look at what we have written here.

If you are lovers of any age, looking for the time of your lives, then this guidebook is for you. Take the "road less traveled," the path to a magical and romantic adventure. Let us show you the Walt Disney World for lovers.

Finding Romance at Walt Disney World

Daylight was fading as we made our way across the deserted beach. The blazing reds and brilliant ochers of the fleeting sun ignited the fiery clouds and spilled onto the lagoon, setting it afire with shimmering lights. The sand beneath our bare feet still held the warmth of the day. Hand in hand, we passed empty cabanas to a large swing, where we sat together, savoring those final moments of daylight.

Dinner at a nearby restaurant had been elegant and intimate. We had decided to kick off our shoes and find some place to enjoy the sights and sounds of the evening when we discovered the secluded swing. We watched the boats make their way across the lagoon. We could hear the people aboard them, laughing and talking. Their voices and the thrumming of engines faded as the boats disappeared in the distance. There was something special about being here, away from everything. It seemed dreamy and blissful.

We sat silently, swinging slowly. This was a contentment so powerful that we simply shared it in a knowing silence. Just when we were sure that it couldn't possibly get better, fireworks began to flash in the sky across the water. We could hear the dull thuds of rockets as they exploded over Cinderella Castle, igniting the sky with clouds of gold and showers of red. Huge and brilliant flowers of sparks blossomed in the darkening sky only to be carried gently away in the breeze. We squeezed each other's hands just a bit harder.

It *was* a special moment for us. Relaxing, romantic, *magical.* It was that kind of moment that we take vacations hoping to find. If we were going to rate it as a romantic experience, we would consider it special and sublimely romantic.

Romance is a personal thing, and we do not pretend to know what will make everyone experience it. We do feel that there are ingredients conducive to romance, as well as elements that are incompatible with it. This kind of intimacy can occur when you are alone on a beach at sunset, or it can happen in a crowded theater. It is a special feeling of closeness that transports you together to a place away from the everyday. It is something special and out of the ordinary, that seems to occur just for the two of you.

As you read through this guidebook, look for heart symbols (♥). The more ♥'s you see, the more likely we think you will be able to ignite this chemistry. We have tried to savor a place for its ability to enhance our own feelings of togetherness, for its potential to elevate us above the everyday and to let us know that this special thing is happening just for us. Not surprisingly, Disney has a real knack for creating these moments. Sometimes romance just happens, and sometimes we can help it happen.

♥	**A hint of romance**
♥♥	**An air of romance**
♥♥♥	**Intimate and enchanting**
♥♥♥♥	**Unforgettable, sublimely romantic**

Also look for the NEW symbol. These mark those things at Disney that are new to this book or restaurants that have totally new menus. The symbol will be your guide for budget tips.

List of Maps

PART I

What You Can Do Before You Leave Home

CHAPTER 1 

Making the Decisions

In this chapter, we'll get you started on planning your Disney vacation, on making it more relaxed and, we hope, setting the stage for some real romance. We'll help you make the big decisions: when to go and where to stay. If you are making your romantic holiday a family affair, we'll give you lots of information about bringing kids: the special accommodations for families, and how the two of you can get off by yourselves for some special time together. We will also describe the many tickets and passes, the variety of discounts available, and how to fit everything into your budget. In short, we'll help you do everything you can do *before* you leave home to make your Disney vacation all that it can be.

A Work in Progress: What's New at Disney

OK, so this year we're *not* going to tell you what a big year for change it's going to be (even though it is). We realize now that we repeat this year after year. And for good reason: Walt Disney World is as much a process as a place. Always looking for new and better things to do, the Disney Imagineers are constantly adding new attractions and tinkering with old ones. If you think Disney World is the same year after year, you should try writing a guidebook. The Disney process is one of continually new displays, rides, resorts, and restaurants. Menus are constantly being freshened, existing shows are being improved, and shops are offering new and better merchandise.

1998–99 will best be remembered as the opening year of Disney's Animal Kingdom, the long-awaited fourth theme park. Expect to see new attractions arriving here on a regular basis during the coming years. There will be new rides, new lands, and the Animal Kingdom Lodge, a resort overlooking a wild animal savanna.

Debuting in the Magic Kingdom this year is The Enchanted Tiki Room: Under New Management, which is a brand-new version of a Disney World favorite, and Buzz Lightyear's Space Ranger Spin. Disney–MGM Studios will see the opening of a spectacular nighttime light and music show called Fantasmic!, the Copperfield Magic Underground restaurant, the Rock'n Roller Coaster, and a new animation studio tour. At Epcot, we expect to see Test Track open after nearly a year of disappointing delays. Also new at Epcot will be a totally redesigned Coral Reef Restaurant.

Downtown Disney will continue its exciting expansion with the Cirque de Soleil circus, DisneyQuest interactive entertainment center, the Wildhorse Saloon, the Copperfield Magic Underground—The Store, and the BET SoundStage Club.

Other premiers include Cítricos restaurant at the Grand Floridian, the All-Star Movies Resort, and the long-awaited Disney Cruise Line. Then in October of 1999, Disney will begin its 15-month-long Millennium Celebration. And of course, there will be New Year's Eve 1999. We'll tell you more about these things later.

When to Go

When the two of you head off to Disney, you will discover more seasons there than the old and familiar summer, fall, winter, and spring. These seasons describe the weather, but the Disney seasons take into account other important considerations such as crowds, holidays, and special events. Simply stated, when Walt Disney World is busiest, the resort rates are highest. When it is slowest, the resorts offer lower rates. From most expensive to least, you will find the following seasons: holiday, peak, regular, and finally, value season, the least expensive of all.

There is a slight difference in seasons from one resort group to another, and we have outlined it below, along with the features of each season. The following dates are for 1999:

Holiday, Peak, and Regular Seasons

- More people, bigger crowds, longer lines
- Few, if any, discounts
- Peak season rates are higher than regular season rates, and holiday season rates are higher than either
- During these times, parks open early and stay open later
- Numerous special events, such as fireworks and parades

For Value, Moderate, and Wilderness Lodge Resorts

- Holiday season: December 26 through December 31
- Peak season: February 12 through April 24
- Regular season: April 25 through August 28

For Deluxe, Home Away from Home Resorts, and Fort Wilderness Campsites

- Holiday season: December 26 through December 31
- Peak season: February 12 through April 24
- Regular season: April 25 through July 4

Value Season

- Fewer people; every place is less crowded
- Rates are lower and there are numerous special rates, offers, and discounts
- Parks open later in the day and close earlier
- Fewer special events such as fireworks and parades

For Value, Moderate, and Wilderness Lodge Resorts

- January 1 through February 11
- August 28 through December 25

For Deluxe and Home Away from Home Resorts

- January 1 to February 11
- July 5 to December 25

Good Times to Visit

During the course of the year, there are many special and seasonal events. Whether it's the Fourth of July or Chinese New Year, the folks at Disney love a party. Most of these events are memorable. Besides the usual holidays are celebrations of Mother's Day, Mardi Gras, a spring garden festival, a summer swing music celebration, and even a winter kite festival. For more information and dates of special events, call Disney Information at (407) 824-4321. If you are planning to visit Disney World on a big holiday, such as Independence Day, be forewarned: park attendance hits record highs on these days.

Our favorite time of year has always been during the three weeks after Thanksgiving and before Christmas. At least several of the deluxe

Disney resorts offer greatly reduced rates, and the World is dressed in its finest holiday attire. There are special events, such as the Jolly Holidays Dinner Show, nightly tree-lighting ceremonies, wandering carolers and musicians, and the Very Merry Christmas Party. It is beautiful, festive, and fun. During these weeks, you may enjoy all the benefits of the holiday season without the crowds.

Other times of year attract fewer people as well. The week following Labor Day is the slowest of the Disney year. January to early February are good months and the weather is generally quite nice. The final week of August, though hot, is not usually crowded. The entire fall, except for Thanksgiving weekend, is a wonderful time for a Disney visit.

OUR RECOMMENDATIONS

- If possible, go during value season.
- Take advantage of numerous resort discounts, smaller crowds, and discount vacation packages.

New Year's Eve 1999 and the Millennium Celebration

The Disney Imagineers have big plans for the Millennium, and if you are thinking about going, we have some good news and some bad news. The bad news is that as far as New Year's Eve 1999 is concerned, the Disney Resorts have been booked-up for years. The good news is that this event is going to be such a big deal that the party is going to last for the entire year.

While specific plans for either New Years Eve 1999 or the 15-month-long Millennium Celebration have not yet been finalized, we do know that there are many people involved in the planning. The year-long celebration will center around Epcot and will include a new nighttime spectacular with fireworks, music, and special effects. Exceptional entertainment and exhibits of breakthrough technologies will be part of this daily event, which will begin in October of 1999 and continue throughout the first year of the new millennium.

As for New Year's Eve 1999, plans are just now being made for parties in all of the hotspots of Disney. We have heard that there will be a huge gala at Pleasure Island and suspect that similar parties will be happening at the BoardWalk's Atlantic Dance, the California Grill, and Downtown Disney. Reservations will likely be a must so keep your ears open for announcements and be ready to make your plans early.

TIPS FOR NEW YEAR'S EVE 1999

- At the time we go to press, rooms are still available at many of the hotels along Hotel Plaza Boulevard and at the Swan and Dolphin. Know that, like the Disney Resorts, rates are high and that certain minimum stays are required.
- Check with Central Reservations very early in 1999 to see what may be available for parties.
- Given the magnitude of this event and that Disney World will be completely booked-up, expect Epcot to be extremely crowded on this night. We would expect that the gates will close early in the day on December 31, 1999, to all but Disney Resort guests.
- September 1999 marks the month that full payment of resort reservations is due. We would expect some cancellations at this time, although we suspect that these rooms will not be released for the general public. It may be worth a try, however.

Weather

Weather-wise, central Florida is a mixed bag, encompassing all of the four seasons without the severity of, say, New England. Although this past winter was unusual due to El Niño, winters at Disney are usually cool and balmy with occasional cold snaps. If you are coming from colder climes, you will likely find the winter weather at Disney World to be most agreeable. Summers in Florida range from hot to HOT. Spring and fall land somewhere in between with a mix of warmer and cooler days, a sort of leftovers time.

OUR SUMMER RECOMMENDATIONS

- Prepare for heat: brings lots of light, loose clothing, hats, and bathing suits.
- Make full use of Disney pools and water attractions.
- Be ready for brief afternoon thundershowers.

OUR WINTER RECOMMENDATIONS

- Expect any kind of weather except very hot; be prepared clothing-wise; try layering clothes.
- Don't forget your bathing suits: most pools and water attractions are heated, and there are always the hot tubs.
- Avoid holidays or college break periods, to keep crowds low.

OUR SPRING AND FALL RECOMMENDATIONS

- Pack for almost any weather except very cold or very hot.

Here's a month-by-month look at weather and crowds:

January

Weather: Usually cool nights and balmy days but be prepared for occasional cold spells. Average high: 70°. Average low: 50°.

World Conditions: After January 1, everything slows down beautifully. Value season all month. An excellent time for a romantic visit.

February

Weather: A very likely month for wintery cold snaps. Still, February can be a nice month for weather. Expect more balmy days and cool evenings. Average high: 72°. Average low: 51°.

World Conditions: Attendance is lower through the first week and average for the remainder of the month. Things begin to pick up a bit in the last few days of February. Value season lasts until about the eleventh of this month. After this, the peak season begins and runs until about April 24. Parks are open late for the busy Presidents' Day week.

March

Weather: March can be a blustery month with a mix of weather. It's usually one of the wetter winter months. Rarely will March be very cold. Average high: 76°. Average low: 56°.

World Conditions: Attendance begins to pick up, getting busy during the spring break season. This month is all peak season.

April

Weather: This is a nice month! The climate is usually breezy, with warm days and balmy nights. Average high: 82°. Average low: 60°.

World Conditions: The weekend of April 4, 1999, is Easter. Busy peak season until April 24, then regular season.

May

Weather: A month of pretty good weather. The days become warmer than April but only occasionally does it get really hot. This is spring in central Florida. Average high: 88°. Average low: 66°.

World Conditions: Fewer crowds and wonderful spring weather make this a great time for your romantic Disney getaway. Just watch out for the busy Memorial Day weekend and you'll have it made. Regular season all month.

June

Weather: Summer begins to arrive and with it . . . HEAT. Evenings are still fairly pleasant. Average high: 90°. Average low: 71°.

World Conditions: The first week is not too crowded, but after that, watch out. School gets out, the summer season begins full-tilt, and the hoards arrive. It is still regular season all month.

July

Weather: This is summer—expect it to be HOT. Afternoon thundershowers are fairly common. Average high: 92°. Average low: 73°.

World Conditions: Summer is in full swing now, and Disney World is about as crowded as it gets. The weekend of the fourth is the busiest of the year. If there is one month to avoid, this is it. Regular season all month in moderate and value resorts; the value season for deluxe and home away from home resorts begins after the first week.

August

Weather: This is definitely a hot month: hot days, hot nights. A good chance of afternoon thundershowers, too. Average high: 92°. Average low: 76°.

World Conditions: The first two weeks are very busy and then the crowds begin to leave. By the last week of the month, things are starting to get pretty nice. Regular season lasts until about the third week for moderate, value, and Wilderness Lodge resorts; value season all month for the other resorts. It's still hot but getting to be a good time to visit, due to fewer people.

September

Weather: Don't forget, it's still summer here in Florida, which means more hot days and hot nights. Also, the rainy season begins. This mostly means afternoon thundershowers, not the monsoons of India. Average high: 89°. Average low: 72°.

World Conditions: The week after Labor Day is the slowest week of the year at Walt Disney World. The rest of the month is also slow: few crowds, short lines. Value season all month long.

October

Weather: Still warm, but the real heat of the summer has passed. Nights are beginning to get balmy. Average high: 82°. Average low: 68°.

World Conditions: A nice month for a visit. The weather is pleasant and the crowds are still elsewhere. Another month of discounts: it's value season.

November

Weather: The weather is really starting to get nice now. Days are balmy and evenings are cool. Don't forget your bathing suit. Average high: 76°. Average low: 57°.

World Conditions: This is a nice month to visit, with few crowds until Thanksgiving week (a good week to stay home). After this: our favorite time of year. Value season all month.

December

Weather: This is usually a very nice month but occasionally cold. Average high: 72°. Average low: 52°.

World Conditions: Crowds are less than normal until about December 18. After this, the World is very crowded. Swimming suits are still useful, especially in a hot tub. Value season until December 25, then it's expensive holiday season.

Deciding Where to Stay

Yes, this is the big decision. Selecting where to stay will set the backdrop and mood of your entire visit. Convenience, luxury, and even romantic atmosphere are all very much related to your resort.

Basically, you have two choices if you are visiting Walt Disney World: you can stay inside the World or you can stay outside. Inside, known to cast members (the Disney Folks) as "on-property," means staying in one of the many and varied Disney resorts. Staying outside, or "off-property," means staying in one of the many hotels or motels located in the surrounding areas, such as Kissimmee, Lake Buena Vista, or Orlando.

There are, indisputably, many fine hotels and even a few resorts in the areas surrounding Walt Disney World. Many of them may be cheaper than staying inside Disney, but they all share one thing in common: they are *not* in Disney World.

Outside, you will be staying at least several miles from the fun. Even though an off-property motel may advertise that it is "five minutes from Disney," this doesn't mean that it will take you only five minutes to make the trip. The motel may actually be a five-minute drive from Disney's front gate, but by the time you add parking, walking, traffic, and a host of other impediments, we seriously doubt that you will be able to leave your off-property room in the morning and get to the park of your choice in less than 45 minutes.

If you stay off-property, you'll quickly discover that all of this going back and forth eats up valuable vacation time. And staying outside usually means that it isn't very practical to drop back to your hotel room for an hour's rest or an afternoon together. If you are driving, the dense crowds at the gates in the morning and at closing time spell H-A-S-S-L-E.

If this doesn't sound so discouraging, consider what it is like to stay inside Disney. Every bed on property is located in what Disney calls a "themed resort." At a Disney resort, you'll find yourselves the pampered guests of lodgings that have been carefully themed to enfold you in the very Disney magic that you have come looking for. Each Disney resort has its own specially designed atmosphere. Everything at Dixie Landings, for example, reflects the Mississippi River theme of the resort. The look of the resort, the Bayou cuisine of its restaurants, the dress of the cast members, the room furnishings—everything down to the smallest detail enriches that theme. Each resort is designed to enhance your Disney visit, to make it easier and more fun. Once you have left the theme parks and returned to your resort, you will not feel as though you have left Disney World. It will mean exciting days and luxurious and intimate nights.

And this is really just the beginning. Disney resort guests get special benefits such as early admission into the theme parks, special passes, and full use of Disney transportation.

But, you are thinking, it costs a fortune to stay at a Disney resort. Not true. There are now Disney resorts for most every budget, with prices beginning at $74 per night. There are campsites, trailers, suites, multiroom villas, treehouses, vacation homes, and much more. There is a tremendous offering of truly nice places in a range from $119 to $250 per night, and up to $1,600 for the Roosevelt Suite at the Grand Floridian (yes, that's per night!).

OUR RECOMMENDATIONS ON WHERE TO STAY

- Stay on-property. It will make for a more relaxing vacation. You'll have the time to see more of Disney and to do it without the frustration of traffic jams, long lines at park entrances, and a lot of time spent coming and going. We are convinced that staying at a Disney resort will make a more memorable vacation. If you've already done it, you know what we are talking about.
- If you feel like you simply must stay off-property, we suggest that you do your homework first. Find out exactly how much it will cost and precisely what you will get for your money. Extra persons and miscellaneous charges might bring up the price of your bargain room more than just a few dollars.
- To make your Disney resort stay more affordable and to get just the room you want, make an extra effort to make your plans as far in advance as you can. Disney resorts will actually take reservations *years* in advance.

The Disney World of Discounts

Disney offers a large variety of discounts for both resorts and vacation packages. Experience has shown us, however, that these discounts must be pursued. They are usually not widely advertised or generally known. With a bit of research, though, you should be able to find something that suits your needs.

To begin with, discounts are affected most by the season. Of course, we are talking about value season. During the regular, peak, and holiday seasons, discounts become hard to come by and, if you are able to get one, it will not be as large as during value season. So, if you are looking for a deeply discounted resort or package rate, begin by planning an off-season visit.

The following sections describe sources of Disney discounts.

Disney Central Reservations Office (CRO)

Yes, discounts are available through the regular reservation process, and to get one you must ask your reservationist about specials or discounts for the dates that you have selected. Remember that most discounts are scheduled for value season. Try a variety of dates to see what you can get. Call Disney Central Reservations at (407) W-DISNEY (934-7639).

The Magic Kingdom (MK) Club

Membership to the Magic Kingdom Club is available to state employees (usually any state), employees of hospitals, large corporations, or businesses, and often university employees. Check with your employer's human resources or personnel department to see if one is available for you.

If you are not eligible, you may purchase a Magic Kingdom Club Gold Card for $65. Persons over 55 and Walt Disney Company stockholders may purchase the Gold Card for $50. The Gold Card offers the same discount as the Magic Kingdom Club, with a few extras. Gold Card membership is good for two years.

The Magic Kingdom Club is the most widely used discount. Using it can mean big savings. Even if you have to pay the $65 for a Gold Card, you will likely discover that the card will pay for itself in a single visit, especially during value season. Call or write:

Magic Kingdom Gold Card
P.O. Box 3850
Anaheim, CA 92803
(800) 893-4763

DISCOUNTS AND PRIVILEGES

- Disney resort discounts up to 10% or 20% on select resorts for select dates and for select vacation packages.
- Other discounts include admission tickets and passes, golf, dinner shows, select theme park restaurants, merchandise at Disney stores nationwide and shops at Downtown Disney, and Disney Cruise Lines.
- Gold Card membership includes a two-year subscription to *Disney Magazine,* a tote bag, luggage tag, and newsletter.

American Express

If you book a Disney package vacation for a deluxe resort through American Express, you'll get a host of worthwhile features. For details, call American Express Disney Reservations at (800) 297-2849.

DISCOUNTS AND PRIVILEGES

- $250 Disney dollars, worth $250 anywhere at Walt Disney World
- 10% of Disney merchandise at select stores at Walt Disney World
- Mickey 'n You photo
- Free fanny pack
- 10% discount on boating activities and select dinner shows
- 20% discount on select Disney tours and programs
- An assortment of discount coupons

Walt Disney World Annual Passes

The Theme Park Annual Pass is available to anyone willing to spend $299 for it (about $254 for children). Besides providing an entire year's worth of admission to the four theme parks—Magic Kingdom, Epcot, the Animal Kingdom, and Disney–MGM Studios—it can be a source of outstanding resort discounts, during both the regular and value seasons. The Premium Annual Pass adds Discovery Island, the water parks, and Pleasure Island to the admissions. The price is $399 for adults (about $339 for children). There is even a discount on any of the annual passports for both Magic Kingdom Club members and Florida residents.

Only one of you needs an Annual Pass to get the resort discount, and you may book your discounted room before you even buy it. Just be prepared to present either your pass or its voucher at check-in. To obtain information and book reservations for Annual Pass discounts, call Disney Central Reservations and tell them you are a pass holder. Discounts during value season are always greater than those offered during regular season. Call Disney Central Reservations at (407) W-DISNEY (934-7639).

DISCOUNTS AND PRIVILEGES

- A hodgepodge of seasonal resort discounts, some very good. Discounts may be as much as 50% off regular resort rates.
- Bearer gets unlimited admission to the four theme parks for one full year.
- Seasonal "Mickey Monitor" newsletter with discount dining coupons and advance notice of special events.
  - Special renewal prices for pass
  - 10–15% discounts on select Disney tours
  - 10% discount on Richard Petty Driving Experience "Rookie Experience"
  - 20% discount at Seasons Dining Room at the Disney Institute

American Automobile Association (AAA)

Because this organization functions as a travel agency, it offers a variety of resort and package discounts to its members. Some are quite good. These are worth looking into.

DISCOUNTS AND PRIVILEGES

- Resort rate and vacation package discounts (available to AAA members only)

Delta Airline Dream Vacations

Delta is the official airline of Walt Disney World and offers its own assortment of Disney vacation packages. Some are on-property, and others are not. These are sold in conjunction with airline tickets, usually to Orlando. Because Delta's packages and promotions change throughout the year, we suggest that you call for their current offerings. Call Delta Airlines Dream Vacations at (800) 872-7786.

DISCOUNTS AND PRIVILEGES

- A variety of vacation packages that include airfare with Delta

Your Local Travel Agent

Several years ago, Disney began discounting vacation packages to travel agents. This has enabled travel agents everywhere to be competitive in a previously closed market.

Florida Resident Discounts

Mickey loves Floridians. After all, he lives in Florida, doesn't he? A number of benefits are afforded to Florida residents. Usually offered during value season, discounts include resort rates, packages, and admission tickets. If you are Florida residents planning a visit, you will certainly wish to take advantage of one. Simply call Disney Central Reservations at (407) 934-7639 and ask when Florida residents' specials are being offered.

These discounts are available to anyone with a Florida driver's license or other proof of residency, such as a rent receipt or a utility bill. Disney also offers discounted Theme Park Annual Passes and Premium

Annual Passes for Florida residents and even Magic Kingdom Florida resident discount passes.

The **Florida Resident Seasonal Pass** is one of the best bargains for Floridians. It provides unlimited admission to all four theme parks for an entire year from first use, excluding mid-June to late August, the Christmas holiday season, and around Easter. The price is a mere $159 ($135 for ages 3 to 9). This pass also entitles the bearer to the same resort discounts available to Annual Pass holders. It's a great deal.

The **After 4 P.M. Epcot Pass** is another ticket for Florida residents. For $69 ($59 for ages 3 to 9), owners of this pass can visit Epcot on any evening for a full year.

The Disney Dining Experience This little-known organization is for Florida residents only. Membership, which is priced at around $40, provides a 20% discount in a large selection of Disney restaurants and half-price admission to Pleasure Island. This includes both food and alcoholic beverages and is good for the cardholder's entire party. It also entitles the bearer to buy tickets to a series of Disney Dining Experience special dining functions scheduled throughout the year. If you are a Florida resident and enjoy dining at Walt Disney World, this card will pay for itself in short order. Call (407) 828-5792 for information.

DISNEY DISCOUNT TIPS

- Be comparative shoppers. Look around for the best deal. Check out every source possible. Be persistent.
- Don't pass up a good deal waiting for a great one. You can make a reservation and cancel it later when a better deal arrives.
- When talking with a CRO reservationist, be sure to ask a lot of questions. Carefully explain what you are looking for. These people know a lot, but they also seem trained to not offer the cheapest alternative unless you ask for it.
- For best-room availability, try calling Central Reservations around 10 A.M., eastern time. This really works.
- Book early and book during value season.

Admission Options: Which Ticket Is for You?

Although you don't have to purchase your attraction tickets before you get to Walt Disney World, you'll want to know enough about what options are available so you'll know which best suit your needs.

If you are a couple with children, you'll want to know that children under 3 years of age do not require admission passes to any of the Disney attractions. There is a children's pass for ages 3 to 9 years and a general pass for all other visitors.

Following is the assortment of Disney tickets and passes (note that the prices are subject to change and do not include a 6% Florida sales tax).

One-Day/One-Park Ticket This ticket is the simplest one of all: buy one and get admission to one of the four theme parks for one day only.

- General admission price: $42 ($34 for ages 3 to 9)
- Cost per day: $42 ($34 for ages 3 to 9)

Tips: Good for short visit or to fill in days not covered by other passes. Expensive per day cost.

4-Day Value Pass This pass can save nearly $20 compared to the price of four One-Day/One-Park tickets. It provides one day in each of the theme parks for any four days, and unused days never expire. This pass does not allow park hopping (visiting more than one park in a day).

- General pass price: $149 ($119 for ages 3 to 9)
- Cost per day: $37.25 ($29.75 for ages 3 to 9)

Tips: This is a good deal if it fits your vacation and you can live with no park hopping. Spend additional days at a water park ($26) and/or Downtown Disney (free).

5-Day Park Hopper Pass This pass provides five days of admission to the Magic Kingdom, Disney–MGM Studios, Epcot, and the Animal Kingdom. Visit one or all of these four parks on any of the five days. Unused days never expire.

- General pass price: $189 ($151 for ages 3 to 9)
- Cost per day: $37.80 ($30.20 for ages 3 to 9)

Tips: For only pennies a day more than the 4-Day Value Pass, you get park hopping. Save the extra day if you don't need it.

All-in-One Hopper Pass The All-in-One Hopper Pass provides the pass holder unlimited admission to *all* Disney attractions. This includes all four theme parks, Blizzard Beach, Typhoon Lagoon, Pleasure Island, the Wide World of Sports, Discovery Island, and River Country.

With this pass you can visit any or all of these attractions on any of the days of this pass. Unused days never expire.

- Six-day pass price: $249 ($199 for ages 3 to 9)
  Seven-day pass price: $274 ($219 for ages 3 to 9)
- Cost per day, six-day pass: $41.50 ($33.17 for ages 3 to 9)
  Cost per day, seven-day pass: $39.14 ($31.29 for ages 3 to 9)

Tips: For a few dollars a day more in average cost per day than the 5-Day Park Hopper, you'll get admission to all the rest of the Disney attractions: water parks, Discovery Island, Pleasure Island, and the Wide World of Sports. Save any unused days for your next trip.

Length of Stay Pass Available only to Disney resort guests, this pass provides unlimited admission to *all* Disney attractions for the duration of your Disney visit, no matter the length. This includes all four theme parks, Blizzard Beach, Typhoon Lagoon, Pleasure Island, the Wide World of Sports, Discovery Island, and River Country. The longer your stay, the less the average cost per day. Length of Stay Passes are available for any length of stay. Here's the breakdown for general passes (and for ages 3 to 9), plus the average cost per day:

- One-night/two-day pass price: $111 ($89); cost per day: $55.50 ($44.50)
- Two-night/three-day pass price: $152 ($122); cost per day: $50.67 ($40.67)
- Three-night/four-day pass price: $191 ($153); cost per day: $47.75 ($38.25)
- Four-night/five-day pass price: $219 ($175); cost per day: $43.80 ($35)
- Five-night/six-day pass price: $245 ($196); cost per day: $40.83 ($32.67)
- Six-night/seven-day pass price: $269 ($215); cost per day: $38.43 ($30.71)

Tips: The Length of Stay Pass is the cheapest admission to *all* attractions except for the Premium Annual Pass. Remember that having admission to all the attractions here at Walt Disney World makes financial sense only if you actually *use* them. The Length of Stay Pass could be overkill for a visit of three or fewer days, as it would be hard to make use of all the admission features.

Water Park 1-Day Pass This ticket provides admission to either Blizzard Beach *or* Typhoon Lagoon for one day.

- Pass price: $26 ($21 for ages 3 to 9)

River Country 1-Day Pass This pass gives admission to River Country for one day.

- Pass price: $16 ($13 for ages 3 to 9)

Discovery Island 1-Day Pass This is the Discovery Island one-day admission ticket.

- Pass price: $12 ($6.50 for ages 3 to 9)

Pleasure Island 1-Evening Pass This pass provides admission for one evening to Pleasure Island.

- Pass price: $19; there is also an annual pass for $51.

Disney's Wide World of Sports This ticket gives admission for one day to the Wide World of Sports. Does not include admission to premier or special events.

- General pass price: $8 ($6.75 for ages 3 to 9)

Disney offers a selection of passes for an entire year of admission. Of course, you need to visit often enough to make one worth the investment, although there are annual pass holder discounts for resorts that can help one of these passes to pay for itself. Some of these discounts can be as high as 50% off room prices. For details, see the section on the Disney World of discounts in this chapter.

Theme Park Annual Pass This pass provides unlimited admission to all four theme parks for one year from date of first use.

- Pass price: $299 ($254 for ages 3 to 9)

Tip: If you are going to be spending more than eight days in a given year at Walt Disney World, this pass makes sense.

Premium Annual Pass Providing unlimited admission to *all* Disney attractions except the Wide World of Sports for one year from date of first use, this pass covers all four theme parks, Blizzard Beach, Typhoon Lagoon, Pleasure Island, Discovery Island, and River Country.

- Pass price: $399 ($339 for ages 3 to 9)

Tip: Not counting resort discounts, you'll have to spend a couple of weeks at Disney within one year for this pass to earn its keep. With resort discounts, this pass can pay for itself in a single visit. Try making your next year's visit within the next 12 months. For details on both annual pass holder resort discounts, see the section on the Disney World of discounts in this chapter.

TIPS FOR DISNEY ATTRACTION ADMISSIONS

- The above costs will give you a good picture of the relative expenses of these passes. Unannounced price increases during 1999 are possible, even likely. To get the exact figures for your visit, call (407) 934-7639.
- The Magic Kingdom Club provides discounts on *all* Disney admission tickets and passes, including Annual Passes. See the section on the Disney World of discounts in this chapter.
- To fill in days not covered by your passes, consider spending a day at Downtown Disney. There's plenty of fun there for at least one day. Other options that would save the cost of a theme park ticket would be Discovery Island or one of the water parks.
- See the section in this chapter on Florida resident discounts and the Florida Resident Seasonal Pass.
- All tickets and passes can be purchased at one of the 500 Disney Stores across the U.S. We recommend doing this, as it will eliminate standing in line to get your tickets after you've arrived at Walt Disney World. If you are opting for an annual pass, you'll only be able to get a voucher at the Disney Store and you'll have to stop in a Guest Services at the entrance to one of the theme parks to have it turned into the actual pass. Tickets and passes can also be ordered by telephone by calling (407) 934-7639.

Vacation Packages: Are They for You?

Like the Disney characters, Walt Disney World vacation packages come in many shapes and sizes. Typically, they include at least room accommodations and admission tickets. Some include much more. Some offer airfare to Orlando and others offer meals as well as unlimited recreation. There are even plans that include virtually everything that you might want to do at Walt Disney World, from golf and boating to spa treatments. There are family packages, cruise packages, holiday packages, golf and sports packages, honeymoon and wedding plans, and the ultimate in vacation experiences, Disney's Grand Plan. This assortment of packages is priced for either value season or regular season.

There are basically two sources for packages to Walt Disney World: the first is independent agents and tour guides, and the second is Disney. Independent packages usually provide accommodations in off-property locations. Many also include air or bus transportation. Most provide Disney admission tickets and frequently little else. This is the type of package deal that you are likely to find in your local newspaper. If you are considering one of them, we can only warn you to be very careful. Off-property accommodations are often not what they're described to be or what they look like in photos. And once you get to Walt Disney World, you may be amazed at what these "all-inclusive" package deals don't include.

Vacation plans created by Team Disney will be our focus. With these, you will be able to stay in one of the many themed Walt Disney World resorts.

The Nuts and Bolts of Packages

Disney vacation plans are figured on a per person, per day cost. Youngsters are accounted for at either of two cost levels: juniors (10 to 17 years old) or children (3 to 9 years old). Children under 3 years of age are free. Different packages and prices are available for the entire spectrum of Disney resorts. If you opt for a vacation package, you should know that after your initial deposit, the complete balance of your package cost is due no later than 21 days before the first day of your vacation.

The first step in the quest for your vacation package should be to call the Walt Disney World Travel Company. Request their catalogue of vacation packages. This booklet will give you all of the basic package combinations and their list prices. To get your booklet, call the Walt Disney World Travel Company at (800) 828-0228.

Walt Disney World Travel Company is not the only source of vacation packages. A growing number of companies and travel agents deal in Disney vacation packages. What they offer and how much they charge vary greatly. Armed with the Walt Disney World Travel Company list price booklet, you will be ready to shop around and select a package that is priced right.

SOURCES OF DISNEY VACATION PACKAGES

- WDW Central Reservations Office (CRO): (407) W-DISNEY (934-7639)
- Walt Disney World Travel Company: (800) 828-0228
- The Magic Kingdom Club: (407) 824-2600
- The Magic Kingdom Club Gold Card (800) 446-5365
- American Automobile Association: call your local AAA travel agent
- Delta Airlines Dream Vacations: (800) 872-7786
- American Express: (800) 297-2849
- Your local travel agent

Three Types of Vacation Packages

There are three basic types of resort packages: the Disney Resort Magic Plan, the Deluxe Plan, and the Grand Plan. The Resort Magic Plan is the most basic and provides accommodations, unlimited admission to all Disney attractions, and one Disney "flex feature" per person, per stay. Flex features include the following:

- Admission to DisneyQuest with 30 play units
- One round of golf at Oak Trail, 9-hole executive course
- Mickey 'n You Photo session
- Resort or character breakfast
- Choice of theme park tour
- Golf or tennis clinic
- *Fantasmic!* Cap
- Choice of logo tee shirt

A five-night Resort Magic Plan for two at the Yacht or Beach Clubs would cost $1,846. To this you could add the Disney Dining Plan, which would cost an additional $55 per adult, per day ($16 per child) and would provide $60 worth of food ($18 for children) at select Disney World restaurants, a savings of nearly 10%. Thus a five-night Resort Magic Plan with dining option for two would cost $2,346. The World of Recreation Plan is no longer being offered.

The other two package plans are "all-inclusive," which means that they include virtually everything but souvenirs. The Deluxe Plan includes accommodations, admission to all Disney attractions, three meals daily in a large variety of Walt Disney World restaurants, and use of Disney recreation, including golf, tennis, motorized watercraft, bikes, and more. A five-night Deluxe Plan at either Yacht or Beach Clubs, for two adults, would cost $3,482.

The Grand Plan provides even more: private golf and tennis lessons, three 25-minute spa treatments at the Grand Floridian Spa ♥♥♥, a day of activities for each person at the Disney Institute, babysitting services, and an IllumiNations fireworks cruise. Dining provisions for the Grand Plan are grand indeed and include virtually all Disney restaurants, even Victoria and Albert's ♥♥♥♥, as well as daily snacks and room service. A five-night Grand Plan at the Yacht or Beach Club would cost $4,211.

The Grand Plan is available only for stays at one of the deluxe resorts, while the Deluxe Plan is available at any resort. A five-night, deluxe Plan for two at the Wilderness Lodge would cost $3,100, at Dixie Landings, $2,750.

Both the Deluxe and Grand Plans would leave you feeling privileged and pampered. The Grand Plan is special and sublime. Expensive, yes, but if you can afford it, either would provide an unforgettable Disney holiday.

Specialty and Seasonal Packages

Besides the three vacation packages, Disney also offers a variety of packages designed both for special interests and for special events. The Golf Getaway features accommodations and one round of golf daily with transportation to any of Disney's six courses. There are packages for the Disney Institute, the Indy 200 auto race, the Night of Joy Christian music celebration, and a host of other events. There is even a baseball school package for the Wide World of Sports (see Chapter 7). From the Epcot Garden Show to the Disneyana Convention, the possibilities are too numerous to list here. For details and dates, call Disney Central Reservations at (407) 934-7639 or Disney Information at (407) 824-4321.

There are also packages for the many seasonal events at Walt Disney World, including the Fall Fantasy package and the winter Sunshine Getaway. Both offer good seasonal discounts. One of our favorites is the Magical Holidays package. Often an outstanding bargain, this package includes accommodations and a choice of one of the World's marvelous holiday events. Choose from Mickey's Very Merry Christmas Party with a dinner at a select restaurant, the Jolly Holidays Dinner Show, or Epcot's Candlelight Processional with dinner at an Epcot restaurant. We have always enjoyed the Jolly Holidays Dinner Show, a real extravaganza and turkey dinner with all of the fixings. The Magical Holidays package usually runs from late November to Christmas.

It is worth noting here that Disney's Dining Plan is available only with the Resort Magic Plan or the Honeymoon Escape (see Chapter 9). It is not available with any of the seasonal or specialty packages.

Are Packages a Bargain?

The first question to ask yourselves about vacation packages is "Can we do better by ourselves?" This can usually be answered by adding up the features of a package plan and comparing the total to what you are able to get on your own. If we were to compare a Resort Magic package with making your own reservations and carefully looking for a bargain room, we'd have to say that the package will most likely cost more.

The all-inclusive packages are, most certainly, expensive. If you make use of all the features, you could actually save money, but if you are thinking about one of these plans as a bargain, you'd be missing the point. The Deluxe and Grand Plans simply provide a special and lavish way to experience the magic of Walt Disney World and allow you to do anything you wish without worrying about how much it costs. This is the real intangible benefit of the all-inclusive plans: the carefree and relaxed feeling either provides. Knowing the total cost up front is one of the real advantages of an all-inclusive vacation plan.

Tip: If you book a Disney package at one of the deluxe resorts through American Express, you'll get a variety of discounts, including $250 Disney dollars (worth $250 at Walt Disney World). For details, see the section on the Disney World of discounts in this chapter.

The Romantic Family Trip

If having children meant the end to romance for married couples, then everyone would be an only child. We hope that if you have children, romance is alive and well in your lives. If it isn't, may this be your wake-up call. With a bit of planning, you will be able to visit Walt Disney World as a family and still have romantic moments for just the two of you.

Making a family trip to Disney World is a large undertaking, one that will take even more planning than a visit for two. It will be more expensive, and there will be a greater number of logistical concerns, especially if you are traveling with very young children or an infant. Consider, though, that it's a free ride for kids under 3 years of age at Disney World. No admission tickets are necessary, they do not count as people in resort rooms, and they eat for free at buffet meals. Walt Disney World has been Imagineered with families in mind. When it comes to meeting the needs of a family, the facilities are nearly limitless.

Making Plans: When to Go

The best time to visit Walt Disney World is during the off-season. Unfortunately, this means while schools are in session. Yes, we are suggesting that you take the kids out of school for your Disney vacation.

Fall is the perfect time for Walt Disney World. It is still early in the school year and it should be an easy time to arrange a short absence. Off-season is also the value season. Resort rates, packages, and admission tickets are all available at discounted rates. While people are still at the parks, they will be significantly fewer in number. You will see much more, do much more, have a more relaxed time of it, and spend less money. Need we say more?

Accommodations: An Even Bigger Decision for a Family

For us, staying off-property with children is even less appealing than doing it by ourselves. There's a lot of travel, a host of logistics, and a lot of lost time. It's a lot easier to get the kids back to a Disney resort for an afternoon of rest than it is to get them back to a motel on Highway 192.

Along with the choice of off-property or on, you will be faced with the decision of how to accommodate all of you. There are more options than you think.

One Family, One Room Sharing a room with your family will not make having a romantic time impossible; it simply makes things more of a challenge. Getting a room in a Disney resort is expensive enough. Getting two may be a fatal blow to an already stretched budget. While we cannot speak for accommodations outside of Disney World, we can tell you that children younger than 17 stay for free at all Disney resorts. Standard resort rooms feature two large beds, and cribs are available at every Disney resort at no extra cost.

Most Disney resorts permit a maximum of four people in each room. The Wilderness Lodge, besides its standard room with two queens, has a number of rooms with one queen bed and a set of bunk beds, which is a more interesting option for a family of four. Many of the deluxe resorts allow five. This is usually managed with two queen beds and a daybed/sofa. Dixie Landings features a trundle bed in many rooms that will accommodate a fifth person, and most of the hotels at Downtown Disney's Hotel Plaza can also sleep five. If you have a family larger than five, you'll have to do something besides share a standard resort room.

One Family, Two Rooms Two rooms is another way to go. All Disney resorts offer connecting rooms, and some feature a room with two beds connected to a room with one king-size bed. This sounds to us like the perfect layout for a small family. If you are considering sharing a room at one of the premium resorts, we would suggest that, for about the same expense, you get two rooms at one of the more moderately priced resorts, such as Port Orleans or the Caribbean Beach, or at Hotel Plaza.

A Suite for a Family Suites offer yet another route to accommodate a family. Virtually all of the premium resorts offer a selection of suites, some with as many connecting rooms as you might care to add. While these can be the perfect place for a family, they are expensive.

Family-Sized Accommodations These are Disney's home away from home accommodations, and each features a kitchen, providing an economical alternative to restaurant dining. For about the cost of a single room at the Yacht or the Beach Clubs, you can get a luxurious one-bedroom villa at either Old Key West or the BoardWalk. Here you can enjoy a washer and dryer, a living room with fold-out queen bed, and your own king-size bedroom. Add to this a balcony and an oversized Jacuzzi tub, and your romance family vacation begins to take shape.

The Villas at the Institute offer another variety of family accommodations. The compact bungalows feature a bedroom with two queen beds and a living room with a sofa, and the Treehouse or Fairway Villas can each sleep six in luxurious and woodsy surroundings for under $400 nightly. Deep discounts are often available off-season, some reducing the prices to that of a single deluxe resort room. On the budget end of the spectrum are the Fort Wilderness Homes or Cabins, both of which can sleep six. Here you can enjoy a double bed in your own room and bunks for the kids. We particularly like the newer Cabins. Another more affordable choice is the DoubleTree Guest Suites in Downtown Disney. These two-room suites can accommodate two adults and two children with ease and are available off-season at very reasonable rates.

All of the Disney home away from home accommodations feature maid service, which includes washing your dishes. Now that's a vacation!

Family Necessities

If you have an infant, bring all the baby supplies that you might need. Though widely available at Disney, choices are limited and prices are high. Extra pacifiers are a good idea. We would also suggest bringing snacks and drinks for the kids. Boxed juice drinks and refillable plastic drink cups with straws will come in handy too. And, if you are able, bring your own folding stroller. While these are easily and inexpensively rentable at the theme parks, you will frequently find yourselves standing in line to get one. Besides, a stroller will come in handy at your resort and at Downtown Disney. Be sure to mark it with your name and your resort.

Kids and Food

Disney knows what picky eaters kids can be. Fast-food outlets seem to specialize in all the favorites. Milk and chocolate milk are available virtually everywhere. Buffets provide a good way for children to find something they want to eat and to try new things. And of course, there are children's menus, even at the fine dining places. These offerings include just the kind of stuff most kids like: burgers, hot dogs, chicken strips, macaroni and cheese, and other finger foods.

You'll also want to know about character meals. Whether for breakfast, lunch, or dinner, these are usually buffets that feature Disney characters who will go from table to table for visits and memorable photos. We've even enjoyed character meals without kids. For more about them, see Chapter 6.

Preparing the Kids

When our kids were young, we took them to Walt Disney World as a surprise. "Let's go out for donuts," we told them as we dragged them out of bed at 6 A.M. All the way to the front gate (it was 120 miles), we pretended that we had no intention of actually going in. We just want to *look* at it, we told them. Meanwhile, the kids whined and cried. By the time we'd gotten our tickets, they were beginning to smell a rat. Or at least, a Mouse.

This was certainly a memorable adventure but, in reality, none of us were prepared for our visit, and pandemonium reigned supreme. We suggest that you do a few simple things to prepare your children for the kind of visit to Walt Disney World that you wish to have. Get them set to enjoy spending some leisure time at the resort and, if you plan to take advantage of the many and varied children's activities, you might prime them for these. We are sure that you know just how to do it.

You might also ask Central Reservations what attractions will be closed (in rehab, as insiders say) during your visit. Better to head off expectations now than later.

Setting Your Pace

Let your family know that this visit will not include spending every waking moment trying to cram in one more attraction. You'll spend plenty of time in the theme parks but you'll also take time to relax around the pool and to explore other areas of Walt Disney World. Take them for a boat ride or explore Discovery Island. Try to keep to your child's regular schedule. If naps are the rule at home, then they should be at Disney too. Try to eat and snack at the normal times. Remember how much energy this kind of stimulation will demand from your children and do your best to keep them rested and therefore happy. This goes for yourselves too.

Logistical Concerns

If you have children, you know what an art it is to travel with them. We always enjoyed finding ways to make travel with our kids easier and more fun. When our children were younger, we traveled so much that they were in correspondence school, but that's another story.

Disney World is built to accommodate families, so you should find facilities for almost every situation. Each of the theme parks has a baby care center where you will find facilities for heating formula, rocking chairs for bottle- and breast-feeding, and an assortment of expensive baby supplies and formulas. Diaper-changing stations are available in both men's and women's restrooms throughout Walt Disney World.

Getting Some Time Alone Together

Being here in "The Happiest Place on Earth" will be paradise for you and your family. There are lots of things to do here together, and there should be no shortage of time to enjoy each others' company. We have always found that being here with our kids somehow made us feel even more like a family. Having this kind of fun together is something that none of you will ever forget. A Disney vacation will bring you nearer to your children and it will make you, as a couple, feel closer. If this isn't romance, we don't know what is.

Still, having time alone together is both natural and healthy for a couple in love. You may wish to spend an evening together, have a romantic dinner and go out for some grown-up entertainment. No problem. Depending on the age of your children, there are a number of alternatives.

If you are traveling with an infant or very young children, KinderCare, Disney's sitting service, will be your best alternative for an afternoon or evening out. With older children, the options increase to include activities ranging from Disney activity centers to educational programs.

KinderCare This service provides in-room baby-sitting and is the only option for children under 4 years of age. We tried this once with our grandkids, Ben and Guin, and the baby-sitter showed up with a bag of toys. The kids felt comfortably at home and by the time we returned, they were having such a good time that they wanted the sitter to spend the night.

Reservations should be made at least 24 hours in advance. Cost is $11 per hour for one to three children, with a four-hour minimum. Charges for four or more children will be dependent on their ages. If you have a sitter for eight hours or more, you will be required to provide a meal. This service is particularly good for younger children and may even be more economical if you have more than one child.

For information or to make arrangements ahead of time, call KinderCare at (407) 827-5444.

Disney Children's Entertainment Centers If your child is at least 4 years old and potty-trained, then one of these "clubs" will be your best bet. Each will provide your child with a memorable evening of entertainment and his or her very own Disney experience. There are six such centers for the children of Disney resort guests. We have heard many wonderful things about them and can tell you, firsthand, that children love them—ours did, during our visit to the Polynesian years ago.

Neverland Club The Neverland Club at the Polynesian is open nightly from 4 P.M. to midnight and features a dinner buffet from 6 to 8 P.M. Foods usually include chicken strips, pizza, hot dogs, and ice cream. Activities include a live animal show from Discovery Island, video games, films, and a picture with Goofy. $8 per hour per child with a four-hour minimum and $6 for each additional child. This imaginative

Peter Pan experience begins with a trip through an open window of Wendy's bedroom and into Neverland—fun and memorable.

Cub's Den The Cub's Den at the Wilderness Lodge also offers a buffet dinner. The cost here, though, is only $7 per child per hour and includes a Discovery Island animal show, video, games, and movies. The menu usually includes hamburgers, hot dogs, pizza, macaroni and cheese, corn on the cob, and peanut-butter-and-jelly sandwiches. Hours are 5 P.M. to midnight, with dinner from 5:30 to 7:30 P.M. Open to guests of all Disney resorts, this western-themed adventure is great for boys and girls.

Sandcastle Club This children's center is located at the Beach Club and is available to guests at the Yacht and the Beach Clubs. While the Sandcastle Club does not include a buffet, it has plenty for kids to do. Computers, video games, a large library, and arts and crafts are a few of the offerings here. Hours are 4:30 P.M. to midnight and cost is $5 per hour per child. Meal arrangements must be made through room service if your child is visiting during mealtime or for more than four hours.

Harbor Club Located at the BoardWalk, this children's activities center features both day and evening programs. Evening programs are for ages 4 to 12, run from 4 P.M. to midnight, and cost $5 hourly per child with a one-hour minimum. Activities include board and video games, Disney movies, supervised arts and crafts, and snack time. Dinner can be arranged at 6 or 7 P.M. for additional cost.

For more information or to make reservations at the above Disney clubs, call (407) WDW-DINE (939-3463).

Mouseketeer Clubhouses There are two Mouseketeer Clubhouses: one at the Contemporary and the other at the Grand Floridian. At $5 per child per hour, these activity centers do not offer as much as either the Cub's Den or the Neverland Club and have facilities for far fewer children. While the clubhouse at the Contemporary is open to all Disney resort guests, the one at the Grand Floridian is available only to its guests. Reservations are strongly suggested and may be arranged through the Mouseketeer Clubhouses at the Contemporary after 4:30 P.M. by calling (407) 824-1000, extension 3038, and through guest services at the Grand Floridian at (407) 824-1666. Dinner is available for an additional charge at the Contemporary and is a must for stays of four hours or longer. There is a four-hour maximum at the Grand Floridian.

Camp Dolphin Both the Dolphin and the Swan offer this program for children, which include arts and crafts, movies, music and books, and other supervised activities. Afternoon camp is $12 per child per hour, from 1:30 P.M. to 4:30 P.M. The Dinner camp runs from 6 P.M. to 11 P.M., and the cost is $45 for one child and a bit less for each additional youngster; dinner in one of the hotel restaurants is included.

Vacation Station Kids Hotel This center at the Hilton features children's activities from 5 P.M. to midnight for ages 4 to 12. Cost is $6 for one child, $11 for two. For Hilton guests only; reservations are recommended.

Kids' Stuff Clubhouse Located at the Buena Vista Palace, this is this resort's headquarters for children's activities and includes meals, games, and arts and crafts. Daytime hours are 9 A.M. to 4 P.M. with costs beginning around $5 per hour. Ask about the Kids' Stuff family packages. In the evening, themed activities are available on Mondays, Wednesdays, Fridays, and Saturdays, 6 to 11 P.M., for $25 per child. Discounts are available to Palace guests who are dining that night at one of the resort's restaurants.

Camp Disney Youth Discoveries

This assortment of children's programs includes hands-on activities, behind-the-scenes locations, and interactions with Disney cast members. Cost is $89 for a two-program day with lunch or $59 for single programs without lunch. For 7- to 11-year-olds the programs featured include Broadway Bound, Face Magic, Discovery Island Kidventure, Swamp Stomp, and Art Surround. Programs for 11- to 15-year-olds are Art Magic, Discovery Island Explorers, Showbiz Magic, The Funny Papers, and Rock Climbing. For information about available times and days and to reserve your child's Camp Disney Experience, call (407) WDW-TOURS (939-8687). We recommend making your plans at least six weeks in advance. American Express cardholders and annual pasholders are entitled to special rates, usually a 10% savings. These plans are included in Grand Plan and Disney Institute vacation packages.

OUR RECOMMENDATIONS FOR ROMANCING WITH KIDS

- Take your vacation during the off-season. It will be less expensive and more relaxing.
- Thoroughly explore the possibilities of getting your own room or your own bedroom. It will make a big difference.

- Keep your pace a relaxed one. Don't wear yourselves out. Spend time at your resort. The kids will play happily in the pool and not get cranky and overtired. Same for you.
- It is important that both of you share the chores involved in taking care of your children. It's no fun for one person to be stuck with all of the work while everyone else is vacationing.
- Be sure to make your reservations for the Entertainment Centers when you book your room, especially for the Neverland Club.
- If you haven't made reservations or if you have more than one child, KinderCare is a good choice.
- Try a family activity such as bike riding or boating. Do something special together.

Taking Your Pet to Disney

If you are traveling with a member of the family who just happens to be an animal, you'll need to know a few important things. First, none of the Disney resorts will allow you to keep your pet with you in your room. The closest you'll be able to get is a pet-designated camp site in Fort Wilderness (for more details, see the section on Fort Wilderness in Chapter 2). If you're not camping, the only choices are one of the five Disney kennels or something outside of Walt Disney World.

There is one Disney kennel at the Ticket and Transportation Center near the Magic Kingdom, another at Fort Wilderness, and one each at Epcot, Disney–MGM, and the Animal Kingdom. There are a total of 700 animal spaces at Walt Disney World. The rules are the same for each kennel: $9 per pet for overnight ($11 for non-Disney guests), and $6 per pet for day boarding. You must bring your pet's current shot record and you will be expected to walk your pet twice a day (three times for puppies). In order to make your pet more at home, it is suggested that you bring the food your pet is used to, and for overnighters, pet beds and toys are also suggested. No farm animals are accepted but the folks here at Disney have had some strange boarders: fish, iguanas, and even a basket of hermit crabs. For details and reservations, call (407) 824-2735.

Doing It All on Your Budget

We are sure that you, like most couples, are planning your Disney vacation to fit a budget. It is important that you know ahead of time how much your Disney vacation is going to cost so that you will be able to enjoy yourselves without worry. Nothing can ruin a vacation like the nagging concern that you are overspending. If you have elected to purchase one of the all-inclusive packages, then you will be enjoying one of its greatest advantages: you will already have a very good picture of what your Disney vacation will cost.

If you are making your own plans, you will have to do some figuring to know what your Disney adventure is going to cost.

The Major Expenses

After the cost of getting to Walt Disney World, the major expenses fall into three categories: resort expenses, admission ticket costs, and food expenses.

Resort Expenses Resort and admission expenses are the expenditures easiest to factor. Take a look at our guide to the Disney resorts in Chapter 2 and see which resort looks good to you. Modest price increases are yearly events at Disney, so you might want to check with Central Reservations to make sure that you have the most current rates. Don't forget to add a combined Florida state sales and resort tax of 11% to your room.

Admission Ticket Costs Admission tickets will also be a simple matter to calculate (see the section on admission options in this chapter). Once you have made your admission choice, you should have a clear figure to deal with.

Food Expenses Figuring your food expenses will be a bit more complicated. Whatever your tastes, you should know that dining out, three meals a day, at Disney World will constitute a significant part of your vacation budget. Just how big a part will depend on you.

It is *possible* for a couple to eat at Walt Disney World for $70 per day. However, it will have to be done carefully. A $70 per day food allowance will require dining largely at the more inexpensive, counter-service restaurants with one moderately priced meal per day. Dining exclusively in the fast-food eateries is not our idea of a romantic vacation.

For a more realistic figure for a couple's food expenses, we suggest planning on $120 per day. Allowing for this amount, you will be fairly free to eat in all of the moderately priced restaurants and even include one or two expensive restaurants during your vacation. Needless to say, a larger budget will mean more lavish meals in fancier restaurants. Please note that this $120 includes gratuities but does not include alcoholic beverages in significant amounts. For tips on where to dine, how to eat at the finer restaurants without spending a fortune, bargain meals, and a host of other information, see what we have to say about the Disney dining experience and the Disney restaurants in Chapter 6. Remember, of the big three expenses, food is really the only one that can be difficult to predict.

Putting It All Together: What Will It Cost?

Now that you have some idea of what the major costs will be, all that remains is to add them up and to see what you can get. To give you a good idea of the scope of possibilities, we have constructed two sample budgets. Don't forget to add your transportation expenses getting to and from Walt Disney World and any other anticipated expenses such as memorabilia, alcoholic beverages, or child care. All prices include tax.

Four-Night/Five-Day Stay for Two at the Beach Club (Peak Season)

Standard view room	$1,394
Resort gratuities	20
Meals and gratuities	600
Length of Stay Passes	465
TOTAL	$2,479

Four-Night/Five-Day Stay for Two at the Beach Club (Value Season), with Annual Pass Discount

Standard view room with 30% pass holder discount	$820
Resort gratuities	20
Meals and gratuities	600
Premium Annual Pass for one	423
Length of Stay Pass for one	232
TOTAL (saves $384)	$2,095

TIPS FOR DOING IT BEST ON A BUDGET

- Take advantage of off-season specials and lower rates to get the most for your money. Plan ahead.
- Book ahead for a value season special to get the best resort rate.
- Try a variety of resorts and admission ticket combinations before making your final decision.

Making Your Resort Reservations

There are over 700 cast members at the Disney Central Reservations Office (CRO) taking an incredible 20,000 reservations daily. The special rates and least-expensive rooms are the first to go, so we suggest that you have plan A, plan B, and even a plan C in the event that your choice is not available. Here are the numbers to call:

Disney Central Reservations Office (CRO) (407) W-DISNEY (934-7639)

Magic Kingdom Club (407) 824-2600 (members only)

Magic Kingdom Gold Card (800) 446-5365 (Gold Card holders only)
- Open 7 A.M. to 10 P.M. (Monday through Friday); 7 A.M. to 8 P.M. (weekends and holidays)
- Reservations for all resorts and Disney vacation packages

Walt Disney World Travel Company (800) 828-0228
- Open 8:30 A.M. to 8 P.M. (Monday through Friday); 8:30 A.M. to 5 P.M. (Saturday)
- Reservations for Disney vacation packages only

Before you make your call, here are some things to think about beforehand:

- Views: A variety of views are available in all of the Disney resorts. Selecting one of these will be part of making your reservations. Expect to pay more for rooms with views of water, castles, and theme parks. Standard view usually means the least scenic one available, often the parking lot or a busy side of the resort. Somewhere between the premium view and the standard view, you are likely to find courtyard views, woods views, and pool views.
- Types of beds: Most resort rooms come with two queen beds or two doubles, but as we have mentioned, there are a number of king-size beds available at most of the Disney resorts. This is the time to reserve one of these if that is your choice. Making a king-size bed reservation usually means that the view cannot be guaranteed. In some resorts a king bed can no longer be guaranteed.
- Room location: In our guide to the Disney resorts in Chapter 2, we describe the various choices of room locations for each resort. If you have a preference for a certain location, you should make this request when you reserve your resort room. Although no guarantee can be made, a mention of this will be attached to your reservation.

- Smoking or nonsmoking room: Be sure to mention your preference when making your call.
- Connecting rooms: If you are bringing your children along, consider a room that connects to your own. Disney reservations can guarantee connecting rooms.
- Discounts or specials: Always ask about specials or promotions when you make your reservations.
- Dinner show reservations: If you're planning on a dinner show, you should make reservations at this time.
- From October to April, if you are interested in playing golf, reserve your tee times when you book your room.
- Children under 17 years of age stay for free in Disney resorts.
- Disney resorts charge extra for more than two adults per room. The charge is $10 per night at the value resorts, $15 per night at the moderates, and $25 per night at the deluxe resorts. There are no extra charges at Old Key West, the BoardWalk Villas, and the Villas at the Institute.
- Special comments: If this is your honeymoon or anniversary, be *sure* to tell your reservationist. This will come up when you check in, and most Disney resorts will do something—usually a card, a rose, or a small gift.

Making Reservations

You will probably want to begin your reservation odyssey by simply gathering the most current information. Once you get a Disney reservationist on the telephone, you will immediately discover that the system is designed to make reservations, not to dispense information. The very first thing that you will be asked for is a date. If you are simply shopping for prices and have no date, pick any date during value season to get those prices, any date during regular season to compare prices, and so forth.

RESERVATION TIPS

- Make your reservations in the morning, around 10 A.M. For some reason, resort availability seems best at this time.
- Keep trying if at first you are unable to get what you really want. There are plenty of cancellations that produce more available rooms.
- A CRO reservationist can act as your intermediary in reserving a suite. Simply call and spell out what you want. There will be some

communicating back and forth, but eventually you'll get what you want. Suite availability is limited.

- Reservations that begin with a value season rate maintain that rate for your entire visit. The lower rate remains good as long as you wish to stay, up to the maximum reservation limit of 30 days. Since some value season discounts can be as much as 50%, simply arriving a day earlier for the last day of value season can pay for several nights of your holiday visit.

What to Bring with You

Don't forget a liberal amount of sunscreen with a minimum SPF of 15 or higher for the summer. The Florida sun can burn you even on an overcast day. We recommend that you not only bring sunscreen but that you *use* it, too.

Be sure that you have a handful of dollar bills for tipping, especially if you are staying in one of the deluxe resorts.

You can always bring your own snacks, liquor, or wine. Ice machines are convenient to all rooms, and an ice bucket and glasses are standard furnishings.

If you are interested in having some of your favorite music in your room, you might want to bring a small portable stereo. It might be just the thing for creating that special mood.

Available Items in Disney Resorts

Housekeeping will be happy to provide you with an assortment of items. Available at every resort, for no charge, will be extra pillows, blankets, iron and ironing board, and hair dryer.

If you need a refrigerator in your room, whether for pleasure or medical reasons, you should know that some resorts charge $5 per day for them and some do not. A limited number of microwave ovens are available at the Grand Floridian. Coffeemakers are standard at the Caribbean Beach and Coronado Springs and come with some of the rooms and suites at the Dolphin and most concierge rooms elsewhere.

Some of the deluxe resort rooms have minibutlers. These small refrigerators are stocked with wines, liquors, soft drinks, candy, and snacks. The selection is impressive. So are the prices.

Each Disney resort has a "general store" section in one of its shops. In this area, you will find sunblock, magazines and newspapers, film, insect repellent, Band-Aids, and a whole gamut of items dealing with everything from a headache to the munchies.

Your First Day at Walt Disney World

On your first day, you'll need to make arrangements to get to your resort. If you are arriving by automobile, you will be delighted to know that the roadways are well marked. Once on property, you will find that Walt Disney World has its own system of road signs. They are large and easy to read.

If you are staying in a Disney resort, all that you really need to know is which resort area your resort belongs to. Simply follow the Florida highway signs to the exit for that area and then follow the red and purple Disney signs to your resort.

If you are flying or taking the train into Orlando, you may be surprised to learn that Disney World is not there. It is 20 miles south, near Lake Buena Vista. Fear not. An entire industry has evolved solely to transport guests from the airport or train station to Disney. You will find a variety of cabs, limousines, and van services that will take you directly to your resort (or not so directly, if that is your wish). Several transportation options are available.

Florida Town Cars is a service that has many repeat users. With a fleet of Lincoln town cars, this company provides a personalized option for getting to the Disney resorts from either the Orlando airport or the Amtrak station. All you have to do is to make arrangements via a toll-free number, and you will be met at the gate by a friendly driver holding a sign with your name on it (we've always wanted to do that). Round-trip fare for five persons or less is $75. Ask for this special Internet rate. You are promised the same driver on both ends of your vacation. We have heard glowing reports of this company. Arrangements and inquiries from out of Florida should be directed to Florida Town Cars at (800) 525-7246. The Orlando number is (407) 277-LIMO (5466). Town car service is particularly personal and even a bit romantic.

Mears is the other company providing a similar service and offers both van and town car service. Van service (round-trip) is $25 for each adult and $17 for each child. Limousine service is $165 round-trip. Arrangements should be made in advance with Mears at (800) 759-5219. A Mears booth can be found at the Orlando International Airport on the second level. Passengers may make arrangements upon arrival at this kiosk. Because this service is used by the Walt Disney World Travel Company for its packages, lines here can get long.

Cab fare from either the Orlando train station or airport to a Disney resort is about $43 each way, making the round-trip fare no bargain.

Getting Your Own Wheels

A rental car is yet another option for transportation between airport and resort. Rental car rates vary greatly during the course of the year, from company to company, and with special deals and packages.

So, is having a car while you are at Walt Disney World a good idea? This is a tough question to answer simply. If you are able to find your way around easily, then it might be a convenience to drive from your resort to other resorts. A car would also come in handy at either Fort Wilderness or the Villas at the Institute. As for us, when on vacation, we prefer to leave the driving to Disney.

If you are flying into Orlando and are planning on renting a car, National, Budget, Avis, and Dollar are located right at the airport and do not necessitate a shuttle or bus ride to get your car.

Arriving at Your Disney Resort

Check-in time at the Disney Resorts is 3 P.M. (4 P.M. at Old Key West and the BoardWalk Villas). If you arrive earlier than this, you'll be able to register, have your luggage put in storage, and get started with your Disney vacation. You'll be able to get your resort cards (see Chapter 2) and admission tickets and return later to settle into your room. On occasion and subject to availability, we've even managed to get into our room early in the day.

Special Requests and Last-Minute Changes

If you were unable to reserve the room that you had wanted, this may be a good time to remedy that situation. When you check in, remember to ask for what might not have been available earlier. While there is no guarantee, cancellations and last-minute changes may pay off.

Your Last Day at Walt Disney World

It seems cruel to have to think about this before you even arrive at Disney, but your last day, like your first, demands a few considerations. Check-out time at Disney resorts is 11 A.M. If you plan to leave Disney World before that time, no problem. Simply get packed up and depart. Give yourselves an hour to get to the airport from your room (add a little more time during a holiday). If you are returning to the train station or to the airport, the process is pretty much the same as arriving.

If you are departing later in the day, morning check-out will mean that you will have to vacate your room no later than 11 A.M. Again, you will be able to place your luggage in storage until you actually leave. Your resort ID cards and Length of Stay Passes will be good until midnight of your last day, so you will be able to carry on with your Disney adventures.

Late Check-Out

Disney resorts are usually able to grant a 1 P.M. check-out each day for a limited number of rooms. These two extra hours can make a big difference. If you want late check-out, call the front desk at your resort on your last night to see what that resort's policy is. There is no late check-out at either Old Key West or the BoardWalk Villas.

Some Things You Might Need to Know

A Few Tips on Gratuities

For some reason, tipping situations tend to make both tipper and tippee uncomfortable. However, knowing when to tip and what amount is appropriate should alleviate the awkwardness.

- Cab, limo, town car drivers: 15%
- Valet parking: $1 to $2
- Bellpersons: $.50 to $1 per bag
- Housekeeping, maid service: $1 to $2 per day
- Room service: 15% included in bill, add more as desired
- Housekeeping, delivery: $1
- Table-service restaurants: 15%–20%
- Buffet restaurants: 10%
- Cocktail service: 15%–20%

Banking Around Walt Disney World

Running out of cash at Walt Disney World should pose no problem (as long as you are still solvent). Banking facilities and automated tellers are convenient and numerous. There are ATMs in the lobbies of each resort except the BoardWalk, where you'll find it on the promenade near Wyland Gallery. At the theme parks, you'll find one near each park entrance. Both Epcot and the Magic Kingdom have several others, and there are four ATMs at Downtown Disney, two on the West

Side and one in each of the other areas. All can be easily located on the guidemaps for each park and Downtown Disney.

Banking facilities can be found at several locations:

- For full service, try Sun Bank on Buena Vista Boulevard, directly opposite the Downtown Disney Marketplace.
- Foreign currency is exchanged at the Guest Services of all four theme parks. Also at the Sun Bank and at all Disney resort front desks.
- Disney resort front desks will cash personal checks for all resort guests.

Food Shopping

If you are staying in one of the many Disney home away from home lodgings that offers a kitchen or even if you are simply looking for a place to buy beverages and snacks, you'll probably need a supermarket. While the Gourmet Pantry at the Downtown Disney Marketplace is certainly handy for limited groceries, lots of baked goods, and a good selection of wines, it is expensive. An alternative is not far away: Gooding's Market is a large and modern supermarket located at the Crossroads Shopping Plaza at the end of Hotel Plaza Boulevard. To find it, drive a bit past the Downtown Disney Marketplace until you come to Hotel Plaza Boulevard. Turn onto it and continue through the intersection at Route 535 and into the shopping plaza. By the way, you'll still be on Disney property.

CHAPTER 2

Our Guide to the Walt Disney World Resorts and the Disney Cruise Line

Over the years and our many stays in the resorts of Walt Disney World, we've discovered that it's not easy to have a favorite. Each year, as we visit in search of what's new and improved, we marvel at Disney's ability to get it right. Each of these resort creations is a masterpiece of detailing and theming. "So well done, so well done" seems to be our mantra as we make the rounds.

Yes, each of the Disney resorts is perfectly conceived and each has so much to offer that is unique, entertaining, and memorable. Beautiful landscaping, engaging architecture, and quality are the hallmarks of the Disney resorts, and constant refurbishing, upgrading, and redecorating keep each in splendid condition. We honestly believe that staying on-property makes for a better, more relaxing, and "more Disney" vacation. If you are skeptical about what we are saying, we can only tell you to give it a try. After a stay in one of Walt Disney World's fabulous resorts, we think you'll be a convert.

For your Disney resort vacation, you'll want to know as much as you can about them all before deciding which is the one for you, and we know how difficult that is to do before actually staying in them. How convenient each is to the parks and to the attractions that *you* will be visiting, the atmosphere of its guest rooms, what kind of facilities are offered, where in the resort you should book your room, and what kind of room you should book are just a few of the many things you'll wish to know ahead of time.

This chapter is an inside look at the fabulous resorts of Walt Disney World. We have made the effort to stay everywhere and most places many times. We have firsthand experience with suites, villas, and virtually every kind of lodging available. We do not rely on surveys, press releases, or the judgments of others. We have simply been there ourselves, seeking out what is special for your Disney vacation. Our dogged determination to get it right is, we think, what sets ours apart from the other guide books.

Services Available to Disney Resort Guests

Certain services are provided by all of the Disney resorts. Note that although they are on Disney property, the Dolphin, the Swan, Shades of Green, and the seven hotels along Hotel Plaza at Downtown Disney are not Walt Disney World resorts. Therefore, the following discussion of available services will not apply to these establishments, although they may well offer such services. See the following descriptions of each of these resorts for its list of available services.

Resort ID Cards

When you check into your Disney resort, you will each receive a resort ID card. These plastic cards will be your tickets to unlimited use of the Walt Disney World transportation system and free parking at any of the attractions, and, if guaranteed with a credit card, they will be your Disney credit cards. Your resort cards will allow you to cover your Disney expenses virtually everywhere simply by charging everything right to your room account. If you purchase a Length of Stay Pass, these cards will admit you to all of the Disney attractions. From fast food and fine dining to transportation and theme park admission, you simply won't believe how easy and magical these cards will make your vacation.

On the morning of your departure, or at any time during your visit, a fully detailed bill can be prepared to give you a complete picture of what you have spent. These cards are valid from check-in or preregistration to midnight on the day of your departure.

The Length of Stay Pass

For Disney resort guests only, this pass provides unlimited admission to all Disney attractions for the exact length of your Disney vacation. It is the least costly pass that will provide daily admission to *all* Disney attractions for just the days of your vacation.

Surprise Mornings

The Surprise Mornings program is a powerful perk that will admit you to a different theme park each day, 90 minutes before the general public. For more details, see Chapter 4.

The E-Ticket Express

Magic Kingdom E-Ticket Express is available only to resort guests with either Length of Stay, Park Hopper, Seasonal, or Annual passes. This $10 ticket admits the bearer to three hours of riding the big ones after closing time on select dates. Rides open include Space Mountain, Splash Mountain, Big Thunder Mountain Railroad, Pirates of the Caribbean, Alien Encounter, The Haunted Mansion, the Astro Orbiter, Country Bear Jamboree, and Timekeeper. Lines are very short and tickets are very limited. See Guest Services for available dates and your E-Tickets.

Guest Services

This essential service, usually located in the lobby or main building of each resort, will be invaluable in planning and executing your stay at Walt Disney World. You can go to Guest Services to buy tickets or to make your reservations for dinner, tennis, golf, or for entertainment. Guest Services will also be your source of Disney information. Brochures, menus, and schedules for virtually everything are available here. Whether you want to know the time for a parade or ignition time for a fireworks show, your Guest Services should have it all.

The Resort Newspaper

Each resort has its own little themed information "newspaper" that you should receive at check-in. The Polynesian's paper is the "Island Palm Press" and Dixie Landings' newspaper is called "The Sassagoula Times." Each paper will give you lots of information about your resort, its restaurants and shops, and its services. We suggest that you read the one for your resort so that you'll be familiar with what's available to you and where and when you'll find it.

The Refillable Resort Cup

Each of the Disney resorts offers its own logo thermal cup. It's a quality and useful souvenir, and with it you get refills at your resort's fast-food outlet. At the All-Star, Caribbean Beach, the Contemporary, the Wilderness Lodge, the Polynesian, and Coronado Springs, refills of soft drinks, tea, and coffee are free for your length of stay. Refills are discounted at Dixie Landings and Port Orleans and with drink prices starting near $2, it won't take long for this cup to earn its keep.

Romance Photo Session ♥♥♥

Take a stroll with a Disney photographer and bring home an album of the two of you in your favorite Disney locations. Included are 20 professional-quality color photographs in a deluxe album with Cinderella Castle on the cover. This is the perfect memento for a

Disney honeymoon. Cost is $275. This photographic service also includes a Family Portrait Around the World, with prices beginning under $300. Reservations for these services should be made before arrival at Walt Disney World. For more information or to make arrangements, call Disney Photographic Services at (407) 827-5029.

First Aid

Emergency service and in-room health care are available on a 24-hour basis. Guests are responsible for any charges.

Wake-up Service

If you need to be up early, simply press the appropriate button on your room telephone to arrange a wake-up call. You won't believe who will call to wake you.

Wheelchairs

Each Disney resort has a limited number of wheelchairs for the use of its guests. There is no charge, but a credit card guarantee is required. The chair may be used everywhere throughout Walt Disney World and can be kept throughout the length of your visit.

Additional Services

- Guest messaging system
- Pager rental
- Walt Disney World Foreign Language Center
- Same-day dining reservations by telephone
- Four full-service barber and beauty shops
- Luggage assistance
- Overnight use of Walt Disney World kennels; for information, call (407) 824-2735
- Package delivery to your resort room from any Disney shop
- Sunday church services held at Luau Cove at the Polynesian
- Children's activities centers and in-room baby-sitting
- Coin-operated laundry and laundry service
- Quality two-hour film developing
- Walt Disney World Florist is available to deliver a variety of floral arrangements, food baskets, and wine or champagne to any Disney resort room, including your own; call (407) 827-3505. Send someone you love a rose.

Types of Disney Resorts

There are four types of Disney accommodations: deluxe, moderate, value, and home away from home. Each has unique offerings and each has its own price range.

As you would expect, the rooms are larger and have more lavish furnishings in the deluxe, full-amenities resorts. "Amenities" mean services, and here at Walt Disney World, you will get what you pay for. The grounds and lobbies of the deluxe resorts are the most lavish and elaborately styled. The choices of dining and recreational activities are always greater at the deluxe resorts. These accommodations offer room service as well as bell service, and many provide a nightly turndown as well. Some even feature luxurious bathrobes for guests. With the exception of the Dolphin, deluxe resorts offer either two queen-size beds or a single king (the Dolphin features a choice of two doubles or a single king). Most deluxe resorts rooms also include a daybed.

While the moderate accommodations do not enjoy quite this level of luxury, rooms are comfortable, well appointed, and, though not as large as rooms at the deluxe resorts, lodgings are still spacious. Moderate resorts offer either two double beds or a single king.

Theming at the moderate resorts is always enchanting. Dining options here typically mean one table-service restaurant and a food court. Recreational offerings, while not as extensive as the deluxe resorts, are usually quite good.

The value resorts, while offering yet smaller rooms and simpler furnishings, still manage to be themed and quite "Disney." Rooms feature either one king bed or two doubles. Resort grounds and pool areas are all exciting but, besides swimming pools, recreational offerings are minimal. Value resorts offer only food courts.

All the accommodations of the home away from home category offer some type of kitchen, either a wet bar with small refrigerator and microwave oven or the whole works. Many include accommodations for an entire family, and a host of these lodgings even feature complete kitchens, washers and dryers, and entertainment centers.

There is, we feel, one important advantage to staying in a deluxe resort. Here, the entrance to each room is through a hallway inside the resort. This makes for large windows that look onto landscaped grounds, often onto a lagoon, a forest, or even a castle; most include a balcony or patio. Home away from home accommodations also offer a high degree of privacy, some with even a degree of seclusion. The moderate and value resorts, on the other hand, have outside walkways. Windows look onto these and, with curtains open, the result is a loss of privacy. Neither the moderate nor value accommodations feature balconies or patios.

Deluxe Resorts

Prices begin at $180 per night.

- Disney's Contemporary Resort
- Disney's Polynesian Resort
- Disney's Grand Floridian Resort and Spa
- Disney's Yacht Club and Beach Club Resorts
- Disney's Wilderness Lodge Resort
- The Walt Disney World Swan and Dolphin
- Disney's BoardWalk Inn

Moderate Resorts

Prices range from $119 to $184 per night.

- Disney's Port Orleans Resort
- Disney's Dixie Landings Resort
- Disney's Caribbean Beach Resort
- Disney's Coronado Springs Resort

Value Resorts

Prices range from $74 to $104 per night.

- Disney's All-Star Music Resort
- Disney's All-Star Sports Resort
- Disney's All-Star Movies Resort (opening January 1999)

Home Away from Home

Prices begin at $179 per night.

- Disney's Old Key West Resort
- The Villas at the Disney Institute
- Disney's Fort Wilderness Resort
- Disney's BoardWalk Villas

Concierge Service

Available at most of the deluxe resorts, this service is known by many seasoned travelers as "the hotel within a hotel." A comfortable lounge with day-long offerings of snacks, beverages, hors d'oeuvres, and wines is the usual service. Some concierge areas offer even more. Concierge rooms are usually located on a private floor and offer such upgraded amenities as sumptuous bathrobes, fancy toiletries, and a private desk staff dedicated and knowledgeable in making your stay go as smoothly as possible. Once, while staying at the Royal Palm Club concierge at the Grand Floridian, we requested dinner reservations for 7 P.M. at Narcoossee's. The computer said "no," but our concierge wasn't about to disappoint us. A phone call to the restaurant, and our reservation was assured. We've even had the concierge staff have a watchband repaired, get us a birthday card signed by Mickey Mouse, and set up a Christmas tree in our room.

Of course, concierge service will add to the cost of your day's stay. But is it worth it? We love concierge service and think that it can be a good choice for a family, as the lounges all offer continental breakfasts that include cold cereals and milk. You'll have to decide for yourselves if this and the rest of the perks are something for you. If you are looking for something truly special though, we'd recommend this wonderful upgrade.

The Resorts by Area

There are four resort areas at Walt Disney World. Each occupies its own little piece of Disney turf, and each has a unique offering of resorts.

THE MAGIC KINGDOM RESORTS

- Disney's Polynesian Resort
- Disney's Contemporary Resort
- Disney's Grand Floridian Resort and Spa
- Disney's Wilderness Lodge Resort
- Disney's Fort Wilderness Resort and Campground
- Shades of Green

It should come as no surprise that all of the Magic Kingdom resorts are near the Magic Kingdom. If you want to be as close as possible to Cinderella Castle, than take a careful look at this group. The Grand Floridian, the Polynesian, and the Contemporary are all right on the famous monorail loop that runs around the Seven Seas Lagoon. Although they're nearby, the Wilderness Lodge, Fort Wilderness, and Shades of Green do not enjoy a location on the Seven Seas Lagoon. Shades is located over on the golf courses near the Polynesian, and both the Wilderness Lodge and Fort Wilderness Resort and Campground can be found on Bay Lake, not far from the Contemporary.

THE EPCOT RESORTS

- Disney's Yacht Club and Beach Club Resorts
- Disney's BoardWalk Inn and BoardWalk Villas
- The Walt Disney World Swan and Dolphin
- Disney's Caribbean Beach Resort

Except for the Caribbean Beach, these are all deluxe resorts, and all surround Crescent Lake and are adjacent to Epcot and Disney–MGM. Convenience to both parks, the BoardWalk Promenade, and Fantasia Gardens is as good as it can get. Bus service to all other Disney destinations is outstanding. Without a doubt, this is our favorite corner of Walt Disney World. The Caribbean Beach is a short distance away and is a charming, moderately priced resort.

THE ANIMAL KINGDOM RESORTS

- Disney's Coronado Springs Resort
- Disney's All-Star Sports Resort
- Disney's All-Star Music Resort
- Disney's All-Star Movies Resort (opens January 1999)
- Disney's Animal Kingdom Lodge (opens 2001)

These were once the Studio Resorts, but with the opening of Disney's Animal Kingdom and with their proximity to it, this name change seems natural. Besides the Animal Kingdom, the resorts here are convenient to Blizzard Beach, the new McDonalds's, Fantasia Gardens, the BoardWalk, and Disney–MGM Studios.

THE DOWNTOWN DISNEY RESORTS

- Disney's Port Orleans and Dixie Landings Resorts
- Disney's Old Key West Resort
- The Villas at the Disney Institute
- Buena Vista Palace Resort and Spa
- Courtyard by Marriot
- DoubleTree Guest Suites Resort
- Grosvenor Resort
- The Hilton
- Hotel Royal Plaza
- Travelodge Hotel

With the opening of the fantastic Downtown Disney, a new resort area has been created to encompass the nearby resorts on the east side of Disney World. Please note that the last seven on the list are not Disney owned and operated. They do, however, provide unequaled convenience to the excitement of Downtown Disney, the Disney Institute, and to the Lake Buena Vista golf course as well as a few other advantages we'll discuss later.

The Magic Kingdom Resorts

Disney's Polynesian Resort

One of the most popular of the Disney resorts, the Polynesian is a fanciful recreation of the South Seas. It was Walt Disney World's first resort (it opened two weeks before the Contemporary), and it was also our first experience staying on-property. Having enjoyed a recent refurbishing, this wonderful creation is even more beautiful now than it was on the day it first opened. In the last few years, under the careful direction of a general manager who is a native Hawaiian, it has been reborn to better represent the real cultures of the South Pacific rather than an imaginary Disney version. The resort and grounds have now been decorated with colorful Polynesian paintings and sculpture, and even the room decor tells a story in authentic designs and colors of South Seas fabrics. The resort also features authentic Polynesian storytellers, "Island Guides," a torch lighting ceremony, a luau, and coconut races for the kids. It's all designed to entertain and to educate, and it is what Disney does so well.

Located on a pristine white sand beach directly across the lagoon from Cinderella Castle, the "Poly" enjoys one of the most spectacular views in all of Walt Disney World. It is an exciting and romantic place to visit. The lush grounds of this resort have over the years grown dense with tropical foliage. Candlenut trees, gardenias, banana trees, hibiscus, and orchids are but a few of the more than 75 species of exotic plants that make this resort a veritable garden. Its many meandering footpaths invite an evening stroll, and we can tell you it is a magical one. The flickering torches, balmy lagoon breezes, and scents of flowering foliage all combine to create a potent piece of Polynesia. Kick off your shoes and walk along the lagoon to discover the quiet beach areas at either end of the resort. Here you will find hammocks and bench swings where you can relish a few quiet moments alone late in the evening.

The Great Ceremonial House lies at the center of life in Disney's South Seas. It is surrounded by a profusion of exotic plants and fish

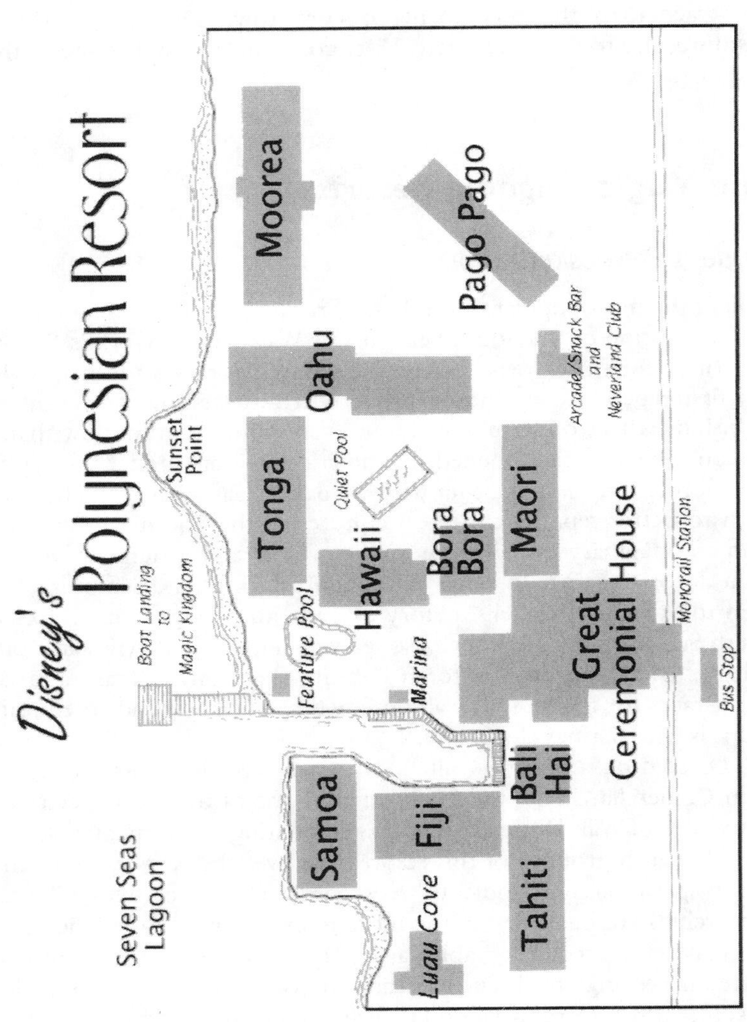
Disney's
Polynesian Resort
Seven Seas Lagoon
Boat Landing to Magic Kingdom
Sunset Point
Moorea
Oahu
Tonga
Quiet Pool
Pago Pago
Arcade/Snack Bar and Neverland Club
Maori
Bora Bora
Hawaii
Feature Pool
Marina
Great Ceremonial House
Monorail Station
Bus Stop
Bali Hai
Samoa
Fiji
Tahiti
Luau Cove

ponds. Native statues stand sentry at the entrance. Inside, the mingling of Hawaiian music and rushing water set the stage for your Polynesian adventure. Mammoth hewn beams and woven bamboo are the makings of this place, all trimmed carefully with hanging baskets of brightly colored orchids and birds of paradise.

The centerpiece of the Great Ceremonial House is its towering garden of palms, volcanic rock, and splashing water. It reaches to the domed glass ceiling three stories above. The gurgling waterfalls, brilliant blossoms, and verdant foliage produce a sensation that is both cool and soothing. Large wooden ceiling fans spin slowly, and a pair of brightly colored scarlet macaws squawk in the branches of a tree.

The Great Ceremonial House is home for this resort's front desk, Guest Services, shops, and several of its restaurants and lounges. "Aloha" is the usual greeting here at the Polynesian, where there is a Hawaiian word for nearly everything. The real theme of this tropical paradise may be best expressed by "Ho'Onanea," which means the passing of time in ease, pleasure, and peace.

The Polynesian's guest rooms are located in colorful "longhouses" that surround the Great Ceremonial House. With names such as Tonga, Moorea, Tahiti, and Bora Bora, the longhouses offer not only a variety of locations but also an assortment of accommodations. Some of the buildings are near the Great Ceremonial House, others surround the pools, and still others can be found along the sparkling sand beach of the lagoon. The Bali Hai houses the Polynesian's suites, while Tonga is home to the Royal Polynesian concierge service. Given the lay of the land and the size of this resort, you will find that certain longhouses are closer to some things and farther away from others. But nothing is very far, and walking around the Polynesian is one of its greatest pleasures.

There are two pools, one "quiet" and one themed. The quiet pool is located in a lovely garden area in the center of the resort complex. The themed swimming pool is located along the Polynesian's beautiful beach. Nestled amidst dense tropical foliage and bordered by huge rocks and waterfalls, it is lavish and tropical. There is one small water slide, intended for children. This is a fairly small pool, considering both the size of this resort and the fact that most guests come here to swim and play. It and the rooms that surround it get pretty noisy, especially in the evening hours of summer. The beach features cabanas, swings, and hammocks. While away the afternoon here catching a few rays as colorful sailing catamarans whisk around the lagoon and boats come and go from the dock, carrying guests to and from the Magic Kingdom.

Rooms at the Polynesian

After the Great Ceremonial House, the lovely guest rooms at the Polynesian should come as no surprise. Each is spacious (409 square feet) and splendidly themed. Fabrics feature traditional Polynesian designs of browns and greens. Furnishings are tropical creations of wicker and bamboo. A room at the Poly does not provide a mere hint of tropical paradise but will immerse you in the romance of Polynesia.

Guest rooms each have two queen-size canopy beds and a daybed. None of the standard rooms feature king beds. Each room also has a small table and several handsome wicker chairs. A large tropical armoire hides the television and, along with the closet, provides room enough even for travelers like ourselves, who can never seem to decide what not to bring. Large marble baths feature counters of green and black with a spacious vanity and shower-tub combination.

There are 11 three-story longhouses around the grounds and along the lagoon. Oahu, Moorea, and Pago Pago (pronounced pongo-pongo) all have rooms that enjoy either patios or balconies. The remainder of the longhouses have ground-floor patios and balconies on the third floors only. Second-floor rooms have sliding glass doors that open onto wooden railings. Selections can be requested when you make your reservations, and we advise asking again at check-in.

Polynesian rooms feature garden, marina pool, or lagoon views. Naturally, the most expensive overlook the lagoon, its white, sandy beach, and Cinderella Castle. If you can afford the difference, you will find the view memorable and romantic. At night, the lights of the monorail make their way around the lagoon and fireworks sparkle above the Castle. Garden rooms are beautiful as well; at night, the torchlit footpaths and dense greenery will transport you.

1999 Room Rates for Disney's Polynesian Resort

Accommodation	Regular Season	Peak Season	Value Season	Holiday Season
Garden view	$294	$324	$274	$360
Lagoon view	$370	$395	$345	$420
Concierge garden	$370	$395	$345	$440
Concierge lagoon	$455	$485	$425	$530

Royal Polynesian Concierge Service

The Tonga longhouse is home to the Polynesian's concierge service. It is located right on the lagoon, and rooms on that side of the building boast extraordinary views. Determined to get a firsthand experience of everything, we happily stayed here in the tropical lap of Polynesian luxury. Royal Polynesian concierge service provided additional room amenities such as bathrobes, a coffeemaker, and a full array of toiletries.

As concierge guests, we relished the use of Tonga's lounge. Amidst the plush Polynesian furnishings, we savored a day-long offering of foods with a tropical touch, snacks, beverages, and desserts. Each evening found us sipping cordials, nibbling desserts, and watching the fireworks over the lagoon. Like passengers on a small cruise ship, we were able to chat with other guests, some of whom we had seen at breakfast.

A knowledgeable and dedicated staff was ready to spring into action for reservations, transportation, and any of our other concerns. We found the Polynesian's concierge service to be romantic and unforgettable—the perfect choice for us or for any other couple in love.

Suites at the Polynesian

The Bali Hai longhouse, located next door to the Great Ceremonial House, accommodates the Polynesian's suites. The Bali Hai is much smaller and more intimate than the other longhouses. It has only two stories and a dozen or so suites.

While all of the suites and rooms at the Bali Hai include concierge service, the concierge lounge is far enough away to make it less than convenient. To accommodate guests of the suites, a continental breakfast from room service is standard. The concierge staff is available, and use of the Tonga's concierge lounge is encouraged.

The smallest and least expensive suite here is not really a suite at all; it is a single oversized room. While considerably larger than the regular resort room, this luxurious accommodation is grand enough to accommodate a comfortable sitting area, a small desk and chair, and a dining table. The bathroom is large and offers a shower-tub and bidet. With either a single king bed or twin queens, this room comes as a garden-view room only. Marina-view versions are available on the lagoon side of the building, but they offer only dual queen-size beds. Garden kings or queens cost around $425 per night. These rooms are exceptionally nice and are on our small list of favorite Disney accommodations. The marina queen version is about $30 more per night and features a waterfront panorama.

The King Kamehameha suite is one of the most lavish in Walt Disney World. This two-level set of rooms commands a panoramic view of the marina area and lagoon. At over $1,200 per night, it is the stuff that dreams are made of. It has a large living room downstairs with a wet bar and enough space for a small wedding reception or party. The upstairs king bedroom is luxurious and perfectly themed. The bathroom features an oversized Jacuzzi tub. By adding adjoining rooms both upstairs and downstairs, this suite could accommodate the largest of families.

Transportation and Convenience

The Polynesian is right on the main monorail loop that runs around the lagoon. The monorail station is located on the second floor of the Great Ceremonial House and is a relatively short walk from most of the longhouses, giving this resort a real convenience to the Magic Kingdom and the other resorts around the lagoon. A boat also runs from the Magic Kingdom to the Grand Floridian and then to the Polynesian and back to the Magic Kingdom. From the longhouses along the lagoon, getting to the Magic Kingdom by boat is especially pleasant and convenient.

If you are staying at either Moorea or Pago Pago, you might find that walking to the Ticket and Transportation Center (TTC) or to the ferryboat landing might provide more convenient transportation to either Epcot or the Magic Kingdom. Other Disney destinations are reachable by bus from a bus stop near the main entrance of the Great Ceremonial House. We found bus service to be typically good.

- To the Magic Kingdom: monorail, boat from dock, or by foot to ferry from TTC
- To Epcot: monorail or by foot to TTC with transfer to Epcot monorail
- To Discovery Island, River Country: boat from the Magic Kingdom
- To Disney–MGM Studios, the Animal Kingdom, Blizzard Beach: direct bus
- To Downtown Disney and Typhoon Lagoon: 8 A.M. to 4 P.M., by monorail to TTC and transfer; after 4 P.M., by direct bus
- To BoardWalk: Bus to Downtown Disney and take Board-Walk bus

Dining at the Polynesian

With three restaurants at the Polynesian and many others at nearby resorts along the monorail, your dining options are considerable. Guests enjoy two table-service eateries and two snack bars. There's even a dinner show, called the Polynesian Luau. 'Ohana offers a character breakfast and Disney-style dinner feast. The Polynesian has an all-purpose restaurant, the Kona Cafe. Serving three meals daily, its menu has a definite Polynesian accent and specializes in coffees and pastries. For in-room dining, 24-hour room service is available. No resort would be complete without some sort of fast-food offering, and at the Poly it's Captain Cook's Snack Isle. It's open 24 hours with the usual selection of Disney fast foods.

For reviews and more information about the table-service restaurants and dinner shows at the Polynesian Resort, see Chapter 6.

Lounges at the Polynesian

There are two tropical lounges at the Polynesian: the Tambu Lounge and the Barefoot Bar. Both offer a tantalizing selection of specialty drinks. The Tambu Lounge, which adjoins 'Ohana, has been recently redesigned. Appetizers are from the firepit of 'Ohana. The Barefoot Bar is the Polynesian's poolside bar and features snacks as well as a selection of refreshing tropical concoctions.

Shops at the Polynesian

Trader Jack's is located on the second floor of the Great Ceremonial House. It offers character merchandise, toys, gifts, films, postcards, and Polynesian logo items, and an assortment of beers, wines, liquors, sundries, and snacks. There is an excellent selection of clothing shops on the ground floor of the central building. Whether you are looking for something special for yourselves or for a gift to bring home, these places definitely have nice stuff. Kanaka Kids, Robinson Crusoe, Esq., and the Polynesian Princess all make for good browsing.

Recreational Activities at the Polynesian

- Two heated swimming pools
- Watercraft rentals
- Evening fireworks cruise
- Moana Mickey's Video Arcade
- The Neverland Club children's activity center and dinner club
- 1.5-mile jogging and walking path

Our Impressions of the Polynesian

- This is a beautifully themed resort. Its guest rooms are large and some of the finest at Disney. We think that the Polynesian is both memorable and romantic. It is a first-class place to stay, and its motto says it all: "Aita Peatea" (there will be another day tomorrow just like today).
- Convenience to the Magic Kingdom is good to very good; convenience to other Disney destinations is only average.
- The main pool, although beautiful, well themed, and fun, is small and, given the high percentage of families that stay here, quite noisy. The quiet pool is a sensible alternative. There is no hot tub at the Polynesian.
- Many families with small children stay at the Polynesian, and we found that the resort's beaches and pools remain busy throughout the day.

Recommendations for Reservations

- Themed pool-view rooms are considerably noisier than other rooms. Try a quiet pool-view room, if you must.
- Spring for a lagoon view. You'll be happy you did.

Romance at the Polynesian

- The rooms at the Polynesian: ♥♥♥
- Royal Polynesian concierge service or garden king room at the Bali: ♥♥♥♥
- Breakfast in bed: ♥♥♥♥
- Breakfast on your balcony or patio: ♥♥♥
- Dining by a window at 'Ohana at Papeete Bay: ♥
- Strolling around the grounds after dark, especially the two quiet beaches at either end of the resort: ♥♥♥
- In the evening, taking the walkway around the lagoon to the Grand Floridian, having dinner, enjoying a cocktail in one of the lounges there, or simply seeing the sights: ♥♥♥
- The Polynesian Luau: ♥
- Viewing the Electric Water Pageant or fireworks from Sunset Point, a small grassy area along the beach near the Oahu longhouse, or one of the two quiet beaches: ♥♥♥
- Fireworks cruise for two, available at the marina: ♥♥♥
- Renting a boat and taking a cruise: ♥♥

Disney's Contemporary Resort

In the early 1970s, when the Contemporary first opened, it was at the forefront of architectural innovation: modular construction, a cavernous atrium lobby, and a monorail that ran right through it all. It was an impressive display of the vision and imagination of Walt Disney. During the last quarter of a century, while the rest of the architectural world has been playing catch-up, the Contemporary has still remained an impressive site on the Disney horizon. It is a marvel of glass, steel, and concrete and it is itself a Disney icon.

This may be one of Disney's oldest resorts, but it is no dowager. Constant improvements and refurbishing have kept it seeming as new as the day it opened. During the past 25 years, the Contemporary has maintained a firm grip on its first-rate status. It offers a variety of spacious rooms and suites as well as a complete package of resort amenities. These, and its unequaled proximity to the Magic Kingdom, are what this exciting place is all about. The ambience here at the Contemporary is definitely modern. It is fast-paced, fun, and high-energy.

The resort's main building is called the Tower. Adjacent to it are two newer additions called the Garden Wings, which lie along the north and south sides of the Tower building and are connected to it by short, covered walkways. The Tower building is an enormous 15-story, A-frame structure. Its atrium-style lobby is the Grand Canyon Concourse. Tiers of guest rooms hang suspended from its sides. The ends of the building are large, open expanses of glass. Within them is an entire world of restaurants, shops, and lounges. A dazzling mosaic leaps hundreds of feet from floor to ceiling.

Rooms at the Contemporary

The rooms at the Contemporary, at 422 square feet, are some of the largest standard rooms at Disney. Compare them to the All-Star's 260 square feet. Each room is light, airy, and spacious. The decor is modern with a color scheme of beige trimmed with black. The bedspreads are light, with a splash of brightly colored, confetti-like patterns. There is a large, Danish modern armoire with plenty of drawer space and a television. The vanity area is large and has a single sink. The bathroom features the usual shower-tub. While well appointed and comfortable, the rooms lack the charm and fantasy that are so present at other Disney resorts.

All of the rooms in the Tower have balconies; none of the standard rooms in the Garden Wings do. Rooms in the Tower building face

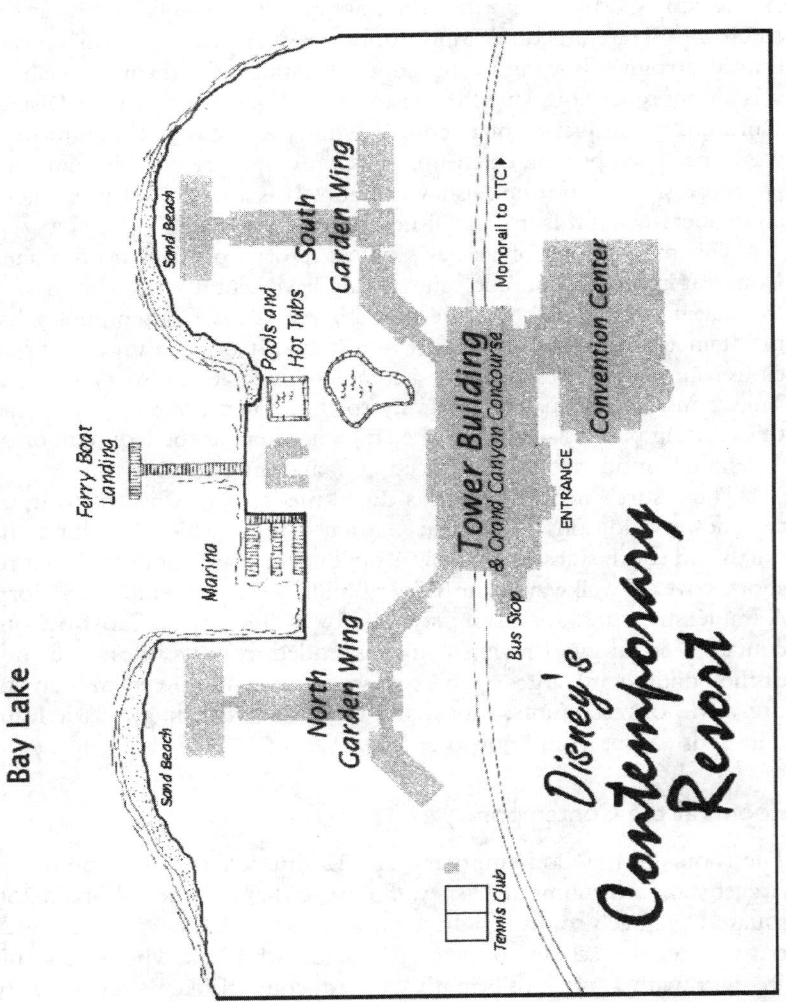
Bay Lake
Sand Beach
Marina
Ferry Boat Landing
Pools and Hot Tubs
Sand Beach
North Garden Wing
South Garden Wing
Tower Building
& Grand Canyon Concourse
Monorail to TTC
Bus Stop
ENTRANCE
Convention Center
Tennis Club
Disney's Contemporary Resort

either the Magic Kingdom or Bay Lake with views that range from very good to astounding. Furnished with several chairs and a small table, balconies in the Tower are large and comfortable. Our room was located on the twelfth floor overlooking the Magic Kingdom. After dark, the view was spectacular. Tower rooms with panoramas of the Magic Kingdom are the most requested at the Contemporary. So, if this is your wish, reserve early.

Rooms of the Garden Wings overlook the parking area or landscaped gardens and Bay Lake. With only three floors here, views are pleasant but not panoramic. The larger Garden deluxe rooms feature a small foyer and spacious bath with either a single king bed or one queen with foldout sleeper/sofa. Views from these rooms are particularly pleasant. Not as convenient to the services of the Tower building, these rooms do offer a certain tranquillity and sense of seclusion not found in the Grand Canyon Concourse.

Most rooms at the Contemporary offer the usual two queen beds and a daybed/sofa. There are only 33 rooms with king beds, counting both the Tower and Garden Wings, and many of these are suites. The standard rooms at the Contemporary do not have minibutlers.

1999 Room Rates for Disney's Contemporary Resort

Accommodation	Regular Season	Peak Season	Value Season	Holiday Season
Garden Wing, standard	$234	$264	$214	$290
Garden Wing, garden	$260	$290	$240	$320
Garden Wing, deluxe	$295	$325	$275	$355
Tower room	$330	$360	$300	$385
Tower Club	$380	$410	$350	$460

Concierge Service and Suites at the Contemporary

On the fourteenth floor are this resort's impressive suites, and guests here also enjoy the Contemporary's fine concierge service. Included are continental breakfast, midday snacks, afternoon hors d'oeuvres and champagne, and evening cordials and desserts. Guests will also have private check-in and check-out, their own private lounge, and a concierge staff. The two presidential suites each offer spacious king beds and Jacuzzi tubs (the only rooms with whirlpool tubs at this resort). With wet bar, dining area, large parlor room with sofa and chairs, and two oversized balconies, one of these beauties will run $1,200 per night. There are other suites on this floor, beginning around $925. More than once, an Arab prince and entourage have occupied this entire floor.

The twelfth floor of the Contemporary is the Tower Club. A serving place and small sitting area have been set up near the elevators, and here guests can enjoy a continental breakfast and some light snacks in the afternoon. There is a concierge staff here from 7 A.M. to 4 P.M. Rooms on this floor also feature refrigerators.

There are suites in the Garden Wings too, but they do not include concierge service. With 1,313 square feet, you will certainly not feel cramped in one of these luxurious rooms. Each provides a large bedroom with adjoining parlor and sico bed and, depending on view and season, cost from $740 to $815 nightly. This is plenty of room for a family, but at these prices, you might be better off with two Tower rooms.

Transportation and Convenience

With the Contemporary right on the monorail loop, travel to and from the Magic Kingdom is both easy and exciting. Arrivals and departures are from the monorail station on the Tower's fourth floor. Be advised that during peak hours the trip to the Magic Kingdom can take upwards of 20 minutes. There is also a short walking path to the Magic Kingdom. This is a pleasant stroll past some amusing topiary. The walk is especially convenient from the north Garden Wing.

Except for the pleasant monorail ride to Epcot, travel to other Disney destinations is not quite so much fun. It is relatively easy, though. Several areas require transferring buses at the Ticket and Transportation Center (TTC), which can be reached easily from the Contemporary by either monorail or by direct bus.

- To the Magic Kingdom: monorail or a pleasant walk
- To Epcot: monorail with transfer at TTC to Epcot monorail
- To Discovery Island, River Country: boat from the dock at the lakeside of resort
- To Disney–MGM Studios, the Animal Kingdom, Blizzard Beach: direct bus
- To Downtown Disney and Typhoon Lagoon: 8 A.M. to 4 P.M., by monorail to TTC transfer; after 4 P.M., by direct bus
- To BoardWalk: Bus to Downtown Disney and take BoardWalk bus

Dining at the Contemporary

Dining here is outstanding. Along with the Contemporary's three full-service restaurants, room service, and fast-food eatery, you will find many fine choices at the other resorts around the Lagoon. Atop the Contemporary is the California Grill, Walt Disney World's finest and most exciting dining destination. The Concourse Steakhouse is another good dining choice, with a variety of well-prepared breakfasts and lunches. Evenings here feature fine dining with seafood and cuts of beef. Chef Mickey's Buffet is the Contemporary's place for Disney character meals with both breakfast and dinner buffets. For more information and our reviews of these table-service restaurants, see Chapter 6.

On the first floor, located near the front desk, is the Contemporary's new espresso bar, offering fresh-brewed coffee concoctions and a small selection of pastries and biscottis. The Food 'n Fun Center is nearby, adjacent to the video arcade. A bit noisy, the Food 'n Fun Center offers a typical selection of Disney fast foods and is open from 6 A.M. to 1 A.M.

Lounges at the Contemporary

The California Grill Bar is located right inside the restaurant and shares the Top of the World view. Besides an extensive wine list and a full complement of liquors, it offers a menu of appetizers, sushi, taster plates, and pizzas from the Grill. The Grill Bar is open from 5 P.M. to 1 A.M. and offers wine tasting on Fridays at 6 P.M.

The Outer Rim Cocktail Lounge is on the fourth floor of the Tower building, overlooking Bay Lake and Discovery Island. Open from 12 P.M. to 11 P.M., this lounge offers an assortment of cocktails and appetizers. It is often crowded with guests waiting to get into Chef Mickey's Buffet, however, and it is also noisy, due largely to its location in the Grand Canyon Concourse.

The Sand Bar is located in the marina complex near the pool, on the lakeside of the resort. This lounge operates seasonally.

Shops at the Contemporary

Except for the Bay and Beach and the Racquet Club, all of the Contemporary's shops can be found on the fourth floor in the Grand Canyon Concourse.

Concourse Sundries and Spirits should pretty much take care of any loose ends. Whether you are in search of souvenirs, snacks, newspapers or magazines, film or tobacco products, or nonprescription medicines, here is where you will go. Concourse Sundries has a large offering of beers, wines, and liquors. Bayview Gifts is the perfect place to stop for that little something special. Fresh flowers and unique gifts are the specialty here, so you can surprise someone you love. Other shops offer character merchandise, jewelry, and men's and women's sportswear.

Recreational Activities at the Contemporary

- Two heated swimming pools
- Two hot tubs
- Kiddie pool and play fountain
- The Olympiad Health Club and Tanning Salon
- Marina Pavilion with watercraft rentals
- Water-skiing, parasailing, and fishing excursions
- Six lighted tennis courts, backboards, ball machine
- Volleyball and shuffleboard
- Lakefront beach area
- Children's playground and spray fountain
- Food 'n Fun Center video arcade
- Free Disney movie every night in the theater at the Food 'n Fun Center
- Fireworks cruises

OUR IMPRESSIONS OF THE CONTEMPORARY

- While this resort may not offer the same sense of storytelling as other resorts and is not romantic in the same sense as the Grand Floridian, it is nonetheless a very exciting place to stay.
- This resort is very convenient to the Magic Kingdom.

RECOMMENDATIONS FOR RESERVATIONS

- Neither Garden Wing is convenient to the Tower building or the monorail. The north wing is, however, convenient to the tennis courts and the footpath to the Magic Kingdom. Both Garden Wings offer pleasant and quiet surroundings.
- Garden deluxe rooms in the Garden Wing are quiet and beautiful. Add-ons to the suite at the end of the wing, these rooms enjoy king beds and upgraded amenities.

ROMANCE AT THE CONTEMPORARY

- Resort theming: ♥
- Breakfast in bed: ♥♥♥♥
- Breakfast on your balcony overlooking Disney World or Bay Lake: ♥♥♥
- Having a drink or dinner at the California Grill during the evening fireworks show: ♥♥♥

- The eleventh-floor observation deck at night, especially during the fireworks shows at any of the parks: ♥♥
- King bed Garden deluxe room: ♥♥
- A stroll on the beach behind either Garden Wing, then watching the Electric Water Pageant from the beach: ♥♥♥♥

Disney's Grand Floridian Resort and Spa

Even from a distance, there is something very romantic about this place. Its red-shingled roofs, ornate turrets, and intricate latticework all seem to belong to a time long past. We confess gladly to a little thrill each time we are near it. In our hearts, this lovely resort represents an unhurried age when the quality of life was held dear and when time was something to be savored. Here amidst the stately palms and gas lamps and among the verandas and the rose gardens, old-world craftsmanship has been brought to life.

This is the Grand Floridian, and it is the jewel in the Disney crown. A stay here will immerse you in a richness and elegance that will be the stuff of your romantic dreams. Details are everything at the Grand. From flawless service to sumptuous bathrobes, the luxurious and the lavish come standard.

Arriving at the Grand Floridian is definitely exciting, and it is likely something that you will never forget. The tree-lined drive leads through manicured gardens and up to an entrance where a dozen costumed valets and bellpersons scurry about. Knickers, knee socks, and pastel jackets are the uniforms of the day. Once inside the huge lobby, you begin to understand why this place is called Grand. Level upon level of formal balconies surround this great hall and lead the eye upward towards the domed ceiling high above. Rows of turned white posts are capped with rails of gleaming mahogany. Light filters through stained-glass skylights onto sparkling chandeliers.

Fabrics, decor, and design are all in perfect harmony. Details attract your eye: A topiary Cinderella Castle occupies one space, while above it an old-fashioned cage elevator ascends slowly. This striking Grand lobby is an awesome and even a dizzying sight. Everything about the Grand Floridian appears to be first-class, and everything most certainly *is* first-class. A stay here will be, for both of you, a celebration of everything that is special and memorable.

Set perfectly along a combed, white sand beach on the Seven Seas Lagoon, the Grand Floridian is but a stone's throw from Cinderella's

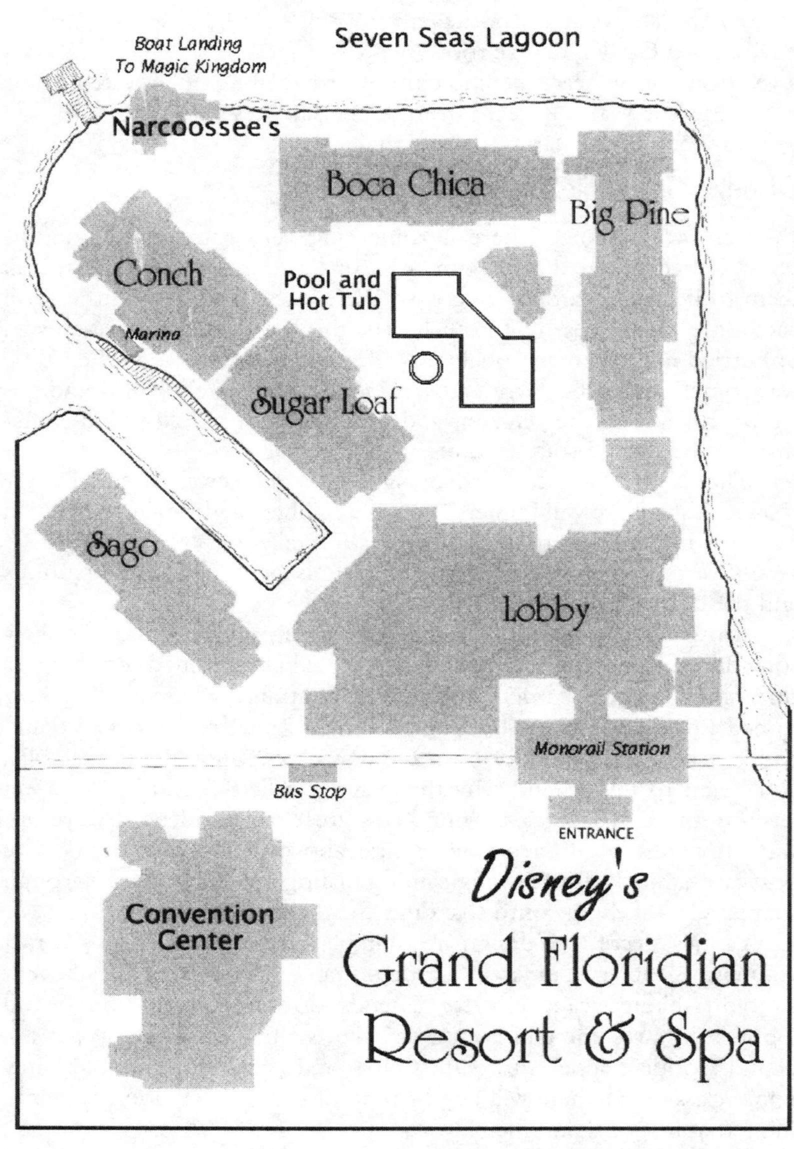
Seven Seas Lagoon
Boat Landing
To Magic Kingdom
Narcoossee's
Boca Chica
Big Pine
Conch
Pool and
Hot Tub
Marina
Sugar Loaf
Sago
Lobby
Monorail Station
Bus Stop
ENTRANCE
Convention
Center
Disney's
Grand Floridian
Resort & Spa

front door. The monorail slips quietly from the station and whisks guests away to Disney adventures.

The Grand's five lodge buildings are neatly arranged around a large pool area. Connected by garden walkways, these buildings reflect the Victorian charm of the lavish Grand lobby and house the resort's luxurious guest rooms. Each building is named for a Florida key: Sago, Boca Chica, Conch, Big Pine, and Sugar Loaf.

Rooms at the Grand Floridian

Each charming and luxurious room in this resort is decorated much as it might have been a century ago, with marble-topped sink, ceiling fan, and antiqued armoire. Each marvelous remembrance is made complete with plush carpets, pastel floral fabrics, and lightly colored woodwork. Large glass doors open onto a spacious balconies that look onto the lovely garden grounds. Costumed housekeepers arrive daily with wicker baskets of fresh linens.

Rooms here are large (400 square feet) and comfortable. They are the perfect marriage of the elegance of yesterday and of the creature comforts of today. Each has two queen-size beds, several chairs, and a small table. A daybed/sofa lends the perfect place to lounge. Every guest room features twin marble vanities in a spacious and well-lit area adjacent to the bathroom.

Because of the unusual shapes of the lodge buildings, standard room sizes and shapes vary slightly within each building. Top-floor attic rooms, while a bit smaller, feature quaint dormer balconies and vaulted ceilings. Lodge tower rooms are a bit more expensive and are a little larger than the standard rooms; a comfortable sitting area substitutes for the balcony or patio.

Rooms at the Grand enjoy two different views, of either the garden or lagoon. Each has its charm. Many of the rooms overlooking the lagoon feature an impressive panorama of Cinderella Castle. The sparkling water, fireworks, and the Electric Water Pageant all make evenings here magically romantic. Whatever your choice, the Grand Floridian is a luxurious place to celebrate your honeymoon, anniversary, or romantic Disney vacation.

Rooms here are scheduled to begin a cycled "rehab" beginning in May of 1999. Word is that Disney animated character theming is planned for each room, with such Disney favorites as Ariel, Belle from *Beauty and the Beast,* and Alice in Wonderland. Each lodge building will feature its own theme, and decor will include bright pastel fabrics and character wallpaper. Although we haven't seen it ourselves, we have been assured that it will not alter this resort's tasteful and Victorian theme.

1999 Room Rates for Disney's Grand Floridian Resort and Spa

Accommodation	Regular Season	Peak Season	Value Season	Holiday Season
Garden view	$319	$349	$299	$390
Lagoon view	$385	$415	$365	$465
Lodge tower	$390	$420	$370	$470
Lodge concierge	$435	$465	——	$520
Concierge	$540	$575	$510	$630
Concierge deluxe	$555	$590	$525	$645
Honeymoon, Clarendon	$555	$590	$525	$645
Honeymoon, Turret	$555	$590	$525	$645

Concierge Service and Suites at the Grand Floridian

The luxurious concierge rooms at the Grand are located on the private, upper floors of the main lobby building. All 90 rooms include plush bathrobes, slippers, VCRs, and complimentary movies. This is the life! The beautiful and comfortable concierge lounge is located on the fourth floor, and here you will enjoy a sumptuous offering of treats served throughout the day: continental breakfast, midday refreshments, afternoon tea, and hors d'oeuvres and wine before dinner. Drop by in the evening, sip cordials, and share a dessert while you listen to the music of the Grand's orchestra waft up from the landing below. Once you have been a guest here, you will understand why so many who have visited before will not even consider a stay elsewhere. Visitors returning here will find that their personal preferences have been "remembered" by a daily staff of six that is dedicated to making the concierge stay all that it can be.

There are a variety of rooms here in concierge that range from a standard resort room to the elegantly modern Roosevelt suite (where Princess Diana and her sons stayed during their Disney holiday). There's a concierge deluxe room too, and it's larger than the standard. The Grand Floridian also features two types of exceptionally romantic concierge rooms, and our favorite is the Turret honeymoon suite. Six of these octagonal rooms are located in the two towers of the main building. Each features a large bathroom, walk-in closet, and a bedroom with a spectacular panorama. Several command views of Cinderella Castle right from the four-poster king bed. From our own experience, we can tell you that, for sheer magic, one of these suites has no equal here at Walt Disney World. The other honeymoon rooms are on the secluded Clarendon concierge level. Room amenities here include a Jacuzzi tub and love seat. These too are enchanting and romantic. Know that the Turret rooms do not have balconies.

There are other suites as well, but none so perfect a place for a couple in love. With names such as the Biscayne, the Cypress, and the Sanibel, they offer a variety of bedrooms and parlors each with enough space for a family. Prices begin around $1,000 nightly. A handful of one- and two-bedroom suites are also located on the top floors of the lodge buildings. These are simply attic rooms with adjoining parlors. Each parlor features a pull-out queen, sitting area, and bathroom. A second bedroom can be added. Prices begin around $775 per night and concierge service is not included.

Lodge concierge is something new here at the Grand, and it means a room in the Sugar Loaf Key building. Each day, a continental breakfast is served here along with a small variety of snacks and beverages throughout the afternoon. This is all done in the downstairs lobby area and is available only to Sugar Loaf guests; it costs an additional $115 per day. Lodge Concierge is not available during value season.

Transportation and Convenience

Guests at the Grand Floridian enjoy the same monorail and bus transportation as the Contemporary and the Polynesian. The motor launch that makes the trip from the Polynesian stops at the dock near Narcoossee's restaurant on its way back from the Magic Kingdom. We suggest that you monorail to that park and return by boat.

- To the Magic Kingdom: monorail or water taxi
- To Epcot: monorail with transfer at the Ticket and Transportation Center (TTC) to Epcot monorail
- To Discovery Island, Fort Wilderness, River Country: monorail or boat to Magic Kingdom, then boat
- To Disney–MGM Studios, the Animal Kingdom, Blizzard Beach: direct bus
- To Downtown Disney and Typhoon Lagoon: 8 A.M. to 4 P.M., by monorail to TTC and transfer; after 4 P.M., by direct bus
- To BoardWalk: Bus to Downtown Disney and take BoardWalk bus

Dining at the Grand Floridian

Some of Walt Disney World's finest eateries are located here. Victoria and Albert's ♥♥♥♥, a gourmet dining experience, is considered by many to be one of Florida's best places to dine. There is also the Mediterranean cuisine of Cítricos ♥♥♥ and the wonderful Grand Floridian Cafe. And one of our very favorite places to dine at Disney is the lakeside Narcoossee's.

As if these weren't enough, 1900 Park Fare is a delightful breakfast and dinner buffet-style restaurant. It features Disney characters galore at both meals. For snacks and fast food 24 hours a day, visit the Gasparilla Grill, which serves a large variety of counter foods that are a notch or two above the standard Disney fare. To complete the largest selection of restaurant offerings in any Disney resort, the Garden View Lounge offers a continental breakfast each morning and an elegant afternoon high tea ♥♥♥. The Grand also offers round-the-clock room service. For more details regarding these and other Disney dining spots, see Chapter 6.

Yet another dining option available to guests of the Grand Floridian is the Romance Dinner. This special service provides an unforgettable private dining experience delivered to the Grand Floridian location of your choice. Enjoy it in your room, on your balcony, on the beach, in the garden, on the lagoon in one of the resort's Flote boats, or even on the resort's private yacht, *The Grand One*. Just about any location is possible. There are not set menus and virtually anything is possible, depending on what you'd like to order from this resort's selection of restaurants. This is an unforgettable experience, served white-gloved with crisp linens and candlelit table setting. For information, call room service.

Lounges at the Grand Floridian

The Grand Floridian is home to three quite different lounges. The charming and comfortable Garden View Lounge is on the ground floor of the lobby building. It features not only the lavish afternoon high tea but also a full service bar from 11 A.M. to 11 P.M.

Mizner's is located on the second floor of the main building. Specialties here include ales, ports, and select brandies. Each evening, a small orchestra plays on the landing right next to this handsome and comfortable lounge.

There is also a poolside snack bar with beer, wine, specialty drinks, and a small assortment of sandwiches.

Shops at the Grand Floridian

A good selection of shops can be found at the Grand Floridian, all of which are located in the lobby building. As you might expect, though, the emphasis is on classy and expensive. Still, you will find a good selection of Disney character merchandise, in addition to some rather fancy clothing and accessories for both men and women. Sandy Cove is the resort's gift and sundries shop, where you will find film, sunblock, and other such items. There's also a hair salon, the Ivy Trellis, and Bally's, offering some of the world's finest leather goods.

Grand Floridian Spa ♥♥♥♥ and Health Club

Get yourselves in the perfect mood for your romantic holiday with pampering treatments at this luxurious spa. From a sensual variety of massages to mineral soaks, facials, wraps, and aromatherapy, this first-class spa offers a truly special experience. For more details, see Chapter 7.

Recreational Activities at the Grand Floridian

For boating fun, the Grand offers the Captain's Plan. For $100, guests get four hours of assorted boating rentals. Not a bad deal considering that a typical power boat costs nearly $20 per half hour. *The Grand One* is this resort's 44-foot power yacht, and it can be chartered for a cruise, a dinner, or a fireworks cruise. With crew, cost is around $275 per hour. Booking should be done in advance by calling (407) 824-2439.

- One large, heated swimming pool, open 24 hours
- One large hot tub
- White sand beach on Seven Seas Lagoon
- Marina complex with watercraft rentals
- Grand Floridian Spa and Health Club
- In-room massage, by appointment
- Jogging and walking path
- Wingfield tennis courts
- Golf shuttles to golf courses throughout the day
- Children's activity center
- Video arcade
- Fireworks cruises
- Live music afternoons and evenings in the lobby

OUR IMPRESSIONS OF THE GRAND FLORIDIAN

- The Grand Floridian is an enchanting and romantic resort. The rooms are luxurious, and a stay here will have you feeling special and pampered. It is almost the dining capital of Disney World.

- Service here at the Grand is exceptional.
- Lodge Concierge service seems expensive considering what is offered.
- The downside is that the Grand is expensive. Specials and discounted rooms are available, but rates are rarely outstanding. The exception to this rule is the Magical Holiday Package.

RECOMMENDATIONS FOR RESERVATIONS

- For a good view of Cinderella Castle, the best views are from the Boca Chica Cay lodge building. The next best view is from Conch Cay, with rooms ending in 25 to 31. After that, Big Pine Cay rooms ending in 41 to 47 have great views. Both Big Pine and Conch are no-smoking buildings.
- Make your reservation for Victoria and Albert's when you reserve your room.
- The Turret suites with the views of the castle are 4021, 4221, and 4321 (we still call this one *our* room).

ROMANCE AT THE GRAND FLORIDIAN

- Unsurpassed theme, service, accommodations, and ambience: ♥♥♥♥
- Restaurant selection (the best in the World): ♥♥♥♥
- A Honeymoon or Turret room: ♥♥♥♥
- A lagoon-view room: ♥♥♥♥
- Breakfast in bed: ♥♥♥♥
- High tea at the Garden View Lounge: ♥♥♥
- Eating at Cítricos: ♥♥♥
- An intimate dinner at Victoria and Albert's: ♥♥♥♥
- The Romance Dinner: ♥♥♥♥
- Watching the fireworks or Electric Water Pageant from one of the swings on the beach: ♥♥♥♥
- A late-night swim in the pool or hot tub: ♥
- A fireworks cruise: ♥♥♥

Disney's Wilderness Lodge

Located in the woods near the Magic Kingdom is one of Disney's most majestic resort creations, the Wilderness Lodge. It is a magnificent tribute, both architecturally and thematically, to the great lodge houses built by the U.S. Park Service around the turn of this century. We have

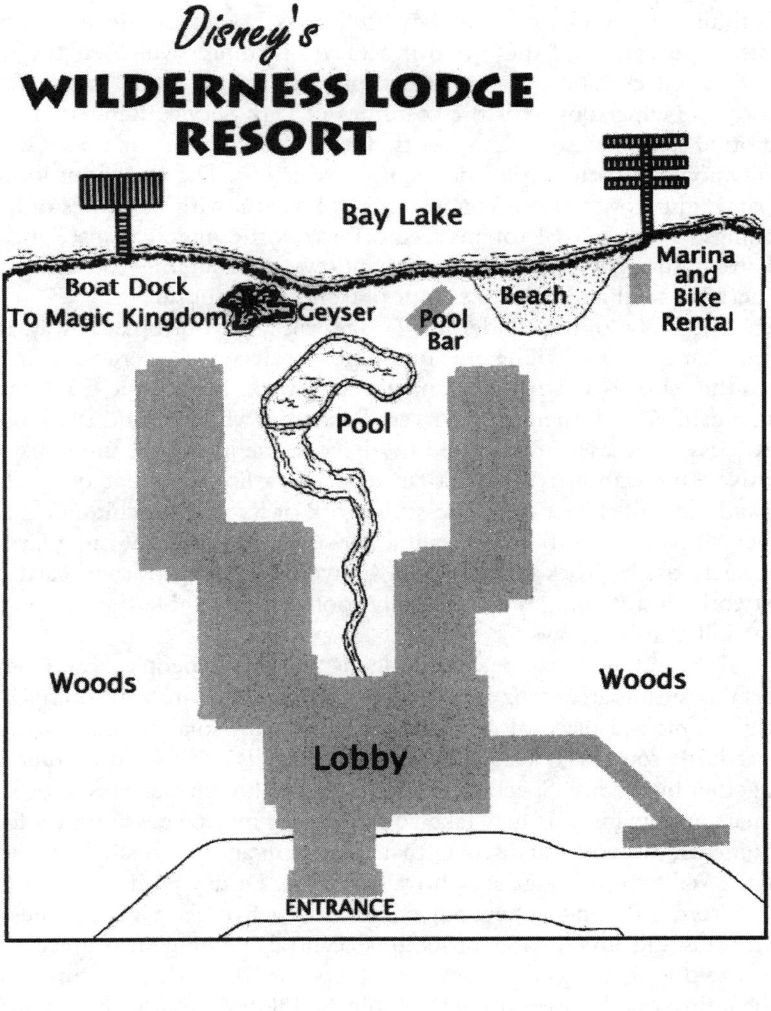

Disney's

WILDERNESS LODGE RESORT

Bay Lake

Boat Dock
To Magic Kingdom

Geyser

Pool
Bar

Beach

Marina
and
Bike
Rental

Pool

Woods

Woods

Lobby

ENTRANCE

actually visited many of the lodges after which the Wilderness Lodge was styled, such places as the Ahwahnee at Yosemite, the Lake McDonald Lodge at Glacier National Park, and Yellowstone's Old Faithful Inn. We know that the Wilderness Lodge has been created with great care, and the mood it achieves is impressive. Near the resort's front entrance, a whimsical topiary buffalo and calf graze. The Lodge's bellpersons wear the costumes of Park Service Rangers, from knotted kerchiefs to hiking boots. Once inside the great doors, you will know that you have made the right selection. The cavernous lobby soars eight stories above you and surrounds you with balconies of log railings. Two colossal totems face off across the huge expanse, and a shaft of sunlight enters through windows high among the timbers. There is a faint and delicious scent of campfire in the air.

The lobby of the Wilderness Lodge will take your breath away. Its grandeur and its detailing are stunning. The decor is American Indian, and the lobby is a showcase of native craft work. Behind the front desk is an exhibit of authentic Indian cradleboards, while around the lobby are glass showcases of feathered headpieces, the intricate handiwork of native American artisans. In a far corner is a fireplace that befits the grand scale of the Lodge. The stonework of its massive chimney rises over 80 feet to the beamed ceiling above. A multitude of hued layers simulate the bedrock of the Grand Canyon. The forged iron hearth is artwork, and its hinges are carefully tooled to resemble quivers, each one full of iron arrows.

As grand as it may be, the Lodge is a place for people, too. Comfortable sitting areas, cozy corners, and fireplaces invite you to linger a while. This is a place of creature comforts, with sofas, ottomans, and hearthside rockers. It's a place for holding hands and for sitting quietly together by the fire. Spectacular and huge, the Lodge manages to be intimate and inviting. It may take you days or it may take you only a few moments, but you will discover that the charm and the rustic ambience of the Wilderness Lodge are unrivaled at Walt Disney World.

From a distance, the Lodge resembles a frontier fort. The hewn log walls and green roofs of its great central building turn gracefully into two long wings. The swimming pool is formed by a man-made hot spring that bubbles up in the lobby and flows out into the Lodge's rocky courtyard. As the stream builds to a torrent, it becomes a waterfall, splashing noisily over huge artificial granite boulders and tumbling into the swimming pool.

The resort overlooks Bay Lake and Discovery Island. Every evening, the Electric Water Pageant passes by; with its music and lights, it is the perfect end to each magical day. The Disney Imagineers have even provided a steaming geyser that erupts hourly.

The pool at the Lodge is themed and beautiful. During the summer months, there is one hot tub and one cold tub. During the cooler seasons, the cold tub is heated. The lakefront forms a small, sandy swimming beach, and its marina rents a variety of boats and bicycles. Walking, jogging, and cycling paths will take you around the lake to Fort Wilderness or to River Country. It's a trip you should take the time to make.

Rooms at the Wilderness Lodge

The standard rooms at the Lodge have a high-timber, western sensibility. Though a bit smaller than those of the other premium resorts, the rooms are comfortable and well appointed. Each is woodsy and charming. The furniture is simple and natural and includes two queen beds and a colorful "quilted" spread. There is a large pine armoire with ample drawer space and a large television set. A small table and several chairs provide the ideal place for in-room dining. The bathroom is fairly standard, with a twin vanity and the usual tub-shower.

Each room at the Wilderness Lodge has its own balcony, and there are a variety of views. Standard-view rooms overlook small parking areas, while woods-view rooms open onto the dense forest surrounding the resort. Our woods-view room was on the side of the resort that faces the Magic Kingdom. At night, we were able to see the fireworks above the treetops.

Courtyard rooms provide views of the courtyard and pool, while lake-view rooms enjoy magnificent vistas of Bay Lake. Most of the standard rooms come with the usual dual queen-size beds, and two other offerings are available in limited numbers. There are about 40 rooms with single king beds. These have been designed for the physically challenged, and they are handsome rooms. Some rooms also offer a single queen bed and a bunk bed. These seem to capture the western feeling of the Lodge and are ideal for families with one or two children.

1999 Room Rates for Disney's Wilderness Lodge Resort

Accommodation	Regular Season	Peak Season	Value Season	Holiday Season
Standard view	$200	$230	$180	$249
Woods view	$219	$249	$199	$270
Courtyard view	$250	$280	$225	$310
Honeymoon "suite"	$255	$285	$230	$310

Suites at the Wilderness Lodge

A small assortment of suites is available at the Lodge. On the top balcony of the lobby are four charming Honeymoon "suites." While not really a suite, each has a king-size bed and a large bathroom with Jacuzzi tub. These reasonably priced rooms are special, intimate, and private. They are the only ones on this floor, high atop the vast lobby, and you will enjoy the feeling of being away from and above the rest of the world.

The deluxe room costs about $330 per night and may be even less during value season. This room has a standard bedroom with two queen beds or one king and a small sitting room and wet bar. A standard adjoining room may be added to this suite.

The remaining two suites here are the Yellowstone and Yosemite, which are the presidential and vice-presidential suites, respectively. We think both are among the best-themed suites here at Walt Disney World and, at $720 and $615 per night, they are something of a bargain. The Yellowstone features an elegant, western motif. From the suite's double doors and large foyer with elkhorn chandelier to the lavish, marble bath, this place is first-class all the way. The suite's four-poster king bed is a unique sculpture of wood, and the spacious suite of rooms is furnished with a large, wooden dining table, stuffed leather chair, and antique books. The Yosemite is nearly as large and enjoys much more of a cowboy sensibility. Rawhide curtains, branding-iron towel racks, and saloon doors on the kitchen/wet bar are just a few of the memorable and whimsical details. Either suite comes with a large whirlpool tub (the Yellowstone's is bigger). We have promised ourselves to stay in one of these suites but, as yet, have not been able to decide which one.

Transportation and Convenience

Convenience is not, we are sorry to tell you, one of the strong suits here at the Wilderness Lodge. Still, transportation is acceptable, although we still hear the occasional complaint.

- To the Magic Kingdom, Fort Wilderness, River Country, Discovery Island: by boat, arrivals and departures from the lakeside dock; the Magic Kingdom can also be reached by bus to the Ticket and Transportation Center (TTC) and then monorail
- To Epcot, Disney–MGM Studios, the Animal Kingdom, Blizzard Beach: direct bus

- To Typhoon Lagoon and Downtown Disney: 8 A.M. to 4 P.M., by bus to TTC and transfer; after 4 P.M., direct bus
- To BoardWalk: Bus to Downtown Disney and take BoardWalk bus

Dining at the Wilderness Lodge

The Lodge has three western-themed restaurants; two have table service, and one has fast food. The Artist Point ♥♥ is the Wilderness Lodge's premier eating place. Dinner specialties are the freshest of meats, seafood, game, and wines from the Pacific Northwest. The Artist Point also features a character breakfast.

The all-purpose restaurant is the Whispering Canyon Cafe. It's a fun place to eat and the food is good. Each of the day's hearty meals is served family-style, all you care to eat, or a la carte. For reviews and more information about these restaurants, see Chapter 6.

The Lodge has a themed counter-service eatery called the Roaring Fork. Open 24 hours, this self-serve restaurant offers a selection of breakfasts, sandwiches, salads, and desserts. And the Lodge also serves complimentary coffee in the lobby during the morning hours.

The Lodge also has 24-hour room service with a menu that includes barbecued ribs, pizza, grilled fish, and prime rib. Foods come from either the Artist Point or Whispering Canyon. Wines, beers, and mixed drinks are also available.

Lounges at the Wilderness Lodge

The picturesque Territory Lounge is located adjacent to the Artist Point and serves a selection of microbrewery beers, specialty drinks, and wines from 11 A.M. to 1 A.M. This year, it once again features a menu of interesting sandwiches and finger foods that would make for a light dinner. If the Artist Point is too crowded or if you simply prefer it, you may order anything from the Artist Point menu in the lounge after 4 P.M.

The Trout Pass Pool Bar enjoys a nice view of the Lodge and of the lake and beach and offers an interesting selection of specialty drinks and a small variety of snacks and sandwiches.

Shops at the Wilderness Lodge

There's only one shop at the Lodge, but it's a good one. Just outside the front door of the Lodge Mercantile sits one of the comic sites of the Lodge: a totem pole of Disney characters. Inside, you will discover one of the nicest on-property places to browse. Besides some handsome Lodge logo merchandise, you'll find an impressive array of western craft items as well as quality fashions and the usual assortment of sundries.

Recreational Activities at the Wilderness Lodge

- Swimming pool with small water slide
- One hot and one cold spa
- White sand beach and marina with assorted boat rentals
- Bicycle rentals
- Video arcade
- Fishing excursion
- The Cub's Den children's activity center

The Wilderness Lodge Tours

Each day, the Lodge conducts two free tours that begin in the lobby, one at 9:30 A.M. and the other at 3:30 P.M.. The morning tour is rich with details and lodge lore. The afternoon tour features samples of food from the Lodge's eateries. Even if you aren't staying here, we'd highly recommend either tour.

OUR IMPRESSIONS OF THE WILDERNESS LODGE

- A beautifully themed resort. The fantasy element here is so powerful that a visit will be a real adventure. As elusive as romance is, we'd have to say that the Lodge has it.
- The selection of restaurants here could be better. Some real improvements have been made in offering a la carte items at the Whispering Canyon, but if you are visiting for a week, you might get tired of the eateries here.
- The Lodge is an outstanding value. It falls in cost somewhere between the premium resorts and the more modestly priced ones, yet it offers extraordinary theming, well-decorated rooms, and most of the services found at the more expensive places.
- The four Honeymoon suites could be the best on-property room bargain.
- The pool is a bit small for a hotel with nearly 800 rooms. Even during the winter months, two hot tubs are simply not enough.
- A car would come in handy here, especially for dining at other Disney resorts.

RECOMMENDATIONS FOR RESERVATIONS

- If you want to have your room located in the main lobby building, ask for it when you make your reservation. A room that is on one of the lobby's balconies is considered a woods-view room. Occasionally, noise from the lobby can be heard in these rooms.
- Courtyard-view rooms can be noisy.
- Some of the lower-floor lake-view rooms have stunning balconies of "granite."

ROMANCE AT THE WILDERNESS LODGE

- Resort theming: ♥♥♥
- The Honeymoon "suite": ♥♥♥
- Having your morning cup of coffee in front of the fireplace on the third-floor landing above the main door: ♥♥
- The Artist Point restaurant: ♥♥
- The Territory Lounge: ♥
- Taking a stroll or a bike ride over to Fort Wilderness: ♥
- Searching for the hidden Mickeys in the lobby: ♥

Disney's Fort Wilderness Resort and Campground

If you've never been to Fort Wilderness, you'll find that there's a lot more going on out there than a campground. More than any other Walt Disney resort area, Fort Wilderness is a world unto itself. With 750 beautifully wooded acres, Fort Wilderness would have little trouble drawing guests even without the nearby Disney attractions. What this amazing place has to offer includes a sandy beach, two swimming pools, a host of watercraft, sports activities, a petting farm, a water park, two popular dinner shows, a restaurant, and a couple of shops. And besides offering a real variety of quality campsites and motor home hookups, Fort Wilderness even has its very own lodgings, the Wilderness Homes and Cabins. To say that Fort Wilderness is a campground would be like calling the Magic Kingdom an amusement park. Fort Wilderness is a campground, but it is much, much more.

Fort Wilderness has a distinctly western flavor. Weathered log buildings, rough hewn timbers, split-rail fences, and meadows filled with wildflowers are set amidst a shady forest of slash pine, cypress, and

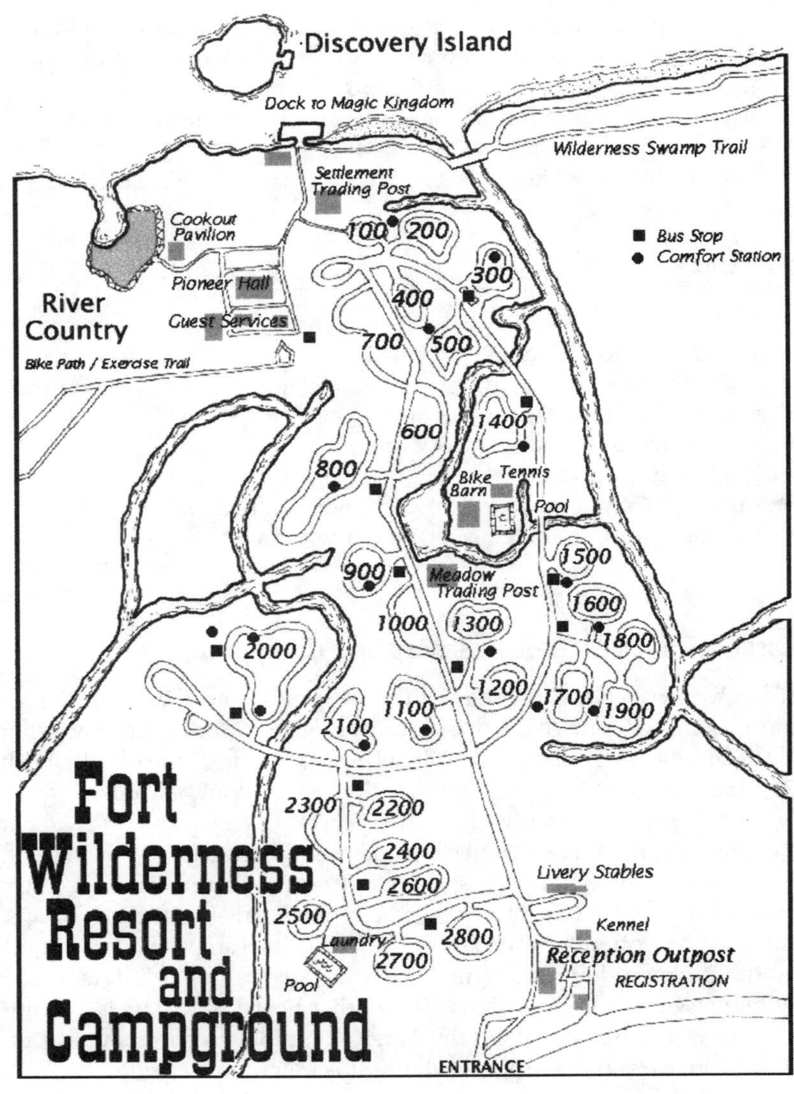
Discovery Island
Dock to Magic Kingdom
Wilderness Swamp Trail
Settlement Trading Post
Cookout Pavilion
Bus Stop
Comfort Station
Pioneer Hall
River Country
Guest Services
Bike Path / Exercise Trail
100
200
300
400
500
700
600
1400
800
Bike Barn
Tennis
Pool
1500
900
Meadow Trading Post
1600
1000
1300
1800
2000
1200
1700
1900
1100
2100
Fort Wilderness Resort and Campground
2300
2200
2400
2600
Livery Stables
2500
Kennel
2800
Laundry
2700
Reception Outpost
REGISTRATION
Pool
ENTRANCE

live oak. Fort Wilderness does not feel much like Florida. It would not be an exaggeration to say that for us, it recalls the many national parks we've visited in the west.

There are three basic types of accommodations at Fort Wilderness: campsites and the Wilderness Homes and Cabins. Each offers something quite different. Both the Wilderness Homes and Cabins are Disney resort lodgings. The campsites, of course, furnish a place to either pitch your tent or hook up your motor home or trailer.

Fort Wilderness Campsites

Fort Wilderness is Disney, and that means everything is something special. The campsites, whether for tents, motor homes, or travel trailers, are all large and relatively private. Each comes with either a full or partial hookup. Full hookups include water, sewer, electric, and cable television. Partials supply only electric and water. All offer ample space, a small barbecue grill, and a picnic table, and all provide 110 and 220 electricity.

Wherever your campsite, you won't be far from an air-conditioned Comfort Station. Each of these features private showers and restrooms, an ice machine, and a coin-operated laundry. They are all clean and well maintained.

There are also a small number of campsites where guests are allowed to have pets. Availability is limited, and these sites all offer only partial hookups. Cost is an additional $5 per night for each pet. If you want to bring your pet on a Disney adventure, be sure to reserve one of these (loops 1600–1900) when you make your reservation.

Fort Wilderness Homes and NEW Cabins

The Fort Wilderness Homes and Cabins are something altogether different. Each is really a small, air-conditioned 12-by-50-foot structure and each has a full kitchen with utensils, pots and pans, a microwave oven, and a dishwasher. All include color TVs with cable and large bathrooms. Living rooms feature pull-down, double Murphy beds, and both the Homes and Cabins are offered with a choice of one of two different bedroom designs. One style features a double bed and a set of bunk beds; the other has one double bed. Each Home or Cabin has a raised, outside deck, a picnic table, and an outdoor grill.

The real difference between the two is that the Cabins are the latest versions of the Homes. Each is new and features log siding and a rough-hewn beam interior. Theming here is at its best and so are creature comforts. We highly recommend a stay in one.

While certainly not equal to the luxury found at Old Key West, the Wilderness Homes and Cabins have their charm. Furnishings are quaint and homey. Chairs and table are woodsy and rustic. The overall feeling is surprisingly pleasant. Each is large: around 500 square feet.

If you are visiting Disney with your children, a Wilderness Home can provide the privacy for your romantic Disney holiday. Being able to prepare many of your own meals will save you some serious money as well. Maid service is included and, amazingly, this means dish-washing too. So cook up a storm and leave the cleaning to Disney.

Location, Location, Location

As the old adage goes, there are three important elements to real estate. The same is true for Fort Wilderness. The central area is around Pioneer Hall, and it is here that you will find the resort's restaurants, Guest Services, the Settlement Depot, beach, River Country, and most of the other recreational activities. We suggest that you locate yourselves as close to it as possible in one of the preferred campsites.

Fort Wilderness is large. The roads here wind lazily through the resort's 700 forested acres. The campsites and homes are all located on small "loop" roads that connect to the larger streets. There are nearly 30 such loops. Some are closer to things than others. Some offer a bit more seclusion. Others offer convenience to the pools or to the beach or bus stops. Each loop is numbered, with the series beginning at Loop 100 and ending with Loop 2800.

Loops 100 through 500 are the Preferred Campsites, and you will pay about $6 more per night to stay in one. They are all full hookups. It is well worth the extra expense, and we suggest that you request one when you make your reservation. We also suggest that you make your reservation as far in advance as possible. These puppies go fast.

If you are planning a stay in one of the Wilderness Homes or Cabins, you'll be a bit farther away. These occupy loops 2100 through 2800. The partial hookup campsites are also a little farther out, occupying loops 1500 to 2000.

1999 Accommodation Rates for Disney's Fort Wilderness Resort and Campground

Accommodation	Regular Season	Peak Season	Value Season	Holiday Season
Wilderness Home	$199	$214	$179	$254
Wilderness Cabin	$229	$249	$204	$275
Preferred Campsite	$60	$66	$49	$74
Campsite, full hookup	$55	$61	$39	$70
Campsite, partial hookup	$45	$51	$35	$59

Occupancy rates are based on two adults per accommodation; children under 17 years of age are no extra charge. A maximum of six persons are allowed in each Home or Cabin, with 10 persons maximum at any one campsite. Extra adults at the Homes or Cabins are $5 each per night and $2 each per night at the campsites.

Transportation and Convenience

Transportation to the Magic Kingdom and Discovery Island is quite convenient from the Settlement area. All other destinations are by bus to the Ticket and Transportation Center (TTC), followed by a bus transfer or, to Epcot, a monorail trip. If there is a problem with Fort Wilderness, this is it. Such trips are time consuming, especially during the busy seasons. A car here would be helpful getting to such places as Downtown Disney, the BoardWalk, or to other Disney resorts for dining.

There are two bus services at Fort Wilderness: one that carries guests around the resort and another that takes guests to the TTC. Buses come and go about every 20 minutes. For complete bus directions, see your resort information and check-in newspaper, "The Gazette," and the Disney Transportation Guidemap.

Since Disney asks that you not drive your car around in Fort Wilderness except to arrive and depart, you'll want to give some thought to getting around this large resort. Rental electric carts are available either for your length of stay or by the day. At $23 per day or $36 for a 24-hour period, these carts are expensive, but if you are in one of the more distant areas, one will come in handy. There are also rental bicycles, available either by the hour or for $12 per day. With miles of peaceful, wooded paths, a couple of bikes would be nice. During our time at Fort Wilderness, we noticed many people riding around on their own bicycles. So, if you are driving and can bring your bikes along, do it. Don't forget a couple of good locks. Otherwise, transportation around the resort will be by Fort Wilderness' internal bus system. Be sure to allow a little extra time to reach your destination.

- To all Fort Wilderness areas: by internal bus
- To Magic Kingdom, Discovery Island: boat launch from Bay Lake dock
- To River Country: internal bus or walk
- To all other Disney destinations: bus to Ticket and Transportation Center, then transfer to other buses; monorail from TTC to Epcot

Restaurants and Eating at Fort Wilderness

Many guests staying at Fort Wilderness fix their own meals. Whether you are visiting in your motor home or staying in a Wilderness Home or Cabin, one real advantage of Fort Wilderness is being able to feed yourselves economically.

We suggest then, on your way through one of the surrounding communities, that you stop for groceries. There are two Trading Posts here at Fort Wilderness, and while they offer a decent selection of basic foodstuffs, they do so at Disney prices. If you are looking for a real supermarket, Gooding's at the Crossroads Plaza near the Downtown Disney Marketplace is convenient.

There are three restaurants at Fort Wilderness, and two of them offer dinner shows: the Hoop-Dee-Doo Musical Revue and the All-American Backyard Barbecue (see Chapter 6 for details). The third restaurant, Trail's End, is located next door to Pioneer Hall and features reasonably priced buffet meals for breakfast, lunch, and dinner. There's plenty of good food at each, and dinners even include hand-carved roast beef.

Crockett's Tavern is Fort Wilderness' picturesque lounge. It features the usual mix of specialty drinks and even offers a barbecue sandwich, nachos, and hot wings. One of us used to be a real Davy Crockett fan, so for us a stay at Fort Wilderness wouldn't be the same without a visit here. It even features some "genuine" Davy Crockett television artifacts. Crockett's is open from 4 to 11 P.M.

Recreational Activities at Fort Wilderness

- Two heated swimming pools and white sand beach
- Marina with rental craft
- River Country water park
- Two lighted tennis courts

- Jogging and walking paths
- Video arcade
- Swamp Trail nature walk
- Petting farm
- Horseback riding and nightly hayrides and campfire program
- Volleyball, tetherball, basketball, horseshoes, and "yolf"
- Fishing excursions
- Hayrides
- Evening movies and marshmallow roast

OUR IMPRESSIONS OF FORT WILDERNESS

- No doubt, this is a super campground. The facilities are first-rate—sparkling and clean. Everything seems new. There is so much to do here that you hardly have to go anywhere for fun.
- We love the Wilderness Cabins and think that they are a great family lodging.

RECOMMENDATIONS FOR RESERVATIONS

- To get either a preferred campsite or one that permits pets, make your reservations as far ahead of time as possible.
- Ask for a Cabin instead of a Home, if it is available.
- At various times throughout the year, there are frequent discounts on both the cabins and the homes.

ROMANCE AT FORT WILDERNESS

- Taking an evening stroll around the resort: ♥♥
- Having a nightcap at Crockett's Tavern: ♥
- Taking a late-afternoon dip in the lake on a hot summer day: ♥
- Having your privacy when you bring your family to a Wilderness Home: ♥
- Watching the Electric Water Pageant from the beach: ♥

Shades of Green Resort

This resort, once known as the Disney Inn, is now reserved for use by active and retired military personnel, employees of the Department of Defense, and members of the National Guard and military reserves. Owned by the U.S. government, Shades of Green

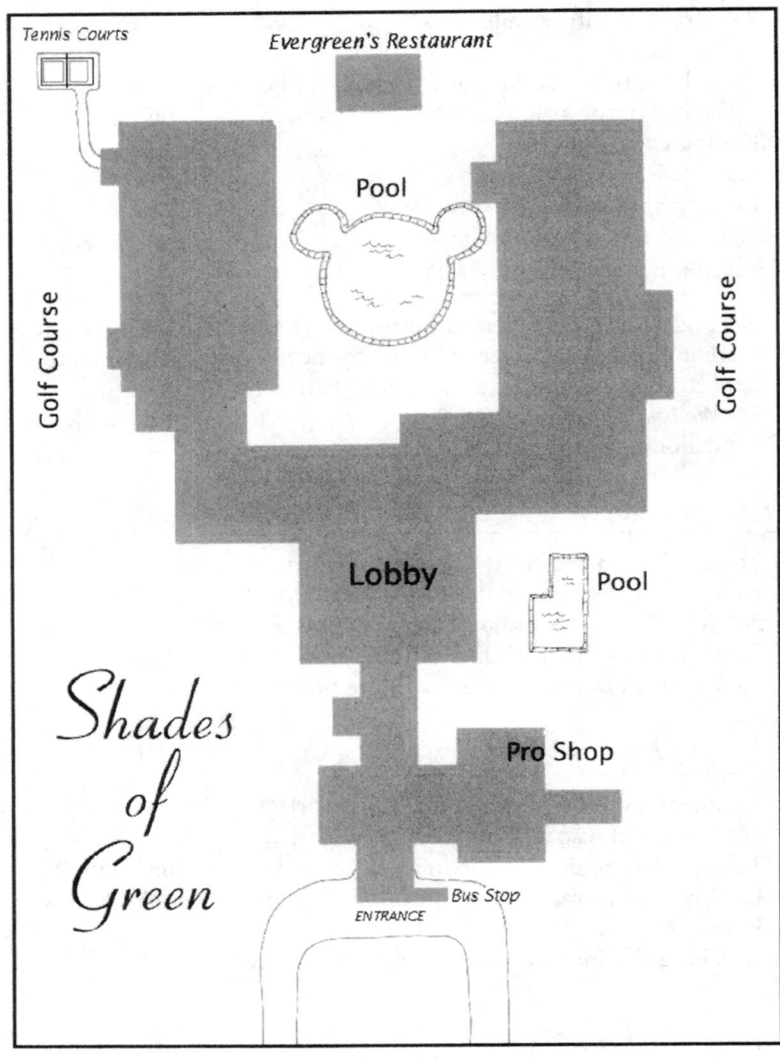
Tennis Courts
Evergreen's Restaurant
Pool
Golf Course
Golf Course
Lobby
Pool
Shades of Green
Pro Shop
Bus Stop
ENTRANCE

provides an affordable Disney vacation for the men and women of the U.S. armed services and their families.

This lovely resort is nestled between two of Disney's championship golf courses, the Magnolia and the Palm. It features a woodsy and quiet ambience. Rates are based on rank and range from very reasonable to downright deserving. Special passes are available to guests at a discount, and Shades of Green restaurants offer meals at reduced prices. Every effort at Shades is made to make the Disney experience an affordable one for our people in uniform.

The long entry drive at Shades of Green seems more like one to an exclusive country club than to a Disney resort. The grounds are beautifully landscaped, and the resort is handsome and well maintained. Theming isn't an element here, but the atmosphere is unmistakably Disney. While guests at Shades of Green do enjoy Surprise Mornings, they do not get Disney resort ID cards.

The staff members at Shades of Green are not Disney employees. We found them to be genuinely dedicated to delivering the best service possible. Employees have all been trained to Disney standards so that the magic Disney hospitality is definitely a presence here.

Special arrangements can be made for small weddings at the resort's own garden gazebo. Family reunions and modest parties are also easily handled by the resort's eager staff. These events can be as grand or as modest as you can afford, and the many rules and regulations regarding such happenings at Disney resorts are not a consideration here. Staff members make a real effort to get to know their guests, and we suspect that repeat customers are the rule rather than the exception.

No taxpayer funds are used to support this resort. Shades of Green and all other Armed Forces Recreation Centers are self-supporting.

Rooms at Shades of Green

The resort consists of one large building with two three-story wings. Guest rooms face either the pool courtyard or the golf course. There is no such thing as a bad view here, and the rooms, at 450 square feet, are among the largest standard rooms in Disney World. Furnishings are light oak, and bedspreads are a floral pattern. Of the 287 rooms, 284 have two queen beds. Two of the remaining three rooms have one queen-size bed, and the last is a large suite. Each room has a sofa bed, small table and chairs, and balcony or patio. A large, remote-controlled color television occupies a colonial armoire, and the bathroom has a vanity and separate shower. Shades of Green is every bit a luxurious Disney resort.

The one suite at Shades of Green has a living room, master bedroom, and a large bath. There is a four-poster king bed in the bedroom and a foldout queen-size sofa bed and two Murphy beds in the living room. This suite can accommodate up to seven persons and has two full bathrooms, one with a small Jacuzzi and bidet.

Suite furniture is of light pine with a ceiling that features varnished, decorative beams. Baskets of crisp linens and objects of art make this lovely suite quite elegant. At $180 per night (regardless of rank), this is an excellent opportunity for honeymooners. It is spacious, luxurious, and romantic. The large patio overlooks the golf course.

Shades of Green is such a bargain that demand is beginning to exceed room supply. We have heard reports that overbooking has caused some Shades of Green guests to be relocated to other Disney resorts, such as the All-Star Resorts, which although they are bargains at $59 per night, are no match for the accommodations at Shades of Green. Other guests have been located at other resorts, mostly the moderately priced resorts such as the Caribbean Beach or Dixie Landings. These resorts are much nicer than the All-Star Resorts. Still other guests are being put up at some of the seven hotels along Hotel Plaza boulevard at Downtown Disney.

Shades reservation personnel have assured us that those guests who are going to stay at a resort other than Shades will be told so at the time of reservation. Since this resort is so nice, we suggest that you make your reservations as early as possible to avoid staying someplace less luxurious.

Valid military ID or current LES and Department of Defense (DOD) pay grade verification is required at check-in. Room rates at Shades of Green are based on rank and civil service rate and double occupancy:

- E1–E5: $59 per night
- E6–E9, O1–O3, WO1–CW3, GS1–GS10, NF1–NF3, widows, disabled veterans: $84 per night
- O4–O6, CW4–CW5, GS11–GS15, NF4–NF5: $89 per night
- O7–O10, retired DOD civilians, NF6: $98 nightly

Special package rates are now available. Reservations can be made by calling Shades of Green reservationists at (407) 824-3600.

Transportation and Convenience

Transportation to all Disney destinations is by Shades of Green buses. These are not Walt Disney World buses. They run on a schedule that is available at the front desk. Service is on par with that of Disney, and having a printed schedule should take the guesswork out of travel.

Dining at Shades of Green

There are two restaurants at Shades of Green. The Garden Gallery has a delightful garden decor with large potted trees. It features American cuisine in a table-service setting with a breakfast buffet and an a la carte dinner of steaks, seafood, and pastas. The Garden Gallery offers discounted dinner prices for Shades guests.

If you're looking for lunch, you'll find it poolside at Evergreen's. Open at 11 A.M., this sports bar and eatery features a selection of salads and sandwiches. The hamburger is quite good. Decor here is interesting, with a collection of antique sports equipment and a tennis court, complete with players, fixed to the ceiling. It's a popular place with the golfers. For our review and more information about Evergreen's, see Chapter 6.

Special Ticketing to Disney Attractions

Along with the usual selection of Disney tickets and passes (all discounted), Shades of Green also offers its own Length of Stay Pass called the Stars and Stripes Pass. It's good for your whole visit and will admit you to all of the Disney attractions. A three-day pass is $115 for an adult; each successive day adds about another $20. Compared to the Length of Stay Pass, this is a considerable savings.

Shops at Shades of Green

One small Army–Air Force Exchange Store features a selection of Disney merchandise at discount prices. Also available are a generous selection of sundries, magazines, and books. Military and DOD identification cards are required to purchase goods at this shop. There's also Made in the Shade, which features popular souvenir items and this resort's logo merchandise.

Services Available at Shades of Green

- Room service from 7 A.M. to 11 P.M.
- Coin-operated laundry facilities
- Small refrigerators ($5 per day)
- Video camera rentals ($6 for 24 hours)
- Travel services

Recreational Activities at Shades of Green

- Two large standard swimming pools
- Two tennis courts
- One kiddie pool
- A children's playground
- A small health club
- Video arcade

OUR IMPRESSIONS OF SHADES OF GREEN

- This is a very nice resort and provides an affordable way for military personnel to visit Walt Disney World and to stay on-property.
- There is no hot tub here at Shades, but the management has assured us that plans are under way to have one built. Just how long the government wheels of progress will grind before this happens is anyone's guess.

ROMANCE AT SHADES OF GREEN

- Resort theming: ♥
- The suite: ♥♥♥

The Epcot Resorts

Disney's Yacht Club and Beach Club Resorts

Next door to Epcot and along the shores of Crescent Lake lie two of Disney's most enchanting creations. Both are visions of nineteenth-century luxury where guests are immersed in a setting that is perfectly exciting, lavishly relaxing, and splendidly romantic. The gray and blue clapboard buildings of the Yacht and Beach Clubs perfectly evoke a bygone era of grace and hospitality. These picturesque resorts share a quaint, turn-of-the-century New England seaside theme. One reflects a more formal nautical charm, while the other radiates the casual ambience of the shore.

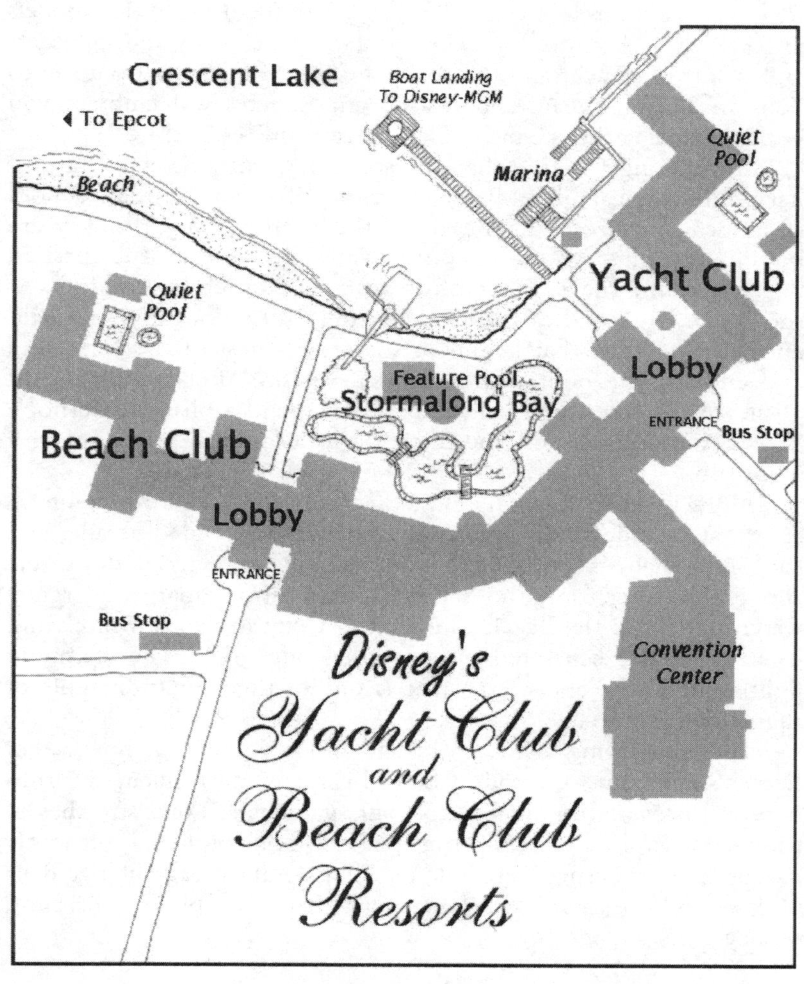
Crescent Lake
To Epcot
Boat Landing
To Disney-MGM
Marina
Quiet Pool
Beach
Quiet Pool
Yacht Club
Lobby
Feature Pool
Stormalong Bay
ENTRANCE
Bus Stop
Beach Club
Lobby
ENTRANCE
Bus Stop
Convention Center
Disney's Yacht Club and Beach Club Resorts

Lakeside, a rope-slung boardwalk, beached shipwreck, lighthouse, and a white sand beach with colorful cabanas complete the seaside illusion. The Disney magic is everywhere, from the antique "woody" station wagon at the front door of the Beach Club to the detailed ship models in the Yacht's elegant lobby. The overall effect is classy and unforgettable. Both the Yacht and the Beach are first-rate resorts from top to bottom. Their intimate and relaxed atmospheres will embrace you both, enhancing the chemistry for your romantic escape.

Stormalong Bay, the shared water playground, is an extraordinary and magical place. It seems more like a river than a pool as it meanders from the Beach to the Yacht. Along the way are bubbling springs, whirlpool eddies, waterfalls, and hot tubs nestled in surrounding rocks. It even features a sand beach for children. At the Beach Club end of the sand-bottom Stormalong Bay is a wild and winding slide that begins in the crow's nest of the shipwreck and ends in the pool with a sudden splash. After a morning of Disney excitement, you will be ready to spend a blissful afternoon here, swimming and sunning. Each resort also has a quiet pool with a hot tub.

Along with Stormalong Bay, the resorts also share a common area that includes Periwig's Salon and Barber, a video arcade, and the Ship Shape Health Club with its old-fashioned indoor spa. Along the waterfront, the Yacht Club features a marina of rental watercraft, while the Beach Club enjoys a lazy stretch of white sand. These areas are separated by a long wooden pier. The charming lighthouse at the end of the pier is one of the signature sights of these idyllic resorts.

The landscaping at the Yacht and Beach Clubs is a showcase of Disney's penchant for details. Colorful gardens and manicured shrubbery will prove an inspiration to home gardeners. Long stretches of trimmed lawns lead gracefully to the lake. On one of them is the lovely gazebo used by Disney Fairy Tale Weddings. Amidst beguiling gardens of roses and the carved, wooden cupids, happy couples tie the knot, Disney-style.

Disney's Beach Club Resort

The relaxed and romantic atmosphere at the Beach has lured us back time and again. We like to think of this place as our home away from home. We confess that staying elsewhere has been done with some reluctance. The casual atmosphere here is elegant yet informal. For us, the Beach Club is simply inviting.

The Beach's lobby is a canvas of pastels, pink marble, and fine woodwork. Large windows facing the lake make the lobby airy and bright. Comfortable wicker furnishings are everywhere on plush carpets of floral designs, and wooden bird cages and large potted palms add just the right touches of warmth.

Around the resort are porches with rockers, beaches with cabanas, and lovely gardens with benches. Enjoying the Disney attractions for a few hours at a time will not be hard. After a morning in the parks, you'll be ready to return.

Rooms at the Beach Club The "seaside" rooms here are sunny and bright. Ensconced amidst the luxurious furnishings and relaxing shades of turquoise, you will not for a minute forget that you are enjoying a romantic vacation at the beach. The verdigris-finished bedsteads and seahorse lamps seem weathered by their "years" at the seashore. The corals, greens, and aquas of the seahorse fabrics convey a pleasant sense of shoreside tranquillity, and the muted prints of beach scenes complete the image. This is a place of creature comforts; it is your own intimate and private retreat. You have landed in the lap of luxury and, if you are like us, you will not be anxious to depart.

Beach Club rooms are indeed inviting. With a choice of either a single king or double queen beds, each room features a large vanity area with twin sinks. The attractive armoire is of light wood. Inside it you will find not only the usual television but also a stocked minibutler. Each room has a small table and several chairs—just the place for breakfast or intimate dining. Many rooms include a daybed/sofa. Balconies are either full-size, with patio furniture, or standing room only. Ground-floor resort rooms all have patios.

There is the usual Disney complement of views. Standard-view rooms look out onto well-landscaped gardens, beyond which are the resort's parking lots. Ground-floor, standard-view rooms have charming little patios that open onto beautiful gardens. Water-view rooms at the Beach overlook Stormalong Bay or the quiet pool area. Other rooms command views of the various gardens on the lakeside of the building, and some rooms provide excellent views of Epcot and IllumiNations, the laser light show.

1999 Room Rates for Disney's Beach Club Resort

Accommodation	Regular Season	Peak Season	Value Season	Holiday Season
Standard view	$284	$314	$264	$350
Water or pool view	$340	$370	$310	$405

Suites at the Beach Club From the luxurious to the lavish, the Beach Club offers a variety of suites. The Newport is this resort's presidential suite. It features a king bedroom with a large vanity, bath, and large Jacuzzi tub. The formal living room is arranged around a fireplace and includes a spacious dining area, wet bar, and room enough for a small party. Located on a corner of the fifth floor, the Newport has a narrow balcony that runs the entire width of the living room and bedroom. The view of Stormalong Bay and of the lagoon is commanding. So is the price: $965 nightly.

The Nantucket is the Beach's vice-presidential suite. With a beautiful king bedroom and a smaller and less formal living room, it seems better suited for a honeymoon or anniversary. Located on the second floor, the Nantucket overlooks a pleasant garden area. It is charming and is conveniently located near the lobby. Price is $690 nightly.

The Beach also offers a deluxe room. At $455 nightly, there are two varieties, each with a large king bedroom. Deluxe A features a sitting area that is part of the bedroom, and Deluxe B offers a separate sitting area with French doors and a daybed. Deluxe B is a nice choice for a family with one child.

Disney's Yacht Club Resort

The lobby of the Yacht Club showcases its nautical theme. A large antique globe sits in the center of the elegant splendor. You will wonder where the Disney folks get things like this. There are intricate ship models in glass cases that invite more than just a casual glance. Ornate brass chandeliers, polished hardwood floors, and decorative ropework recalls the finery of New England's old yachting establishments. Tufted leather sofas and chairs will tempt you with the promise of luxurious comfort. Muted reds, whites, and blues herald the colors of the grand old yacht clubs of Cape Cod, Marblehead, and Bar Harbor.

This lobby area is more formal but is no less inviting than that of the casual Beach Club. There is a certain classiness to this place and, as one of our mothers said when we arrived, "Now, this is the style I'm accustomed to!"

Rooms at the Yacht Club Like the rooms at the Beach, guest rooms at the Yacht Club are light and airy. The furnishings have a bit more formal charm, though. Bedsteads and armoires are of white antiqued wood; the lamps are of polished brass. The nautical decor is made complete with fabrics of blues and whites with accents of pale red. Like her sister ship, the Yacht Club will embrace you with the luxurious comforts found only at first-class hotels: large, soft towels, signature toiletries, and a host of other details.

Each room at the Yacht Club has a vanity area with twin sinks. There are chairs and a small table, and some rooms even have daybeds. Every room has a large balcony with several chairs and a small table where you can sit and enjoy an early morning breakfast, read the newspaper, or simply sit and watch Disney World awaken.

Most rooms at the Yacht Club are configured with two queen beds, but like the Beach, it has a number of king bedrooms. Here at the Yacht, the assortment of views is the same as that at the Beach, except that no rooms here provide a view of Epcot.

1999 Room Rates for Disney's Yacht Club Resort

Accommodation	Regular Season	Peak Season	Value Season	Holiday Season
Standard view	$284	$314	$264	$350
Water or pool view	$340	$370	$310	$405
Concierge garden view	$425	$455	$395	$500
Concierge lagoon view	$460	$490	$430	$540

Concierge Service at the Yacht Club While both the Yacht and the Beach offer a variety of suites, at this time only the Yacht Club features concierge service. However, there is some movement towards a Beach Club concierge floor, and this might be a reality during your visit.

All of the rooms and suites on the Yacht Club's fifth floor feature this wonderful service. Concierge guests enjoy upgraded room amenities, which include a different room decor and terry bathrobes. Of course, they also enjoy use of the luxurious lounge overlooking a pleasant garden area. The continental breakfast each morning features pastries, croissants, cereals, and muffins. Midday snacks are of chips and salsa, fruit, and cookies and milk. Late afternoons mean wine and cheese, a vegetable tray, and a marvelous selection of hors d'oeuvres. In the evening, cordials and desserts are offered.

Suites at the Yacht Club Our favorite Yacht Club suite is the Commodore. It is charming and romantic—the perfect accommodation for a honeymoon, anniversary, or a romantic getaway. The Commodore is large and lavishly furnished. With a comfortable sitting room, a large bedroom with a king-size sleigh bed, and concierge service, a stay here will make your time dreamy and idyllic.

The Commodore's bathroom is spacious and luxurious, more of a room than a bath. Complete with television, vanity areas, walk-in shower, and Jacuzzi tub, it is world-class. If you can afford the $690 per night price tag, we are sure that it will not disappoint you.

The Turret suites occupy the first three floors of the resort's beautiful tower-like structure. Each includes an octagonal sitting room in the turret, a large bedroom, and a spacious living room. The Turret room is sunny and bright, offering a thrilling panorama of Stormalong Bay and Crescent Lake. At over $625 per night, these accommodations are unique and lavish.

If you're looking for something really spectacular, there is the Presidential, which is the fourth floor of the Turret suites. Highlights include a large dining area, Jacuzzi tub, and two full balconies. The basic suite is around $965, with an additional double-queen bedroom adding nearly another $460. Disney CEO Michael Eisner stays here during his Disney visits.

The Yacht's premier suite is the Admiral. It is one of only a handful here on Disney property that offer such luxury. We have taken to calling it "Arnold's Room" after one of its celebrity guests. The Admiral includes furnishings more lavish than even those found in the other Yacht Club suites. Furniture is dark and varnished. There is enough room here for a large family or a small meeting. In the dining room, the table will easily seat a dozen, and the wet bar is designed to be a serving area for a large room-service event.

The dark wood theme is carried throughout, with a large armoire and four-poster king bed in the master bedroom. The bath has an oversized shower and tub. This suite of rooms also has a 40-foot-wide patio, which opens onto its own secluded garden and pond. An additional five rooms can be connected through adjoining doors. We know that Arnold must have liked this place: when he left, he must surely have said, "I'll be back." At nearly $1,000 per night, we have no doubt that he can afford it.

Transportation and Convenience

Both the Yacht and the Beach are only minutes from almost any Disney destination. Whether by boat, foot, or by bus, transportation to anywhere is about as easy as it gets.

Reaching Disney–MGM Studios or Epcot from either resort is by *Friendship* motor vessel. Arrivals and departures are from the lighthouse dock on the beach side of the resorts. The trip to Epcot takes only a few minutes by boat and even less time by foot. All other Disney destinations, except Discovery Island and River Country, are reached by direct buses. Each resort has a bus stop near its front entrance.

- To Disney–MGM Studios: short boat trip from resort dock
- To Epcot: short walk or boat ride to International Gateway
- To Magic Kingdom, the Animal Kingdom, Typhoon Lagoon, Downtown Disney, Blizzard Beach: direct bus
- To Discovery Island, River Country: bus to Magic Kingdom and boat to either; River Country, bus to the Ticket and Transportation Center (TTC) and transfer to River Country bus
- To the BoardWalk: a short stroll around the lake

Dining at the Yacht and the Beach

One of the many advantages here is the outstanding dining. Because these are "Siamese" resorts, guests at either the Yacht or the Beach will find that strolling over to dine at the other resort will be both pleasant and convenient. Each resort boasts its own array of themed restaurants and lounges.

At the Beach, you will find the Cape May Cafe and its delightful beach decor. It serves breakfast and dinner, both buffet-style. Breakfast is a character affair, and dinner is a New England clambake. At the Yacht are the Yacht Club Galley and the superb Yachtsman Steakhouse. The Galley serves a large and varied menu for breakfast, lunch, or dinner, including a wonderful breakfast buffet. The Yachtsman is open only for dinner with its specialty of fine cuts of aged, prime beef. Other entrees include lamb, grilled seafood, and poultry.

In and around the pool area are two other restaurants: Beaches and Cream Soda Shop and Hurricane Hanna's. Beaches is one of our favorite things about these resorts. This delightful fifties-style soda fountain offers a mean double-chocolate ice cream soda, and it is always a part of our visits here. Hamburgers and Disney's finest hot dogs are also featured here. Hanna's is the Y & B's poolside bar and eatery, serving an assortment of drinks, coffees, beer and wine, and good sandwiches. Either of these places is ideal for a light meal while relaxing around Stormalong Bay. Along the beach is a Joffrey coffee wagon, featuring a selection of specialty coffees and pastries. This is some of the best coffee at Disney.

The Yacht Club Galley is the source of in-room dining at both resorts. We have made good use of it on our numerous visits and have always found both the food and the service outstanding.

For more details and our reviews of the table-service restaurants, see Chapter 6.

Lounges at the Yacht and the Beach

Each resort has two lounges. In a quiet corner in the lobby of the Beach, you will find the Rip Tide Lounge. Martha's Vineyard Lounge is the Beach's other lounge and it is a charming and quiet hideaway. Its soft lighting, wicker furnishings, and rose hues create a pleasant atmosphere.

At the Yacht, you'll find the Ale & Compass adjoining the lobby. Varnished brightwork and polished brass are the decor here. Plush sofas and chairs invite you to sit awhile and sample the outstanding selection of imported ales and beers. During the breakfast hours, both the Ale & Compass and the Rip Tide feature coffee, teas, juices, and a small continental breakfast. Either one is a comfortable place to sit and to make plans for your day's adventure.

The Crew's Cup Lounge is next door to the Yachtsman Steakhouse. Offering a complete selection of beers, wines, and mixed drinks, the Crew's Cup features a cozy clubhouse ambience. Comfortable booths, sofas, and plenty of varnished wood and polished brass make it charming and inviting. There's even a rowing shell overhead. With a varied offering of appetizers, finger foods, and sandwiches from the Yachtsman, this is a cozy place to consider for lunch or a light evening meal.

Shops at the Yacht and the Beach

Each resort features its own shop. The Atlantic Wear and Wardrobe Emporium can be found at the Beach Club, and Fairings and Fittings is over at the Yacht. Both shops offer a large selection of sundries, character merchandise, and gifts. Each features its own line of logo resort wear and a unique line of men's and women's apparel. There's some very nice stuff at these shops, making them two of our favorite shopping places. Both shops often feature sale racks.

Along the beach, you'll also find a few interesting "shops." The Pearl Factory offers a selection of pearl jewelry as well as live oysters, each with a pearl inside. Nearby are Temporary (Disney character) Tattoos and Hair Wraps.

Recreational Activities at the Yacht and the Beach

- Stormalong Bay pool complex: ♥♥
- Five hot tubs/spas: ♥♥♥
- Two quiet pools: ♥
- Sand beach on the lake (no swimming) with cabanas

- Lafferty Place video arcade
- Fireworks cruises: ♥♥♥
- Complimentary tennis courts (at the Beach Club)
- Jogging and walking paths (map available at the front desk)
- Ship Shape Health Club, state-of-the-art fitness center with sauna and spa
- Bayside Marina with a variety of rental boats
- Volleyball (ball at health club)
- Bocci ball and croquet court (at the Beach Club)
- The Surrey quadricycles at the BoardWalk

OUR IMPRESSIONS OF THE YACHT AND THE BEACH

- These are lovely, charming, and romantic resorts. Most certainly, our favorites.
- With such proximity to the BoardWalk, Epcot, and Disney–MGM a stay here will have you in the middle of all the fun and excitement. This is the best corner of Walt Disney World to be in.
- Dining is outstanding. To these choices add the convenience of the restaurants at Epcot, the Swan, Dolphin, and the BoardWalk, and you'll have to narrow your choices down from nearly 30 restaurants, all within walking distance.
- Our penchant for hot tubs is most certainly satisfied here. There are two lovely hot tubs near Stormalong Bay, one more at each of the quiet pools, and one in the health club.
- Both resorts have recently enjoyed total "soft good" rehabs: new spreads, curtains, and fabrics.

RECOMMENDATIONS FOR RESERVATIONS

- Standard-view rooms on the ground floor of the Yacht and the Beach enjoy quiet garden areas. Parking lots are not very visible from them. This is not true for upper-floor standard-view rooms. Ground-floor standard rooms at the Beach are smoking rooms.
- The fifth floor at the Beach used to be concierge service. The rooms are a bit different and feature a few added amenities and upgraded fabrics. Concierge service may be offered again here at the Beach Club. Ask.
- If you want real convenience to Epcot and the BoardWalk, ask for a room near the Beach's quiet pool.
- If you wish to be in one of the upper-floor rooms facing Epcot, ask for it when you reserve and again when you check in.

- Real versus tiny balconies at the Beach Club are hit or miss. On your reservation and at check-in, be sure to request a room with a real balcony.
- Some of the rooms can be a walk from the main elevators. If this is not to your liking, mention it at check-in.

ROMANCE AT THE YACHT AND THE BEACH

- Overall resort theming: ♥♥♥♥
- Room ambience: ♥♥♥
- Yacht Club concierge service: ♥♥♥♥
- The Commodore suite, with concierge service: ♥♥♥♥
- Stormalong Bay pool area: ♥♥
- Room-service breakfast in bed: ♥♥♥♥
- Hot tubs at day's end or late night: ♥♥♥
- Taking a stroll over to the World Showcase for IllumiNations: ♥♥
- Taking a swim in Stormalong, then going to Beaches and Cream for a double-chocolate ice cream soda: ♥
- The *Breathless* IllumiNations Cruise for Two (see Chapter 7 for more information): ♥♥♥♥
- Watching IllumiNations from the beach: ♥♥♥
- A "*Breathless* Burst" (see Chapter 7): ♥♥ (See our coupon in the back of this book for a 10% discount.)

Disney's BoardWalk Inn and BoardWalk Villas

This resort is a charming remembrance of America's bygone era of seaside holidays. It is the golden years of such places as Coney Island, Atlantic City, Cape May, Nantasket, and Revere Beach brought marvelously to life. If in your youth you were lucky enough to enjoy a vacation at one of these shoreside gems, you'll find the BoardWalk to be a powerful piece of nostalgia. If you never did, you'll discover here a magical re-creation of a time you may have only imagined.

The BoardWalk is both a resort and an entertainment district, and it brings together more than just a few of our favorite elements. It is a delightful and exciting period piece and after dark it comes alive with romantic magic: dining, dancing, and entertainment. You'll find it all here as you stroll the BoardWalk Promenade. Located directly across Crescent Lake from the Yacht and the Beach Clubs, the BoardWalk is the perfect creation to cohabit this, our favorite corner of Walt Disney World.

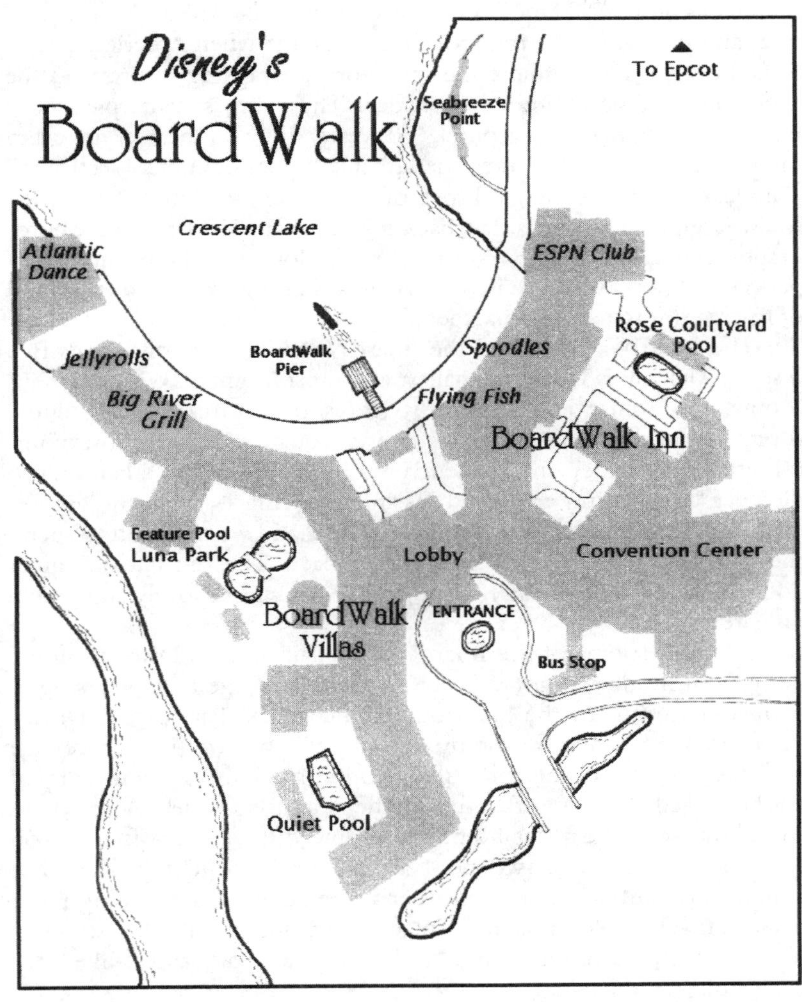

Disney's
BoardWalk
To Epcot
Seabreeze Point
Crescent Lake
Atlantic Dance
ESPN Club
Rose Courtyard Pool
Jellyrolls
BoardWalk Pier
Spoodles
Big River Grill
Flying Fish
BoardWalk Inn
Feature Pool
Luna Park
Lobby
Convention Center
BoardWalk Villas
ENTRANCE
Bus Stop
Quiet Pool

The BoardWalk features two very different resorts joined by a bustling, barrel-vaulted, and Victorian lobby. The elegant entrance reminisces an era of American culture. This is the 1930s Atlantic seaside, and here you'll be transported to that age when Americans vacationed on the shore amidst the splendor of sprawling resorts and the excitement of oceanside promenades. The lobby's centerpiece is a magnificent miniature carousel, 70 years old and perfect in every minute detail. Overhead, the indescribable "Hoppocampus Electrolier" chandelier weaves its magical spell of wonder and delight. Overstuffed sofas, large potted palms, fan-back wicker chairs, and the old photographs and curious relics of this period's long-vanished amusement parks create a powerful sense of nostalgia. Disney's knack for this kind of re-creation remains unmatched.

The BoardWalk Inn and the BoardWalk Villas are this area's two resorts. The Inn is Disney's smallest and most intimate. With only 378 rooms, this romantic, Victorian-style resort features well-appointed rooms, awning-covered balconies, private courtyards, and a host of unforgettable "seaside" and garden views. Explore the Inn's hallways to discover cozy sitting areas and fascinating artifacts from the amusement parks of this era. Everything has a tale, and we urge you to spend the time learning the story behind this place. The Inn has one quiet pool and an accompanying hot tub/spa, both set in a lovely and peaceful garden area.

The 532 rooms of the BoardWalk Villas fall into Disney's home away from home category. Accommodations range from the single-bedroom studios to the luxurious Grand Villas. Part of the Disney Vacation Club, these accommodations will be for time-share sale and for rental. All of the Villa's lodgings feature some sort of cooking facility; most offer full kitchens and laundries. A stay here will allow you to eat "at home" and dine out only as often as you wish. The Villas have two pool areas: one is a quiet pool with a community clubhouse and another more resembles an amusement park. Luna Park is an exciting place, featuring a roller coaster–like water slide, a carousel lounge and eatery, and a carnival-like children's play area.

More than a resort, the BoardWalk's charm is that of a seaside village of the mid-Atlantic. Its grounds are beautiful, hospitable, and relaxing. Mowed lawns, picket fences, beguiling gardens, and manicured shrubbery carefully accentuate its varieties of architecture. The effect enhances the sensation that this place evolved over time, that it truly *is* a small coastal town.

Once settled into your room, the excitement begins. The magic of the BoardWalk comes alive after dark. Its lively Promenade features a world that you have only imagined. You'll find shops, restaurants, nightclubs, sidewalk vendors and entertainers, and boats arriving and departing from the Promenade Pier. And there's more: magicians, games of skill, fire-eaters, and portrait artists. Everywhere is the magic that you have been expecting, and it is all right outside your door. Stroll the Promenade, then enjoy a quick snack or some fine dining. Rent a bicycle "surrey," or walk to Epcot. You can dance the night away at Atlantic Dance or simply sit and enjoy the nightlife. This is one of the neatest places at Disney. For more details about the BoardWalk, see chapter 5.

Rooms at the BoardWalk Inn

This is a deluxe resort and a stay here means that you'll be immersed in both the luxury and magic of Disney. The Inn is a showpiece of Victorian charm, featuring an eclectic blend of elegant furnishings styled to create the ambience of a bed and breakfast. Iron and brass bedsteads, antique photographs of old seaside resorts, vintage furniture, and papered wainscoting all evoke an enchanting sense of the past. Accommodations at the Inn feature either twin queen beds or a single king. Standard rooms are large (390 square feet), and most feature child-size daybeds. Marble baths are roomy, and spacious vanities feature large mirrors and dual sinks. Draperies have been created using the images of actual postcards of this period. The Inn's rooms feature the colors of blue and white, with bedspreads of botanical specimens accented with floral greens and pastels.

All rooms at the Inn have balconies; those with standard views overlook the front of the resort and its reception area. From the water view rooms, you'll be right on the Promenade, enjoying all the charm and romance of the BoardWalk. Lodgings here are surprisingly quiet when the balcony doors are closed. The Inn's garden view rooms are adjacent to the lovely Rose Courtyard, one of the most unique and quiet places at Walt Disney World. Here, among flower-covered trellises and picket-fenced gardens, in the shadow of Epcot's Eiffel Tower, your Disney romance will come to life. Sit a while amidst this garden splendor or take a dip in the quiet pool. The Rose Courtyard only *seems* a world away from the excitement of the nearby Promenade.

1999 Room Rates for Disney's BoardWalk Inn

Accommodation	Regular Season	Peak Season	Value Season	Holiday Season
Standard view	$274	$304	$254	$329
Garden view	$284	$314	$264	$350
Water view	$355	$385	$325	$405
Concierge	$425	$455	$395	$500
Concierge deluxe	$495	$530	$465	$580
Garden suites	$645	$675	$615	$770

Concierge Service and Suites at the BoardWalk Inn

Known as the Innkeeper's Club, the Inn's concierge service is small and sublime. From our own blissful experience here, we know you'll relish the plush bathrobes, the luxurious lounge, and the highly personal service. A continental breakfast with coffees, teas, and a variety of pastries, bagels, fruit, and cereals will be the perfect beginning to each morning. Available throughout the day are a variety of beverages and snacks. After 3 P.M., enjoy tea, sandwiches, and pastries. Late-afternoon snacks include wine, cheese, and a hot dish from one of BoardWalk's fine restaurants. The friendly and helpful concierge staff will be most pleased to make all your arrangements. After dinner, you'll want to return to the lounge's balcony to sip cordials, nibble desserts, and enjoy IllumiNations. This is romantic Disney at its finest.

The Innkeeper's Club offers only three king beds among its standard rooms. The remainder have two queen beds. Concierge deluxe rooms feature two queen beds and a large sitting area with a pull-out queen. Junior suites, at around $630 nightly, each have a king master bedroom and Jacuzzi tub with adjacent parlor room featuring a plush sitting area, pull-out queen, and second bath.

The Inn's presidential suite is called the Steeplechase, and it is the most elaborate and grandest on the property. Extravagant furnishings, a Promenade view, and its incredible size combine to make this suite of rooms ($1,245 per night) something unique even among presidentials. Canopied king bed, giant Jacuzzi tub, and a full patio with potted palms are but a few of its many memorable features. The Sonora, at $1,060 nightly, is the vice-presidential suite, and though scaled back a little, it is nearly as stunning.

The Inn's garden suites are some of the most unique on-property accommodations. Perfect for any honeymoon or romantic getaway, each features a private entrance through the gate of its own unique rose garden. Complete with birdhouse, mailbox, arbor, and picket fence, each suite is the quintessential love nest. Just a bit secluded, all 14 garden suites offer downstairs sitting areas and upstairs king bedrooms with couple-sized Jacuzzi baths. Furnishings are typically luxurious and follow color schemes similar to standard rooms.

Except for several of the concierge deluxe rooms on the third floor and the garden suites, which are in the Rose Courtyard, all suites and concierge rooms are located in the fourth floor's exclusive Club area. All garden suites and concierge deluxe rooms, regardless of location, include concierge access.

Rooms at the BoardWalk Villas

The sunny seaside accommodations of the Villas come in a variety of shapes and sizes, each with a roomy balcony. These bright and colorful lodgings all offer a simple decor of casual comfort. Floral prints, brass fixtures, and gleaming white woodwork reminisce the family vacation cottage at the beach. Ceiling fans, large tiled baths, and cozy creature comforts will have you feeling right at home.

The studio features a single king bed and a queen sleeper/sofa. A small wet bar provides refrigerator, microwave oven, and coffeemaker. Request a toaster from housekeeping, if you like. Some studios also offer a child-size daybed, providing enough sleeping space for four adults and one child.

The spacious one-bedroom villa is one of our favorite accommodations at Disney. It is the perfect place for a small family, a romantic escape, or both. These villas each feature the complete villa kitchen with dishwasher, toaster, blender, range, refrigerator, and enough equipment to cook just about any meal you might desire. The living area features an entertainment center with VCR and TV as well as several chairs and a pullout queen sleeper. Let's not leave out the breakfast bar, dining area, washer and dryer, or the rest of this splendid place. The master bedroom's king bed adjoins the tiled bath and its Jacuzzi tub. This villa's comfortable 720 square feet and its location at the BoardWalk make it one of the World's most attractive accommodations.

By adding a connecting studio to a one-bedroom villa, you'll get a two-bedroom villa. The Grand Villa is a luxurious, three-bedroom apartment. It includes two baths, a living area with sleeper/sofa, dining room, complete kitchen, master bedroom with a four-poster king, and a large Jacuzzi tub.

There is the usual assortment of views here at the Villas. The standard view overlooks the front of the resort and parking areas; preferred views can be either overlooking the BoardWalk or one of the pool areas.

1999 Room Rates for the BoardWalk Villas

Accommodation	Regular Season	Peak Season	Value Season	Holiday Season
Studio				
Standard view	$274	$304	$254	$330
Preferred view	$284	$314	$264	$350
One-bedroom villa				
Standard view	$345	$375	$315	$405
Preferred view	$385	$415	$355	$450
Two-bedroom villa				
Standard view	$555	$679	$440	$615
Preferred view	$595	$729	$480	$685
Grand Villa	$1,250	$1,350	$1,150	$1,540

Transportation and Convenience

Located in our favorite corner of Walt Disney World, the BoardWalk shares the same transportation system as the Yacht and the Beach Clubs and the Swan and the Dolphin. Whether by foot, bus, or boat, you'll feel right next door to every Disney destination.

- To Disney–MGM Studios: short boat trip from the Promenade Pier
- To Epcot: short walk or boat from Promenade Pier
- To Magic Kingdom, the Animal Kingdom, Downtown Disney, Typhoon Lagoon, Blizzard Beach: direct bus
- To Discovery Island, River Country: bus to Magic Kingdom, then boat

Dining at the BoardWalk

Dining choices here at the BoardWalk are so good that you might not care to venture elsewhere for a meal. But if you do, be ready to make a decision, because there are more than 20 good restaurants within walking distance.

At the BoardWalk, try the fine dining and imaginative cuisine of the Flying Fish Cafe. This is one of the World's hottest places for a great meal and one not to miss. Spoodles and its "cuisine of the sun" is another outstanding BoardWalk eatery. Featured here is an outstanding breakfast menu and Mediterranean tapas and wood-fired pizzas for both lunch and dinner. There's more, too: try the super sandwiches, pastas, and salads at ESPN Club or the Big River Grille & Brewing Works' pleasing selection of entrees, pub pies, salads, gourmet burgers, and five handcrafted beers. For more detailed information and reviews of these and other Disney eateries, see Chapter 6.

The BoardWalk also offers 24-hour room service, delivering food from its variety of restaurants. If you don't see what you feel like eating on the menu, ask for it. Room service also features a sumptuous assortment of themed "amenities baskets" such as might be left in your room while you are out. Just a few of these treats include a chef's special chocolate turndown, elaborate welcome baskets, and cookies and milk.

The BoardWalk Promenade also features an interesting and often amusing selection of treats more suited to a nibble, a quick lunch, or snack. The BoardWalk Bakery will tempt you with muffins, bagels, croissants, and a luscious offering of pastries. The Bakery also manages a selection of juices, coffee, milk, espresso, and cappuccino. Seashore Sweets is the Promenade's old-fashioned sweet shop. Saltwater taffy, soft-serve ice cream, and a selection of beverages and coffees make this a place to check out. Spoodle's sidewalk cafe even has an "express" breakfast window, which becomes a pizza cafe after 5 P.M.

In the evening, along the Promenade are a host of vendors and carts offering an entertaining variety of treats: popcorn, hot dogs, fried onion rings, shaved ice cones, crepes-on-a-stick, and fresh fruits and juices. There's even a Joffrey coffee wagon with a variety of excellent specialty coffees and pastries.

Lounges at the BoardWalk

Besides the entertainment district of the Promenade, the BoardWalk is home to two lounges. The BelleVue Room is the Inn's 1930s-style sitting room. Drop in here for a flight of single-malt scotch, small-batch bourbons, or Grand Marniers. Cozy, comfortable, and quiet, this full-service bar is open from 11 A.M. to midnight, with the nostalgic music and radio shows of the 1930s. Leaping Horse Libations is the pool lounge at the Villas. Looking more like a carousel, the Leaping Horse offers an assortment of sandwiches and alcoholic or nonalcoholic specialty drinks.

Shops at the BoardWalk

Adjacent to the lobby is Dundy's Sundries, the place for BoardWalk logo merchandise and the usual variety of film, souvenirs, and gifts. Looking to take home a soap dish like the one in your room? Find it here. The Promenade's Screen Door General Store is just the place for packaged drinks, snacks, and modest selection of groceries. Thimbles and Threads is the BoardWalk's source for swimwear and resort apparel, while character merchandise can be found at the Character Carnival.

For the serious collector and interested browser alike, Wyland Gallery displays and sells a truly amazing collection of stunning marine artwork. Both sculptures and murals here are not to be missed.

Recreational Activities at the BoardWalk

- Luna Park swimming area with the 250-foot-long Keister Koaster water slide and large pool
- Two quiet pools
- Three hot tub spas, one at each pool area
- Muscles and Bustles Health and Fitness Center
- Children's playground at Luna Park
- Harbor Club, evening and daytime children's activity center
- Bicycle rentals at the Villas Community Hall
- Surrey rentals on the BoardWalk Promenade (four-wheeled pedal cars for two, four, or six persons)
- Two lighted tennis courts (equipment and lessons available)
- Rentals at Villas Community Hall: video movies, bikes, pool floats
- Fantasia Gardens miniature golf (see Chapter 7 for details)
- BoardWalk two-hour guided bass fishing excursion (see Chapter 7)
- BoardWalk fireworks cruise
- Sideshow Games video arcade

OUR IMPRESSIONS OF THE BOARDWALK

- The Inn is luxurious and romantic—a first-class establishment in every way
- The Villas offer unique and comfortably homelike accommodations. The one-bedroom villa is a real gem.
- Overall, this resort is really something special: beautifully themed, romantic, and exciting. There is so much to do here that you could keep busy without ever visiting a single theme park. One of

Disney's premier destinations.

Recommendations for Reservations

- At the Inn, go for either water or garden views. The garden view is the most romantic.
- For couples with children, try a one-bedroom villa or a junior suite.
- Try a one-bedroom villa or studio to save money on meals. Look for off-season specials.
- If you want a room with a Jacuzzi: go for a one-bedroom villa, junior suite, garden suite, Steeplechase, or Sonora.
- If you're on your honeymoon, be sure to mention it on your reservation.

Romance at the BoardWalk

- Overall theming: ♥♥♥♥
- King bed at the Inn: ♥♥♥
- A stay at the Innkeeper's Club: ♥♥♥♥
- A garden suite: ♥♥♥♥
- Dinner at the Flying Fish: ♥♥♥
- Rent a surrey for two and ride around the lake: ♥♥♥
- Sinatra Night at Atlantic Dance: ♥♥♥ (See the coupon in the back of this book for 20% off your bill at Atlantic Dance.)
- A nightcap and radio show at the BelleVue Room: ♥♥♥
- A late-night swim at the quiet pool or hot tub: ♥♥♥
- A drink and appetizer on the outside patio of Atlantic Dance: ♥♥♥
- Breakfast in bed: ♥♥♥♥
- IllumiNations from the second-floor outside balcony of Atlantic Dance: ♥♥

The Walt Disney World Swan and Dolphin

These unusual resorts are the product of Michael Eisner's unwillingness to settle for less. When he came aboard as Disney CEO, he insisted on something quite different than the structures planned for this site. "Come meet my architect," he told the planners. And of course, he was talking about the world-renowned Michael Graves. What ensued was an architectural competition that produced this unique resort complex.

The Swan and the Dolphin are perfectly aligned, set together like sisters and nestled neatly between Epcot and the Disney–MGM Studios. Separate, yet part of a greater whole, these two share some-

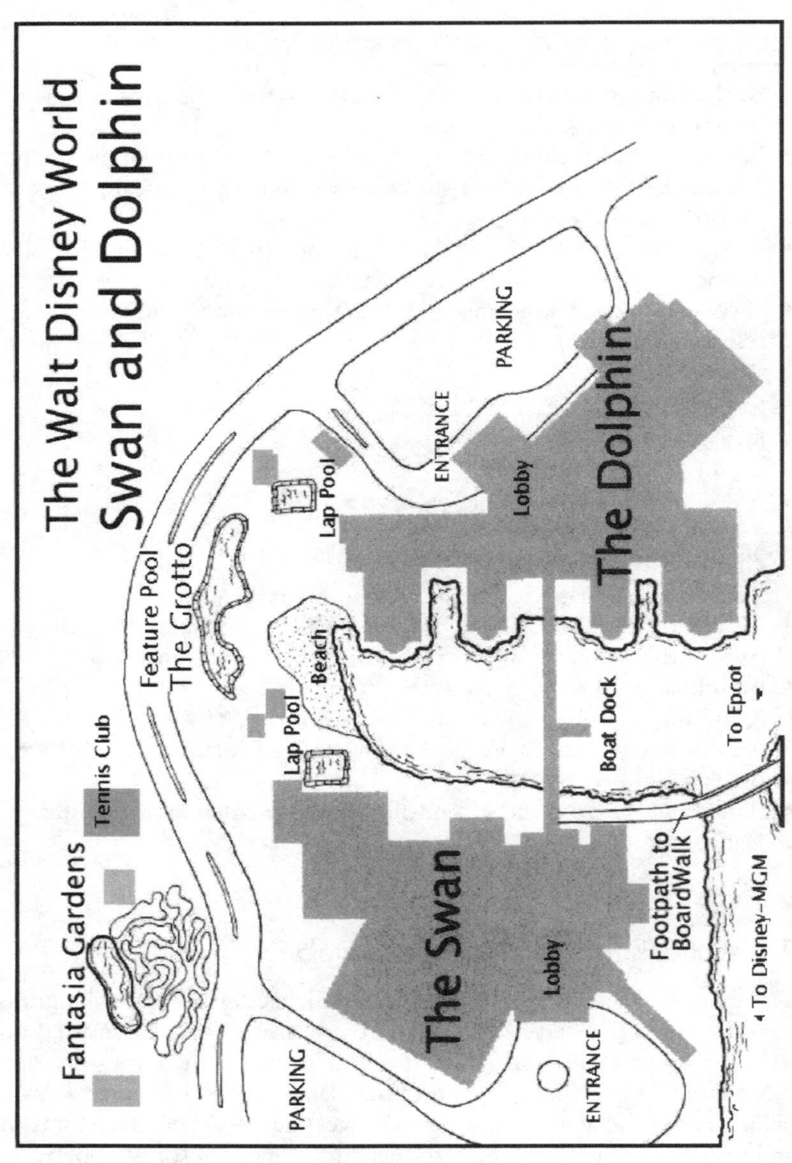
The Walt Disney World
Swan and Dolphin
Fantasia Gardens
Tennis Club
Feature Pool
The Grotto
Lap Pool
Beach
Lap Pool
PARKING
ENTRANCE
Lobby
The Dolphin
Boat Dock
To Epcot
The Swan
Lobby
Footpath to BoardWalk
To Disney-MGM
PARKING
ENTRANCE

thing special. The coral and aquas of their exteriors and the perfect convergence of shapes tell us that there is a juncture happening. These fantastic structures were designed from the ground up to occupy each other's space, to be seen together and from each other. The theme of these resorts is fantasy and fun. Everything from the 47-foot swans perched atop one resort to the nine-story cascading waterfall at the other serves to evoke a feeling of whimsy and delight. A visit here after dark will work its magic spell.

Virtually no expense has been spared in the landscape design of these resorts. Date palms, magnolias, and other well-tended foliage abound. Driveways, walkways, and paths are all integral pieces in the big and beautiful picture.

Each resort has its own Olympic "lap" pool with hot tub. Both resorts share a water playground that ranks second only to the Yacht and the Beach Clubs' Stormalong Bay. The Grotto is a long and narrow lake/pool. Waterfalls, secluded hot tubs, and a water volleyball court are several of its highlights.

A recent merger has brought these two sisters together. They are now managed by the same company, and since neither is a Disney resort, you will find a few differences. Most noticeable will be the Length of Stay Pass, which is not available for guests of the Swan or Dolphin. Each resort maintains a Guest Services desk that offers the usual selection of tickets and passes. Your Swan and Dolphin resort card will be limited to charging at both resorts only. Aside from these, you will enjoy all of the benefits of staying at a Disney resort: Surprise Mornings, preferred tee times, same-day dinner reservations, and guaranteed park admission, to mention only a few. These two resorts seem to cater to conventions and businesspeople and seem a little more adult-oriented than Disney resorts. But make no mistake about it, both feature first-class, deluxe accommodations and services typical of the world's finest resorts.

Transportation and Convenience

The Swan and the Dolphin enjoy the same wonderful transportation that serves the Yacht and the Beach Clubs and the BoardWalk. This group of resorts is the most convenient of all Disney resort areas.

Both the nearby Epcot and Disney–MGM are reached by boat from a dock on the walkway between the resorts. The BoardWalk is a short stroll away and all other Disney destinations are via direct buses, leaving from the bus stops near each front entrance.

The Walt Disney World Swan

The Swan was the first Disney resort that we visited without our kids. We hadn't been to Disney World in more than 10 years when we arrived here. We'd never seen Epcot, and Disney–MGM Studios had just opened. We had no idea what to expect and were ready for just about anything. What we got was a few days of intimate and relaxing fun. We had a wonderful time strolling around and discovering the parks and we had an even more memorable time at this classy resort. We enjoyed hot tubs, swimming, and fine dining, all accented with occasional touches of Disney magic. We were hooked.

On this first trip, we slowed our car as we approached the Swan. We marveled at the elaborately complex landscaping and ornate cast-iron street lamps. Above and around us loomed a building the likes of which we had never seen. The huge, twin swans sitting on its roof were not even its most unusual details. The resort's paint job seemed more like a giant mural: huge, aqua waves broke on hues of coral. The balconies included ironwork so intricate that it appeared to have been carved.

So intriguing was this place that we felt more like exploring than registering. The tropical theme of the grounds and building were carried gracefully into the interiors. A fountain of swans and a flock of parrot chandeliers were but a few of the many delightful decorations. The furnishings featured carved swans, and even the sand in the ashtrays was imprinted with the seal of the swans. Hallways, windows, and porticos were all in symmetry. This confluence, we were to discover, was one of the essentials of Michael Graves' design.

Rooms at the Swan Our first room at the Swan had two queen beds. It would take a few more visits before we would discover king-size sleeping accommodations. The room's bright array of tropical colors was cheerful and gay. Woodwork was lightly colored and trimmed in pastel aquas and pinks. Our balcony looked out onto a small lake and, across it, to an as yet unfinished Dolphin. A quick look around our room revealed a large armoire with a color television, a massage showerhead, and a basket of luxurious toiletries. In the closet were bathrobes with embroidered swans. The level of luxury, we knew at once, was something that we were going to get very used to.

Many of the resort rooms look out onto the Dolphin, which is a very attractive and impressive sight. From some upper-floor rooms, guests can get an impressive view of IllumiNations. Many more have views of Disney–MGM Studios, and others look out over the swimming areas. There really aren't any bad views here, simply better ones. Rooms are available with either a king-size bed or two queens. Not all rooms, however, have balconies. Value season at the Swan is considerably longer than it is at Disney resorts and includes summer.

One of the features we enjoy here at the Swan is paying $5 per day and getting use of the health club and free local calls.

1999 Room Rates for the Walt Disney World Swan

Accommodation	Value Season	Peak Season
Standard view	$275	$310
Lake view	$300	$355
Resort view, no balcony	$315	$375
Resort view, balcony	$330	$395
Royal Beach Club (concierge)	$405	$430

Concierge Service and Suites at the Swan Concierge service at the Swan is known as the Royal Beach Club and is located on the exclusive east end of the twelfth floor. A continental breakfast is served each morning, and beverages and fruit are offered at midday. Hors d'oeuvres and cocktails begin before dinner, and coffee and desserts are served in the evening. Alcoholic beverages are served at reduced prices. In all, you receive a day's worth of delights. The Swan's dedicated concierge staff is available to assist with all of your reservations and special needs. There is even a complimentary shoe shine service. All you have to do is ask.

There are five different suite designs at the Swan. Each has something unique to offer. The Junior suite is the most affordable. Each comes with a lavishly furnished bedroom, a king bed, desk, and sofa and chairs. The ample living room and dining area feature a round table and four cane-back chairs. Cloth robes, private bar, and live plants are a few of the indulgences.

The color scheme of these suites is that of the resort: aqua and rose. Fabrics are soft and plush. Each occupies the end unit of the Swan's wings. This corner position provides for many windows and an outstanding panorama. At around $400 a night, the Junior suite has a lot going for it. A stay here will be indulgently romantic.

From this modest start, the suites become considerably more expensive. Beginning with the Grand suite at nearly $1,000 per night, followed by the Governor's suite at nearly $1,300, and reaching all the way to one of the two incredible presidential suites at around $2,000 nightly, these suites are well suited to those able to afford them. The two presidential suites each feature a theme. One is the Oasis room, the other is the Southwestern room. With over 1,000 square feet, these multiroom suites each feature a marble entryway, grand piano, fully stocked bar, king-size bed, Jacuzzi tub, and full kitchen stocked with assorted beverages. Furnishings are lavishly extravagant. It is hard, even for us, to imagine traveling in this style.

Dining at the Swan As we have mentioned, dining options at this resort are exceptional. With memorable eating places at the neighboring BoardWalk and the Yacht and the Beach Clubs as well as those at the nearby countries of Epcot, the choices begin to look limitless. And they are. For convenient, varied, and outstanding dining, this is the corner of Walt Disney World to be in.

The Swan offers its guests three interesting table-service eateries. The all-purpose restaurant is the Garden Grove, which serves every meal in a pleasant garden gazebo. At dinner, it becomes Gulliver's Grill, featuring seafood and steaks. Disney character breakfasts are served here on weekends, and a variety of dinnertime entertainment, including characters, is featured throughout the week.

Palio offers fine Italian dining in a romantic atmosphere. Featuring strolling musicians and outstanding food, Palio is one of our favorite dining spots at Disney. The dessert cart here features an exceptionally large and inviting selection. The Splash Grill and Deli is the Swan's convenience-food location. Located near the lap pool, this small restaurant features a variety of lunches, dinners, and snacks. Even more convenient is the Swan's 24-hour room service. Its large menu can furnish snacks, meals, beverages, or the makings for intimate in-room dining. For reviews and information about these and other restaurants, see Chapter 6.

Lounges at the Swan Kimonos is a beautiful and stylishly created retreat that features an Oriental flair. Relax and watch the sushi chefs perform their graceful art. Kimonos is a romantic place to have some fine sushi, tempura, or a drink.

The Lobby Court Lounge, besides offering a selection of wines and spirits, also offers an outstanding cup of coffee. Open in the morning and again in the evening, the Lobby Court Lounge also features a decadent assortment of pastries and chocolate desserts, more than enough to tempt the stalwart. This is a delightful place to sit in the evening and listen to the lounge's player piano.

Shops at the Swan Disney's Cabana is the Swan's souvenir and Disney character merchandise store. It also offers a large selection of casual men's and women's sportswear.

Services Available at the Swan

- Valet parking
- Full bell service
- Valet and laundry service
- Beauty salon
- Concierge desk
- Nightly turndown service
- Pay-per-view movies
- Refrigerators

Recreational Activities at the Swan

- Lap pool with spa and the Grotto (a three-acre water playground)
- Kiddie pool
- White sand beach with watercraft rentals
- Health Club at the Swan
- Jogging and walking path
- Tennis club and basketball court
- Camp Dolphin and Camp Swan children's activity centers
- Video game room
- Fantasia Gardens miniature golf

RECOMMENDATIONS FOR RESERVATIONS AT THE SWAN

- Reservations for this hotel are handled by Disney CRO at (407) 934-7639; by Westin Reservations at (800) 228-3000; and by the Swan/Dolphin reservation system at (800) 227-1500. For the best rates, we recommend calling the Swan/Dolphin number.
- The farther ahead you book, the better the rate.
- Try checking with Westin for its yearly variety of special rates, promotion, and honeymoon packages.
- For a free room upgrade on a romance package, see the coupon in the back of this book.

OUR IMPRESSIONS OF THE SWAN AND DOLPHIN

- These are beautiful and fanciful resorts. Both seem a bit more adult-oriented than the Disney Resorts.

- A beach, beautiful pools, hot tubs: you have it all at these resorts.
- These resorts are right in the middle of our favorite corner of Walt Disney World, near great dining, entertainment, and nightlife.
- Both resorts offer convenience to all Disney attractions.
- Not being able to charge everything around Disney to your room account is a drawback here, though not a serious one.

Romance at the Swan

- Resort theming: ♥♥♥
- Room amenities: ♥♥♥
- Fine dining: ♥♥♥
- Breakfast on your balcony: ♥♥♥
- Dinner at Palio, listening to the music of a strolling violinist: ♥♥♥
- Hot tubs: ♥♥♥
- Evening walks to BoardWalk, Epcot countries, and the Yacht and the Beach Clubs: ♥♥
- Watching IllumiNations from your balcony: ♥♥♥
- Beach hammock, under the stars: ♥♥♥

The Walt Disney World Dolphin

Water is the theme of this beautiful resort, and it is everywhere. From rows of fountains at the front gate to trickles that flow down the stone walls of the foyer, the pleasant sound of rushing water is music for Dolphin guests. One of the sights here is the waterfall on the Swan side of the resort. Overlooking Crescent Lake, this giant fountain cascades along nine stories of huge, shell-shaped levels and into a 60-foot-wide clamshell.

The scale of everything here is grand. The most prominent part of the resort's main building is the 27-story pyramid that has become a fixture of the Disney skyline. Nearby sit the two 56-foot fish sculptures that celebrate this resort's aquatic theme. Next to the Statue of Liberty, they are the tallest free-standing sculptures in the U.S. From their perch high atop the resort, they stand watch upon a colossal creation of tulip-shaped floral fountains that adorn the tower wings. At night, this array seems too large to be real.

Keeping to the color theme of the two resorts, the building's coral hues are swathed in painted, turquoise banana leaves. Reaching from ground level to the tenth floor, this outrageous mural took six months to complete. It creates a fantasy aura that is part of the Dolphin's mystique.

The lobby too is whimsical and entertaining. Brightly colored fabric hangs from its 10-story ceiling to create a cavernous tent. Flowering vines climb trellises that encircle the lobby floor, and arranged symmetrically around the central fountain are clusters of sofas and chairs. You see artwork everywhere: murals, paintings, and sculptures; the works of Picasso, Matisse, and Rousseau. Even the elevator seems bright and tropical.

Rooms at the Dolphin The rooms are bright and cheerful. A large and well-appointed vanity and a cozy sitting area will make you feel at home. From the floral drapes to the coral and turquoise bedspread, your romantic Disney vacation will take on the fun and tropical theme of the Dolphin. One look out the window and you know that you are in the middle of all of the magic that Disney has to offer.

The variety of resort rooms at the Dolphin come with a choice of either one king bed or two doubles. That is two doubles, not two queens. As with hotels everywhere, the more spectacular the view, the more spectacular the price. Our favorite room at the Dolphin is called the Premier King View. Located on the ends of the wings of the main building, these charming rooms look out in two directions with an unmatched view of the lake, the Swan, Epcot, and Disney's BoardWalk. Each has a king-size bed and twin balconies. A coffeemaker will make mornings a pleasure. At $380 during the brief regular season, this room enjoys many specials during the remainder of the year.

Value season at the Dolphin does not mimic Disney's. It is much longer and runs from early January to mid-February and again from mid-April to the end of the third week in December.

1999 Room Rates for the Walt Disney World Dolphin

Accommodation	Regular Season	Value Season
Standard view	$275	$310
Lake view	$300	$355
Resort view, no balcony	$315	$375
Resort view, balcony	$330	$395
Club level (concierge)	$405	$430

Concierge Service and Suites at the Dolphin The 77 spacious and lavishly decorated guest suites of concierge service are located in the Dolphin Tower. Private check-in will begin your journey here, and along the way you will learn the meaning of "pampered." You'll be treated to a host of luxurious toiletries, Dolphin bathrobes, hair dryer, special stationery, and coffeemaker.

The plush Tower Lounge is available exclusively for the use of Tower guests. This area features a large entertainment center, magazines and newspapers, and a small library. A continental breakfast will be the perfect way to start each day. If you desire, fresh coffee and orange juice can be delivered to your room. Hors d'oeuvres and cocktails service are offered before dinner. After dinner and before your romantic evening out, don't forget to stop by and have a dessert while you watch the fireworks. There is a charge for all concierge alcoholic beverages.

Complimentary use of both the Dolphin's health and fitness center and the tennis courts are also part of your romantic Dolphin Tower visit. A light pressing service is also available upon request. And, of course, the concierge staff eagerly awaits your every request.

The Dolphin boasts that it offers more suites than any other resort at Walt Disney World. While this may be true, many of them are better suited for business purposes. The two types of suites worth mentioning are the junior and the presidential.

The junior suites are in various places throughout the resort. Each consists of a parlor connected to a regular resort room with either a single king bed or two doubles. The parlor offers a sitting area with a pull-out sofa bed and several comfortable chairs.

While you might not feel the need for an extra room, you might find it a good place for the kids if they are with you. During the brief peak season, a junior suite will cost around $650 per night. Most of the year, the same suite is about $550.

There are four presidential suites at the Dolphin. Each has been extravagantly decorated with its own exotic personality. At nearly 3,000 square feet, these suites are larger than many private homes. Named Los Presidentes, the Pharaoh's suite, the Emperor's suite, and Caesar's suite, each is the final word in luxury. Service even includes a round-the-clock butler. These two-bedroom suites offer a large entertainment center, gold-plated bathroom fixtures, ten telephones, four VCRs, and a fully stocked kitchen. Some of the famous persons who have occupied these rooms are Dustin Hoffman, Macauley Culkin, Eddie Murphy, Dolly Parton, and Michael Jackson. This suite costs $2,500 nightly.

Dining at the Dolphin As guests of the Dolphin, you will enjoy a large variety of eateries. Five restaurants provide everything, from the poolside Cabana Bar and Grill to the seafood and steaks of exotic Harry's Safari Bar and Grill. The Coral Cafe is the Dolphin's all-purpose restaurant and features a mix of buffets and a la carte offerings throughout the day. The Dolphin Fountain is a 1950s-style soda shop with a menu of American classics, while Juan and Only's offers Mexican cuisine. For more details and reviews of these restaurants, see Chapter 6.

The Dolphin offers the option for fast food too. Tubbi's Buffeteria is a cute little cafeteria that offers a pretty standard selection of convenience foods. Snacks, breakfasts, lunches, and dinners are the offerings, and there is even a small convenience store that offers a variety of snacks and sundries.

Room service at the Dolphin should not be overlooked as a dining option. The menu is large. We love having our dinner served to us on a white tablecloth right in the privacy of our own room. We suggest that you give it a try. Also available for delivery are Chinese food and pizza. To order breakfast the night before, turn your television set to Channel 88 and follow on-screen directions. A Japanese-style breakfast is also available.

Lounges at the Dolphin When it comes to nightlife, only Downtown Disney and the BoardWalk have more to offer than the Dolphin. The Copa Banana is the Dolphin's nightclub and it frequently features live entertainment. Dance the night away to the rhythm of the islands and enjoy a fruitful selection of tropical drinks. Harry's Safari Bar and Juan's Bar and Jail are two other exotic lounges to visit. Both offer a large selection of wines, beers, and cocktails. Have a yard of ale at Harry's or sip a rare tequila at Juan's. Both are fun and colorful places and well worth your time.

You shouldn't have any trouble finding the Lobby Lounge. Drop by this quiet bistro for a glass of wine or aperitif while you enjoy the music of a live pianist. And at poolside, you can enjoy beer, wine, or tropical cocktails at the Cabana Bar and Grill.

Shops at the Dolphin There are four shops in the lobby of the Dolphin. From gourmet chocolates to jewelry and fine apparel, these shops should provide some interesting browsing and even something special to celebrate your visit here.

Services Available at the Dolphin

- Valet parking
- Full bell service
- Beauty salon

- Multilingual concierge
- In-room massage
- Valet and laundry service
- Pay-per-view movies

Recreational Activities at the Dolphin

- Heated pool and the Grotto (a three-acre water playground)
- Kiddie pool
- White sand beach with watercraft rentals
- Body by Jake Health Club
- Jogging and walking path
- Tennis club and basketball court
- Camp Dolphin and Camp Swan children's activity centers
- Video game room
- Fantasia Gardens miniature golf

RECOMMENDATIONS FOR RESERVATIONS AT THE DOLPHIN

- Reservations for this hotel are handled by Disney CRO at (407) 934-7639; by Sheraton reservations at (800) 325-3535; and by the Swan/Dolphin reservation system at (800) 227-1500. We recommend booking through the Swan/Dolphin number for the best rates.
- The farther ahead you book a room in this resort, the better the price will be.
- Being a member of the Sheraton Club will provide some interesting perks. Call (800) 325-3525 for details.
- For a free room upgrade on a romance package, see the coupon in the back of this book.

ROMANCE AT THE DOLPHIN

- Resort theming: ♥♥♥
- Room amenities: ♥♥
- Premier King View room: ♥♥♥
- Breakfast in bed: ♥♥♥♥
- Hot tubs: ♥♥♥
- Evening walks to BoardWalk, Epcot countries, the Yacht and the Beach Clubs: ♥♥
- IllumiNations from your balcony: ♥♥♥

Disney's Caribbean Beach Resort

When we first arrived at the Caribbean Beach and were greeted by a valet dressed like a Nassau policeman, we knew that we were about to

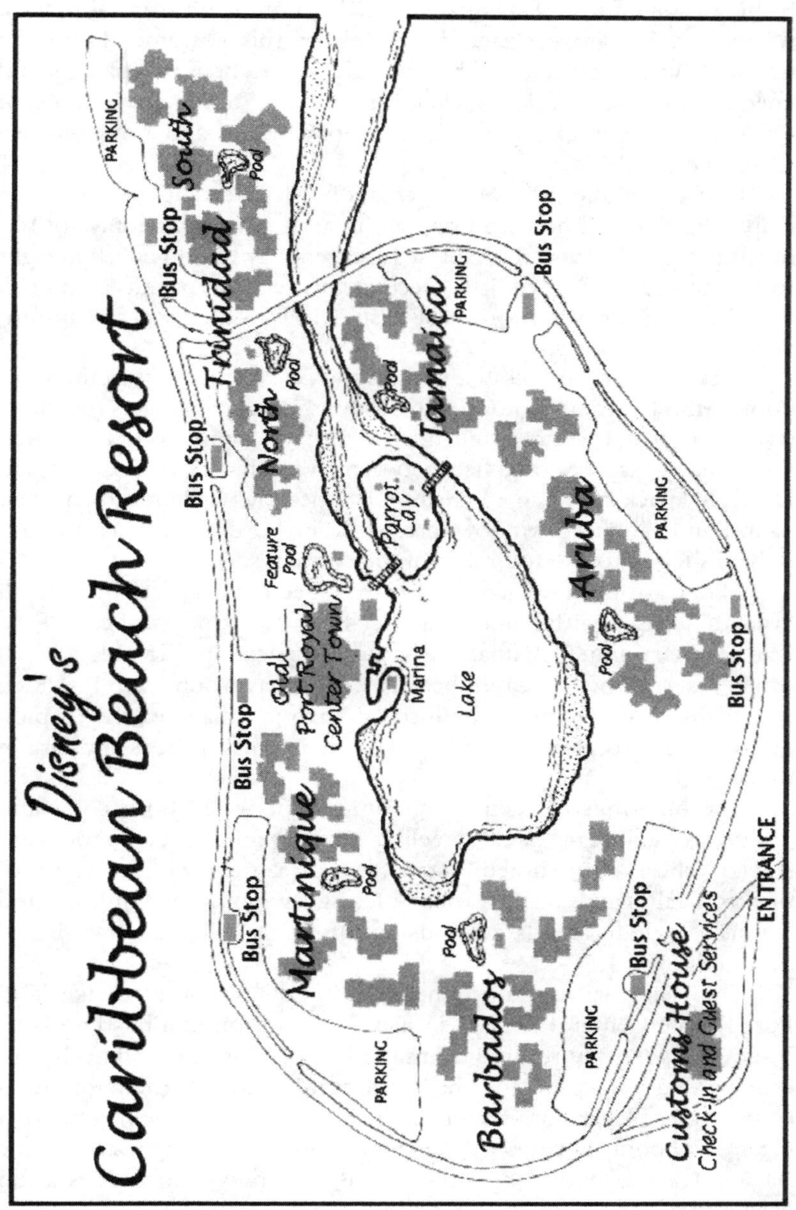
Disney's
Caribbean Beach Resort
PARKING
South
Pool
Bus Stop
Trinidad
North
Pool
Bus Stop
Bus Stop
PARKING
Jamaica
Pool
Parrot Cay
Feature Pool
Old Port Royal Center Town
Marina
Lake
Aruba
PARKING
Pool
Bus Stop
Bus Stop
Martinique
Pool
Bus Stop
Barbados
Pool
PARKING
PARKING
Bus Stop
Customs House
Check-in and Guest Services
ENTRANCE

really go somewhere. Having spent many months on tropical islands, we were able to appreciate the details of this costume. From the starched, white jacket and brass whistle to the braided epaulets and knee socks, here, we knew, was a bit of the authentic Caribbean. Once out of our car, the fragrances of jasmine and bougainvillea embraced us.

Like all fantasies, this Disney creation will take a bit of willing participation. You will need to bring along a bit of imagination. Not too much though, because this fantasy is real enough. From check-in right to the door of your own little piece of this relaxing paradise, you will both be entering yet another of Walt Disney World's perfectly rendered themed resorts.

When you arrive, follow the signs for Guest Check-In to the front door of the Customs House. The Customs House re-creates the lobby charm of an old-world island hotel. Trust us when we tell you that these places are few and far between even in the real Caribbean. Disney's knack for such re-creation is uncanny. Ceiling fans, potted palms, and shuttered windows are but a few of the details typical not only of the Customs House but of the entire resort.

The Caribbean Beach Resort has been created as five small "island" villages with names that recall the exotic ports of call of the Caribe: Martinique, Aruba, Barbados, Jamaica, and Trinidad. Each offers its own white sand beach, pool, playground, and shaded courtyard. Everywhere is the lush and exotic foliage of the tropics: hibiscus, mango, jasmine, and palms. The scents of the islands are in the air.

The buildings of each village are distinctive in both color and design, to give each area a feeling of uniqueness. Two-story and stucco, these "tin-roofed" structures are rich with a taste of the tropical islands. The variety of brightly colored buildings and whimsical gingerbreads reminds us of some favorite down-island destinations.

The island villages surround Barefoot Bay, a 50-acre lake. Old Port Royale Center Towne, a Disneyesque version of a bustling West Indies village, is the resort's central hub. Colorful, gay, and lively, this little "town" is home for the Caribbean's shops, restaurant, food court, water playground, and marina. Enjoy a soak in the hot tub or a dip in the pool, hop on a bike, rent a boat, or lounge around the Banana Cabana pool bar to the strains of Jimmy Buffet. It is a fun place to be.

In the middle of the lake is Parrot Cay, an island connected by foot bridges to the villages on one side of the lake and Old Port Royale

Center Towne on the other. Narrow paths, live parrots, gazebos, a kiddie playground, and picnic area are all set against a lush backdrop of dense bamboo and a tropical garden. It is just the place for a quiet breakfast or a romantic evening stroll.

The colors, the foliage, and the ambience will relax you. Take your time to savor this place and your time here. The Caribbean Beach does exactly what the best of resorts anywhere do and what Disney resorts do better than anyone: it takes you above the everyday and transports you to that unforgettable place called "vacation."

Rooms at the Caribbean Beach

Our king bedroom was located in the island village of Aruba. Some resort rooms with king-size beds are located on the corners of the buildings. This gave our sitting area two windows, one on either wall, rather than the usual single window. With the curtains open and the sheer drapes drawn, the room was bright and airy.

While color schemes vary from one island village to another, the room furnishings are similar. Our room had pale sage walls, bordered at the ceiling by a strip of flowered wallpaper. Its deeper greens and hints of pinks matched the flowered bedspread. The posts of the wooden bedstead featured carved wooden pineapples, the symbols of hospitality.

A large armoire with television was opposite our bed. Next to it was placed the minibutler, stocked with soft drinks, beers, wines, and lots of snacks. One bonus was a coffeemaker, complete with a daily filter pouch of coffee. For us, having our first cup of coffee while still in our room (or bed) was heavenly.

The vanity area featured double sinks and a large mirror. Plenty of room for both of us to get ready for an evening out. The bathroom, a bit on the small side, had the usual shower-tub combination.

Overall, the room was pleasant and comfortable, and we enjoyed our time there. Everything seemed rather new and extremely well maintained, even though this resort is not one of Disney's newest. This, you will find, is the trademark of all Disney resorts.

There are two basic room configurations at the Caribbean Beach: rooms with king-size beds and rooms with twin double beds. All of the king bedrooms here at the Caribbean have connecting doors to adjoining rooms with two doubles. If you are visiting Walt Disney World with your children, this may be an enticing choice.

There are a small variety of views here. Water-view rooms overlook either the lake or the pool. Since pool views seem to look onto the walls that surround the pools, we suggest that if you are looking for a water view you should opt for one of the lake; ask at check-in. Standard-view rooms feature views of either the courtyard or the parking lots. When you check in, we suggest that you ask for (and be prepared to wait for) a courtyard view. Our courtyard view was quiet and beautiful, and it greatly enhanced our visit here.

1999 Room Rates for Disney's Caribbean Beach Resort

Accommodation	Regular Season	Peak Season	Value Season	Holiday Season
Standard view	$134	$149	$119	$164
Water view	$154	$169	$139	$184
King bed	$154	$169	$139	$184

Transportation and Convenience

Service from this resort is quite good, with buses running at least every 20 minutes throughout the day and every 10 minutes during peak hours.

- To all Disney destinations: by bus

Dining at the Caribbean Beach

If there is a drawback to this resort, it is the limited dining options. At Old Port Royale Center Towne is a single table-service restaurant and a food court. The Captain's Tavern is open only for dinner, from 5 P.M. to 10 P.M. It is a small but quaint table-service restaurant and is moderately priced. For reviews and information about this and other restaurants, see Chapter 6.

The Old Port Royale food court is called Market Street, and it is a rather cute little avenue of food shops. Decorated with palms, colorful kites, and other Caribbean artifacts, these exotic storefronts come complete with balconies and "roofs." The effect is delightful. Counter-service shops have names such as Cinnamon Bay Bakery, Montego's Deli, and Bridgetown Broiler.

The seating here is more comfortable and private than most food courts, and with the choice of eating outside on a pleasant porch, we think that this place rates well for a Disney fast-food outlet. Open from 7 A.M. to midnight, Market Street serves a large variety of foods for each of the day's meals.

While the Caribbean Beach does not offer room service, it does offer a delivery service that features pizza, sandwiches, and beverages.

Shops at the Caribbean Beach

Several shops are located in Old Port Royale Center Towne. The Straw Market offers a selection of Caribbean Beach logo merchandise and a variety of tropical and pirate souvenirs and toys. Also found here is a nice collection of tropical sportswear, as well as a small selection of fruits and snacks and Jamaican Blue Mountain coffees.

Adjacent to the Straw Market is the Calypso Trading Post, where you will be able to purchase the usual variety of Disney character merchandise, postcards and stamps, books and newspapers, and a variety of snacks, souvenirs, and sundries such as sunblock and nonprescription medications.

Recreational Activities at the Caribbean Beach

Recreational activities are one of the Caribbean's strong suits. In addition to a themed main pool area are six more quiet pools. The central pool at Old Port Royale boasts a themed swimming area that includes a spa, water slide, and kiddie pool. The surroundings are an "old" Spanish fort, complete with turrets, cannons, and waterfalls. A short slide runs from the ramparts to the water. The pool is exactly the kind of thing that we love so much about Disney resorts: it resembles a movie set more than a hotel pool. The hot tub is, unfortunately, rather small. Although the Caribbean offers sparkling white sand beaches, no lake swimming is allowed. With chaise lounges, cabanas, and some nice hammocks, the beaches are attractive places to catch some sunlight or moonbeams.

The Caribbean also offers a selection of motorized and nonmotorized boats, bikes, and "surrey" quadricycle, pedal cars. A family recreational package is available for about $70 per day, providing unlimited use of bikes and boats. Considering that most motor boats are $20 for half an hour, this package is reason enough to set aside a day to spend away from the theme parks.

OUR IMPRESSIONS OF THE CARIBBEAN BEACH

- Guest Services is located far away in the Customs House, and dining options are minimal. This is more of a problem at breakfast time, when the food court is the only option.
- A car would be of some advantage here, especially for traveling to other resort areas to dine.
- This is a very attractive resort.

Recommendations for Reservations

- Barbados and Trinidad South are a bit far from the central resort area and should probably be avoided (or resort guests in these areas should be given complimentary bicycles). We prefer either Jamaica or Aruba. Both are a short walk from the central areas, and the walk takes you across Parrot Cay. We found this stroll pleasant and, in the evenings, even a bit romantic.
- There are no passenger elevators here, so if you have a problem with climbing stairs to a second-floor room, be sure to request one on the ground floor.

Romance at the Caribbean Beach

- Resort theming: ♥♥
- Courtyard-view room: ♥♥
- King bed resort room: ♥♥
- Early picnic breakfast on Parrot Cay: ♥♥
- Late-night swim at a quiet pool: ♥♥
- Beach hammock by starlight: ♥♥♥♥
- Evening stroll around the resort: ♥♥

The Animal Kingdom Resorts

Disney's Coronado Springs Resort

In his quest for the fabled seven cities of Cibola, Spanish conquistador Francisco de Coronado should have come to Florida. While he wouldn't have found the legendary lost cities of gold, he would have discovered 16 of the most fanciful resorts in the New World, the latest of which bears his name.

Disney's Coronado Springs features the flavor and architecture of the Southwestern U.S. and Mexico and is set on 125 wooded acres between MGM Studios and the Animal Kingdom. Spread lazily around Lago Dorado, a picturesque 16-acre lake, Coronado Springs is comprised of three "villages," each a unique taste of the old Southwest. Disney's first moderately priced resort to include a convention center and fine dining, Coronado Springs offers a colorful diversity of resort experiences all wrapped neatly into one.

If you arrive here with just the right amount of imagination, you'll find yourselves journeying to another place and time. The resort's en-

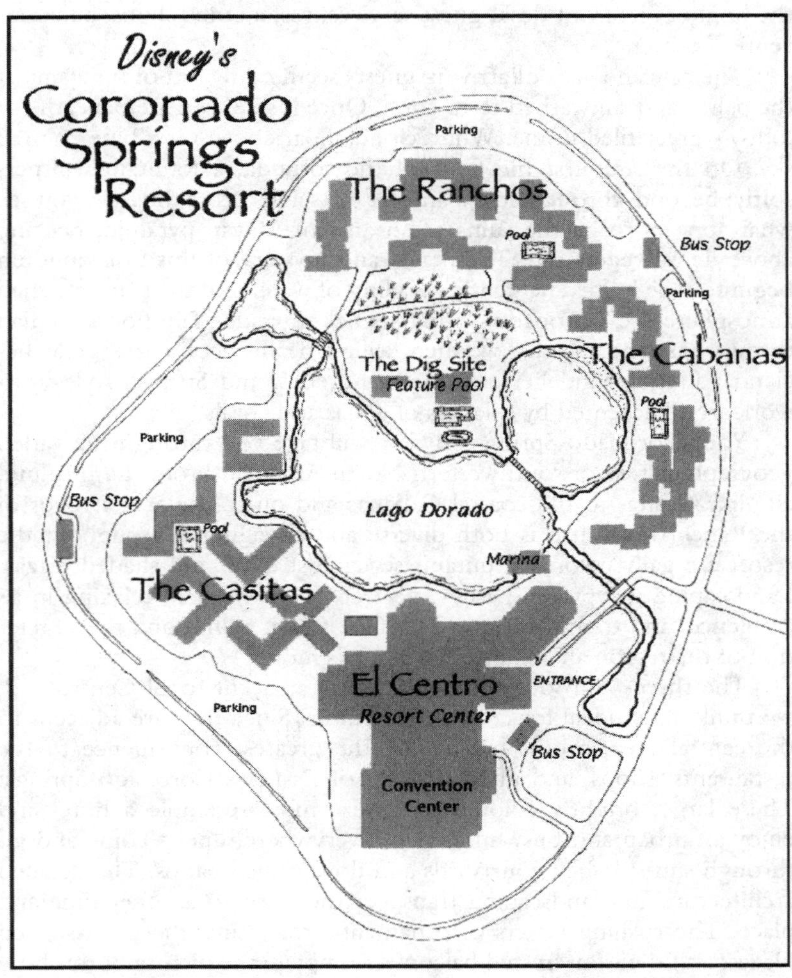
Disney's
Coronado Springs Resort
Parking
The Ranchos
Pool
Bus Stop
Parking
The Cabanas
The Dig Site
Feature Pool
Pool
Parking
Bus Stop
Pool
Lago Dorado
Marina
The Casitas
El Centro
Resort Center
ENTRANCE
Parking
Bus Stop
Convention Center

tranceway leads across a small stone bridge and up to the central building's grand and tent-like porte cochere, where you will be welcomed by a costumed staff. This is El Centro, Coronado's hub of activity and the home of its front desk, guest services, restaurants, shops, and convention center.

The cars and vans of arriving guests seem oddly out of time amidst the palms and sunwashed terra-cotta. Once inside, you are beneath the lobby's great tiled dome. White clouds float above on a blue painted sky. On the sunburst tile floor of the rotunda, a fountain whispers softly; beyond, through an expanse of glass and across the lake, you see what appears to be the ruins of an ancient Mayan pyramid, peeking above dense vegetation. The magic and mystery of this lost kingdom begin to take hold. The gentle gurgling of water and the sun-drenched atmosphere are Coronado Spring's stock-in-trade. Tile floors, Indian throw rugs, and massive wooden ceiling beams accent this great hacienda. Large chandeliers, tile-framed arches, and Spanish-style ironwork are all accented by splashes of aquas and corals.

Your Coronado Springs odyssey will take you through the varied geographic areas of southwestern North America. From the bustling, city-like Casitas to the coastal Cabanas and on to the arid arroyos of the Ranchos, the trip is both diverse and engaging. Throughout the resort are gaily colored fountains set amidst quiet and shaded plazas. Landscaping is typically Disney: perfect in every detail, relaxing in its ambience, and transporting in its effect. Cacti, palms, and the vegetation of the region all enhance the resort's motif.

The three- and four-story Casitas are adjacent to El Centro and, we think, most ideal for convention guests. Since they are adjacent to the central area, rooms here enjoy the greatest convenience to the restaurants, shops, and guest services of Disney's Coronado Springs. These large, brightly colored haciendas most resemble a hotel and enjoy an urban and busy ambience. Everywhere, guests come and go through sun-splashed courtyards and flower-filled patios. The detailed architecture and landscaping transport the spirit to another time and place. The rushing waters of ornamental fountains, the palm-shaded plazas, and the iron-crested balconies complete the picture of this little south-of-the-border city.

Across the lake, Coronado Springs takes on yet another mood altogether. Forgotten now is the hustle and bustle of El Centro. Here, a pleasant stroll away, across picturesque footbridges, you will discover the quiet and enchanting countryside of southwestern North America.

Your journey will take you first to a small rocky cove of Lago Mar, around which are scattered the tin-roofed Cabanas. They are a picturesque celebration of coastal Mexico. Half of the rooms in these two-story, terra-cotta bungalows enjoy stunning vistas of the lake, the ruins of the ancient pyramid, and at night, the dazzling lights of the central area. Life here in the Cabanas is leisurely and romantic.

Not far away, you'll come across this resort's exciting feature pool, the Dig Site. Here, surrounded by the ruins of a vanished civilization, an "ancient" Mayan pyramid appears only partially unearthed. A tangle of jungle vines seems intent on reclaiming it while water tumbles gently down its steep staircase and into the swimming pool that lies at its base. From somewhere behind, the Jaguar Flume water slide whooshes its riders beneath the steely gaze of a giant jungle cat and into the cool waters below.

In the shadow of this great pyramid lies a unique children's play areas. One of its many features is a large sandbox where little archeologists can dig to uncover Mayan antiquities. Other "excavations" amidst these ruins include a large hot tub, arcade, and poolside bar and snack shop, Siesta's. The Dig Site even features a volleyball court and children's wading pond. It is the discovery of the Lost Kingdom of Gold come to life.

Past the Dig Site, you'll enter a small wildlife area. The dense foliage, wooden walkway, and iron lamps are the ideal elements for an evening stroll. Further along, this mythical journey will take you into the arid regions of the pueblo-style Ranchos. Rocky buttes, cactus gardens, hitching posts, and red tile roofs accent this, the best-themed of Coronado Spring's three villages. This village may be farthest from the central area but it is the one not to miss. Throughout the Ranchos runs a dry and stony river bed. Add to all of this the Florida sunshine and you'll easily imagine that you are visiting a grand hacienda of Old Mexico.

Each of the three villages has its own uniquely landscaped quiet pool and a network of walkways connects them all to each other, to El Centro, and to the Dig Site. The Esplanade walkway runs around the entire lake. It's perfect for a romantic evening stroll.

Rooms at Disney's Coronado Springs Resort

This is a moderately priced Disney resort, and rooms here are all comparable to other resorts of this category. With 314 square feet, you should find them spacious for two and fairly comfortable for a small family. Each has a large vanity with a single sink and the usual shower-tub bathroom. All of the rooms at this resort feature coffeemakers and irons and ironing boards. Refrigerators are available for a small daily charge. There is the usual mix of single king beds and twin double beds. Elevators and both ice and vending machines are conveniently located in every building.

Each of the three villages features its own special decor that has been created to enhance its theme. Rooms at the Casitas are casually formal and accented with turquoise and salmon. Bedspreads are a colorful Mexican pattern and bedstead and armoire are antiqued aqua accented with Mayan sunbursts. Rooms at the Ranchos have a decidedly Indian motif. Blues, golds, and the triangular patterns of Navajo artistry accentuate these rustic lodgings. Furniture is of dark wood and room décor includes a hammered metal mirror. The ambience of Old Mexico comes alive in the bright and comfortable Cabana rooms. Bedspreads are of reds and golds, while the Spanish-style furnishings are antique gold with brightly painted accents.

Because this resort features a large convention center, it also offers an assortment of suites. The junior suites, VIP suites, and executive suite seem to us, though, to be aimed largely at the convention market.

1999 Room Rates for Disney's Coronado Springs Resort

Accommodation	Regular Season	Peak Season	Value Season	Holiday Season
Standard view	$134	$149	$119	$164
Water view	$154	$169	$139	$184
King bed	$154	$169	$139	$184

Transportation and Convenience

Transportation to all Disney World destinations is by bus. There is one bus stop at the central area and another at each of the three areas. Because of its location in Walt Disney World, service to the Animal Kingdom, Disney–MGM Studios, and the Magic Kingdom is all outstanding. Transportation to all other Disney attractions is typically good.

- To all Disney destinations: by bus.

Dining at Coronado Springs

Food choices here are unlike those found at any of the other Disney moderate resorts. Because of the convention trade, Coronado Springs features the exotic "Nuevo Latino" cuisine of the Maya Grill. The outstanding menu offers an array of grilled seafood, poultry, and steaks that are an exciting fusion of the cooking styles of a dozen South

American countries. It is one of our favorite dining spots and worth the trip from anywhere at Disney. You can read more about the Maya Grill in Chapter 6.

Instead of a food court, Coronado Springs has the Pepper Market. This unique restaurant features a festive "marketplace" of open kitchens. Food is prepared to order here at nine colorful stands, and all you have to do is to decide what you want and have your ticket stamped. Everything we've tried here has been fresh and tasty. The Pepper Market is fun *and* a good place to eat. It's an amusing version of a Mexican open-air marketplace with a inviting selection of Tex-Mex offerings that include fajitas, tacos, salads, and an overstuffed burrito. There's even burgers, sandwiches, pastas, and pizza as well a kid-friendly station with macaroni and cheese, hot dogs, and chicken fingers. This is not your usual paper-plate-and-plastic-flatware eatery, so expect prices to be a bit higher than at other resort food courts (there's also a 10% service charge).

Coronado Springs also features a limited room service with continental breakfasts, taco and Caesar salads, deli subs, and pizza. At the Dig Site there's Siesta's, the poolside lounge and grill. Here you'll find a selection of specialty drinks as well as fajitas, tortilla wraps, burgers, and hot dogs. It is worth noting that this resort's refillable cup can be filled at either the Pepper Market or at Siesta's.

Francisco's is this resort's colorful lounge, and it is adjacent to the Pepper Market. It's the perfect place to unwind after a day at the parks.

Shops at Coronado Springs

Besides the usual Disney merchandise and resort logo-wear, Panchito's offers a small selection of Southwestern and Mexican artwork and curios. Of course, you'll also find the usual resort selection of sundry items such as film, magazines, snacks, and nonprescription medications.

Recreational Activities at Coronado Springs

- One feature pool area, the Dig Site, with water flume
- Hot tub/spa for 22 people
- Three quiet pools, one in each area of the resort
- La Vida Health Club and Tanning Salon
- Two video arcades: the Jumping Bean and the Iguana Arcade
- Children's wading pool and playground area
- Jogging and walking path (0.9 mile)
- Rental bicycles, paddle boats, kayaks, and canoes

- This resort is currently experimenting with a small fleet of powered watercraft
- Nature walk in preserved wetlands
- Look for the "Mickey-cacti" at the Ranchos
- Fun photo opportunities around the pool and children's playground

OUR IMPRESSIONS OF CORONADO SPRINGS

- This is another star in the firmament of Disney resorts.
- The central area and the Casitas are where the action is. The Ranchos and Cabanas are much more laid-back and quiet.
- The central area, with restaurants and guest services is convenient to the Casitas but a bit of a walk from the Cabanas and even a little further from the Ranchos. The Dig Site is located adjacent to both the Cabanas and the Ranchos and is a bit of a hike from the Casitas. It all seems to balance out.
- Because of the convention trade, this resorts seems to be the most adult oriented of the moderate resorts.

RECOMMENDATIONS FOR RESERVATIONS

- For a romantic experience, we'd suggest a king bed in either the Ranchos or Cabanas.
- For proximity to the Dig Site, stay in the Ranchos or Cabanas.
- Cabana building 9B is particularly convenient to the central area.
- The Ranchos is the best-themed of the three villages.
- Corner rooms, with windows on two walls, offer more light.

ROMANCE AT CORONADO SPRINGS

- A evening stroll along the lakeside Esplanade: ♥♥♥
- Breakfast in bed: ♥♥
- Late-night hot tub or swim: ♥♥
- Cabana with water view and king bed: ♥♥
- Dinner at Maya Grill: ♥♥

Disney's All-Star Resorts: Music, Sports, and NEW Movies

(Movies opens January 1999)

The All-Star Resorts are Disney's foray into the budget market. Rooms here are the most inexpensive on-property and, as you would expect, the All-Star Resorts are one of Disney World's busiest destinations.

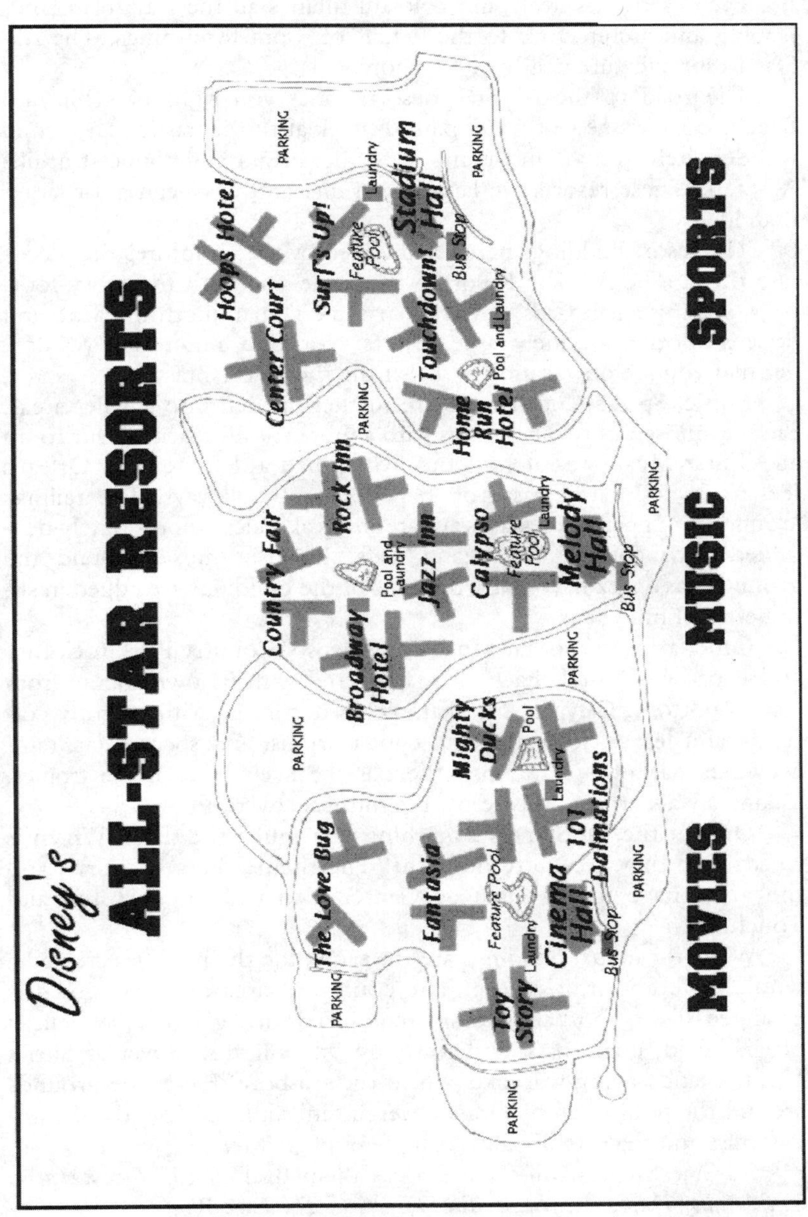
Disney's
ALL-STAR RESORTS
MOVIES
MUSIC
SPORTS
Hoops Hotel
Center Court
Surf's Up!
Feature Pool
Laundry
Stadium Hall
Bus Stop
Touchdown!
Pool and Laundry
Home Run Hotel
PARKING
Rock Inn
Country Fair
Pool and Laundry
Jazz Inn
Calypso
Feature Pool
Laundry
Melody Hall
Bus Stop
Broadway Hotel
Mighty Ducks
Pool
Laundry
101 Dalmations
The Love Bug
Fantasia
Feature Pool
Laundry
Cinema Hall
Bus Stop
Toy Story

Each carries its lively and colorful themes all the way from landscaping and architecture to the details of room furnishings. The All-Star Resorts feature nearly 6,000 rooms.

The road to the All-Star Resorts takes you right past Blizzard Beach, Disney's newest water park. A peek at this fantastic playground will definitely get you in the mood for the bright and comic-strip-like All-Stars. These resorts are larger than life, and we mean a lot larger than life.

The resort buildings here are dwarfed by the sculptures that decorate them. The All-Star Resorts will dazzle you with five-story footballs, soaring surfboards, towering trumpets, mammoth maracas, and dozens of other uniquely large objects. Not for a minute will you forget that you are on vacation and that the theme is fantasy.

Music, Sports, and Movies are further divided into smaller areas, each comprised of two buildings with a more specific theme. Our room at All-Star Music was at Jazz Inn, which had a definite New Orleans feel to its fountains, cast-iron benches, and walkways. The railings around the upper-floor walkways are musical scales, appropriately decorated with colorful notes and clefs. Piped-in music around the grounds has a jazz flavor, and the tops of the buildings are edged in silhouettes of musicians.

Other areas in All-Star Music are Calypso, Country Fair, Rock Inn, and Broadway Hotel. Each is Imagineered with its own theme from top to bottom. Calypso, for example, is decorated with brightly colored palm leaves, four-story-tall conga drums, and spectacular, rainbow-like marimbas. The music here is the lively beat of the tropics. Taking a walk around this resort is a musical adventure.

Over at the All-Star Sports, things are much the same. Which is to say that they are quite different. The theme there is sports, and the areas have names such as Center Court, Hoops Hotel, and Touchdown.

While the actual buildings are the same, the theming has created a whole different atmosphere. The courtyard area at Touchdown is arranged like a football stadium, complete with gigantic helmets, a playing field, goal posts, and towering "floodlights." Over at Surf's Up, the landscaping will take you to the seashore. Here, the grounds around the pool resemble grass-covered sand dunes. Mounds of pampas grass and thickets of palms complete the picture.

All-Star Movies will feature areas themed after *101 Dalmatians, The Mighty Ducks, Fantasia, Toy Story,* and *The Love Bug.*

Music, Sports, and Movies each have a central area with a front desk, Guest Services, food court, shop, video arcade, and lounge. The central areas are called Melody Hall at Music, Stadium Hall at Sports, and Cinema Hall at Movies.

If you elect to stay at the All-Star Resorts, whether Music, Sports, or Movies, we suggest that you take a stroll around all the properties. There are a lot of wonderful little touches that have been created to delight you. And they will.

Rooms at the All-Star Resorts

There are two basic types of rooms, standard with two double beds and rooms with a single king bed. The king room is also the room equipped for handicapped people. All-Star rooms are on the small side, 260 square feet, which is to say that they are about the same size as most budget motels. The room furnishings are decidedly more Disney than off-property rooms but, by Disney standards, they are pretty modest.

Our king bedroom at Jazz Inn lacked many of the amenities of even the Disney moderately priced resorts. The room decor was festive and modern. The "quilted" bedspread and bathroom wallpaper both featured patterns of jazz musicians, and the drapes were decorated with musical scales. The room furniture is similar throughout the All-Star. Modern and cartoon-like, it seemed entertaining. The theming in the rooms was simple. Creature comforts were minimal.

Each room at the All-Star has a rather small vanity. Our king bedroom had only a shower. Wonderfully designed for the use of those physically challenged, it was very spacious with a handy seat right under the water. The double room has the more conventional shower-tub. King bedrooms each come with a small refrigerator.

1999 Room Rates for the Disney's All-Star Resorts

Accommodation	Regular Season	Peak Season	Value Season	Holiday Season
All rooms	$89	$94	$74	$104

Transportation and Convenience

With so many rooms here, we were concerned that transportation would be slow. We are delighted to report that service to all Disney destinations is quite good. Each of the All-Star resorts has its own bus fleet, and we found service to be frequent and convenient.

- To all Disney destinations: by bus

Dining at the All-Star Resorts

The End Zone Food Court at Sports, the World Premier Food Court, and the Intermission Food Court at Music offer a complete array of food for breakfast, lunch, and dinner. All of the food served here is cooked on the premises, and much to our surprise, it was somewhat better than many other Disney food court offerings. The hamburger was actually quite good.

The dining areas here, like most food courts, are noisy and at peak hours are crowded. Try taking your trays the few steps out to the pool area and eat at a table, under an umbrella.

There are several other interesting options for eating at All-Star. One is ordering out. There is a pizza delivery at All-Star, and while this pizza is nothing to write home about, it is decent. The menu also includes beers, wines, salads, and subs. There are also food trucks that drive around during the day, hawking breakfast stuff in the morning and sandwich goodies later.

Lounges at the All-Star Resorts

Each central area has a lounge that serves beers, wines, and specialty drinks, both alcoholic and nonalcoholic. The Singing Spirits Pool Bar is the lounge at Melody Hall; at Sports, it's the Team Spirits Pool Bar; and at Movies, it's Silver Screen Spirits. As their names imply, each is adjacent to the main pool.

Shops at the All-Star Resorts

Sport Goofy Gifts and Sundries is at All-Star Sports, and Maestro Mickey's is at Music. Each offers a selection of its own logo merchandise, and both have the usual Disney character products, sportswear, gifts, souvenirs, sundries, and even a small selection of liquor. Also available is a small offering of magazines, books, and newspapers. And if you are planning to snack in your room, each shop has a modest selection of chips, beverages, and groceries items.

Recreational Activities at the All-Star Resorts

Each of the All-Star Resorts has two pools—one large main pool and one smaller, less centrally located pool. At All-Star Music, the large pool is shaped like a huge guitar. An island in the center features a frolicking gang of sculptured Disney characters who occasionally spray nearby swimmers with jets of water. It is a delightful sight gag. The quiet swimming area at Music is the Piano Pool and is—you guessed it—shaped like a huge piano. At Sports, the main pool is called Surfboard Bay and is located amidst the beachside landscaping of Surf's Up. It has a California beach theme. A bit farther away is the quieter swimming area, the Grand Slam Pool. Movies' pool is the Fantasia Pool and is styled after the animated film *Fantasia*. Movies' quiet pool is the Duck Pond. Each main swimming area also has a nice kiddie pool.

It is worth noting that because recreation is so minimal here, guests of the All-Stars can purchase a day of unlimited recreation (motor boats, bikes, canoes, etc.) at the Caribbean Beach. Cost is $70 for your entire party.

OUR IMPRESSIONS OF THE ALL-STAR RESORTS

- For the cost-conscious, the All-Star Resorts are an affordable way to stay on-property. Each is a charming and themed Disney resort, albeit a bit spartan.
- Many of the rooms are a hike from the parking lots. The luggage assistance system is awkward and runs on its own schedule, not yours. A stay here will teach you the real meaning of LUGgage. Plan on carrying your own bags to your room unless you simply cannot. If so, speak with the front desk upon check-in.

RECOMMENDATIONS FOR RESERVATIONS

- At Music, the Calypso area is closest to Melody Hall and is adjacent to the main pool. It is also the noisiest area. Country Fair is the most secluded but it is a hike from the parking area. Rock Inn, Broadway Hotel, and Jazz Inn seemed to be the most convenient, are relatively quiet (for this resort), and are near the quieter pool. We would recommend that you request one of these areas if you are staying at All-Star Music.
- At Sports, the busier area is Surf's Up. All other areas seemed quiet by comparison. Touchdown and Home Run Hotel would be our recommendations. Both are convenient to the quieter pool area and to parking.
- At Movies, Fantasia and 101 Dalmatians will be adjacent to the central Fantasia Pool. Mighty Ducks and The Love Bug will be a bit farther away. All Movie buildings appear to be convenient to parking areas.

ROMANCE AT THE ALL-STAR RESORTS

- Separate room for the kids: ♥♥

The Downtown Disney Resorts

Disney's Port Orleans and Dixie Landings Resorts

It's not the mighty Mississippi, but it's a river and it's known as the Sassagoula. If you hop a boat at Downtown Disney and head upstream past the grand old paddle wheeler, *Empress Lilly*, and past the Disney Institute, you might just imagine yourself on the Ol' Mississippi. Upriver, you'll make harbor at Disney's Port Orleans resort. This quaint and colorful little city, with its shady, cobbled streets, gas lights, and relaxed French Quarter ambience, will make you feel as though you've gone back in time to walk the streets of old New Orleans.

Further up the Sassagoula, you'll enter Magnolia Bend, part of Disney's Dixie Landings resort. The banks of the river here are lined with stately magnolias and graceful willows. Here and there, an occasional footbridge crosses the waterway, leading off to the grand "old mansions" of the resort.

A bit farther upstream, the boat will bring you to Alligator Bayou. Now you've entered the back river country and another part of Dixie Landings. Here, the resort more reflects the rural charm of the bayou. The rustic resort buildings are nestled amidst a dense forest of slash pines. Shaded footpaths crisscross in all directions past small ponds and along tiny streams. At night, the crickets "sing" in the bushes, compliments of the Disney Imagineers.

This is what you'll find along Disney's Sassagoula River: three delightfully different areas that together are the Port Orleans and Dixie Landings resorts. While they combine for over 3,000 rooms, the feeling here is anything but that of hustle and bustle. Along the banks of the Sassagoula, you will enjoy a sense of privacy and harmony.

We have grouped Port Orleans and Dixie Landings together not because they are so alike but because, together, they make up this Disney picture of "life on the river." What they have in common is that they are both moderately priced and beautifully themed resorts.

Disney's Port Orleans Resort

This lovely resort evokes the ambience of the old French Quarter. The delight begins the moment you pass through the iron gates and into the tree-lined drive. The Disney artists have been hard at work. The main building is the Mint, and it is a masterpiece of ornate wrought-iron work and glass. Check-in is more fantasy than a chore. The vaulted ceilings and iron railings here more resemble a bank than a hotel lobby, and

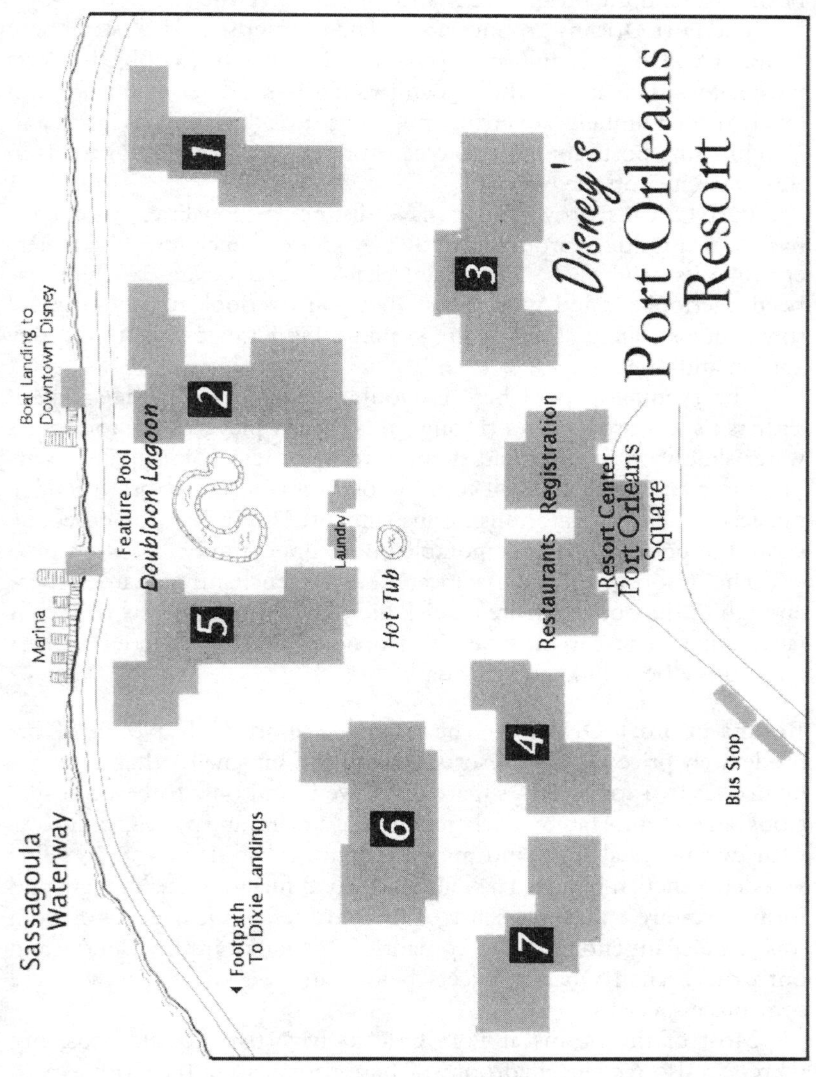
Sassagoula Waterway
Footpath To Dixie Landings
Marina
Feature Pool
Doubloon Lagoon
Boat Landing to Downtown Disney
Laundry
Hot Tub
Restaurants
Registration
Resort Center
Port Orleans Square
Bus Stop
1
2
3
4
5
6
7
Disney's Port Orleans Resort

friendly service is the coin of this realm. The hotel staff is attired in perfect period costume. Not a detail has been missed. The Imagineers have been busy, and the promise of Mardi Gras is everywhere.

The Port Orleans grounds are splendidly landscaped. A stroll here at night will be relaxing and romantic. The narrow, cobbled streets have names such as Rue d'Blues and Rue d'Baga. The small parks and lovely stone fountains are enchanting. Narrow sidewalks, gaslights, and iron hitching posts combine to create a real sense of neighborhoods in this "old city" on the river.

Port Orleans's row houses have distinct personalities, too. Each has its own unique yard, surrounded by an iron fence just a bit different than its neighbor's. The quaint charm is convincing. Nothing has been overlooked, and we suggest that you overlook nothing. Spend some time strolling about in the evening. Find a nice bench in a cozy garden and sit awhile.

The swimming pool here is Doubloon Lagoon. A huge dragon slithers its way around and through this fantasy playground, forming a water slide with its long and slippery tongue. It is colorful and exciting. Here and there you will come across colorful statues of "crocodile musicians," each with a musical instrument. Don't miss the crocodile shower at poolside for a memorable photo opportunity.

The resort's hot tub is located in an enchanting garden near enough to the pool to invite a quick dip but far enough away to keep it fairly quiet. The garden's cast-iron benches and ivy-covered trellises make this a beautiful spot after dark.

Rooms at Port Orleans The rooms here are fairly typical of the moderately priced Disney resorts. Although a bit smaller than Disney's luxury resort rooms (314 square feet), we found ours to be both spacious and comfortable. Each features a small vanity area, complete with two pedestal sinks and mirrors. Beneath the drapes are genuine wooden Venetian blinds. The antiqued wood furniture, ceiling fan, and formal armoire enhance a sense of the old French Quarter. Our room was just elegant enough to be romantic. One look out the window and onto the French Quarter streets below, and we knew that we were someplace special.

Most of the rooms at Port Orleans have two double beds, but there are also 62 king bedrooms. These rooms are a bit more expensive, but we always find a double bed to be rather small. King bedrooms here at Port Orleans are all corner rooms, making each brighter and more airy.

1999 Room Rates for Disney's Port Orleans Resort

Accommodation	Regular Season	Peak Season	Value Season	Holiday Season
Standard view	$134	$149	$119	$164
Water view	$154	$169	$139	$184
King bed	$154	$169	$139	$184

Transportation and Convenience Port Orleans is fairly convenient to the rest of the World. There is one large bus stop in front of the resort; buses run every 20 minutes and even more frequently during the busier hours. For Wide World of Sports, Discovery Island, and River Country, consult your Transportation Guidemap for bus transfers.

A boat service runs to Pleasure Island and the Downtown Disney Marketplace. The small launches are fun and will take you through parts of Walt Disney World that you would never have a chance to see otherwise. Don't miss this trip.

- To Downtown Disney: by boat (from 10 A.M. to 11:30 P.M.) or bus
- To Magic Kingdom, Epcot, Disney–MGM Studios, The Animal Kingdom, Typhoon Lagoon, Blizzard Beach: by bus
- To BoardWalk: bus or boat to Downtown Disney and take BoardWalk bus

Dining at Port Orleans There is one table-service restaurant at Port Orleans, Bonfamille's Cafe, and a Mardi Gras–themed food court called the Sassagoula Floatworks and Food Factory. Bonfamille's is a delightful garden courtyard restaurant that serves both breakfast and dinner. The cuisines here are American and Creole. For more information and our review of Bonfamille's, see Chapter 6.

The Sassagoula Floatworks is a warehouse full of Mardi Gras props. Giant masks and colorful floats are suspended from the ceiling. Food-wise, the choices are many with a definite New Orleans flair. The variety of "shops" offer everything from scrambled eggs and muffins to burgers and home-style jambalaya. There's even fresh pasta and pizza. Don't miss the traditional French Quarter treat, beignets, at the bake shop.

While Floatworks seats 300, the resort has over 1,000 rooms. Of course, this means that if you eat at the more traditional times, you're likely to find it crowded. If the two of you are like us, you may not like to spend mealtimes in such an atmosphere. An alternative is to take your trays into one of the pleasant outside sitting areas or out by the pool.

Another meal alternative is Sassagoula Pizza Express, which delivers pizza, salads, beverages, and desserts from 4 P.M. to midnight.

Lounges at Port Orleans Scat Cat's is a delightful little lounge adjoining the lobby. It has a full bar and in the evening frequently features live entertainment. Hors d'oeuvres are available from the kitchen of Bonfamille's. Mardi Grogs is the poolside bar, serving a variety of nonalcoholic and specialty cocktails during pool hours. Also on the menu are snacks and deli sandwiches.

Shops at Port Orleans Jackson Square Gifts and Desires offers the usual selection of Disney character merchandise as well as a line of clothes and accessories with the Port Orleans logo. This shop also has a variety of general store items as well as offering authentic Creole condiments and New Orleans chicory coffees.

Recreational Activities at Port Orleans

- Doubloon Lagoon, a themed swimming pool with water slide
- Hot tub (spa)
- Boat and bike rentals
- Surrey "quadricycle" rentals
- Walking or jogging paths
- Video arcade

OUR IMPRESSIONS OF PORT ORLEANS

- Of the moderately priced resorts, we think that Port Orleans is quite romantic. After dark, it is simply enchanting.
- The boat service to Downtown Disney is delightful. It turned our trip into an adventure. It is especially pleasant around sunset.
- If you are heading over to Dixie Landings, whether to look around or to have a meal, you'll find that it is a short walk away via a delightful footpath that runs along the river.
- Port Orleans will be getting a "soft goods rehab" during 1999 that will include new bedspreads and draperies.

RECOMMENDATIONS FOR RESERVATIONS

- If you can, avoid the standard parking lot view. The beautiful part of this resort is inside the courtyard.
- Pool-view rooms are convenient for swimming, but you may find that you have sacrificed peace and quiet.

ROMANCE AT PORT ORLEANS RESORT

- Overall theme: ♥♥♥
- Room with king bed: ♥♥
- Doubloon Lagoon: ♥♥
- Bonfamille's Cafe: ♥♥
- Taking breakfast from food court to a poolside table: ♥
- Taking a nice, long hot tub soak at day's end: ♥♥♥
- Taking an evening stroll to Dixie Landings: ♥♥♥
- Taking a late-night swim: ♥♥
- Enjoying a sunset cruise to Downtown Disney: ♥♥
- Renting a boat or surrey and exploring: ♥♥

Disney's Dixie Landings Resorts

With a bit of the old Disney magic, Dixie Landings manages to be two very different resorts in one. The Magnolia Bend area of Dixie Landings reminisces the plantations of the Old South. Stately courtyards, charming fountains, and formal gardens re-create the sweeping grandeur of the antebellum South. Resort rooms here are in large mansion-like buildings with winding stairways and imposing columns. The weeping willows and sloping lawns of Magnolia Bend give way to dense thickets of pine and Florida maple at Alligator Bayou. Here, the "weathered" resort buildings are quaint and small. Their tin roofs peek through the treetops. Footpaths seem narrow and winding and the charm is more rustic and homey.

While Dixie Landings has over 2,000 rooms, the resort is so spread out that it does not feel so large. Still, a visit to the central building, the Sassagoula Steamboat Company, will serve to remind you that this is indeed a big place. During the busier times of day, there is a lot of traffic here.

The Steamboat Company re-creates a small port on the river with docks, warehouses, and a water-driven cotton mill. The Disney penchant for detail is everywhere. Even the bathrooms in the lobby have old-fashioned cisterns and wooden toilet seats. Talk about theming.

Check-in will be the beginning of your Dixie adventure. The reservationists wear the costumes of clerks, and they will help you "book passage" on your trip upriver. The front desk resembles a steamship office more than a hotel. Piles of old steamer trunks and exotic ports of call create a pleasant sense of fun.

The Sassagoula Steamboat Company is home to the Dixie Landings restaurants, lounge, general store, and food court. Also located

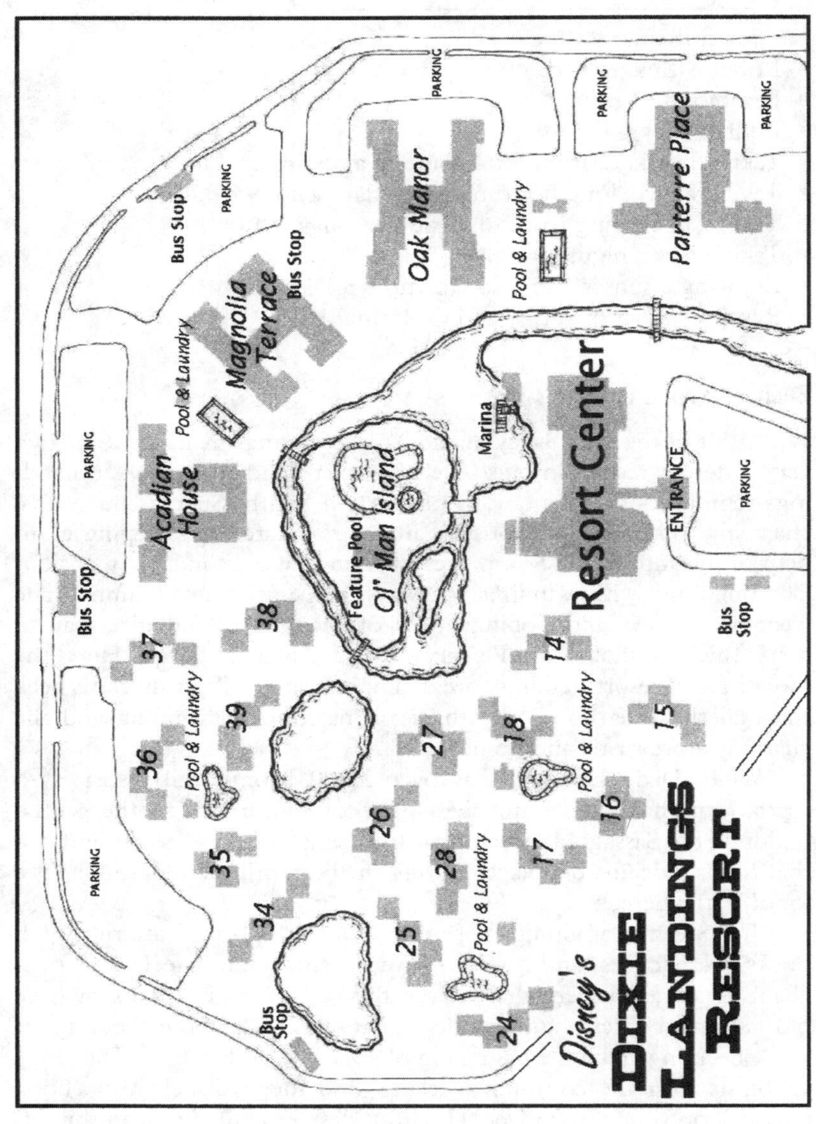
Disney's
Dixie Landings Resort
Oak Manor
Parterre Place
Magnolia Terrace
Acadian House
Resort Center
Ol' Man Island
Feature Pool
Marina
ENTRANCE
PARKING
Bus Stop
Pool & Laundry
14
15
16
17
18
24
25
26
27
28
34
35
36
37
38
39

here is Guest Services. The guest buildings of both Alligator Bayou and Magnolia Bend surround Ol' Man Island, a three-acre water recreation area with pool, playground, spa, and a stocked fishing hole.

Ol' Man Island has one large pool with a short water slide. There are also five quiet pools located around the resort. These are convenient to most rooms, and if you are looking for something a bit more intimate, you're in luck. There is only one hot tub here at the Landings, and we feel that it is not enough. It is located right in the middle of things at Ol' Man Island, minimizing peace, quiet, and privacy.

Rooms at Magnolia Bend Magnolia Bend is made up of four "parishes." With such names as Parterre Place and the Acadian House, each is really a large resort building housing more than 250 guest rooms. The feel here is a bit big for our tastes, especially in the standard rooms that look out onto the parking areas. Views from the river side of the complex are infinitely more relaxing and private.

The rooms at both Magnolia Bend and Alligator Bayou are the same general size and shape and rooms with twin doubles also feature a trundle bed for a fifth person. With 314 square feet of space, each is adequate and comfortable. While the rooms at both the Bend and the Bayou are the same dimensions, they are worlds apart in decor. The ambience at Magnolia Bend is definitely more formal. French Provincial furniture, brocade upholstery, and an antiqued, mirrored armoire are suited perfectly to the antebellum grand manor. Each room has a ceiling fan, a small sitting bench, table and chairs, and a spacious and well-lit vanity area. There are two pedestal sinks and each has its own mirror, giving you both a place to get ready for your evening out. Rooms feature either two double beds or one king.

Rooms at Alligator Bayou Alligator Bayou offers much more of a down-home feeling. Instead of four large mansions, the same number of guest rooms are spread out among 16 rustic and weathered buildings, each housing about 60 rooms. The look here is "backwater cracker" but the ambience translates into something more intimate. The Bayou's buildings are tucked away in a small forest. Each feels a bit hidden and the sensation of being in a large resort is lost.

The Bayou rooms manage an aura of homespun comfort and warmth. The log bedstead frames, patchwork "quilts," and other details give the rooms a feeling of fantasy and fun. In-room theming is at its best here in Alligator Bayou. This is the only moderately priced resort that has accommodations for more than four persons.

1999 Room Rates for Disney's Dixie Landings Resort

Accommodation	Regular Season	Peak Season	Value Season	Holiday Season
Standard view	$134	$149	$119	$164
Water view	$154	$169	$139	$184
King bed	$154	$169	$139	$184

Transportation and Convenience Transportation at Dixie Landings is the same as at Port Orleans. Dixie Landings, though, has four bus stops situated around the perimeter of the resort. The same wonderful boat service runs to Downtown Disney and travel to all other Disney areas is by bus. Service here is quite good, although the buses get crowded during the peak morning and afternoon travel hours.

- To Downtown Disney: by boat (10 A.M. to 11:30 P.M.) or bus
- To all other Disney destinations: by direct bus
- To Wide World of Sports, Discovery Island, and River Country: consult your Transportation Guidemap for bus transfers

Dining at Dixie Landings The restaurants at Dixie Landings are all located in the resort's large central area. While the guest accommodations are organized around this area, it can be a trek from some of them. We found that this made for a pleasant morning stroll; however, you might want to locate yourselves according to your own needs.

At the Landings, you will find one table-service restaurant, Boatwright's Dining Hall, and a colorful food court with five counter-service food outlets. Boatwright's serves hearty breakfasts and dinners, and the food is surprisingly good. For reviews and information about this and other restaurants, see Chapter 6.

The Dixie Landings food court is called the Colonel's Cotton Mill, and it offers a good selection of fast foods for the day's meals. It even manages to provide an interesting ambience. Breakfast offerings run the gamut from a muffin or bagel to French toast or "biscwiches." There's even an all-you-care-to-eat breakfast buffet. Other meals get a hearty treatment of burgers, barbecued ribs, pizza, and Cajun specialties.

If you need to escape the noisy food court atmosphere, go out by the pool and sit at one of the tables there. They are well-shaded and comfortable. In the early morning hours, you are likely to encounter only the occasional swimmer or landscape workman. The Cotton Mill is open from 6 A.M. to midnight, with hours varying for some of the shops. Like its "sister resort," Port Orleans, Dixie offers pizza delivery.

Lounges at Dixie Landings There are two lounges at Dixie. In the central building is the Cotton Co-Op. Its long mahogany bar, leather club chairs, and fireplace make it look like a movie set. Besides the usual beverage offerings, the Co-Op also features a small variety of finger foods prepared at Boatwright's. There is also a live entertainer in the evenings. Muddy Rivers is the poolside bar.

Shops at Dixie Landings Fulton's General Store is located in the main resort building and will be your source for Dixie Landings logo merchandise as well as a fairly good selection of other character stuff. It has a country store feel with a large penny candy counter. It has the usual sundries as well as an interesting selection of wines and liquors.

Recreational Activities at Dixie Landings

- Five quiet pools throughout the resort complex
- Ol' Man Island, a 3.5-acre themed water recreation area
- One hot tub
- Marina with boat and bicycle rentals
- Surrey "quadricycle" rentals
- Guided fishing excursions on the river

Recommendations for Reservations

- For the sake of convenience, you may wish to request a particular building when you reserve your room. Oak Manor would be our choice at Magnolia Bend, and in Alligator Bayou, buildings 14–17 or 27 are our suggestions. All are nearest the central building and Ol' Man Island.

Our Impressions of Dixie Landings

- This is a charming and well-themed resort. We especially like Alligator Bayou.
- Boat Service to Downtown Disney is delightful. Don't miss it.
- The footpath to Port Orleans makes for a very pleasant evening walk, whether for sightseeing or for dining at Bonfamille's.
- Old Man Island pool area is usually quite crowded. The quiet pools are a sensible alternative.

Romance at Dixie Landings

- Overall theming: ♥♥
- Rooms with king-size beds: ♥♥

- Late-night swim in a quiet pool: ♥♥
- An evening stroll to Port Orleans: ♥♥♥
- Sunset boat ride to Downtown Disney: ♥♥
- Renting a boat or surrey and exploring: ♥♥
- Taking the boat to Port Orleans and eating at Bonfamille's: ♥♥♥

Disney's Old Key West Resort

Old Key West is part of the Vacation Club, Disney's time-share venture. And since it is also available as a nightly rental, we thought we'd give it a try. We must admit to being a bit skeptical. It seemed large and not particularly close to anything, and it looked like condos. Whatever reservations that we'd had, however, were quickly put to rest when we arrived at our one-bedroom vacation home.

The Key West theme is executed as only Disney can do it. The Florida Keys should look this nice. The pastel villas, with their "tin" roofs and gingerbread gables, are scattered in clusters throughout the area known as Conch Flats.

Landscaping at Old Key West is lush and tropical. The villas are surrounded by dense stands of foliage and flowering trees, providing a feeling of privacy that you will find hard to equal elsewhere in Walt Disney World. Plants are larger than life. If you are from a northern clime, you will marvel at the variety of greeneries, most of which you've probably only seen as potted house plants. Like much of Walt Disney World, this place is one big garden. Palms, crepe myrtle, blossoming hibiscus, and spider lilies abound. Quaint and narrow Key West streets wander gently among the Florida cracker-style villas. Southern porches, iron streetlamps, and old-fashioned bus stops add the finishing touches to the little taste of Key West created by the Disney Imagineers.

Driving, we followed Old Turtle Pond Road to our villa. Parking was a few steps from the front door. Once inside, our curiosity turned to sheer delight. Our villa was not only surprisingly large but surprisingly beautiful. The ambience was definitely Florida Keys style, open and airy, bright, and casually comfortable. Greeted by a mix of pastels, a splash of florals, and an expanse of open spaces, we hurried from room to room to survey our new abode. Ceiling fans, numerous large windows, and a king-size bed were just the beginnings. The vacation home had a huge living room/kitchen where we found a comfortable chair, love seat, and sofa with queen-size, foldaway bed. Handsome watercolors of island scenery, silk "tropical plants," and a carved wooden conch combined to give our villa a lived-in, at-home feeling.

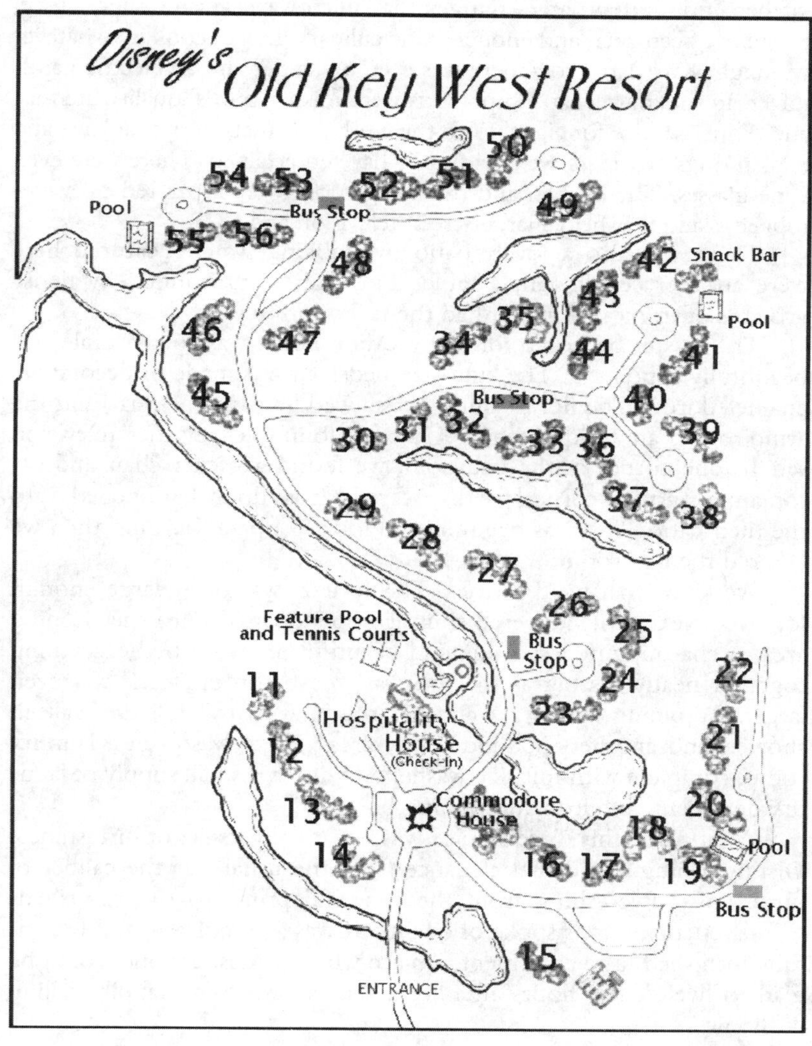
Disney's Old Key West Resort
Pool
Bus Stop
Snack Bar
Pool
Bus Stop
Feature Pool and Tennis Courts
Bus Stop
Hospitality House (Check-in)
Commodore House
Pool
Bus Stop
ENTRANCE
11
12
13
14
15
16
17
18
19
20
21
22
23
24
25
26
27
28
29
30
31
32
33
34
35
36
37
38
39
40
41
42
43
44
45
46
47
48
49
50
51
52
53
54
55
56

The kitchen was integral with the living area, just the way we like it. Furnished with the best of appliances, it surpassed our expectations. It was handsomely tiled and was not only functional but beautiful. The kitchen featured a large refrigerator, microwave, dishwasher, stove, toaster, coffeemaker, and enough basic culinary gear to cook up whatever we might have cared to. There was even a blender and an electric hand-mixer. In the drawers and cupboards were mixing bowls, quality utensils, and dinner service for eight. With the cloth placemats, terry napkins, and napkin rings provided, we could easily have entertained. There were even wine glasses. The kitchen and the living room were separated by a tile-topped island that held a large-screen television and VCR.

There was also a lovely patio overlooking water. Featured here were another ceiling fan, a table, and chairs. Surrounded by dense growths of tropical plants, it had the feel of privacy.

The master bedroom for our vacation home was comfortable and beautifully appointed. The king-size bedstead was made of decorative, enameled iron. The floral "quilt" was a wedding-ring pattern, and the armoire was an antique white. Here we found yet another television set. In one corner of the bedroom, we found a wicker chair and ottoman; in another corner, we discovered a glass door that opened onto the tiled patio. This was beginning to look like paradise. And then we entered the bathroom.

We knew that we'd arrived. The Jacuzzi was easily large enough for two. Next to it, louvered shutter doors opened onto the sleeping area. A charming pedestal sink and beautiful tile work tied everything together neatly. As big as the tub was, the bathroom itself was even larger. Adjoining it was yet another room, with toilet, large walk-in shower, and another sink and vanity area. There was even a laundry room, complete with full-size washer and dryer, a small supply of laundry detergent, and iron and ironing board.

What made this place so nice was not merely its list of furnishings. Distinguishing this casual elegance from the usual was the caliber of furnishings. Everything from the beautiful prints to the varnished-wood venetian blinds spoke of quality. It was a completely and beautifully furnished little apartment, a place where almost anyone would be glad to live. A few hours after we'd arrived, we were happily calling it "home."

Accommodations at Old Key West

There are three basic types of lodgings here at Old Key West: the studios, the vacation homes, and the Grand Villas. The studio offers a single room with two queen beds, an outside patio, and a small kitchen with microwave oven, wet bar, and mini-refrigerator. One of these added to our one-bedroom vacation home would make a two-bedroom vacation home, able to accommodate eight persons.

The three-bedroom Grand Villa is a two-level townhouse, something quite different altogether. Accommodations are for 12. The master bedroom still has the king bed and Jacuzzi tub, but upstairs are two queen-size beds in one room and two double beds in the other. The fine furnishings of the Grand Villa and its cathedral ceiling create an impressive effect.

1999 Room Rates for Disney's Old Key West Resort

Accommodation	Regular Season	Peak Season	Value Season	Holiday Season
Studio	$244	$274	$229	$300
One-bedroom Vacation Home	$325	$355	$305	$390
Two-bedroom Vacation Home	$450	$480	$420	$535
Three-bedroom Grand Villa	$890	$940	$850	$1,050

Transportation and Convenience

We are pleased to tell you that getting places from Conch Flats is fast and easy. To make things even better, the buses follow a schedule, which you receive in your check-in packet.

- To Downtown Disney: by boat or bus
- To all other Disney Destinations: by bus

Dining at Old Key West

There is one table-service restaurant, Olivia's Cafe, and two counter-service snack shops, Good's Food-To-Go and the Turtle Shack. Both Good's and Olivia's are located in the resort's central area, adjacent to the main swimming area. The Turtle Shack is in one of the outlying pool areas. Both fast-food outlets offer a selection of sandwiches and snacks. The poolside bar at the central pool is the Gurgling Suitcase, and it features the usual assortment of wines, beers, and specialty drinks.

Olivia's serves breakfast, lunch, and dinner, offering an intriguing menu of Key West cuisine. It also features a character breakfast on Sunday and Wednesday. Old Key West features room service from Olivia's. For a review of Olivia's and other restaurants, see Chapter 6.

Shops at Old Key West

The Conch Flat General Store will be your source for just about everything at Old Key West. There is even a substantial grocery section. Every room comes equipped with a grocery check-off list that you can drop off at the General Store. They'll do the shopping and deliver the goods for a mere buck. Now we're talking vacation.

Recreational Activities at Old Key West

- One themed central pool area with sauna and hot tub
- Three quiet pool areas, one with a hot tub
- 1.5-mile biking, jogging, walking path
- Children's playground and kiddie pool
- Marina with rental watercraft
- Bicycle and surrey "quadricycle" rentals
- Tennis, basketball, and volleyball
- Fitness center
- Video game room
- Complimentary video tape library
- In-room massage, by appointment

Recommendations for Reservations

- The real beauty here is the one-bedroom vacation home.
- The one-bedroom vacation home is an ideal place for a family, especially during value season when the prices come down.

Our Impressions of Old Key West

- We really liked this resort and found it beautiful and relaxing.
- During our visit, transportation to all Disney destinations seemed particularly easy.
- Don't miss the pleasant boat ride to Downtown Disney from Old Key West.

Romance at Old Key West

- Resort theming: ♥♥
- Villa amenities: ♥♥♥♥

- Jacuzzi in the vacation homes: ♥♥♥♥
- Taking a bike ride or walking on the path to Downtown Disney, and taking a look at the Treehouse villas, too: ♥♥
- Taking a boat to Downtown Disney: ♥♥

The Villas at the Disney Institute

Once known as the Disney Village Resort, this area offers a unique variety of lodgings, all set in the quiet and secluded surroundings of the Lake Buena Vista golf course and the Disney Institute.

Rooms at the Villas at the Disney Institute

There are five basic types of accommodations: bungalows, townhouses, Treehouse villas, Fairway villas, and Grand Vista Homes. They all belong to the home away from home category and provide some sort of kitchen facility. Most provide living space for more than the usual four persons as well as fully furnished kitchens. If you plan to visit Walt Disney World with a large family, then one of these may be just the place for you. All Villa accommodations feature daily maid service that includes dish washing.

Bungalows These one-bedroom, L-shaped suites are scattered around the shores of one of the Institute's lakes. Each has a living room and a wet bar area with refrigerator, coffeemaker, and microwave. The separate bedroom features double queen beds and a small vanity and small bath. The two-story rustic buildings feature patios or balconies for each suite. Recently refurbished, the bungalows are fresh, comfortable, and quite cozy.

Townhouses Available as either one- or two-bedroom units, these well-furnished, two-story apartments feature living rooms, full kitchens, and upstairs sleeping quarters. With a pullout sleeper downstairs, the one-bedroom unit can sleep four, while the two-bedroom model can accommodate up to six guests. Adjacent to the Institute and on the shores of Lake Buena Vista, the townhouses overlook Downtown Disney.

Treehouse Villas Some of the most interesting accommodations at Walt Disney World, these octagonal lodgings are built deep in the woods along the canals that crisscross the Lake Buena Vista area. Called "treehouses" because they are built on stilts, they feature simple, rustic exteriors. Inside, they are modern and luxurious. The Treehouse area

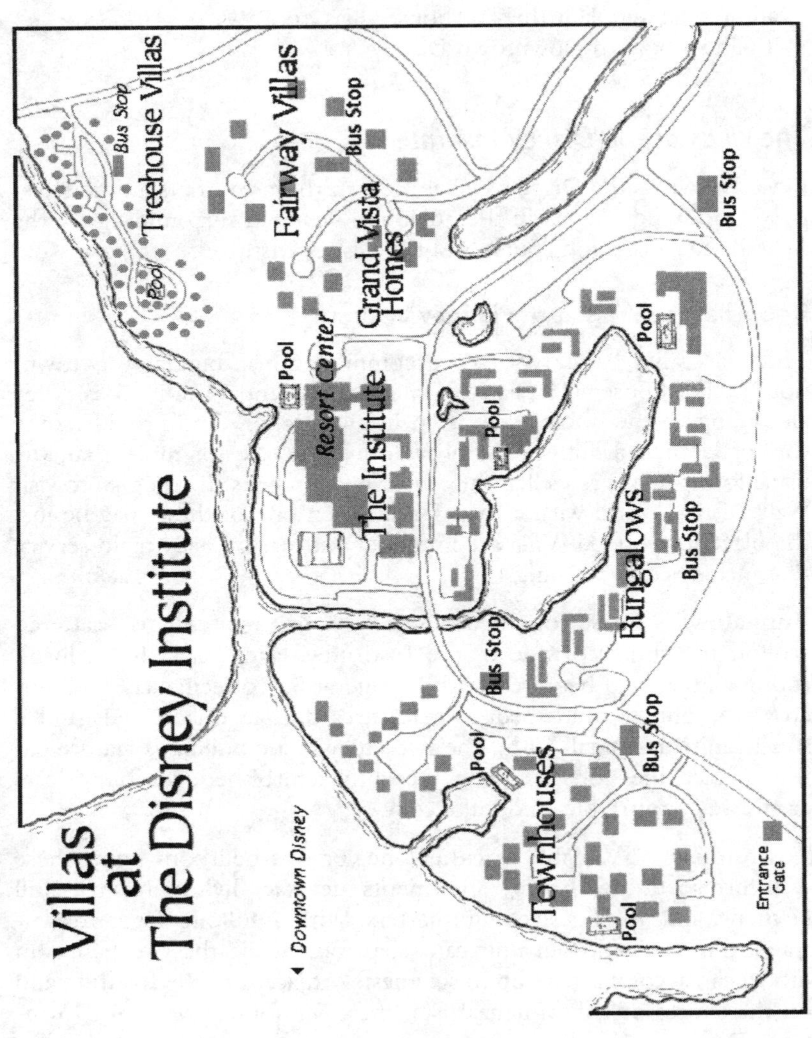
Villas
at
The Disney Institute
Downtown Disney
Treehouse Villas
Bus Stop
Pool
Fairway Villas
Bus Stop
Bus Stop
Grand Vista
Homes
Pool
Resort Center
The Institute
Pool
Bus Stop
Pool
Bus Stop
Bungalows
Bus Stop
Pool
Townhouses
Bus Stop
Pool
Entrance
Gate

seems more like a national park than a Disney resort. It is peaceful and secluded. There are even a handful of peacocks that roam the grounds.

The upstairs area of each Treehouse has two bedrooms, each with a queen bed. It has a small kitchen and living room, and it is almost completely surrounded by a large, elevated deck. It's the perfect place to relax or dine under a canopy of trees. Downstairs is another bedroom with one double bed and a laundry room with washer and dryer. Each "home" has its own driveway and yard. Other Treehouses are barely visible through the dense woods.

Fairway Villas and Grand Vista Homes Both of these types of accommodations offer even more luxury for a large family. The modern, cedar-sided villas are located right along the golf course. Each features two bedrooms and a large living room with cathedral ceiling. With a single queen in one bedroom, two doubles in the other, and a sico bed in the living room, there's sleeping space here for eight.

The Grand Vista Homes were originally designed as model homes for a Disney development that never developed. There are only four of these lavish places: three two-bedroom homes and one three-bedroom home. The two-bedroom homes can accommodate six, while the three-bedroom home can lodge eight. Each comes with a golf cart and bicycles. Refrigerators are stocked upon arrival with snacks, beverages, and milk. Nightly turndown service and newspaper delivery are standard.

1999 Room Rates for the Villas at the Disney Institute

Accommodation	Regular Season	Peak Season	Value Season	Holiday Season
Bungalow	$229	$304	$204	$330
One-bedroom Townhouse	$265	$280	$245	$350
Two-bedroom Townhouse	$360	$380	$335	$430
Treehouse Villa	$385	$399	$365	$475
Two-bedroom Fairway Villa	$430	$450	$395	$510
Two-bedroom Grand Vista Home	$1,025	$1,050	$1,025	$1,240
Three-bedroom Grand Vista Home	$1,200	$1,250	$1,200	$1,475

Transportation and Convenience

The Villas are not centrally located. Despite this, it is an easy matter to reach most Disney destinations. Buses run every 30 minutes but make a great many stops throughout the Villas. For travel within the Villas area, rental golf carts are available for $24 per day or $36 for 24 hours. Twenty-four-hour bike rental is $18.

- Transportation to all Disney destinations: by bus, every 30 minutes

Dining at the Villas at the Disney Institute

There are two restaurants nearby at the Institute. Seasons Dining Room features all-day dining with an interesting menu for each of the day's meals. See Chapter 6 for details. Reflections is a small, lakeside shop that features gourmet coffees, outstanding pastries and muffins, and a selection of quality sandwiches. The Reflections poolside patio is a pleasant stop for lunch.

Recreational Activities at the Villas at the Disney Institute

- Six swimming pools
- Two hot tubs
- Rental bikes and canoes
- Several outstanding walking or jogging paths

OUR IMPRESSIONS OF THE VILLAS AT THE DISNEY INSTITUTE

- It's hard to believe you're at Disney World out here. It's woodsy and quiet.
- This resort is very spread out and transportation is a bit slow. A car would come in handy.
- Both the townhouses and bungalows are within walking distance of Downtown Disney.

RECOMMENDATIONS FOR RESERVATIONS

- During the slower seasons, both the Treehouses and the bungalows enjoy generous discounts.

ROMANCE AT THE VILLAS AT THE DISNEY INSTITUTE

- Resort ambience: ♥
- Treehouse villas: ♥♥
- Taking a walk or a bike ride: ♥

The Downtown Disney Resorts on Hotel Plaza Boulevard

These seven hotels lie along Hotel Plaza Boulevard, and while none are owned or operated by Disney, they offer not only an unequaled proximity to Downtown Disney but also a few other features not found at the Disney resorts. This area lies on the east side of Disney, between I-4 and the Downtown Disney Marketplace. The shady and beautifully landscaped boulevard is a place of high-rise towers, and its urban ambience compliments well the bright lights and excitement of Downtown Disney. At one end of the boulevard is the Marketplace and at the other is the Crossroads Shopping Center, about a mile and a half away. Here you'll find Gooding's Supermarket (the closest market to Disney World) and a variety of non-Disney shops and chain restaurants.

Though none of these hotels enjoys the story-telling themes of the Disney resorts, you'll discover other advantages here. First and most important, each of these hotels offers specials that are simply not available elsewhere on-property. Discounted rooms can be had even during the busy summer months, and values can be outstanding. Room availability here is also good. If you are making a last-minute trip or are simply unable to find a room at a Disney resort, give one of these a try.

Another plus here are the high-rise views. Many of these hotels feature astounding panoramas of Walt Disney World. During our visits here, we were able to see as far as the Magic Kingdom and enjoyed rooms from which we were able to watch the fireworks shows from *all* of the Disney attractions.

If you are planning to visit some of Orlando's other attractions, you'll find that the guest service desks of these hotels are able to provide both tickets *and* transportation to such destinations as Kennedy Space Center, Sea World, Universal Studios, and Silver Springs. And of course, you'll find the usual variety of tickets to all Disney attractions as well, including Park Hopper Passes and the E-Ticket Express. However, guests along the Boulevard do not enjoy Surprise Mornings or the Disney resort card.

Transportation to all Disney destinations from the boulevard is by this area's private fleet of purple and green buses. While every bus once served all seven hotels, service has been improved to minimize the number of stops. The Hilton and Buena Vista Palace now share buses, and the rest of the fleet serves the remaining hotels. Buses run every

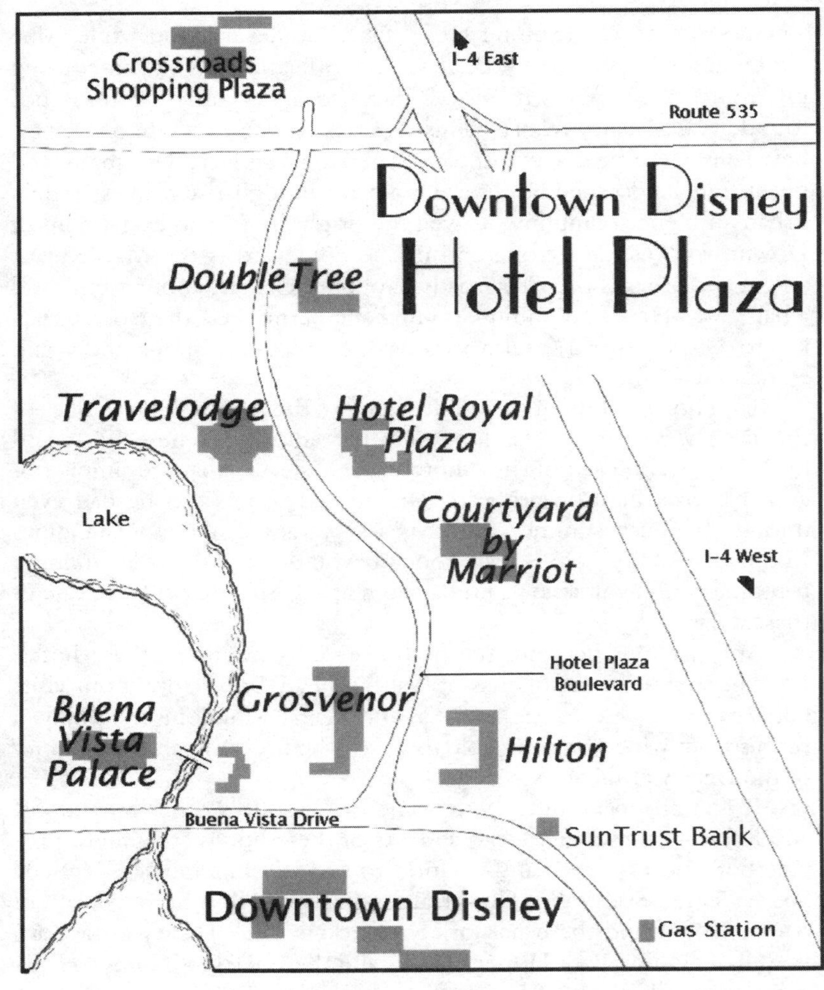
Crossroads
Shopping Plaza
I-4 East
Route 535
Downtown Disney
Hotel Plaza
DoubleTree
Travelodge
Hotel Royal
Plaza
Lake
Courtyard
by
Marriot
I-4 West
Hotel Plaza
Boulevard
Buena
Vista
Palace
Grosvenor
Hilton
Buena Vista Drive
SunTrust Bank
Downtown Disney
Gas Station

30 minutes, and during our stays in these hotels, we found service to be acceptable. While this area has never been known for its transportation, during our recent stays we discovered that getting to other Disney resorts from here was surprisingly easy. From some of these resorts, all we had to do was to walk across the street to the Marketplace and catch a bus to *any* Disney resort, including the BoardWalk. In the evening, there's a Downtown Disney shuttle bus from each hotel along the boulevard. Nowhere else on-property offers this convenience. Dining, dancing, movies, and shopping were so convenient that it has made us rethink this resort group.

It is worth noting that the buses do not drop off guests in the parks at the same bus areas used by Disney buses. While this amounts to only a few dozen yards at Epcot, Disney–MGM Studios, and the Animal Kingdom, it is more noticeable at the Magic Kingdom, where guests are left at the Ticket and Transportation Center. On a busy morning, the trip from here to the turnstiles can take 20 minutes or more.

Generally speaking, these hotels are attractive and well kept. One is even luxurious. Most provide means for five guests per room; several accommodate many more. While none enjoys the theming of such places as Dixie Landings, rooms here on the plaza are generally comfortable and well furnished. Pools and grounds range from good to beautiful, but none begins to approach the likes of Stormalong Bay at the Yacht and Beach or Doubloon Lagoon at Port Orleans.

Each guest on Hotel Plaza Boulevard receives at check-in the "Value Discount Passport," which features a number of discounts at a variety of places, both on- and off-property. One is a card that will allow your party to effectively cut in line at Planet Hollywood to get the next available table. For other good deals in this booklet, we suggest you read it through carefully. There are complimentary desserts, free drinks, and even a discount for the MurderWatch Mystery Dinner Show at the Grosvenor.

Buena Vista Palace Resort and Spa

The Palace is something of a pioneer here at Walt Disney World. It was the first resort on-property to offer true luxury accommodations and then, with the award-winning Arthur's 27, it became the first to feature fine dining. Of course, for the last few decades the Disney resorts have been playing catch-up. But don't for a minute believe that the Buena Vista Palace has been resting on its laurels. With the addition of its European-style spa and the recent total refurbishing of all guest rooms, the Buena Vista Palace Resort and Spa continues to offer everything seasoned travelers like ourselves have come to expect.

The Palace is located directly across the street from the Downtown Disney Marketplace on 27 garden-like acres and alongside a serene, freshwater lagoon. Its 27 stories of mirrored balconies makes it a distinctive sight even here among the other towers of the boulevard. Fountains, manicured beds of flowering plants, weeping willows, and date palms combine to create a real sense of excitement. The long drive brought us to the hotel's shady port cochere and to the beginning of our Palace adventure.

We found the lobby to be an elegantly understated mix of handsome carpets, potted palms, expanses of marble, and crystal chandeliers. Our luggage was immediately whisked away by the bell staff and our check-in took only a few brief minutes. We explored the lobby's "library" area with its stuffed sofas, leather club chairs, and shelves of books. For us, it seemed the perfect place to relax and recap the day or to simply sit and browse our way through the rack of daily newspapers. The view from here onto the quiet lake behind the resort gave everything a sense of ease and comfort. We had arrived.

Rooms at the Buena Vista Palace Resort and Spa

The luxurious guest rooms here at the Palace are in one of its four towers, and all feature balconies or patios and either two queen-sized beds or a single king. There are also 100 suites located in the Palace Island Suites building, a short walk away and adjacent to the pool complex on what is known as Recreation Island.

Our king room was on the twentieth floor of the 27-story main tower building. Once through the door, we noticed at once the wonderful aroma of the spa toiletries. This, we knew at once, was the kind of place where we loved to stay. We were drawn immediately to our balcony and to the panorama of the Institute, Downtown Disney, and Epcot. In the distance, we could even see the Magic Kingdom. We were already making plans to catch the fireworks here later in the evening.

Back in the room, we took a careful look around. Not only did the Palace refurbish, but they did it with quality and with care. The handsome blonde furnishings included a large desk and armoire (with large-screen TV). Bedspread, carpets, and upholstery featured tones of deep blue that contrasted well with the pale yellow wall covering and light furniture. A small tree and beautifully framed prints finished the accents for this, our plush new home. There was even a comfortable sitting area with pullout sleeper sofa and coffee table.

The bath featured a separate vanity area and the usual shower-tub combination. Plush towels, tile floors, and marble trim gave everything a sense of elegance. All rooms here at the Palace feature stocked minibars, hair dryer, and an iron and ironing board.

There are 30 VIP suites here in the tower, each with a kitchen, living and dining area, and one to five bedrooms. There is also a 36-room Crown Level Concierge floor as well as an 18-room Presidential floor that features continental breakfasts from room-service and bathrobes. Here at the Palace you'll also find 65 EverGreen® rooms that offer independent air cleaning systems, filtered water, non-allergic pillows and blankets, and non-dyed towels and linens.

As we've mentioned, there is a special suites-only area of the hotel, and it is adjacent to the pool and recreation area. Each of its 100 suites offers either one or two bedrooms, a balcony or patio, living room with queen sleeper/sofa, microwave oven, refrigerator, minibar, coffeemaker, and hair dryer. This complex features its own lobby area and unequaled proximity to the resort's tennis court, hot tub, and pools. The covered walkway from here to the main building is via a lovely garden path, past the kitchen's herb garden, and across a footbridge that spans part of the lake.

1999 Room Rates for the Buena Vista Palace

Accommodation	Peak Season	Mid-Season	Value Season
Guest room	$189–244	$159–204	$129–174
Crown Level	$264–294	$234–254	$204–224
Suites			
One-bedroom	$289–319	$259–279	$229–249
Two-bedroom	$469–529	$409–449	$349–389

Peak season: Last three weeks of January to end of April; December 25 to 31

Mid-season: May; October to mid-December

Value season: First week of January; June to September; mid-December to December 24

For reservations, call either Disney Central Reservations or (800) 327-2990. Also, check the Palace's web site at http:\\www.bvp-resort.com for some real bargains. See the back of this book for a valuable coupon for this great resort: Stay five nights and get a sixth night free.

Food and Beverage at the Palace

Dining here features a number of options, and they are all quite good. Add to them the many eateries at nearby Downtown Disney, and dining at the Palace becomes nearly limitless. This hotel's premier eatery is the award-winning Arthur's 27 ♥♥♥. An exquisite continental cuisine combined with a romantic twenty-seventh-floor panorama makes this a place where even the locals come to enjoy a fine meal. Adjacent to the lobby is the Australian-themed Outback Restaurant (no relation to the chain). Featuring a large menu of well-prepared steaks, seafood, and other specialties, the Outback Restaurant enjoys an interesting Australian "bush" motif. For our reviews of both restaurants, see Chapter 6.

The Watercress Cafe is the Palace's "all-purpose eatery," and you'll find a good breakfast buffet here each day or you can order a la carte. Sunday mornings feature a Disney character breakfast. The cafe serves from 6 A.M. to midnight each day and the menu is large and includes a generous number of healthy dishes from this resort's spa cuisine. The Watercress Cafe is located on the first floor; its casual ambience and lakeside location make it an ideal place for any of the day's meals.

The Watercress Pastry Shop is another place you'll want to know about. Open 24 hours, this pleasant little cafe features another splendid lakeside view as well as a tempting selection of treats: assorted pastries, cookies, and desserts from the Palace's kitchen, espresso and cappuccino, an Edy's Ice Cream bar, and a breakfast featuring bagels, cold cereal, fresh-squeezed orange juice, and more. It's the kind of place we'd like to see in every resort.

Another "restaurant" here is your room. The 24-hour room service menu is nothing short of huge. We counted nearly 50 items for breakfast alone, and all of the resort's spa menu is also available here. So while you're staying at the Palace, don't forget to enjoy a breakfast in bed or have a romantic dinner in your own room.

Out by the pool, you'll also find the Recreation Island Pool Snack Bar. It serves a selection of burgers, sandwiches, and salads from 11 A.M. to 6 P.M. along with a refreshing variety of specialty beverages. There's even the Courtyard Mini-Market with its gourmet coffee concoctions, snacks, and delightful sitting area.

There are two lounges here at the Palace. The Lobby Lounge is exceptionally comfortable (the "library" is part of it), and besides a large selection of cocktails and fine wines, it offers exotic teas, pastries, and canapés. Stop in here for your own afternoon high tea. Adjacent to

Arthur's is the Top of the Palace ♥♥♥. The Top features a pianist and singer Wednesday through Saturday nights as well as an extraordinary wine list.

Of course, no resort of this caliber would be complete without a nightclub, and here it is: the Laughing Kookaburra Good Time Bar. "The Kook" features live music from Tuesday through Saturday and is the place to go for an evening of fun.

Buena Vista Palace Shops

On the ground-floor level of the lobby is a Disney gift shop with its small selection of character merchandise. Nearby is W. H. Smith's, which features quality men's and women's resort wear and Buena Vista Palace logo merchandise. The spa also features its large variety of Pevonia Botanica spa and health products and EcoCare® toiletries.

The Spa at Buena Vista Palace

Our experiences here were nothing short of blissful. This world-class, European-style spa features a sublime selection of body treatments, massages, whirlpool baths, wet and dry saunas, a lap pool, and a state-of-the-art fitness center. It even has a full-service hair salon. We urge you to take some time to pamper yourselves here. It is what vacations are all about. For more details, see Chapter 7.

Services Available at Buena Vista Palace Resort and Spa

- Full bell service
- Valet parking ($8 daily)
- 24-hour room service
- Concierge desk
- Kid's Stuff child care programs
- Alamo car rental desk
- European-style spa
- Full-service hair salon
- Laundry service

Recreational Activities at Buena Vista Palace Resort and Spa

- Three heated swimming pools
- Hot tub
- Sauna
- Three lighted tennis courts (complimentary)

- Tee times at the six Disney golf courses
- Sand volleyball court
- Marina with bike and boat rentals
- Video arcade
- State-of-the-art fitness center
- Children's playground

Our Impressions of Buena Vista Palace Resort and Spa

- It's a beautiful and luxurious hotel.
- This is *the* place to stay if you are looking to be near Downtown Disney.

Recommendations for Reservations

- Check the back of this book for a coupon for a free night at this resort.
- Get a room high up in the tower with an Epcot view.
- Check the Palace's web site for special discounts (http:\\www.bvp-resort.com).
- Make your reservations through the hotel and ask for specials: (800) 327-2990.
- Reservations can also be made through Disney CRO at (407) W-DISNEY (934-7639).

Romance at Buena Vista Palace Resort and Spa

- The Spa: ♥♥♥
- Breakfast in bed: ♥♥♥
- Dining at Arthur's 27: ♥♥♥
- An evening stroll to Downtown Disney: ♥♥
- A tower room with Epcot view: ♥♥
- A daily free champagne toast at the Top of the Palace lounge: ♥♥♥
- A nightcap at the Top of the Palace: ♥♥♥

Courtyard by Marriot

This familiar name in hotels enjoys a solid reputation for comfortable and well-furnished accommodations. This 14-story, atrium-styled hotel features glass elevators and a tropical-theme lobby. Colors here are bright and airy, and upper-floor rooms offer panoramas of Downtown Disney and nearby Lake Buena Vista.

Our fourteenth-floor room commanded a stunning view of Downtown Disney, and in the distance, we could see both Epcot and the Magic Kingdom. Spacious and comfortable, our guest room featured fabrics of green, burnt orange, and yellow. The bedspread was a tropical jungle print, and the club chairs in our small but comfortable sitting area were a warm blue. With a large balcony and king bed, we quickly made ourselves at home.

Guest rooms here are either in the 14-story tower building or in the adjacent wing that overlooks the pool or I-4. Most rooms feature balconies. Ground-floor, pool-view rooms here at the Marriot are beautiful and offer both patios and a real convenience to the pool and hot tub. These "courtyard" rooms are less expensive than upper-floor tower rooms and would come with our recommendation. Most rooms feature twin queen beds, but there are a few single kings. With a roll-away bed, each room can accommodate up to five persons. All rooms feature pay-per-view movies, iron and ironing board, television with Nintendo gaming, and complimentary coffeemaker (with coffee).

Room Rates at the Courtyard by Marriot

Value season here at the Courtyard means when school is in session, and standard rooms here during those times begin at around $105. Add $10 for pool view in either the tower or the wing and another $10 for "Disney view." During the busy season, when schools are out, expect to pay $175 for standard rooms and the same additional amount for other views. Standard view here at the Courtyard by Marriot means rooms in the back of the hotel, overlooking I-4.

Reservations can be made through Disney Central Reservations or through the Marriot general reservation number. We recommend dealing directly with the Courtyard here at Disney for the best prices available. Hours are 7 A.M. to 11 P.M. and the number is (800) 223-9930.

Food and Beverage at the Courtyard by Marriot

Even with all your comings and goings to Disney, you'll want to know that you can find good food here for any of the days meals. The Courtyard Cafe and Grille is the Marriot's main eatery, and it features either a la carte or buffet breakfasts and a variety of dinner entrees. The Village Deli is another place you'll want to know about. Pizza Hut pizza, sandwiches, and frozen yogurt are featured here. We enjoyed a continental breakfast in the atrium lobby at the 2GO Bar, which had a nice selection of pastries, muffins, cold cereals, and Barney's coffee. 2GO also has a variety of snacks and beverages.

The Tipsy Parrot Lounge is right in the great lobby and features a full-service bar and snacks. Poolside is the seasonal Tiki Bar. All in all, you'll find an ample supply of food and beverage.

Services Available at the Courtyard by Marriot

- Guest services with ticketing to all area attractions
- Disney gift shop with ticketing
- Free parking
- Car rental desk in lobby
- Guest laundry and valet service

Recreational Activities at the Courtyard by Marriot

- Two outdoor, heated swimming pools
- Children's pool
- Quiet hot tub
- Exercise room
- Video game room
- Use of all Disney golf courses and tennis courts

OUR IMPRESSIONS OF THE COURTYARD BY MARRIOT

- This is a quality yet fairly ordinary hotel. Rooms are spacious and comfortable.
- Off-season rooms here can be a real bargain.
- Upper-floor rooms can feature great views.
- It's a comfortable walk from Downtown Disney.

RECOMMENDATIONS FOR RESERVATIONS

- Ground-floor, pool-view courtyard rooms are especially nice.

DoubleTree Guest Suites Resort

Our stay here began with chocolate chip cookies, still warm from the oven. A nice beginning. Next to the front desk, we noticed another nice touch: Kids check-in. While parents are getting registered, so are the kids. A cute sign-in book and small gift pack make this a special moment for everyone. There are other special things about this hotel, too. Most notable is that the DoubleTree is the only all-suite resort on-property at Disney. The 229 lodgings here in the seven-story DoubleTree are all spacious multiroom, one- and two-bedroom suites.

When we arrived in our room on the seventh floor, we were impressed by all the space. The large living room featured a dining area and a comfortable sitting area with pull-out double bed. With television, wet bar, and a desk, we immediately set up shop. Our bedroom featured a king bed, but other suites here are available with twin doubles. The bath and vanity areas were spacious and practical. There was even another TV in the bedroom. We were definitely going to enjoy all of this space. After this book goes to press, the DoubleTree will refurbish its rooms from the carpets up. The new decor will feature shades of blue and deep reds on backgrounds of beige.

While the furnishings here do not lend the luxury and theming found at some of the Disney resorts, the comfortable suites at the DoubleTree have their advantages. Each includes a coffeemaker and complimentary coffee and tea, wet bar with refrigerator and microwave oven, hair dryer, iron and ironing board, and video player with on-demand gaming. Accommodations here at the DoubleTree are most certainly large enough for a family and will provide the privacy that a single hotel room simply cannot. We made breakfast an in-room affair by dropping in at Streamer's Market (in the lobby) and buying milk and cold cereal. It made our first meal of the day both affordable and what we are used to eating.

Room Rates at DoubleTree Guest Suites Resort

The DoubleTree's less-expensive value season is a long one and runs from May to mid-December. Depending on the season, rates for the one-bedroom suites range from a bargain $139 to over $259. The large, two-bedroom suites are more than enough room even for a large family and begin at $375 per night and reach $475 during the holiday season. The DoubleTree also offers a small variety of seasonal and special packages. Discounts for both AAA and AARP are quite good. For reservations, phone the DoubleTree at (800) 222-TREE (8733) or Disney Central Reservations.

Food and Beverage at DoubleTree Guest Suites Resort

Streamer's is the restaurant at DoubleTree. Adjacent to the atrium-style lobby, this eatery offers a large menu for each of the day's meals. Each evening, Streamer's offers an all-you-care-to-eat buffet, and each day's special is announced on signs by the elevator. There's even a breakfast buffet. DoubleTree also has a tropical poolside snack bar and lounge, and for those wishing to do for themselves, there's Streamer's Market. This little store features a good selection of drinks, snacks, and groceries. This is where we went to get our breakfast supply. Using Streamer's Market and your suite's microwave and refrigerator can add up to some real savings, particularly at breakfast.

Services Available at DoubleTree Guest Suites Resort

- Bus schedule given at check-in
- Disney and area attraction ticket desk
- Coin-operated laundry and dry cleaning service
- Budget car rental desk in lobby
- Disney gift shop
- Kids check-in desk and child care services
- Nightly turndown
- Bed boards

Recreational Activities at DoubleTree Guest Suites Resort

- Heated, tropical pool
- Exercise room
- Lighted tennis courts
- Children's playground
- Volleyball court
- Jogging trail
- Video arcade
- Preferred tee times at Disney golf courses

OUR IMPRESSIONS OF DOUBLETREE GUEST SUITES RESORT

- These are very spacious accommodations for the money. Comfortable, but not luxurious. There are no balconies. Decor is pleasant but not themed. This hotel will have gotten a complete room renovation during the summer of 1998.
- A bit longer walk to Downtown Disney than some other hotels here on the boulevard, but it's closer to the Crossroads Shopping Plaza. Bus service is available.
- The pool area here is quite close to the highway.

RECOMMENDATIONS FOR RESERVATIONS

- Look for an AAA or AARP discount.
- Off-season rates can make this place ideal for a small family.

ROMANCE AT DOUBLETREE GUEST SUITES RESORT

- Having your own private bedroom: ♥♥

Grosvenor Resort

Pronounced "grove-nor," this 19-story hotel is one of the nearest to the Downtown Marketplace and features a pleasant British-colonial theme. Throughout its spacious lobby, cooling shades of green, wicker chairs and comfortable sofas abound. There's a constant flow of guests through here, heading for all destinations Disney and otherwise. The Grosvenor is well located for transportation to all of the Central Florida attractions.

The large grounds of the Grosvenor most certainly set it apart from the others here along the boulevard. Located on 13 beautifully landscaped acres, the Grosvenor features two quiet, lakeside garden pools. Here amidst the hubbub of Downtown Disney is an area that is surprisingly serene and marvelously restful. After a morning at the parks, you'll want to get your batteries recharged here for a night on the town.

Rooms at the Grosvenor are located either in the high-rise tower building or in one of its two garden wings. Tower rooms boast an impressive view of Downtown Disney or Lake Buena Vista. Garden wing rooms offer the Grosvenor's only balconies and these overlook either the landscaped front of the hotel or the garden and pool areas. Rooms feature either double doubles or single kings (rollaway beds and cribs are available). Well-stocked minibutlers, coffeemakers with complimentary coffee, and video cassette players are standard items. Room furnishings are of light wood and include a large dresser, desk, and television armoire, and bedspreads are of pastel floral designs. We found our tower room to be quite comfortable and the Lake Buena Vista view quite nice.

Room Rates at the Grosvenor Resort

The peak season at the Grosvenor is February 5 through April 17. Value season is January 1 through February 4 and April 18 to December 16. Standard rooms at the Grosvenor begin at around $175 during value season to $200 during the peak season, with a maximum of five persons per room. Specials and last-minute discounts throughout the year can lower these rates to around $99 per night, and we suggest that you call to see what is available. The most likely times to find bargain rooms are the first 10 days of January, a week before Memorial Day to June 10, the month of September, late August to Labor Day, and December 12 to the 18. We recommend calling Grosvenor reservations at (800) 624-4109 for the best rates, not Disney CRO.

Food and Beverage at the Grosvenor Resort

The Grosvenor makes more of an effort than any hotel along the plaza to give itself something of a theme, and you'll find it most evident in its eateries and lounges. Baskerville's is this hotel's premier restaurant, and it features an authentic Sherlock Holmes museum and re-creation of the famous 221B Baker Street. This eatery's specialty is its prime rib buffet, and on Saturday evenings there is the MurderWatch Mystery Theater dinner show. Baskerville's serves breakfast, lunch, and dinner with a la carte menus. Right next door is Moriarty's Pub. Drop in here before dinner for a cocktail or later for a nightcap. Remember to ask if there is live entertainment here during your visit.

The "very British" theme of the Grosvenor is carried to Crumpet's Cafe, the lobby food court. Here you'll find 24 hours of snacks and beverages—virtually anything you might be in the mood for. It's a great place to grab a quick snack and drink before you head off to your day of park adventures. Also located in the lobby is Cricket's Lounge. Large-screen sporting events are featured here, with a full-service bar and coffee specialties.

And of course, you'll find Barnacle's poolside with snacks, sandwiches, and beverages. During the busy season, you might even find live entertainment here too.

The Grosvenor Disney Store

Naturally, you'll find a selection of Disney character merchandise and souvenirs here as well as a few gifts and sundries.

Services Available at the Grosvenor Resort

- Disney Store with complete ticketing
- Valet parking ($5 daily)
- Valet and dry cleaning services
- Coin-operated laundry facilities
- In-house car rental
- Video camera and cell phone rentals
- ATM
- Child care arrangements

Recreational Activities at the Grosvenor Resort

- Two heated pools
- Hot tub
- Two complimentary lighted tennis courts

- Basketball, handball, volleyball, and shuffleboard courts
- Children's play pool and playground
- Fitness center
- Golf arrangements
- Lakeside gazebo

OUR IMPRESSION OF THE GROSVENOR RESORT

- Nice grounds, but the rooms are pretty unexceptional for the price.

ROMANCE AT THE GROSVENOR

- An evening stroll to Downtown Disney: ♥♥

The Hilton

The very name of this resort has come to be synonymous with fine lodgings. This is an award-winning, Four-Diamond hotel with an impressive list of amenities. The grand marble lobby is vibrant and exciting. From one end to the other, it encompasses a world of shops and restaurants, a sports bar, and even a small grocery and deli. Large saltwater aquariums decorate the area behind the front desk and team with brightly colored and exotic tropical fish. Service at the Hilton is so good that if you simply stand here for a few minutes, someone is bound to ask if he or she can be of some assistance.

The Hilton is located directly across the street from the Downtown Disney Marketplace and it is one of the boulevard's most outstanding travel destinations. It boasts a tropical theme, which is carried elegantly from its lush gardens to its comfortable rooms. With either twin double beds or single kings, each standard room features a small sitting area, perfect for in-room dining. Furnishings here are light oak, and rooms are beige with tropical accents and flowered bedspreads. All rooms feature well-stocked minibars, cable TV with a staggering selection of pay-per-view movies, twin vanities, hair dryer, and iron and ironing board.

The Hilton's Tower Level rooms can be found on the exclusive ninth and tenth floors and feature this hotel's concierge service. Our room here was large and luxurious. As Tower guests, we happily enjoyed the comfortable private lounge, plush bathrobes, continental breakfasts, and beverages and snacks served throughout the day. Our comings and goings were made all the more effortless by a well-trained desk staff that seemed only too happy to fulfill our every wish.

Room Rates at the Hilton

The peak season here at the Hilton is the winter tourist season of January to March. Value season is June through August, and during the rest of the year, prices vary widely based on availability. During the summer value season, expect rooms to cost around $150 and $255 during the busy months. Try booking early to get bargains; inquiries about rates during April, May, and September to December might be rewarded with bargain rates. For reservations, call (800) 782-4414.

Food and Beverage at the Hilton

The Hilton boasts a large selection of restaurants and lounges even for a resort of its size. Finn's Grill is its premier dining place, and each night it offers a different all-you-can-eat special as well as a large menu of a la carte items. Specialties here are seafood and steaks; on the night of our visit, the special was barbecued ribs. Nearby is Covington Mill, which features buffet and a la carte breakfasts as well as varied lunch and dinner selections. The menus here are interesting and the food is well prepared and more than a little above average. It all comes from the Hilton's large kitchen, and that includes everything from homemade potato chips to a tantalizing selection of desserts. Covington Mill enjoys a quaint, New England, back-porch theme and is a pleasant place to enjoy any meal. Ask about its Disney character breakfasts.

Mug's is this resort's gourmet coffee shop. Drop by here to enjoy a pastry, a cappuccino, or an aperitif. Nearby, there's live jazz in the evenings. It is a cozy and comfortable spot. Next door to Mug's is the Mainstreet Market, where you'll find desserts and deli selections to wines, Ben and Jerry's ice cream, and a formidable selection of snacks.

At the other end of the lobby is the Hilton's sports bar. This swingin' place features large-screen TVs, sandwiches and snacks, and a full-service bar. The Hilton also offers its guests Benihana, the well-known Japanese steak house and sushi bar. There's even more: Rum Largo is the poolside bar and cafe, the perfect place for a refreshing tropical concoction or a light lunch. There's even the Old Fashioned Soda Shop. And of course, at the Hilton you'll find complete 24-hour room service. All in all, it's an outstanding selection of quality choices. If you prefer to go out for the evening, the fine restaurants and clubs of Downtown Disney are just a stroll away.

Shops at the Hilton

If you get the munchies or are looking for a snack to take to your room, Mainstreet Market is sure to have something for you. The Disney Store here at the Hilton is large and well-stocked with character merchandise, and On the Green features a classy assortment of men's and women's resort sportswear, with an emphasis on golf. If you want to do some really serious shopping, the Downtown Disney Marketplace is right across the street.

Services Available at the Hilton

- 24-hour concierge service
- Valet parking
- Full bell service
- Vacation Station Kids Hotel
- Valet and coin-operated laundries
- In-house car rentals
- Disney Store with complete ticket offerings

Recreational Activities at the Hilton

- Two heated swimming pools in a beautiful garden area
- Two charming and secluded tropical hot tubs: ♥♥♥
- A children's play pool
- Preferred tee times and transportation for Disney golf
- Nautilus health club
- A championship volleyball court
- Video arcade

OUR IMPRESSIONS OF THE HILTON

- This is a very nice hotel with outstanding service. It's an excellent place to stay in the Downtown Disney area.
- It offers a good selection of restaurants.
- Of this group of hotels, it's one of the closest to Downtown Disney.

ROMANCE AT THE HILTON

- An evening hot tub: ♥♥♥
- A Tower room: ♥♥
- Taking a stroll to Downtown Disney: ♥♥
- Breakfast in bed: ♥♥♥

Hotel Royal Plaza

With a recent total refurbishing, this hotel has become one of the brightest "new" faces here along Hotel Plaza Boulevard. The Royal Plaza's bright and airy tiled lobby expresses a relaxing touch of the tropics. White expanses of wall that soar to high ceilings, wrought-iron accents, large potted palms, and bellpersons in starched-white uniforms and epaulets brought this theme together handsomely. It seemed a little touch of Old Bermuda.

The 394 guest rooms here are either in the 16-floor Tower building or in the two-story Lanai building adjacent to the pool. Rooms are bright and colorful and feature pastel tropical fish bedspreads. All accommodations feature either two queen beds or a single king, a pull-out sleeper/sofa, coffeemaker, video player, and either a balcony or patio. The large Tower rooms offer a big tub, which can easily accommodate two. During our recent Hotel Royal Plaza visit, we were able to stay in one of our favorite rooms, the Executive King. This spacious two-room suite features a comfortable living room with pull-out queen sofa, a dining area, desk, and armoire with large-screen TV and video player. Our cozy king bedroom had a large TV and small sitting area. There were even dimmers on the lights: a nice touch. Several of these rooms even feature mirrored ceilings.

Like the other rooms of the Tower, our bathroom also had a large tub, but ours added Jacuzzi jets. It was all we could think about as we returned "home" after a day spent scouting the parks. All Royal Plaza baths feature a small vanity area, which we found to be quite adequate. If you're visiting Disney with kids, we would recommend one of these fine accommodations.

Another nice room here is the ground-floor, pool-view Lanai room. Though a bit smaller than a Tower room, each features a private poolside patio.

Room Rates at the Hotel Royal Plaza

The value season here runs pretty much like the Disney resorts, but expect to find exceptionally good rates in the first week of June, all of September, and early October. The 1999 rate of $194 per night should be discounted to near $99 during these times as well as whenever schools are in session. Of course, this is subject to availability.

During peak season, the Executive King is around $230. Off-season, you might be able to get it for nearer to $170. For reservations, we suggest that you call this hotel's reservation desk at (800) 248-7890.

Hotel Royal Plaza Packages

The Royal Plaza offers an interesting assortment of romance packages and, given price and this hotel's proximity to the excitement of Downtown Disney, you'll want to know what is available. The Royal Getaway features a two-night stay in superior Tower accommodations. It includes a welcome cocktail and admission to Pleasure Island. This is the most basic package. Each step up includes more and more, until you arrive at the Super Suite Romance, a seven-night/eight-day package with a welcome cocktail, lodgings in a honeymoon suite with Jacuzzi tub, one breakfast in bed for two, deluxe fruit basket and champagne delivered to your room, an in-suite romance dinner for two, his and hers bathrobes, a rental car, and a special Hotel Royal Plaza memento. All this for around $2,500 per couple. The basic package begins around $350 per couple, and there are a variety of others between the two we've mentioned.

Food and Beverage at the Hotel Royal Plaza

The Verandah Cafe is this hotel's main restaurant, and it features each of the day's meals a la carte as well as buffet breakfasts and dinners. The ambience here is tropical, with potted plants, varnished wood floors, and colorful accents. Nearby is the lobby cocktail lounge and the "Marketessin." This little shop is something of a market and something of a deli. It features an interesting assortment of snacks, sandwiches, beverages, and desserts. It's just the place for a light meal or to cure a case of the munchies.

Sip's Poolbar is a pleasant gazebo right alongside the swimming area. It features a selection of refreshing tropical specialty drinks and snacks.

Services Available at the Hotel Royal Plaza

- Valet parking
- Bell service
- Coin-operated laundry and valet service
- Room service until midnight

Recreational Activities at the Hotel Royal Plaza

- Large heated pool
- Hot tub and sauna
- All-new fitness center
- Four lighted tennis courts
- Video arcade
- Tee times at the Disney golf courses

OUR IMPRESSIONS OF THE HOTEL ROYAL PLAZA

- The rooms were tropical and pleasant.

RECOMMENDATIONS FOR RESERVATIONS

- Check out this hotel's romance packages.
- We loved the Executive King room.

ROMANCE AT THE HOTEL ROYAL PLAZA

- One of the Romance packages: ♥♥
- A (family) visit in an Executive King room: ♥♥

Travelodge Hotel

This hotel is an 18-story high-rise, one that affords stunning views of Disney and Lake Buena Vista. It is located on a small and woodsy lot adjacent to the lake, and its pool and garden areas are exceptionally quiet. The lobby of the Travelodge Hotel is small and a bit dark but it enjoys a pleasant tropical theme. Floral carpets of deep green surround a grand and winding stairway that leads up to a quiet mezzanine sitting area. Here in the lobby you'll find a carousel with scenes from Disney's animated classics and nearby you'll see a Disney Store that features a small selection of Disney merchandise and the full variety of attraction tickets. There's more here too: a small market-cafe, a lounge, guest services desk, and on the lakeside of the hotel, the porch-like Trader's Restaurant.

We're pleased to report that rooms here have been recently refurbished and are bright and pleasant. Floral spreads and fabrics accent the textured beige wall coverings. Furnishings are pleasing and comfortable. All rooms here at the Travelodge feature balconies with a small table and two chairs and a choice of three views: Disney, lake, and Orlando. All were pleasant enough, though we found both the lake and Disney views to be quite special. It is worth noting that both provided views of Downtown Disney.

There are four large suites on the eighteenth floor of the Travelodge, and with prices ranging from $200 to $300 per night (depending on the season), each seems something of a bargain. Besides a spacious bedroom and comfortable living room, each also features a very nice enclosed porch with skylight. It is bright, airy, and one of the most unique features we've seen in any room at Walt Disney World. One of these would make a great romance destination or would provide ample space for a small family. If you are interested in one of these beautiful suites, we would advise that you reserve early.

All rooms and suites include coffeemaker and complimentary coffee and tea as well as a hair dryer, small vanity area, and the usual shower-tub combination. Accommodations feature either double queens or a single king bed with pullout sleeper/sofa. All rooms can accommodate four guests (five with a $10 per night rollaway bed). Other amenities include iron and ironing board, pay-per-view movies, and Nintendo television gaming.

Room Rates at the Travelodge Hotel

The value season at the Travelodge includes January to mid-February, late April to early June, and late August through the third week of December. During peak seasons, room rates at the Travelodge range from $139 to $169. Rooms during the value seasons typically are $119 to $139, with numerous deals as low as $89 per night. To get the best possible rate during your Disney visit, we suggest calling the hotel's reservation number at (800) 348-3765.

Food and Beverage at the Travelodge Hotel

Trader's is the all-purpose restaurant here, and it features a breakfast buffet and a la carte dinner with a Caribbean flair. Steaks and seafood are the specialties of the house, and Trader's features a pleasant garden ambience and an even more beautiful dining porch. For a quick snack or light meal, you'll be happy with the Parakeet Cafe and its homemade doughnuts, croissandwiches, and pizza. There's even a nice "breakfast pizza." The Travelodge also has a 7 A.M. to midnight room service.

Flamingo Cove is this hotel's lounge and it is in the lobby, adjacent to Trader's. There's nightlife here too, with Toppers Night Club on the eighteenth floor. A full-service bar, pool table, free popcorn, and a stunning view of Downtown Disney and Epcot make this a pretty lively place from 8 P.M. to 2 A.M.

Services Available at the Travelodge Hotel

- Convenient self-parking
- Room service from 7 A.M. to midnight
- Baby-sitting services

Recreational Activities at the Travelodge Hotel

- Heated pool and garden sundeck
- Kiddie pool
- Children's playground
- Video game room
- Pool table at Toppers

OUR IMPRESSIONS OF THE TRAVELODGE HOTEL

- The rooms are pleasant, with many good views. It's a reasonable place to stay near Disney.
- It's a healthy walk from the Downtown Disney Marketplace.

ROMANCE AT THE TRAVELODGE HOTEL

- King bed with Disney or lake view: ♥
- Travelodge suite: ♥♥

NEW *The Disney Cruise Line*

The Disney Cruise Line promises something unique amidst a sea of ordinary cruise vacations: a ship that includes all the luxury of the world's finest liners as well as entertainment like nothing else on the seven seas. There's more: unique dining experiences, an entire deck of children's activities, and a visit to Disney's own tropical island. Disney promises not only the best family experience afloat, but also one that affords an intimate and romantic *adult* experience as well. With entire areas of the ship being adult-access only, an adult-only restaurant, and an adult-only beach, the Disney Cruise Line has aimed its sights on both the family and couples markets.

We're happy to report that we were able to take a two-day "warm-up" cruise on the *Disney Magic* before this book went to press. During our brief experience, we got a thorough look at both the ship and Disney's island destination, as well as a glimpse of how things will be working during the ship's first few months. No doubt changes will be made, for there were plenty of glitches. As usual, we'll give you our impressions as well as our recommendations to make your cruise experience the best that it can be.

The *Disney Magic*

Since vessels are spoken of in female terms, let us describe the *Disney Magic*: she is drop-dead gorgeous. Her classic lines and art deco interiors evoke the bygone era of luxurious ocean liners. The *Disney Magic* is a stunning masterpiece of European design combined with the wit and whimsy of the Disney Imagineers. The quality and magic that are the hallmarks of Disney Resorts are everywhere from dining rooms to ash trays, from staterooms to smoke stacks. From stem to stern, this ship is an engaging delight to the senses. She is one of the most beautiful vessels afloat. Not a detail has been overlooked. As you pull out of port and the ship's horn sounds the first seven notes of "When You Wish Upon a Star," you'll know just how potent this *Magic* is.

The Cruises

The Disney Cruise Line offers a Land & Sea Adventure package that combines either three or four days at Walt Disney World with either four or three days aboard the *Disney Magic*. You can also opt for just a three- or four-day cruise.

The Disney World side of the package provides resort accommodations and admission to all attractions, as well as transportation to and from the Disney Terminal at Port Canaveral. It does not include meals.

Cruises and the cruise part of the package provide onboard accommodations, meals, beverages and snacks, entertainment, and children's activities aboardship. Not included are alcoholic beverages, shore excursions in Nassau, port charges, gratuities, and recreational equipment rentals at Castaway Cay.

Prices are based on value, regular, and peak seasons; and the category of stateroom you select will determine your Disney World Resort. Prices also include economy airfare.

Accommodations

There are a variety of staterooms aboard the *Disney Magic*, and it is worth noting that accommodations average 25% larger than cruise industry standards. Most staterooms include something altogether new: a "split bath." This means one bath with vanity and shower/tub and another with vanity and toilet. It's the perfect combination, and each is nautical, charming, and well-designed. Every stateroom aboard the *Disney Magic* features satellite TV, hairdryer, comfortable furnishings, and a generous amount of inlaid, pearwood cabinetry. Even the most modest stateroom offers spacious closets and numerous drawers. But most important is that each provides the quality that we have come to expect from Disney.

There are two categories of staterooms: outside (with ocean view) or inside (no view). Aboard the *Magic* you'll find that three staterooms out of four feature ocean views, and nearly half of those have private verandahs. The *Disney Magic* has ten decks, with staterooms on six of them. Generally, the higher your deck, the higher the price.

There are two types of inside staterooms: the standard (184 square feet) and the deluxe (214 square feet and split bath). These are the least expensive staterooms aboard and offer a variety of sleeping arrangements for two to four persons. For the seven-day package, value season prices begin around $2,600 per couple and for a four-day cruise, around $1,800.

Outside cabins include deluxe oceanview ♥ (with large porthole), deluxe stateroom with navigator's verandah ♥♥ (enclosed balcony with partially obstructed view), and deluxe stateroom with verandah ♥♥♥♥ (268 square feet with an open and spacious balcony). An outside cabin will also include a stay at the Yacht or Beach Club, the Contemporary, the Polynesian, the BoardWalk, or the Swan or Dolphin. Value season prices begin around $3,700 per couple for the seven-day package and $2,500 for the four-day cruise. There are also one- or two-bedroom suites ♥♥♥♥ and the Royal Suite ♥♥♥♥. All come with verandahs, concierge service, and a stay at the Grand Floridian Resort and Spa.

If you are a couple with children, each child age 3 to 17 will cost $999 for the package and about $780 for the four-day cruise. Children under 2 years are $275 for either. Without airfare, subtract $1,000 per couple.

Dining Onboard the *Disney Magic*

Disney Cruise Lines promises a unique dining experience and, to some degree, they deliver. There are three charming dining rooms aboard the *Magic*, and passengers rotate from one to another each night, taking with them their service staff. Lumiere's is the ship's elegant French dining room, and Parrot Cay is a bright and colorful Caribbean eatery. The third dining room is Animator's Palette, and this unusual place is itself something of a show as it starts out the evening in black and white and slowly comes to life and color.

We're sorry to report that during our voyage the food was a constant disappointment. Service was spotty though well intentioned, but the food itself seemed flat and unappealing.

Palo ♥♥♥ is this ship's adult-only eatery and offers a spectacular view off the stern of the ship. Palo is a beautiful and romantic dining destination. The food here was definitely tasty, but on the whole, certainly not up to the standards set by our favorite Disney World restaurants.

Topsiders serves buffet breakfast and lunch as well as a buffet dinner for children. It features a too-small indoor dining room and several patios on-deck. We found the food to be unremarkable.

There are several snack bars that serve hot dogs, hamburgers, and pizza, but when it came to a bite to eat, this ship left a lot of us passengers wishing for some other place to go. Perhaps an afternoon tea would fill this gap. The ship also features a 24-hour "stateroom service" with a modest menu.

Entertainment Aboard the *Disney Magic*

There's so much to do onboard for adults, families, and children that we can't describe it in detail. The center of the *Magic*'s galaxy of entertainment is the Walt Disney World Theater, which presents a different, original, Broadway-style production each evening. For movie lovers there's the Buena Vista Theatre. During our cruise, films shown included *Toy Story, The Man in the Iron Mask*, and *As Good as it Gets.*

Beat Street is an "avenue" of adult-only clubs. It includes Offbeat comedy club, Rockin' Bar D dance club, and Sessions ♥♥, an intimate piano lounge. And located in the forward funnel is the ESPN Skybox showing non-stop live satellite sports events. From a quiet and secluded hideaway to line dancing, you should find something here that interests you.

Studio Sea is the ships family dance club and features a DJ, top-40 band, and TV-style game shows. This place was a real hit during our cruise. The Junkanoo festival with music, dance, costumes, and island fare, takes place only on the four-day cruise.

Children's Activities Aboard the *Disney Magic*

When it comes to children's programming, the *Disney Magic* has almost an entire deck with a total of 50 counselors devoted solely to supervised children's activities. There are three areas, each designed to provide age-specific adventures for children: the Oceaneer Club (ages 3–8), the Oceaneer Lab (ages 9–12), and Common Grounds (teens). During our cruise experience, the kids onboard gave these areas rave reviews.

Onboard Recreation and the Vista Spa and Salon

Besides two pools (one for adults only), the *Magic* offers several hot tubs and an on-deck sports area featuring volleyball, basketball, badminton, shuffleboard, and ping pong. There's a quarter-mile jogging and walking course as well as a state-of-the-art Cybex fitness center.

Also onboard the *Disney Magic* is the beautiful Vista Spa and Salon ♥♥♥, which features a sublime variety of treatments from around the world. Enjoy hydrotherapy, massages, aromatherapy, saunas, whirlpools, and the marvelous Tropical Rain Shower. This is a place you'll not want to miss.

Shops Aboard the *Disney Magic*

Upbeat is the ship's tax-free gift shop and features liquor, leather goods, jewelry, and gifts. Mickey Mates and Treasure Ketch are two shops that cover the field of character and logo merchandise, toys and novelties, and men's and women's apparel. We were surprised to find no magazines or books for sale aboardship.

Nassau, Bahamas

The *Disney Magic* spends one entire day in Nassau. There's plenty of time to explore this lively city and the nearby islands, thanks to a large selection of shore excursions for all ages. There is a teen Junkanoo cruise ($25), scuba diving ($65), and a historic Nassau tour ($22). Other excursions include deep-sea fishing, a glass bottom boat cruise, snorkeling, a beach party, and a harbor cruise.

Castaway Cay

After 20 years of cruising the Bahamas on our own sailboat, we're ready to proclaim this one of the most beautiful islands in the archipelago. Besides a beautifully landscaped tropical paradise, there are activities for all ages: snorkeling, boating, floating, biking, and a variety of gorgeous beaches including Serenity Bay for adults and another exclusively for teens. There are even two beachside massage huts at Serenity Bay.

There are also several tropical bars and beverage places as well as a lunch barbecue. The only complaint we heard was that people simply did not want to leave. This is the perfect mate for the *Disney Magic*. No other cruise line has anything like it.

OUR IMPRESSIONS OF THE DISNEY CRUISE EXPERIENCE

- Both the ship and Castaway Cay are simply too beautiful to describe in the space we have here.
- Staterooms are exceptionally comfortable, quiet, and beautiful.
- We found the food to be surprisingly mediocre.
- We experienced a number of service problems, but we are confident that such things will be worked out in the coming months.
- The children's activities are so good on this ship that the rest of the cruise industry will be scrambling to keep up. Good luck to them.
- We are happy to see that there is no gambling on this ship. You can gamble in Nassau.
- We think the recreational rentals on Castaway Cay are too pricey. Snorkeling equipment is $27, kayaks $12 per hour, and bikes $5 per hour.

OUR RECOMMENDATIONS FOR THE DISNEY CRUISE LINE

- We suggest waiting until the ship has been operating for at least six months before booking your cruise. Perhaps by then all of the problems will be worked out, including (we hope) the quality of the food.
- Discounts are available via the Magic Kingdom Club and by booking early.
- We do not recommend the three-day cruise, either as part of the package or as a standalone vacation. It is simply too little time aboard ship.
- If you love Disney, this is an adventure not to be missed.

- There are a number of "reservation only" activities that you will likely be interested in, and we strongly suggest that as soon as you get aboard, you go to guest services and make your plans for: a romantic dinner at Palo, treatments at the Vista Spa and Salon, and massages on the beach at Serenity Bay. We would also recommend that you make plans for your Nassau shore excursion as early as you can.
- We do not recommend an inside stateroom, especially if you are looking for a romantic experience.
- Consult the information packet in your stateroom to determine gratuities for steward and dining staff.
- For information, brochures, and reservations for the Disney Cruise Line, call (800) 511-1333.

ROMANCE ABOARD THE *DISNEY MAGIC*

- A deluxe stateroom with verandah: ♥♥♥♥
- A romantic dinner at Palo : ♥♥♥
- A late night hot tub or stroll on deck: ♥♥♥
- Treatments at the Vista Spa : ♥♥♥
- Massage on the beach at Castaway Cay: ♥♥♥
- Breakfast in bed or on your verandah: ♥♥♥
- Cocktails at Sessions: ♥♥

PART 2

What to Do Once You Get There

CHAPTER 3

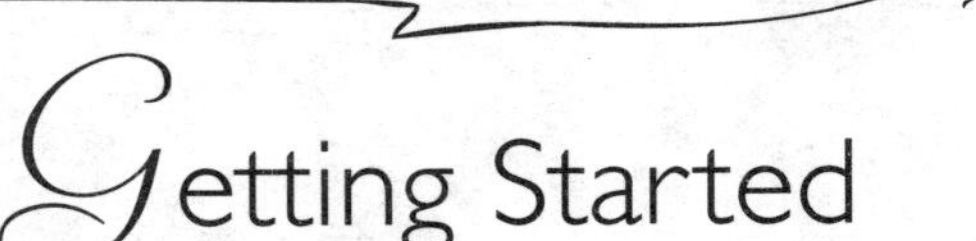

Getting Started

There's so much to do at Walt Disney World that it seems natural for people to want to see it all. Often as not, the average Disney guests spend their entire vacation rushing from attraction to attraction, trying to ride every ride and see every show. Now it seems there is too much to do to fit into even a lengthy vacation. Disney World has grown so large and offers such a diversity of vacation experiences that the fast-lane approach will only keep you in a constant hurry, and all that rushing around will quickly get you to the edge of exhaustion.

We urge you to remember that this *is* your vacation and that you should take it easy enough so you won't need a week off to recover from it. If you want this trip to be something romantic, we hope you know that stumbling back to your resort room after a full-throttle day of running around, only to fall into a deep coma, does not sound to us like romance. In fact, it doesn't even sound like much of a vacation.

So, take our advice and take it easy. Look through this book for the heart symbols. Intersperse your theme park adventures with enough time together doing what is relaxing and intimate. Spend a morning at Disney–MGM Studios, then head back to your resort for a few hours at the pool. Ride a bike or rent a boat. Relax, then go back out and catch a sunset safari at the Animal Kingdom and afterwards an evening of entertainment and excitement. But remember, come home early enough for a nice soak in a hot tub and some time together. Know what we mean? All it takes is resisting the notion that you have to see it all.

Tools of the Trade

Things change constantly at Walt Disney World. We're talking not so much about the big things but about the small ones. Show times, performers, fireworks shows, parades, and even park hours are all subject to seasonal and even daily variations. The first thing you'll want to do after settling in is to get a handle on what's happening and when. There are several useful tools for this.

The World Update

At check-in, you should receive this Walt Disney World general information pamphlet. It provides information on park hours, special events, new attractions, "rehabs" (which attractions are closed for maintenance), and all the latest on Surprise Mornings. Look it over carefully.

The Guidemaps

Available for each Disney attraction, including such places as Downtown Disney and the BoardWalk, any of these detailed maps will be your guide to rides, attractions, rest rooms, shops, and restaurants. Updated weekly, the guidemaps also provide all the information you'll need to find out what's happening and when at Disney, including parades, fireworks, live entertainment, and special events. The guidemaps are available at the Guest Services of your resort and in the attractions themselves. We suggest you pick up all of them early in your stay to help you plan a relaxed and easy Disney visit.

Getting Around at Walt Disney World

Walt Disney World is a big place. Getting around its nearly 40 square miles will be something that you will want to get good at. It will not be hard. The bus system at Disney runs an astounding 200 buses with more than 600 drivers to keep them going. It is the third largest bus system in Florida.

We're not going to tell you that busing around Walt Disney World will be romantic. What we will tell you is that there are a lot of other ways to get around and that some of these are most certainly special and, yes, even a bit romantic. Besides the usual buses, there's the monorail, a fleet of boats, carriages, and trolleys. We encourage you to take the road less traveled.

The Transportation Guidemap

This map and guide will give you all the information you'll need to successfully negotiate your way around the World. The map is large and easy to read. The transport chart will give you virtually every option, be it bus, boat, or monorail. Pick up one of these at Guest Services and keep it with you during your travels.

Disney Bus Service

These past few years have seen some new strategies in Disney bus service. We are happy to report that there seems to be real improvement, and to a system that already seemed to work well. During the Disney rush hours (9 A.M. to 11 A.M. and 5 P.M. to 7 P.M.), buses are running more frequently. With buses promised every 20 minutes, the reality seems more like every 10 minutes. Routes have been altered to make better use of buses. You will find that most buses make a round-about series of stops, and some of them may surprise you.

Bus service at Walt Disney World is really quite good. Buses can get just about anywhere in 10 or 15 minutes. Plan on five minutes to get to your bus stop and, along with a short wait for the bus, you can count on 30 minutes to actually arrive at your destination.

The Disney Fleet

If you enjoy a pleasant outdoor trip, there is nothing like a boat ride. Dozens of watercraft ply the waters of the World, and as Disney resort guests you'll be free to use all of them. From the dock at the Magic Kingdom, boats make their arrivals and departures for the Wilderness Lodge, the Grand Floridian, and the Polynesian resorts, Discovery Island, Fort Wilderness, and River Country. At Epcot's World Showcase Plaza Lagoon, catch a watercraft across the lagoon to either Germany or Morocco. At Epcot's International Gateway, *Friendship* water taxies carry passengers to the BoardWalk, to the Yacht and the Beach Clubs, and to the Swan and the Dolphin. Hop off at any for a meal or to catch a connecting boat to Disney–MGM Studios. And at the Animal Kingdom, there's the Discovery River boats heading to exotic ports of call.

Downtown Disney is located on Lake Buena Vista, which connects to a series of waterways. Here, watercraft leave for trips up the Sassagoula to Port Orleans and Dixie Landings as well as to Old Key West. There's even a water taxi that connects the West Side Esplanade with the Downtown Marketplace.

The Monorail

There are three monorail spurs at Walt Disney World running on more than 13 miles of elevated track. Two spurs run around the Seven Seas

Lagoon. The express carries day guests to the Magic Kingdom from the Ticket and Transportation Center (TTC). The local, for Disney resort guests only, makes stops at the TTC, the Polynesian, the Grand Floridian, the Contemporary, and the Magic Kingdom. The third monorail line runs from the TTC to Epcot. This monorail line is long and scenic, but expect crowds in the early morning hours when Magic Kingdom resort guests flock to Epcot.

The best seats on the monorail are in the front car with the driver. Ask the monorail attendants if seats are available (only four or five can ride at a time). If not, try waiting for the next train. Better yet, try this on the Epcot spur. This is not a loop run, and whoever is in the front car will be getting out.

Travel to Other Resort Areas

Getting to any of the attractions is simple. Traveling to other Disney resort areas is a bit more complicated, though, and you will likely want to do it for a Disney character breakfast, for dining, or for just looking around. If you have a car, then driving may be the simplest thing to do. The roads are exceptionally well marked. But know that busing to other resorts is not difficult. During the day, the easiest way to get to another resort is to go to any park and catch a bus returning to where you want to go. Frequent buses come and go all day long from all resorts. After park closing, this same technique can be used from the bus centers at Downtown Disney, where buses come and go into the wee hours of the morning.

CHAPTER 4

The Attractions

It wasn't long ago that "the Disney attractions" meant three theme parks. Some of us can even remember when Disney World was only the Magic Kingdom. Times have changed. Disney now offers an ever-widening diversity of entertainment. Besides the Magic Kingdom, Epcot, and Disney–MGM Studios, there is now the Animal Kingdom, Disney's newest theme park. And this isn't all. Add to these the Disney Institute, three extraordinary water parks, a wildlife preserve, the BoardWalk Promenade, Disney's Wide World of Sports, and the dazzling nightlife of Downtown Disney and you'll begin to see why it is called Walt Disney *World*.

There's more than just a little something for every taste. If we were to give you one bit of advice about which of these to include in your visit, we'd simply tell you to keep an open mind. Consider everything, especially if you've never heard of it. Often, it's the small and unsung attraction that you'll remember long after the thrill of the Tower of Terror has faded. If you aren't interested in thrill rides, there are countless other things to do. If you do enjoy the more exciting attractions, then fasten your seat belts and get ready for the most exciting rides in themedom.

In this chapter, we will give you an idea of what there is to do now that you have arrived. We'll provide just enough information so that you can discover what best suits your interests and avoid wasting time at attractions that are not your cup of tea.

Tips for the Theme Parks

- Resist the urge to spend all day in the parks. Sure, this is what you've come to see, but remember also that you are on vacation. Visit the parks for a few hours in the morning and then again later in the day. Keep your pace relaxed, and you'll have a better time of it. Save some energy for nightlife and romance.

- Don't forget your guidemaps. If you do, you should have no trouble finding one in any of the parks at front gates or from shops or vendors.
- Surprise Mornings are an important perk for Disney resort guests. Each morning, a different theme park opens an hour and a half before the public onslaught. Only certain attractions are open—you can find out what these will be in the World Update, which you should have received at check-in. Please note that the Animal Kingdom does not feature Surprise Mornings. The schedule repeats itself weekly:
  - Magic Kingdom: Monday, Thursday, Saturday
  - Epcot: Tuesday and Friday
  - Disney–MGM Studios: Sunday and Wednesday
- The first few hours of the day in each park are usually the least crowded. Make use of them.
- The busiest days in each park are that park's Surprise Mornings. Most Disney guests arrive early and stay the day. Don't do this. Come early, but as soon as the park begins to get busy, head over to one of the other theme parks to take advantage of the first few hours of its day.
- Each park has a tip board (usually near its entrance) that provides up-to-the-minute reports of show times and estimated waits. Use them to avoid wasting time in lines.
- Signs at many of the shows will tell you how long the wait will be from a certain point. Always ask the cast members that patrol the line if you are waiting for the next show or the one after it.
- Many attractions have two aisles for their lines, and most people take the one on the right. Don't go with the flow. The left line is usually faster.
- Try arriving at one of the parks a couple of hours before closing. You may feel like salmon swimming upstream, but you'll be amazed at how much you can accomplish while most people are leaving.
- Each of the Disney theme parks has a Guest Services. Most are just inside the front gate.
- Strollers, wheelchairs, and electric convenience vehicles (ECVs) are for rent at each of the parks, just inside the front gates. Strollers or wheelchairs cost $6 per day, and the ECVs are $30. Some deposits apply.
- Storage lockers are located near the entrance to each of the parks and can be used for a nominal amount.

- Walk-Around Photos are another fun feature available at both the Magic Kingdom and Disney–MGM Studios. Roving photographers will take your photo someplace scenic in one of the parks, enhance it with Disney characters, and make it available for you to purchase that day. Cost is around $10, and it is a memorable souvenir. Pick up your photo before the very end of the day to avoid waiting in line.
- Looking to be photographed with the Disney characters? Check each attraction guidemap for the specified locations and times of character encounters. This is *not* just for kids.

The Magic Kingdom

When most people think of Walt Disney World, they think of the Magic Kingdom. Children tend to think of it as the best part of Disney, which often leads adults to think that it is largely for children. While there are many child-oriented attractions here, do not assume that the child in you won't enjoy them.

The Magic Kingdom is made up of seven different areas: Main Street USA, Adventureland, Frontierland, Liberty Square, Fantasyland, Tomorrowland, and Mickey's Toontown Fair.

Magic Kingdom Tips

- The most important thing to know about this theme park is that it is the busiest part of Walt Disney World.
- Don't try to see it all in one day. In fact, don't even try to spend a whole day here.
- If you are interested in seeing the big-name attractions, we suggest that you make them your first effort. Start early. Surprise Mornings at the Magic Kingdom are on Monday, Thursday, and Saturday.
- Try the busier attractions during a parade or fireworks show.
- The E-Ticket Express is for Disney resort guests only. For $10, it provides admission to the Magic Kingdom after closing on select dates only, to ride nine of the "big rides," such as Space, Splash, and Thunder Mountains. See Chapter 2 for details.

Magic Kingdom Special Events

The Daily Parade

Each day in the Magic Kingdom there is a marvelous parade that features floats, song and dance, special effects, and a host of Disney char-

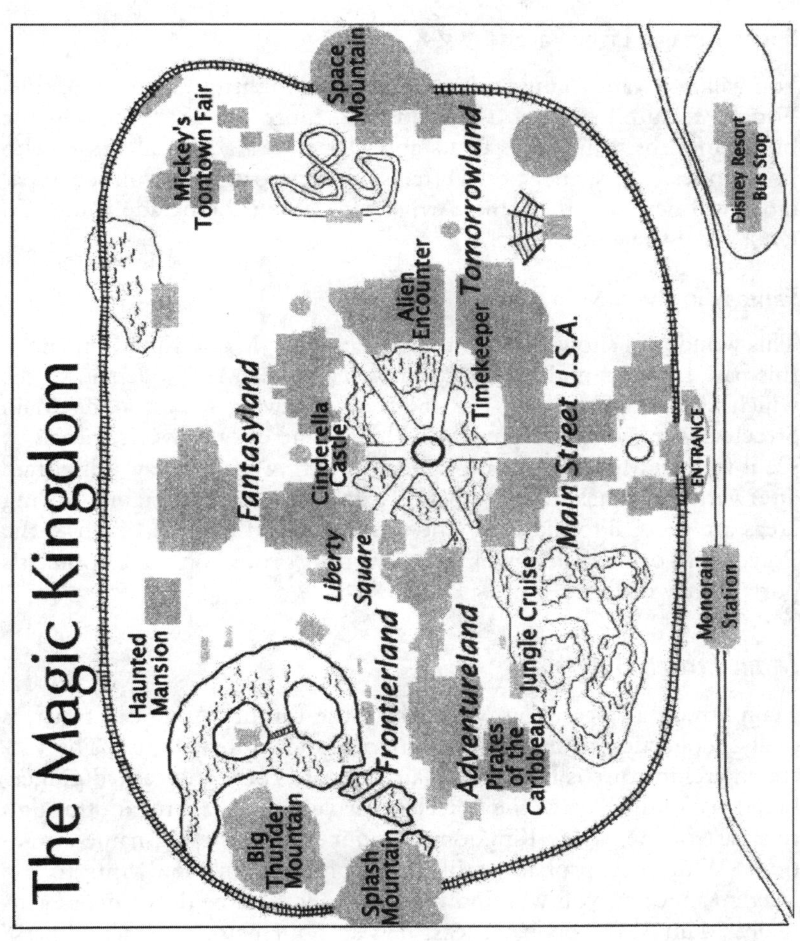
The Magic Kingdom
Haunted Mansion
Big Thunder Mountain
Splash Mountain
Frontierland
Liberty Square
Fantasyland
Cinderella Castle
Mickey's Toontown Fair
Space Mountain
Alien Encounter
Tomorrowland
Timekeeper
Main Street U.S.A.
Adventureland
Pirates of the Caribbean
Jungle Cruise
ENTRANCE
Monorail Station
Disney Resort Bus Stop

acters. It usually begins around 3 P.M., and we suggest that you check your MK guidemap for times and find a place for viewing along the usual parade route (along Main Street and into Frontierland or vice versa) about 30 minutes early.

SpectroMagic Light Parade ♥♥♥

You will not want to miss this unforgettable nighttime musical parade. Usually featured only on weekends and more frequently during the busier months, it includes floats and Disney characters all aglow with fiber-optics, lights, and special effects of every sort. After you see it, parades will never be the same. Arrive early along the parade route and get a good viewing spot.

Fantasy in the Sky Fireworks

This wonderful show is set to the music of the Magic Kingdom and is this park's "good night" attraction. Check your MK guidemap to see which nights during your visit it occurs. Viewing is best along Main Street, but it can get very crowded here. One of our favorite places to see it from is Mickey's Toontown Fair, where we hop the waiting train afterwards and make for the park's exit. Other unforgettable viewing areas are the California Grill (the music is piped in), the beach at the Polynesian, or the balcony of your own resort room on the lagoon. It's pure Disney magic!

Main Street USA

Main Street, a re-creation of a turn-of-the-century American town, is really a collection of shops, small eateries, and a movie house. The Victorian architecture is beautiful. Slate mansard roofs and carved gingerbread evoke the days of the horseless carriage. It is easy to run through this part of the Magic Kingdom on your way to the big-name attractions. While you probably will do so on your first few visits to the Magic Kingdom, you will find it worthwhile to slow down here eventually. Main Street opens at least half an hour before the actual park. Come early and browse, then head for the rides when the park opens.

Walt Disney World Railroad

This is a real steam-powered railway that huffs and puffs its way around the borders of the Magic Kingdom. These authentic old trains were discovered by the Disney people in Mexico, hauling sugar in the Yucatan. The ride takes a bit over 20 minutes and is an entertaining way to get a good overall view of the park. There are three stations, one on Main Street, one in Frontierland, and the other at Mickey's Toontown Fair. All aboard!

Harmony Barber Shop

Who would ever need to get a haircut at Disney? Well, Rick did, and we got an entertaining experience as well as an exceptionally good haircut. It makes for a great photo, as the barbers are in period costumes. If you inquire first, you may find yourself in the barber chair while the Dapper Dans, Disney's barbershop quartet, gather 'round you and harmonize. Now *that's* a haircut.

Main Street Cinema

This theater features nonstop animated classics. It's especially nice if you want to catch Mickey's debut in *Steamboat Willie.*

Transportation on Main Street USA

The trolleys, horseless carriages, and fire engine make a one-way trip up or down Main Street. They are interesting but hardly worth a wait in line.

Main Street Eateries

Main Street is bustling with food establishments. Our favorite is Tony's Town Square, which is next door to the Main Street Depot. The menu here offers a variety of well-prepared Italian favorites as well as some innovative cooking. The Crystal Palace features a pleasant garden atmosphere and character buffets for breakfast, lunch, and dinner. Both lunch and dinner are quite good. The art nouveau Plaza Restaurant is a quiet haven that offers a menu of good deli sandwiches, burgers, and sundaes. For our reviews, see Chapter 6. There are lots of fast-food offerings, too: an espresso wagon, the Main Street Bakeshop, Plaza Ice Cream Parlor, and Casey's Corner, home of the all-American hot dog.

The Shops of Main Street

There are lots of shops along Main Street and, depending on your tastes, you should find at least something that interests you. Some of our favorites are Disneyana Collectibles and Main Street Athletic Club, which features real sports memorabilia. If you're looking for Disney collectibles, from watches to sweatshirts, there's a lot of browsing here. Don't miss Walkaround Photos for some great souvenir pics.

Adventureland

At the end of Main Street, hang a left and cross a small footbridge into another world. With dense jungle on your left and what appears to be Zanzibar on your right, you will head off into the heart of Adventureland. This has always been a favorite of ours. We enjoy strolling about, looking closely at all of the architectural details.

The Swiss Family Robinson Treehouse

✓ Walk-through exhibit
✓ Lasts about 30 minutes
✓ Line moves slowly

Talk about artificial plants. This attraction is a huge treehouse built in a man-made tree. The tree has 80,000 vinyl leaves on it, and the treehouse contains a variety of cute and interesting "inventions" created by the castaway Robinson family.

INTERESTING, but not enough to make it worth a long wait
Tip: Try this attraction when there is hardly any line. Don't attempt this one with cranky kids if there is a wait.

NEW *The Enchanted Tiki Room: Under New Management*

✓ Sit-down show
✓ Lasts 20 minutes
✓ Line moves fairly quickly

One of the Magic Kingdom's oldest attractions now enjoys a riotous new show as Iago, the obnoxious parrot from the feature film *Aladdin,* takes over management. He vows to bring the show up-to-date and, of course, the results are amusing. It's especially good if you're familiar with the old show.

QUITE GOOD, entertaining, and a nice cool place to relax—particularly good for young children
Tip: If you get into the preshow, you'll make it into the next show.

The Jungle Cruise

✓ Boat ride
✓ Lasts 10 minutes
✓ Line moves slowly

This boat ride through Africa (and India) is one of the Magic Kingdom's signature attractions. It is loaded with gags and audio-animatronic animals. Each boat's pilot gives the ride his or her own special brand of groan-a-minute humor. We did this ride once at night, in a misty rain. It was great.

EXCELLENT, especially at night—don't miss it

NEW *Shrunken Ned's Junior Jungle Boats*

- ✓ Remote-controlled boats
- ✓ Lasts about 5 minutes, costs $1

Be the pilot of your own tiny jungle cruise with a radio-controlled jungle boat and a watery obstacle course that includes shrunken heads, a volcano, and other cute features.

OK, especially for kids—miss this one without worrying

Pirates of the Caribbean

- ✓ Boat ride
- ✓ Lasts 8 minutes
- ✓ Line moves quickly

This is a terrific adventure, one of the best that the Magic Kingdom has to offer. It is a boat ride through a Caribbean town that is being plundered by a gang of fun-loving pirates. The special effects and audio-animatronics are some of Disney's finest despite the age of this attraction.

EXCELLENT, not to be missed
Tip: This ride may be too intense for very young children.

The Restaurants of Adventureland

When it comes to eating, you won't find the food very adventurous here. It seems to us that burgers and hot dogs are taking over the Magic Kingdom. The Adventureland Veranda has returned this year with decent quarter-pound burgers and a topping bar. Nearby, you'll find the Eggroll Wagon and the Sunshine Tree Terrace's beverages and frozen yogurt. Other offerings include Pieces O'Ate, with its hot dogs and sauerkraut, and Pirata Y Perico and a small selection of tacos, chili, taco salad, and nachos.

The Shops of Adventureland

Shopping is pretty good in Adventureland, and we recommend some browsing later in the day. Plaza del Sol Bazaar has a fair selection of tropical clothes, while other shops, such as Traders of Timbuktu,

Elephant Tales, and Tiki Tropics, offer some interesting items. The Crow's Nest is this area's film store. It also sells Disney videos.

Frontierland

The Wild West comes alive in this area of the Magic Kingdom. It boasts several outstanding rides and a few good shows.

Splash Mountain

✓ Water-flume ride
✓ Lasts 10 minutes
✓ Line moves quickly

This is one of Disney's best rides and also one of the most popular. Waits here can run as long two hours. Themed after Disney's movie, *Song of the South,* this adventure is essentially a log-flume trip through the world of Brer Rabbit. The music is a pure delight, and the ride tells the tale with more than 100 robotic characters. When you finish this ride, you will be pleasantly spritzed with water and humming "Zippity Doo Dah." We guarantee it. (Or, if you sit in the very front of the log, you may be half-drenched and singing "Blow the Man Down.")

***Excellent,* not to be missed**
Tip: Don't forget to stop in after the ride to see your photo, taken at the moment of the great plunge. We got one of our favorite Disney pictures here. Cost is around $10.

Big Thunder Mountain Railroad

✓ Mild roller coaster
✓ Lasts 3 minutes
✓ Line moves quickly

This ride is one of those attractions that you can go on time after time and still see new things. It is a "runaway" mining train careening through an old-time mining camp. It is loaded with thrills, fun, sight gags, and great special effects.

***Excellent,* not to be missed**
Tip: Try Big Thunder a second time after dark.

Country Bear Jamboree

✓ Audio-animatronic show
✓ Lasts 15 minutes
✓ Line moves slowly

This cute show features bears that sing, dance, and generally horse around. It is entertaining, and we recommend it.

GOOD, especially for children

Tips: Try this one during an afternoon or evening parade. There is a special Christmas version of this show.

The Shootin' Arcade

✓ Electronic shooting arcade
✓ Costs $.25
✓ Line moves slowly

We visited Disney World when our son was 12 years old. He spent virtually all of his time (and tickets) here sharpening his shooting skills. We checked up on him now and then to be sure that he was all right and even dropped by with an occasional hamburger.

OK, if you like this sort of thing

Tip: Walk by and take a look at the Hawken rifles.

Diamond Horseshoe Jamboree

✓ Combination restaurant and live show

This used to be a ticketed show. No longer. Now, the Diamond Horseshoe Jamboree is more like a saloon. There is live entertainment at various times during the day, and all you have to do is stroll in and pull up a chair. A small counter-service restaurant is at the bar, featuring a pretty unremarkable selection. If you wish, you can simply sit and watch the shows. The entertainment varies from magic to music. Entertaining but not memorable.

OK, you could skip this one

Tip: Check your guidemap for show times and arrive a few minutes early.

Tom Sawyer Island

✓ Walk-through playground
✓ No time limit
✓ Line moves slowly

This raft trip to a small island may not be high on our list of things to see, but it isn't such a bad place to bring an overactive child. It's basically an island-playground, complete with caves, fort, and lots of places to explore.

Mostly for kids

Tip: This could be a good place for tired parents to rest.

Frontierland Grub

Pecos Bill's is this area's big restaurant. It is a mega-burger place with hot dogs and a small assortment of sandwiches. Other offerings include Aunt Polly's Dockside Inn, over on Tom Sawyer's Island, featuring a pleasant porch and ham and cheese sandwiches, apple pie, and soft-serve ice cream. Also here in Frontierland is a turkey leg wagon and a churro cart.

The Shops of Frontierland

The shops of Frontierland have a definite western flair. The Prairie Outpost and Supply features penny candy and the Frontier Trading Post has a nice collection of Native American and frontier clothing. After that, there's the Trail Creek Hat Shop, the Briar Patch at Splash Mountain, and Frontier Wood Carving.

Liberty Square

This area, snuggled between Fantasyland and Frontierland, is a small slice of Revolutionary War Americana. Take a look at the Liberty Tree, complete with its 13 lanterns representing the original 13 states. This "father" oak was actually moved here, with great difficulty, from another location at Disney World. Acorns from it have grown more than 500 trees here at Disney.

Liberty Square Riverboat

✓ Boat ride
✓ Lasts 15 minutes
✓ Line moves quickly

This magnificent re-creation of a paddle-wheel steamer was built right on Disney property. The ride makes a short loop on Frontierland's River of the Americas and provides a relaxing view of the attractions along it. This boat, by the way, is pulled along on an underwater track. It is not a thrill ride.

GOOD, pleasant, can be cool and restful

Tip: Try queuing up just when the boat arrives, as it can hold virtually everyone waiting.

Mike Fink Keelboats

✓ Boat ride
✓ Lasts 15 minutes
✓ Line moves slowly

These small boats, which run only during very busy periods, take you along the same route as the riverboat, only you'll have to wait in line much longer for this voyage. There is a cute narrative to this one, but it is hardly worth the wait.

TOO LONG A WAIT; take the riverboat

The Hall of Presidents

✓ Audio-animatronic show
✓ Lasts 25 minutes
✓ Line moves quickly

This show is neither exciting nor funny, but it is interesting, especially if you are history buffs.

INTERESTING, with good audio-animatronics

The Haunted Mansion

✓ Low-speed ride
✓ Lasts 9 minutes
✓ Line moves slowly

We won't tell you much about this one except to say that it is more fun than scary. We'll leave the rest for your delight.

EXCELLENT, do not miss
Tip: May be frightening for young children.

Liberty Square Portrait Gallery

This shady pavilion features a handful of artists ready to draw a caricature of you. The results are quite good and we think make a long-lasting and memorable souvenir of your Disney trip. Cost is $14.95 per person.

The Restaurants of Liberty Square

The Liberty Tree Tavern is a pleasant, colonial-style restaurant. See our review in Chapter 6.

The other restaurant here in Liberty Square is the counter-service Columbia Harbor House. Its compact menu features a loaf of bread filled with either vegetarian chili or clam chowder, sandwiches, and fried fish. Here in the square you'll also find a marketplace of food carts that include hot dogs, baked potatoes, fresh fruit, and drinks. We wouldn't want to leave out the espresso and cappuccino at Sleepy Hollow and the shady and quiet sitting area across the street from it. Sleepy Hollow also features beverages and a few snacks.

The Shops of Liberty Square

Shopping here used to be better; the once-interesting shops now seem to offer the usual Disney merchandise. Even Yankee Traders, one of our favorites, has gone to mainstream Mickey Mouse kitchen accessories. Ye Old Christmas Shoppe does feature a few interesting holiday ornaments and is worth a look.

Fantasyland

Cinderella Castle marks the main entrance to Fantasyland. After more than a year of looking at it painted pink and decorated like a birthday cake, it is good to see it again. For us, it is a magical and romantic sight. The only attraction at Walt Disney World that is taller is the new Twilight Zone Tower of Terror at Disney–MGM Studios.

Cinderella's Golden Carousel ♥

✓ Merry-go-round
✓ Ride lasts 2 minutes
✓ Line moves slowly

This handmade, beautiful old carousel was built in 1917, when "handmade" really meant something. This ride can actually be romantic, especially at night.

QUITE GOOD, more fun and romantic than you might think
Tips: Almost always open for Surprise Mornings. Ask a cast member to snap a picture of you both.

Skyway to Tomorrowland

✓ Cable car ride
✓ Lasts 5 minutes
✓ Line moves quickly

This is a one-way aerial tram ride to Tomorrowland. It provides an interesting view as well as a relaxing, away-from-the-throngs escape. Handicapped visitors are allowed to leave their wheelchairs at one end and take a round trip.

QUITE GOOD
Tip: Try getting on in Tomorrowland—the line there is usually much shorter.

It's a Small World

- ✓ Boat ride
- ✓ Lasts 10 minutes
- ✓ Line moves quickly

This pleasant and upbeat musical boat ride was created for the 1965 New York World's Fair. The music is catchy and it will get you both in the mood for Fantasyland.

QUITE GOOD

Legend of the Lion King

- ✓ Puppet and animated show
- ✓ Lasts 25 minutes
- ✓ Line moves to fill theater

This stage show combines puppets, animation, and impressive special effects to create a simply wonderful miniversion of the animated film. This one may require a wait; it is worth it.

***EXCELLENT*, do not miss**
Tip: Try this early or any time that you see that the line is not huge.

Peter Pan's Flight, Snow White's Adventure, and Mr. Toad's Wild Ride

- ✓ Low-speed rides
- ✓ Each lasts 2–3 minutes
- ✓ Lines move slowly

We put these three rides together because they are so much alike. Despite the fact that these are basically kiddie rides, you might find them fun. Snow White has been redesigned due to complaints that it was too frightening for younger children. It and Mr. Toad's Wild Ride may still be too scary for some young children.

OK, especially if you have small children
Tips: The waits can be long. Any of these rides may be intense for very young children.

Dumbo

- ✓ Midway-type ride
- ✓ Lasts less than 2 minutes
- ✓ Line moves very slowly

This is one attraction that all small children are simply thrilled to ride on. As you would expect, lines here can be very long.

***A MUST* for young children**
Tips: Catch this one early. It is usually open for Surprise Mornings.

The Mad Tea Party

✓ Midway-type ride (spins)
✓ Lasts 2 minutes
✓ Line moves slowly

The speed of rotation of these spinning teacups can be controlled by the riders. Usually, this is a rather mild ride, aimed mostly at younger children.

***OK;* can be fun, especially if you enjoy feeling dizzy**
Tip: Usually open for Surprise Mornings.

Ariel's Grotto

✓ Playground and character encounter
✓ Linger as you wish
✓ Usually a short line

This play area consists of interactive fountains and scenes from *The Little Mermaid*. Our grandkids loved it. There's even a cave where children can meet Ariel. Cute and a good photo opportunity.

GOOD for kids

The Restaurants of Fantasyland

Cinderella's Royal Table ♥♥♥ is a beautiful restaurant located inside the castle and a world away from the crowded streets of Fantasyland. For atmosphere and ambience, it is hard to beat. The food here is good and you'll definitely need priority seating to get in. For our review and a few dining tips, see Chapter 6.

The other Fantasyland eateries offer fast food. The Pinocchio Village Haus is a large indoor restaurant that features burgers, turkey sandwiches, a vegetarian pasta salad, and hot dogs. Lumiere's Kitchen offers hot dogs, fries, and cokes. For snacks and beverages, there's the Seven Dwarf's Mine, Hook's Tavern, the Enchanted Grove, and Mrs. Pott's Cupboard. Scuttle's Landing features flavored, shaved ice cones.

The Shops of Fantasyland

The King's Gallery, inside Cinderella Castle, has an interesting assortment of swords, crystal, and medieval curios. It's easy to miss this place but there's some good browsing here. Tinker Bell's features kids' clothing and some beautiful dolls, while Sir Mickey specializes in adult character clothing. Don't miss this whimsical "Mickey and the Beanstalk" shop. For character costumes for your children, Fantasy Fair is the place to go, and the Seven Dwarf's Mine features Snow White merchandise.

Tomorrowland

Tomorrowland is one of the newest areas of the Magic Kingdom. While the theme here is the future, it has been created as something more of a look at it through the eyes of Jules Verne. It is something like what the Victorian Age might have thought the future would be. It is stylish, imaginative, and whimsical. Several of the old attractions have been replaced, and the whole area, which a few years ago more resembled a shopping center, is fresh and entertaining.

The ExtraTERRORestrial Alien Encounter

✓ Special-effects show (not a ride)
✓ Lasts 20 minutes
✓ Line moves quickly

This attraction got off to a bad start when Michael Eisner, the Disney CEO, rode it during a test run. "Not scary enough," he declared, and it was back to the drawing boards for "Alien." We have ridden it before and after and were impressed both times. The plot, a botched attempt at teletransportation, is good. The show is an awesome display of new technology.

QUITE GOOD, kind of creepy

Tips: The lines here are usually long. If you do not like being in total darkness, skip it. Too intense for young children.

The Timekeeper

✓ Film and audio-animatronic show
✓ Lasts 15 minutes
✓ Line moves quickly

This show, which includes a CircleVision 360 (360-degree) film narrated by a Robin Williams robot, is exciting, clever, wild, and zany in a way that only Robin Williams could have made it.

***Excellent*, not to be missed**
Tips: This attraction is held in a large theater, which, if the lines aren't outrageous, will allow everyone in to see it. Ask the cast members at the door how long the wait will be.

Space Mountain

✓ High-speed roller coaster ride
✓ Lasts 3 minutes
✓ Line moves quickly

This is one of the World's most popular attractions. It is a roller coaster inside of a planetarium. It is fast and fairly rough. The waits in line here can be interminable.

***Excellent*, if you like this type of ride**
Tips: Get here early to avoid long waits. Usually open for Surprise Morning.

NEW *Tomorrowland Arcade*

✓ Video and game arcade
✓ Waste as much time here as you wish
✓ No lines

While this is a large and interesting arcade, we wonder why so many kids would pay to visit the Magic Kingdom and then spend their time here.

***For video game freaks only*; see DisneyQuest at Downtown Disney**

Tomorrowland Transit Authority

✓ Gentle tram ride
✓ Lasts 10 minutes
✓ Line moves very quickly

This is the old WED-Way People Mover, renamed. This was the world's first "MAG-LEV" (linear induction) train constructed for public use.

***Interesting*, but not memorable**
Tip: If you want to see the inside of Space Mountain without riding it, this is the way to do it.

The Astro Orbiter
- ✓ Midway-type ride
- ✓ Lasts about 2 minutes
- ✓ Line moves very slowly

This is a recycled version of the old StarJets ride. It will give you a good view of Tomorrowland. Definitely mild.

OK, more interesting to look at

The Carousel of Progress
- ✓ Show with revolving stage
- ✓ Lasts 20 minutes
- ✓ Line moves quickly

This audio-animatronic show demonstrates how technology has impacted the home over the last three decades.

INTERESTING

Tips: Try this show when the other attractions are busy. Opens one hour after park opening, closes one hour before park closing.

Tomorrowland Speedway
- ✓ Miniature raceway
- ✓ Lasts about 5 minutes
- ✓ Line moves slowly

This is nothing more than a raceway with small, motorized go-karts. The pace is slow, and a runner-track restricts steering. This ride is very popular with children, especially those whose parents don't let them drive the family car.

OK, a kiddie ride

NEW *Buzz Lightyear's Space Ranger Spin*
- ✓ Interactive space ride
- ✓ Lasts 6 minutes
- ✓ Line moves very quickly

This special-effects attraction features a train-like conveyor of space cars in which guests get to shoot at space villains.

FUN, especially for kids

Galaxy Palace Theater
- ✓ Musical stage show
- ✓ Lasts about 30 minutes
- ✓ Line moves to fill large theater

This kids' show features Mickey auditioning a bunch of aliens for a talent show.

***Mostly for kids,* but cute**

Skyway to Fantasyland

✓ Cable car
✓ Lasts 5 minutes
✓ Line moves quickly

This is the one-way aerial tram ride back to Fantasyland.

Food in Tomorrowland

We hope that the future has better food to offer than this area. Cosmic Ray's Starlight Cafe is the Magic Kingdom's largest fast-food restaurant. Besides its usual fare of sandwiches, burgers, and hot dogs, Ray's has added rotisserie chicken and Caesar salad. Still, it is noisy and crowded. The Plaza Pavilion is another large, counter-service eatery and features pizzas, chicken, and sandwiches. Nearby, however, is a charming outdoor patio near the water's edge. Auntie Gravity's Galactic Goodies features a small selection of juices, smoothies, and soft-serve ice cream. The Lunching Pad offers turkey legs and beverages.

The Shops of Tomorrowland

The big store here in Tomorrowland is Mickey's Star Traders. Nothing unusual here: lots of tee shirts and the usual character merchandise.

Mickey's Toontown Fair

If you're coming to Disney World with small children, this is one place you won't want to miss. New in 1996, this area will make you feel like you are *in* a cartoon. It's really a cartoon-like, three-dimensional village, complete with the homes of both Mickey and Minnie Mouse and a small country fair. There's even a kiddie roller coaster, the Barnstormer. This is a must for small children, as there's lots for them to see and do. Attractions include Goofy's Wiseacre Farm, Donald's Boat, and a meeting with the Mouse himself. There's also Toon Park, Pete's Garage, and Mickey's Hall of Fame. We suggest that you arrive early and if you are traveling without young ones, simply take a quick look.

The Barnstormer at Goofy's Wiseacre Farm

✓ Kiddie roller coaster
✓ Short, lasts only a few minutes or less
✓ Line moves slowly

This short roller coaster is intended for young children. Still, it can be too exciting for some youngsters. The ride goes literally *through* Goofy's farm. Some very good sight gags.

***OK*, fun for kids**

Magic Kingdom Dining Suggestions

- For our sensibilities, Tony's Town Square offers the best food in the Magic Kingdom.
- Cinderella's Royal Table ♥♥♥ has a new chef and an interesting menu of good food. It is romantic and beautiful. Priority seating is a must for families, but couples may be able to get in with only a short wait. Ask.
- The Crystal Palace offers character buffets and many interesting dishes. It is a very good choice for families and for salad lovers.
- Plaza Restaurant and Liberty Tree Tavern both have good sandwiches and pleasant dining areas.
- If you want to escape the crowds for a quiet lunch, try taking the boat from near the park's entrance to Narcoossee's at the Grand Floridian.

Magic Kingdom Attractions Not to Miss

- Big Thunder Mountain
- The Haunted Mansion
- The Jungle Cruise
- Legend of the Lion King
- Pirates of the Caribbean
- SpectroMagic Light Parade: ♥♥♥
- Splash Mountain and Splash Mountain photo: ♥
- The Timekeeper
- Fantasy in the Sky Fireworks: ♥♥

Epcot

We love the fantasy of the Magic Kingdom: the rides, the shows, and the delightful and fanciful realities created there. MGM is a celebration of the cinema, and we do love the movies. But there is something more at Epcot. Educating while entertaining is something that Disney does better than anyone, and every area and every exhibit in Epcot is rich with information and fun. This is an exciting place for curious minds.

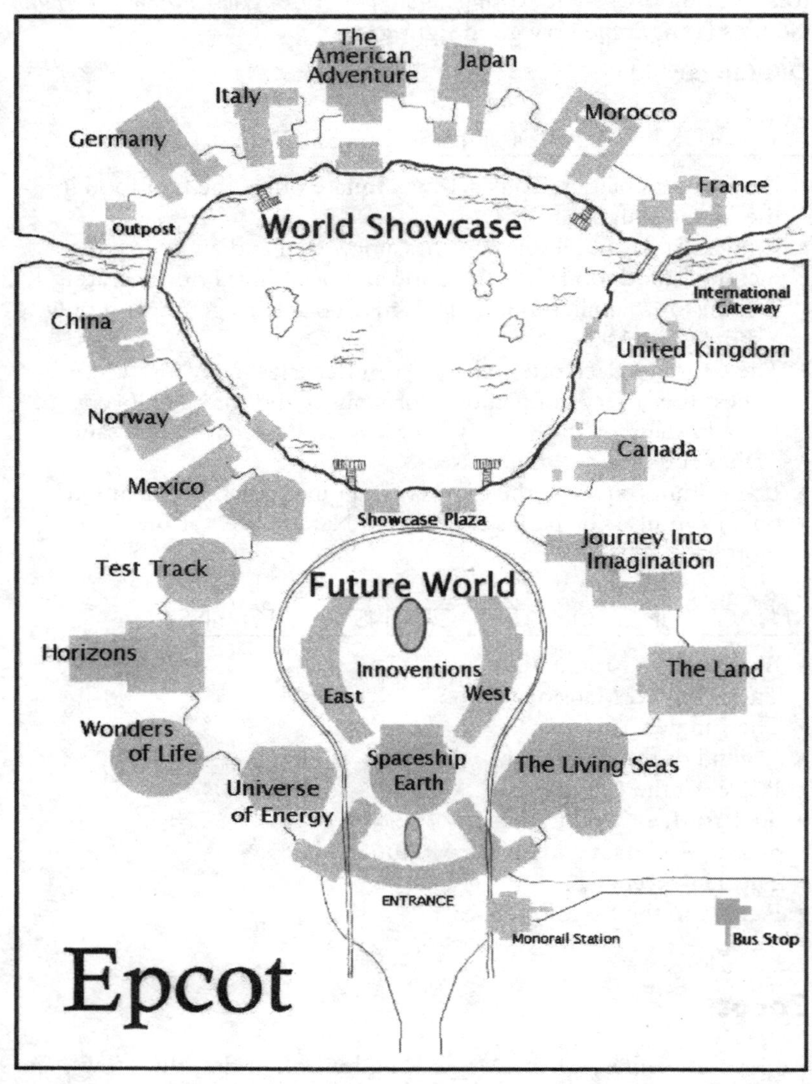
The American Adventure
Japan
Italy
Morocco
Germany
France
Outpost
World Showcase
International Gateway
China
United Kingdom
Norway
Canada
Mexico
Showcase Plaza
Journey Into Imagination
Test Track
Future World
Horizons
Innoventions
East
West
The Land
Wonders of Life
Spaceship Earth
The Living Seas
Universe of Energy
ENTRANCE
Monorail Station
Bus Stop
Epcot

Epcot is nearly twice the size of the Magic Kingdom and is divided into two areas: Future World and the World Showcase. Future World displays the triumphs of science and technology in nine pavilions. The World Showcase is comprised of 11 countries that encircle a freshwater lagoon and together create something of a journey around the world.

Epcot Tips

- Each area of Epcot has different operating hours. Future World opens early and stays open until 9 P.M. The World Showcase opens at 11 A.M. and then closes after IllumiNations, at either 9 or 10 P.M., depending on the season.
- Surprise Mornings at Epcot are on Tuesday and Friday.
- Don't forget your guidemap. You will need it here. You can pick one up at one of the shops just inside either the main entrance or the International Gateway.
- The World Showcase is least crowded right after it opens.
- Future World is busiest in the morning after about 9:30 A.M. and into midafternoon. By late afternoon, the crowds begin to thin out as guests move on to the World Showcase. The hour or two before Future World closes is a good time to visit.
- Try splitting up your Epcot tour. Spend one morning at Future World, then do something fun at your resort. Another day, spend the morning around the pool and get to Epcot in time for the opening of the World Showcase.
- One of Epcot's strong suits is its live entertainment. There are performers here from all over the world and many of them are worth seeing. Be sure to check your Epcot guidemap for details and read what we have to recommend in Chapter 5.

Epcot Old and New

If you're an experienced Disney visitor, you might feel that Epcot has become a bit tired. When it comes to the attractions, it is true that Epcot has been fairly static these few last years. Test Track, when it opens, will be the first totally new attraction in recent years, but its debut has already been postponed for more than a year.

Still, Disney has managed to keep things fresh in Epcot by offering seasonal and special events. There is a winter kite festival, the Spring Flower and Garden Festival, Science Jam, an inventors exposition, and our favorite, the Fall Food & Wine Festival. There are many others too. In fact, there is always something going on here. Each provides a lot to see and do as well as a reason to revisit this park. So if you've gotten bored with Epcot, plan your Disney vacation around an Epcot special event. For dates and information, call Disney Information at (407) 824-4321.

Future World

This part of Epcot is a celebration of human triumphs. Its themes are health, energy, agriculture, the oceans, transportation, imagination, and communications. Each theme is featured in a different pavilion, and each pavilion has its unique attractions and exhibits. It is the busiest part of Epcot and there's lots to do, much more than can be done in one day. If you want to see everything here, count on at least a few days.

Spaceship Earth

Spaceship Earth: The Ride

✓ Slow ride
✓ Lasts about 15 minutes
✓ Line moves quickly

This ride is inside the huge geosphere and will take you through the history of communication.

***Excellent*, one of Epcot's best attractions—don't miss it**
Tips: **This ride is usually open for Surprise Mornings. After the park opens to the public, this is the first place where the entering crowds stop, and it very quickly becomes too busy. Save it for later if there is a long line.**

Global Neighborhood This exhibit is located at the base of Spaceship Earth and features interactive demonstrations and exhibits of the latest in telecommunications developments. You'll find family phones, games, and "near-rides." Some interesting stuff here, but save this one for later in the day, when the other attractions are busy.

Innoventions

If you are into computers or technology, you'll want to see Innoventions. Located in two buildings on opposite sides of a large plaza, you'll find interactive and hands-on displays from all the big names in high tech. From IBM to Silicon Graphics, these companies are all here in force and are anxious to give you an experience with their latest products. Not just for computer nerds, this place and this stuff is way cool. The Sega Company even features an entire free demonstration area of its games as well as an arcade with its latest race cars, motorcycles, and combat games. Bring some money for the arcade: it's the only part of Innoventions where you'll need it.

Displays and exhibits change frequently here at Innoventions, so even if you've visited recently, check it out.

Tip: This area gets very busy. We suggest that you set aside a morning for Innoventions and get here at opening. We've also seen these areas less crowded late in the day, during the hour before Future World closes.

The Fountain of Nations Water Ballet This delightful fountain, located at Innoventions Plaza, is a classic example of Disney imagination. The formula is simple: take one large fountain and add the genius of Disney. The columns of water are controlled by a computer and are timed perfectly to accompanying music. If you think that this is neat in the daylight, try dropping by after dark.

Nighttime on Innoventions Plaza At night, this seemingly plain stretch of concrete takes on a whole new persona. There are fiber-optic lights embedded in the ground all around the plaza and a lot more going on than when you came through here in the morning.

The Wonders of Life

This pavilion is our favorite. It gets very busy, and we suggest that you come right after opening. Inside are shows, films, and dozens of hands-on displays. All of it is good.

Body Wars

✓ Simulated thrill ride
✓ Lasts 5 minutes
✓ Line moves quickly

Like Star Tours at Disney–MGM, this ride doesn't really go anywhere; it merely creates the illusion. The show is a journey into the human body aboard a miniaturized "inner-space ship." It's realistic and exciting. The motion of this ride is jerky.

EXCELLENT

Tip: Lines can get long, but they move quickly.

The Making of Me

✓ Film
✓ Lasts 15 minutes
✓ Line moves very slowly

This cute film ♥♥ features Martin Short, and it is both humorous and touching. If it starts in a few minutes, get in line.

EXCELLENT
Tips: The theater is small and the lines can get long. Make an effort to see it early, or wait until late in the day.

Cranium Command

✓ Show
✓ Lasts 20 minutes
✓ Line moves to fill theater

Another of our favorites, this show features audio-animatronics, animation, and special effects. Throw away your preconceptions about this attraction and see it. It is what Disney does best.

EXCELLENT, not to be missed
Tips: In all but the busiest of times, the wait for this show should not be much of a factor. Don't miss the preshow.

Goofy About Health

✓ Show
✓ Lasts 15 minutes

This low-key multiscreen show features Goofy getting wise about fitness and health.

OK, for children

Hands-on Activities

✓ Various displays and exhibits
✓ No set time limits
✓ Lines move slowly

The Wonders of Life pavilion is full of exhibits that involve your participation. Have your golf swing analyzed, or hop onto a video exercycle and see the sights. There are lots of things to do that are fun and informative. Don't miss the Sensory Funhouse.

GOOD TO VERY GOOD, don't pass by this area

Universe of Energy

Ellen's Energy Adventure

✓ Slow ride
✓ Lasts about 30 minutes
✓ Line moves slowly

In its last incarnation, this attraction was a real snoozer. No longer. Completely revamped, it now features comedian Ellen DeGeneres in a nightmare version of "Jeopardy," during which she appears with Jamie Lee Curtis, Bill Nye the Science Guy, and Alex Trebek. The show includes film, special effects, and audio-animatronic dinosaurs. It is clever and funny.

ENTERTAINING, with well-done special effects

Tips: This ride holds nearly 600 people at a time. The only movement of the line is when one show lets out and another goes in. The wait here looks worse than it is.

Horizons

Horizons

✓ Slow ride
✓ Lasts 15 minutes
✓ Line moves quickly

This ride takes you through a series of sets that re-create past and current visions of the future. The sets and effects are quite good, and the ride is interesting. We hear rumors that this is going to close during 1999 and reopen as some sort of space adventure.

GOOD, but may be closed for rehab in 1999

Test Track

Test Track (scheduled to open in late 1998)

✓ High-speed thrill ride
✓ Preshow lasts 20 minutes; ride lasts 5 minutes

After a great many delays, this ride is scheduled to open in November of 1998. Whenever it does begin running, you can be sure that it will be the fastest ride at Disney, by nearly 40 mph (at least until Disney–MGM Studios' 60 mph Rock'n Roller Coaster makes its debut sometime in 1999).

SHOULD BE GREAT, fast and fun

The Living Seas

The centerpiece of this pavilion is its saltwater aquarium. Some 200 feet across, it is one of the largest fish tanks in the world. It's brimming with reef fish of every sort. The layout of the Living Seas is such that you're nearly surrounded by glass walls, water, and scores of tropical fish. Next to a reef dive, it doesn't get much better than this. The pavilion is divided into three areas, each with its own exhibits and theme.

Tip: Disney features a diving experience here as well as a hands-on dolphin encounter. For more details, read about Disney Adult Discoveries in Chapter 7.

The Caribbean Coral Reef Ride

✓ Slow ride
✓ Lasts 3 minutes
✓ Line moves slowly

This ride is only mildly interesting. It takes you "down" to the aquarium in a "hydrolator" and for a brief ride through an underwater tunnel.

OK ONLY, this pavilion could use some revamping

Sea Base Alpha This part of the Living Seas is the real meat and potatoes of this pavilion. It is a prototype research facility and is chock-full of intriguing displays.

Sea Base Concourse This part of the research facility is an interesting but quick walk-through.

The Land

This is the largest of the pavilions in Future World, and its focus is agriculture. While this may not be on your top ten list of interests, this pavilion has a lot to offer both in entertainment, food, and shopping. Besides the ride, film, and show, it is home to the Sunshine Season Food Fair, which is the largest collection of eateries in Epcot.

Living with the Land

✓ Boat ride
✓ Lasts 10 minutes
✓ Line moves very quickly

This cool and pleasant boat ride takes you through the history of agriculture and into its future. It is scenic and fascinating. The sets and special effects are memorable.

EXCELLENT, not to be missed

Food Rocks

- ✓ Audio-animatronic show
- ✓ Lasts 10 minutes
- ✓ Line moves to fill theater

This show features a kitchen full of rockin' and rollin' fruits and vegetables. The music here is classic rock, with lyrics praising good nutrition.

GOOD and cute
Tip: Waits here never seem too long.

The Circle of Life

- ✓ Film
- ✓ Lasts 20 minutes
- ✓ Line moves to fill theater

The theme of this film is ecology, and the stars are Simba, Timon, and Pumbaa from *The Lion King*. The message is inspiring and upbeat.

GOOD
Tip: This theater seats more than 400. Check for times at the entrance and ask if you will make it into the next show.

"Behind the Seeds": a special guided greenhouse tour

- ✓ Walking tour
- ✓ Lasts 45 minutes
- ✓ By reservation only, $6 per person

This fascinating tour goes through the greenhouses of the Land, where you will see the latest in agriculture techniques. The tours are conducted by real agriculturists.

QUITE GOOD
Tips: Make your reservations inside the pavilion, at the small kiosk near the entrance to Food Rocks. This is a popular tour.

Journey into Imagination

This wonderful pavilion is definitely one not to miss. There are lots of fun things to do here. After you have spent some time inside, don't miss the whimsical fountains outside.

Journey into Imagination

✓ Slow ride
✓ Lasts 13 minutes
✓ Line moves quickly

This ride seems to lack the excitement typical of most Disney attractions. Cute, happy, and warmhearted, yes, but captivating and interesting, no. We hear that this ride is scheduled for rehab soon.

OK

Honey, I Shrunk the Audience

✓ 3-D film and more
✓ Lasts 25 minutes
✓ Line moves to fill theater

Remember Rick Moranis as Professor Wayne Szalinski in Disney's feature film *Honey, I Shrunk the Kids?* Well, he's back. This "movie experience" is one of the most fun things here at Walt Disney World. We'll keep the details a surprise.

***EXCELLENT*, what you came here for—don't miss it!**
Tips: Usually open for Surprise Mornings. Try this early or try it late. Whatever you do, be sure to catch this. Waits here can be long.

The Image Works This area is a fascinating playground of hands-on devices that utilize touch, sound, and light in ways too unusual to even describe. There are no lines and, when it is crowded, you will have to wait to use some of the "games," which unfortunately, children tend to monopolize.

The Restaurants of Future World

There are only two table-service restaurants in Future World. The Coral Reef ♥♥ is located in the Living Seas Pavilion, and it combines an extraordinary atmosphere with good food. This restaurant is scheduled to get a completely new face in late 1998. The Garden Grill at the Land Pavilion is set on a turning carousel and features character buffets for each of the days meals. For our reviews and more details about them, see Chapter 6.

Counter-service offerings here in Future World are numerous but undistinguished. Pure and Simple at the Wonders of Life has a small selection of healthy treats, and you'll find some decent fruit waffles here in the morning and other snacks throughout the day. On Innoventions Plaza is Pasta Piazza Ristorante. It features a typical counter-quality breakfast menu and then pizzas, pastas, chicken, and salad for the rest of the day. Across the plaza at the Electric Umbrella, offerings include hamburgers, hot dogs, chicken sandwiches, and salads. Our favorite on the plaza is the Fountain View Espresso and Bakery. Not a restaurant, it has a tempting assortment of pastries and baked goods and an inviting selection of coffee concoctions.

Future World's largest array of eateries is Sunshine Season Food Fair in the Land Pavilion. This place offers a number of "shops," each with its own variety of foods. From breakfast and baked goods to sandwiches, soups, barbecue, and baked potatoes, you'll find a big selection here. Come early, as it tends to get noisy and crowded. The Joffrey Coffee Company also runs an espresso and cappuccino cart just inside the main entrance.

The Shops of Future World

There are quite a few shops in Future World, although many of them seem to specialize in souvenir items. For more interesting stuff, check out Sea Base Alpha at the Living Seas Pavilion, Field Trips at Innoventions West, and Well and Goods at the Wonders of Life. Our favorite here is the Green Thumb at the Land. It features Disney merchandise for the garden and kitchen.

FUTURE WORLD ATTRACTIONS NOT TO MISS

- Body Wars
- *Cranium Command*
- *Honey, I Shrunk the Audience*
- The Fountain of Nations Water Ballet
- The Living Seas aquarium
- Living with the Land
- *The Making of Me*
- Spaceship Earth
- Test Track (opening late 1998, maybe)
- Ellen's Energy Adventure
- Innoventions

The World Showcase

The World Showcase is a pleasant stroll around a large freshwater lagoon. Each of the 11 areas in this grand walk is a "country," and each has been carefully created to present an architectural, cultural, and culinary taste of that land. Each nation has some sort of exhibit or show, and two even feature rides. All of the pavilions have shops with arts, crafts, and other products that represent each of the countries. Some of the pavilions feature outstanding films.

Don't expect to find the real Norway or the real Japan here. This is Walt Disney World, and these countries are merely interesting concoctions created to provide a taste of Italy or the flavor of Morocco. But neither should you dismiss the World Showcase as totally fanciful. Exceptional care has been given to the landscaping and architecture of each country. From the well-tended version of Vancouver Island's Bouchart Gardens to the real olive trees of Italy, a serious effort has been made to present a horticultural sampling of each nation represented. The landscaping around the lagoon is a gardener's dream. With such attention paid to buildings and streets, it is easy to get the sense of a Japanese garden or a Bavarian village. To complete the travel experience, each pavilion offers a sampling of foods, and many of the cast members around the lagoon are native to the lands they represent. There is also some form of local entertainment at virtually every pavilion, and some are simply delightful. There are food carts everywhere along the lagoon, where you can enjoy such treats as espresso, kaki gori ice cones, funnel cakes, and Italian pastries.

At the end of each day here at the World Showcase, there is IllumiNations, a spectacular laser light fireworks show. Timed precisely to music, this dramatic display is the perfect end to an evening at Epcot. We'll take you clockwise around the lagoon, which is our favorite direction. We won't give you every detail about what you will see here; we'll give just enough information to help you make your own discoveries. Exploration is the operative word here. Spend time in each of the countries, sit awhile, and catch the entertainers. Check your guidemap for times. Look in every nook and alley. You never know what you'll find.

One of our favorite things about strolling the lagoon is what we call the "bush music," the music that seems to be coming out of the shrubbery. Each country features its own; as we depart one, the music fades, and as we near the next, we can begin to hear the strains of its melodies. It is pleasant and transporting.

We'll briefly mention the table-service restaurants here. For details and our reviews, see Chapter 6.

The World Showcase Plaza

This is the gateway to the World Showcase, and the two shops here, the Port of Entry and Disney Traders, offer the usual collection of Disney and Epcot logo merchandise and sundries. Nearby, Epcot's two *Friendship* launches make regular passages across the lagoon to either Germany or Morocco.

There's live entertainment here too and, besides Disney character appearances, you'll find the Junkanoo Bus. The colorful and comical double-decker bus features a live calypso band. It's a real taste of the islands.

Mexico

This pavilion resembles an Aztec pyramid and is surrounded by a lush, tropical jungle, complete with squawking parrots and colorful orchids. Inside, the world of old Mexico comes alive with the beat of mariachi music. Featured is a display of Meso-American artifacts of amazing beauty and workmanship. A plaza of colorful shops offer baskets, hats, piñatas, jewelry, and men's and women's fashions, and an assortment of tequilas, all in great abundance. It is one of the best shopping places here at Epcot.

Also inside is the stunning San Angel Inn, Mexico's restaurant ♥♥♥. Set on the banks of El Rio del Tiempo (River of Time), it enjoys an atmosphere unique even at Disney World. Under a dark sky and surrounded by jungle, you can enjoy Mexican cuisine while a volcano smoulders in the distance.

Outside the pavilion is Cantina San Angel, a counter-service restaurant that has a small but south-of-the-border menu. The Cantina features Mexican beer and is a good place to sit and listen to one of the musical groups that perform here throughout the day. Check for show times.

El Rio del Tiempo (The River of Time)

✓ Boat ride
✓ Lasts 9 minutes
✓ Line moves very quickly

This ride reminds us of It's a Small World except that it travels through the history of Mexico.

GOOD, try not to miss it

Norway

This quaint pavilion features a Viking ship display, a cobbled town square, a lovely Norwegian stave church, and a formidable replica of Akershus Castle. From the sod roof to the tiled cottages, the detail work in this "village" is impressive. Don't miss the exhibit in the Stav Kirke. It is always something of interest. For browsers, Puffin's Roost offers an array of Norwegian products (toys, clothes, jewelry, and hats), making this one of our favorite World Showcase stops.

Inside the miniature castle is the Akershus restaurant, whose menu comes straight from Norway. Kringlas Bakeri og Cafe offers an interesting selection of Scandinavian open-faced sandwiches and exotic pastries as well as Norwegian Ringnes beer.

The Maelstrom

- ✓ Boat ride and film
- ✓ Lasts 15 minutes
- ✓ Line moves quickly

An exciting voyage aboard a Viking ship, this ride is fun and offers one brief thrill. There is lots to see during the trip, and we even recommend a second look. The film is outstanding and has inspired us to put Norway on our list of places to visit.

***EXCELLENT,* don't be afraid of the thrill and don't miss this ride and film**

China

The centerpiece of this beautiful pavilion is the ornate Temple of Heaven, re-created here in intricate and colorful detail. Music and landscaping come together to make the courtyard an exceptionally restful retreat. We recommend that you sit awhile and wait for the entertainment.

Shopping is outstanding at the Yong Feng Shangdian shopping gallery. All things Chinese are found in this large bazaar. Set aside some time, as it is a unique browsing experience. Along the lagoon is a street vendor with an interesting assortment of Chinese toys and novelties.

China features a beautiful sit-down restaurant, the Nine Dragons, and a counter-service eatery, the Lotus Blossom Cafe. The Lotus Blossom has a small and fairly uninspired menu that includes lo mein and sweet and sour pork. Lately, the Lotus Blossom has been offering a few specials that feature more daring regional dishes. The Szechwan chicken dish we sampled lately was quite good.

The Wonders of China: Land of Beauty, Land of Time

✓ Film
✓ Lasts 20 minutes
✓ Line moves to fill theater

This beautiful and poetic 360-degree film delivers just what its title promises. Visitors stand against rails to watch. You'll be so entranced that you'll hardly notice you're standing.

***Excellent*, not to be missed**
Tips: Check at the door for the time of the next show and browse until a few minutes before it begins. The theater will almost always accommodate everyone waiting.

The Outpost and the Village Trader Between China and Germany is the Outpost refreshment stand. It features an assortment of beverages and fresh fruit. Just beyond it is the Village Trader, a small shop of art, handcrafts, and clothing from Africa, India, and Australia. There's some interesting stuff here and the prices are not too bad.

Germany

Browse in the square here while the strolling accordion player is performing, and you'll feel as though you're in a travel documentary. The main attraction in this charming bit of Bavaria is the pavilion's restaurant, the Biergarten, which features a wild and zany rendition of German beer hall entertainment. Germany also features the Garden Railway, a miniature version of the romantic rail that runs from Füssen to Würzburg. Don't miss this amazing "toy" train.

The quaint shops of this Bavarian village offer a large variety of handcrafted German merchandise: cuckoo clocks, glass and porcelain, authentic fashions, and even precision timepieces. There's even a European-style candy shop and a wine cellar with daily wine tastings.

Sommerfest is a counter-service German restaurant. Pick up a meal at the counter and find a nice place to sit in the square.

Italy

Some evening, we'd like to go for a ride in one of the gondolas parked out in front of Italy. It would be so romantic. Instead, we'll stroll in the shadow of the Doge's Palace and perhaps later will enjoy a dinner in the ristorante.

The shops in Italy offer the finest in Venetian glass and crystal, a colorful selection of Italian fashion wear, and a large choice of handcrafted jewelry.

Culinary offerings here include a sidewalk vendor who sells pastries, desserts, and beverages from a small cart; there's also the large and boisterous Italian banquet hall, L'Originale Alfredo di Roma Ristorante. While we do think this is great Italian food (see also Palio, described in Chapter 6), the entertainment is fun. This is a lively place to dine.

The American Adventure

This is the "host" pavilion of the World Showcase, and its charming, colonial-style building is home to the American Adventure Show, the Liberty Inn restaurant, and Heritage Manor Gifts. In the courtyard are a few interesting carts selling souvenirs and curios, and across the plaza is the America Gardens Theatre. Around the side of the pavilion is Mickey's Garden. This quiet little place is an ideal spot to rest and escape the crowds.

With all the interesting food around the lagoon, we wonder what went wrong here. The Liberty Inn offers the usual counter-service hamburgers, hot dogs, and chicken sandwiches that can be found anywhere around Disney. We have recently heard rumors, though, that things may change. Disney is planning to bring fine American cuisine to this pavilion sometime in the next few years.

The American Adventure

✓ Audio-animatronic show
✓ Lasts 30 minutes
✓ Line moves to fill theater

This patriotic journey through American history is narrated by "Mark Twain." It is interesting and even stirring.

QUITE GOOD, especially for history buffs

The America Gardens Theatre

✓ Open-air amphitheater
✓ Live shows throughout the day

This lovely stage features entertainment of every sort throughout the year. Some of it is college bands or orchestras and some of it features well-known performers. Check the Epcot guidemap to determine who is playing here and when during your visit.

Japan

This lovely pavilion is marked by the torii gate on the shore of the lagoon. We always marvel at the Disney Imagineers' attention to detail. The bases of this gate are covered with "oysters," as though the tide had fallen. From the towering pagoda to the Bijutsu-kan Gallery, the rest of Japan has been just as meticulously created.

Don't miss the Japanese garden during your Epcot visit ♥. Try to get here before the crowds to enjoy its serene beauty. Visitors to Disney's Japan will enjoy a choice of three uniquely Japanese dining experiences as well as shopping in the fabulous Mitsukoshi department store. Kimonos, vases, lacquered bowls, and colorful masks are a few of the thousands of items offered in this large shop.

Tempura Kiku is Japan's tempura bar and is an outstanding choice for lunch. The Teppanyaki Dining Room features grill-tables where performance chefs prepare your dinner with a sizzle and a flair. Japan is also home to the Yakitori House, a delightful and authentic Japanese fast-food restaurant that features a lovely garden dining area. The Matsu No Ma Lounge is a full-service bar, and its menu includes a variety of specialty drinks, sake, and a selection of Japanese finger foods including sushi and Kabuki beef. The view of the lagoon from here has no equal in Epcot. Try watching IllumiNations from the Matsu No Ma ♥♥♥.

Morocco

This pavilion, of all the countries, seems to best capture the feeling of being in a foreign land. Back among its winding, narrow streets and shops, you could almost forget that you are at Disney World. This exotic land even reaches out onto the sidewalk with a lively festival of musicians and dancers.

Tons of handcrafted tiles were imported to create the Chellah Minaret, the towering landmark of Epcot's Morocco. There is even an ancient waterwheel that "irrigates" the beautiful gardens along the lagoon. The shops here at Morocco are especially interesting. All things Moroccan are offered in this bazaar: jewelry, native clothing, brassware, leather goods, and more. Prices are fairly reasonable.

Morocco features one of our favorite Epcot restaurants, Marrakesh ♥♥. This exotic eatery boasts a menu of Moroccan cuisine and live entertainment at both lunch and dinner. Also featured here in Morocco each day from 12 to 7 P.M. are the "Treasures of Morocco" guided walking tour and the Fez House exhibit.

France

This pavilion enjoys a perfect location. Set where the waterway from nearby Crescent Lake enters the lagoon, Disney's France captures a sense of the lovely River Seine and the City of Lights. Small boats and artists' kiosks dot the river's edge. The Eiffel Tower rises beyond the mansard roofs. It is not quite Paris, but it is no doubt Gallic.

As you would expect, the emphasis here is on cuisine. This pavilion features a restaurant, the Chefs de France, a pastry shop, and a winery. The shops are distinctly French, with offerings such as men's and women's fashions, original artwork, and the finest of perfumes.

Impressions de France

✓ Film
✓ Lasts 20 minutes
✓ Line moves to fill theater

This film is beautiful, romantic, and unforgettable ♥♥. The theater is cool and offers each guest a seat. Need we say more?

***Excellent*, not to be missed**
Tips: Ask at the door for the next show time. If there is no crowd, browse until just before it begins.

Sidewalk Artisans de Paris Along the lagoon artists are at work. Some do sketches, some create chalk portraits, and yet others will snip your silhouette in black paper. The prices are all reasonable, and the work is good. One of these will make a much better souvenir than a photo taken in front of the geosphere.

The United Kingdom

This pavilion is a charming little slice of Great Britain. From the lakeside dining of the Rose and Crown to Anne Hathaway's cottage, it is a picturesque representation of one of our favorite travel destinations. Shopping here is particularly good, and we always enjoy the fine Scottish woolens, English China, and charming assortment of wooden toys. There's a lot more here too. You can even find an interesting selection of British candy bars. You won't want to miss this pavilion's small garden area, just past the cottage.

If visiting Britain makes you think of pints of dark ale, you won't be disappointed. The Rose and Crown Pub offers all the atmosphere you'll need to enjoy a stout and "pasties."

U.K. Food Carts Two food carts are usually at each end of the pavilion. The cart nearest the International Gateway offers baked potatoes with a variety of toppings. After a potato, if you are still hungry, head over toward Canada and to the next cart. There you'll find a small assortment of desserts. (If you get there after Gayle's mom, there may not be any eclairs left.)

Canada

We enjoy many things in Disney's Canada. The pavilion's 360-degree film is only part of the excitement. After the film, we like to take a walk through the mountain area, past its waterfall, and into the beautiful Victoria Garden that re-creates the famous Bouchart Gardens of Vancouver Island, British Columbia. Colorful beds of flowers, willows, and maple trees make this a little slice of our neighbor to the north.

Shopping here is good, too, in the shadow of the stone architecture of old Ottawa. The Northwest Mercantile has an intriguing selection of Canadian products. Maple syrup, clothes, and wildlife merchandise are only a few of the interesting items. La Boutique des Provinces, Canada's other shop, specializes in goods from the French province.

NEW Canada's eatery is the newly reborn Le Cellier Steakhouse, and it has recently become one of our favorites here around the lagoon. It's the perfect place to escape the crowds and to enjoy one of Epcot's freshest meals. For our review of this restaurant, see Chapter 6.

O Canada!

✓ Film
✓ Lasts 20 minutes
✓ Line moves to fill theater

This is a CircleVision 360 (360-degree) film, like the one in China. All travel films should be this exciting.

***VERY GOOD*, no reason to miss this one**
Tip: If it seems particularly crowded, ask one of the attendants if you'll make it into the next show.

ROMANCE AT THE WORLD SHOWCASE

- A meal at San Angel Inn: ♥♥♥
- The Japanese Garden: ♥
- A drink at Matsu No Ma Lounge during IllumiNations: ♥♥♥

- Lunch or dinner at Marrakesh: ♥♥
- Taking the *Breathless* Cruise from the marina at the Yacht Club (see Chapter 7 for details): ♥♥♥♥
- Having a sketch done by a sidewalk artisan in France: ♥
- *Impressions de France:* ♥♥

EPCOT DINING TIPS

- If you are looking for breakfast in Future World, try Fountain View Espresso and Bakery, Pure and Simple, the Sunshine Season Food Fair, or Pasta Piazza. For a character breakfast, make priority seating arrangements at the Garden Grill.
- Generally, the restaurants around the World Showcase simply cater to numbers too great for the food to be outstanding. Still, we enjoy Le Cellier, Marrakesh, and Akershus for their food. For entertainment, we would recommend Marrakesh ♥♥, the Biergarten, and L'Originale Alfredo di Roma Ristorante. Mexico's San Angel Inn ♥♥♥ is beautiful and one of the most romantic restaurants at Disney. See our reviews of these restaurants in Chapter 6.
- We suggest lunching here at Epcot and dining elsewhere. The same food is less expensive at lunch, too.
- Through the International Gateway between France and the United Kingdom, you can walk to the Epcot resort area. Fine eateries are numerous here. Some of our favorites: the Flying Fish Cafe, Spoodles, Yachtsman Steakhouse, and Palio. There are many more. The restaurants of Epcot are usually pretty crowded, and we would recommend making priority seating arrangements, especially during the dinner hours. Besides calling from your resort room or visiting the restaurant of your choice, you can make "reservations" at a WorldKey terminal. There are three in Epcot, one on the east side of Innoventions Plaza, one on the walkway to the Showcase Plaza, and one between Italy and Germany.
- If you find yourselves hungry in Epcot and without priority seating, the following restaurants are the most likely to be able to accommodate you: China, Morocco, and Canada.

Disney–MGM Studios

This may be the smallest of the four theme parks, but it is a powerhouse of entertainment. With a modest amount of planning, you

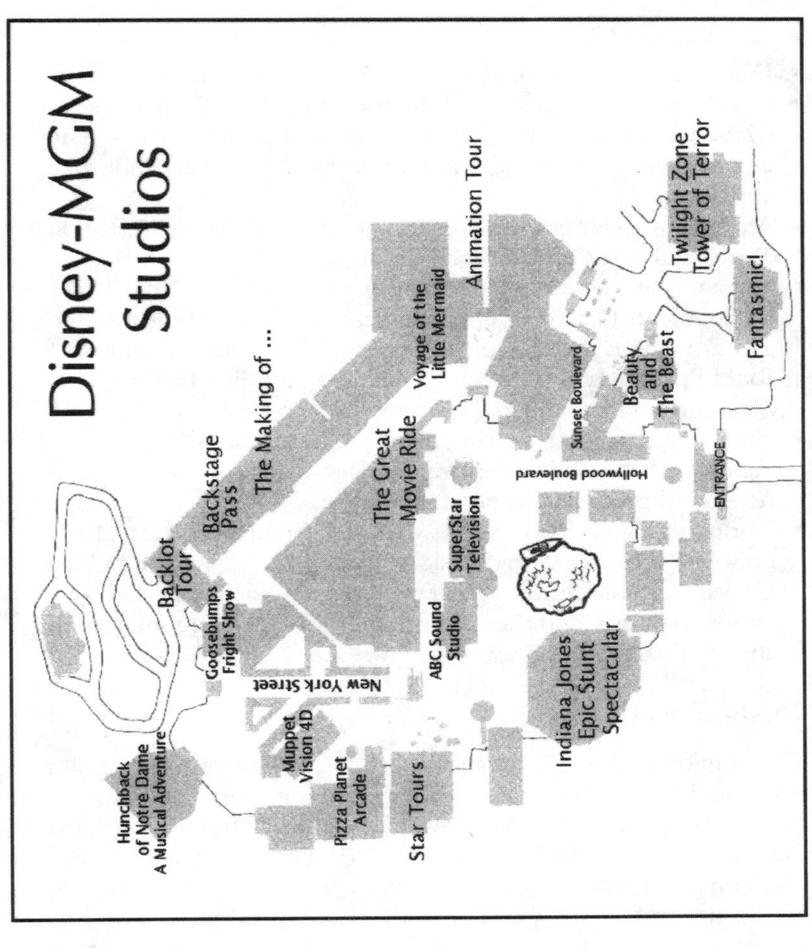
Disney-MGM Studios
Hunchback of Notre Dame A Musical Adventure
Backlot Tour
Goosebumps Fright Show
Backstage Pass
The Making of ...
The Great Movie Ride
Voyage of the Little Mermaid
Animation Tour
Muppet Vision 4D
Pizza Planet Arcade
Star Tours
New York Street
ABC Sound Studio
SuperStar Television
Indiana Jones Epic Stunt Spectacular
Hollywood Boulevard
Sunset Boulevard
ENTRANCE
Beauty and The Beast
Twilight Zone Tower of Terror
Fantasmic!

should be able to take in everything here in a few visits. Most of the attractions are geared to accommodate large numbers of visitors.

Disney–MGM Tips

- Disney–MGM Surprise Mornings are on Sunday and Wednesday.
- Check out the tip board at Hollywood Junction. There is also a window there for making dinner reservations in the park. We suggest that you decide where and when you'd like to eat and make arrangements.
- Attractions to hit first are the Twilight Zone Tower of Terror, Star Tours, and The Great Movie Ride, in that order.
- Some of the attractions ask for participants. Get involved. These are the moments that you will remember most fondly. Trust us on this. The attractions that feature guest participation are the Indiana Jones Epic Stunt Spectacular, ABC Sound Studio One Saturday Morning, and SuperStar Television.
- Take advantage of the roving photographers who will take your picture and then enhance it with Disney characters. These Walk-Around Photos make great memories.
- During the busy times of years, this park features a spectacular fireworks show set to the music of great films. Check the "World Update" or your Studios guidemap to see if Sorcery in the Sky is on for your visit, and then be sure to see it. For more information about this and other fireworks shows, see Chapter 5.

The Boulevards

The Studios is Disney's zany vision of 1930s Hollywood and, like its real counterpart, the main thoroughfares here are Hollywood and Sunset. Along these palm-lined avenues are art deco storefronts, trolley cables, old bus benches, period billboards, fireplugs, vintage cars, and cast-iron street lamps. Evocative of the 1930s, the boulevards bring to life the delightful fantasy of a place that never was.

Along these streets are some interesting shops and more than just a few amusing sights. Watch for the Studios' wacky "streetmosphere" people, a crazy troupe of costumed characters that perform daily. Down Sunset, you'll see the "dilapidated and scorched" Hollywood Tower Hotel, home of the Twilight Zone Tower of Terror. There's lots to see and do along here, but we suggest that you try out some of the park's shows and attractions first, then come back later to explore.

The Attractions of Disney–MGM Studios

We really like this park. There is a lot of thought behind each attraction, and nothing except for the "Honey, I Shrunk the Kids" Movie Set Adventure is aimed solely at children. Things here are intelligent and thoughtful, not to mention fun. We suggest that you give everything a chance. In particular, we encourage you to see the Disney–MGM Studios Backlot Tour and The Magic of Disney Animation Tour. Both are excellent and seem, somehow, to be at the very core of the experience here. Disney–MGM Studios is more than a theme park—it is a working studio, and these attractions will bring you into these working areas to give you an intriguing look at the magic behind the movies.

Twilight Zone Tower of Terror

✓ Special-effects thrill ride
✓ Lasts 10 minutes
✓ Line moves slowly

If you don't mind being taken in an elevator to the top of a 13-story building and dropped several times to street level, then you're ready for this. The special effects along the way are some of the best we've ever seen, and the story line is good. The drops are over quickly and are not as bad as they sound (how many times have you heard *that* line?).

EXCELLENT, if the plunge doesn't frighten you off
Tips: This attraction is very popular and, since the line moves slowly, a long wait is likely. Usually open for Surprise Mornings.

Beauty and the Beast—Live on Stage

✓ Live show
✓ Lasts 30 minutes
✓ Line moves to fill theater

Real people perform this miniversion ♥♥ of the Disney classic film. The costumes, sets, and performances are all good, and the music is, we think, the best ever in a Disney animated feature.

EXCELLENT, do not miss
Tips: The 1,500-seat Theater of the Stars will accommodate virtually everyone in line. The amphitheater is large, and all of the seats provide a reasonably good view of the stage. Seating begins 30 minutes prior to each show. Check for show times.

Star Tours

- ✓ Simulated thrill ride
- ✓ Lasts 10 minutes
- ✓ Line moves quickly

Based on the *Star Wars* films, this ride doesn't really go anywhere. It is a pod-like "ship" that merely simulates flight by coordinating film, sound, and a bit of rocking, tipping, and bucking. It is very convincing and very entertaining.

Excellent, do not miss
Tip: Usually open for Surprise Mornings.

Voyage of The Little Mermaid

- ✓ Live musical show
- ✓ Lasts 20 minutes
- ✓ Line moves slowly to fill theater

This show combines live action and puppetry in a brief version of the Disney animated film. Everything about this show is excellent, especially the special effects.

Excellent, do not miss
Tips: When you first get your guidemap, check for the time of the first show. Arrive 30 minutes before. Better a 30-minute wait early than a much lengthier one later. Only one theater-full of people is admitted at a time, and you may not be in line for the very next show; ask a cast member.

The Great Movie Ride

- ✓ Adventure "train" ride (slow)
- ✓ Lasts 20 minutes
- ✓ Line moves very quickly

This ride takes you through a series of movie scene re-creations. The sets, audio-animatronics, and special effects are all worth seeing again and again. There are even a couple of "live shows" staged along the way. (There are two different versions of the shows, shown to alternating cars.)

Excellent, do not miss
Tips: This ride is usually open for Surprise Mornings. Parts of it may be too intense for very young children.

Indiana Jones Epic Stunt Spectacular

✓ Live show
✓ Lasts 30 minutes
✓ Line moves quickly to fill large amphitheater

This is a live-action stunt show. The special effects and scenery are memorable. This is an attraction executed on a grand scale, and it is exciting and fun.

EXCELLENT, do not miss

Disney–MGM Studios Backlot Tour

✓ Tram tour with some excitement
✓ Lasts 35 minutes
✓ Line moves quickly

This wonderful attraction will provide a behind-the-scenes look at parts of this working studio as well as a special effects adventure. On the tour, you'll see the costume department, prop yard, and experience "Catastrophe Canyon." There's more, too.

EXCELLENT, not to be missed

Backstage Pass

✓ Walking tour and film
✓ Lasts 25 minutes
✓ Line moves quickly

This used to be part of the Backlot Tour. It was, and still is, a look behind the scenes at how special effects are achieved. Now, this attraction shows how the effects in a particular film have been done, and in this case it is Disney's live-action film, *101 Dalmatians.* It features sound stages, actual sets and props, and a film. During the tour you'll also get to see the working set of a Touchstone film currently in production.

VERY INTERESTING and quite entertaining

The Making Of . . .

✓ Walking tour and film
✓ Lasts 25 minutes
✓ Line moves quickly

This attraction features a behind-the-scenes look at how a recent Disney film has been created. Showcased films change nearly yearly, and beginning in summer of 1998, it will be the elaborate sets and props of the action film *Armageddon.*

INTERESTING and enjoyable

American Film Institute Showcase

✓ Walk-through at the end of the Backlot Tour
✓ No time limit

This interesting exhibit features costumes, props, and set pieces from numerous films and television productions, past and present. We've seen some neat stuff here and recommend dropping by if you have an interest.

GOOD
Tip: You don't have to go on the tour to see this exhibit.

NEW *Magic of Disney Animation*

✓ Film and walking tour
✓ Lasts about 35 minutes
✓ Line moves quickly

This tour begins with a film that you will not soon forget. Robin Williams and Walter Cronkite join forces in an introduction so hilarious that you will want to see it again. The tour then takes you through the Disney animators' actual working areas. It is interesting. The grand finale is a memorable film of animation clips from Disney classics. This tour features an entirely new home and a better look behind the scenes, including computer special effects.

EXCELLENT

SuperStar Television

✓ Show with audience participation
✓ Lasts 30 minutes
✓ Line moves slowly to fill theater

This show puts costumed visitors on stage and right in popular television shows. It is especially memorable when one or both of you gets into the show. "Tryouts" are held 20 minutes prior to each show. Get involved in this fun. We've heard that Disney is working on a way to videotape the show and sell the tape to participants. We've been begging for this for years.

EXCELLENT
Tip: If you are honeymooning here, we've heard that they have a special role for you both in this show. Be sure to "try out."

NEW *ABC Sound Studio One Saturday Morning*

✓ Film and show
✓ Lasts 15 minutes
✓ Line moves slowly

This attraction demonstrates the art of creating sound effects. The show includes audience participation. We miss the old version of this show.

OK, more aimed at kids

Jim Henson's MuppetVision 4-D

✓ Film and more
✓ Lasts 20 minutes
✓ Line moves quickly to fill large preshow area, then theater

This 3-D film is a lot more than just a film. We'll leave the rest a surprise.

EXCELLENT, not to be missed
Tips: The line here seems to come and go with the flow of people from nearby attractions, such as Indiana Jones. Try it when there isn't much of a line at various times throughout the day. The preshow should not be missed.

"Honey, I Shrunk the Kids" Movie Set Adventure

✓ Playground for children
✓ No time limit
✓ Line moves very slowly

This is a playground where objects are much larger than usual. Much, much larger. Everything is "rubberized" for safety.

OK, for small children, otherwise avoid it
Tips: Lines here can be long and awfully slow. If this is a must-see for your child, we suggest that you get here early.

NEW *Goosebumps Fright Show and Fun House*

✓ Stage show and walk-through fun house
✓ Show lasts about 20 minutes
✓ Audience stands in street; no line

This show is really for kids so if you have yours along, it should be fun. The fun house is a mirror maze.

OK

Tip: **There are some great gag photo opportunities in and around the Goosebumps shop behind the stage.**

"New York" Street Set

✓ Walk-through
✓ No time limit

Here on the backlot of the studio, Disney has created a huge facade of New York City. It presents some nifty photo opportunities. Parts of the set were used during the filming of *Dick Tracy.*

GOOD

The Hunchback of Notre Dame—A Musical Adventure

✓ Live musical show
✓ Lasts about 30 minutes
✓ Line moves to fill theater

This live "mini" rendition of the animated Disney film features wonderful costumes, colorful sets, special effects, and memorable performances. It is a show not to be missed.

OUTSTANDING, do not miss

Tip: Arrive early. Seating begins 25 minutes before the show.

NEW *Fantasmic! (opens spring 1999)*

✓ Nighttime special effects and music show
✓ Lasts 25 minutes
✓ Line moves to fill 7,000+-seat theater

This incredible show will take guests inside the dreams of Mickey Mouse and into a world of magical effects, dancing waters, and music. The music of the *Sorcerer's Apprentice, Pocahontas,* and *The Lion King* will be featured in this fantastic stage show with shooting comets, animated fountains, and swirling stars. If you've seen the Disneyland version of this presentation, you'll know just how exciting it is.

OUTSTANDING, not to be missed

 *Rock'n Roller Coaster (opens late 1999)*

✓ Thrill ride

✓ Line will move slowly; this ride will be popular

As we go to press, ground has just been broken for this thrill ride. We've heard that this ride will feature a recording studio entrance, where guests will "go on the road" with a rock group in a limousine that will do 0–60 miles per hour in three seconds.

SHOULD BE A MEGA-ATTRACTION

 Mulan Parade

Based on Disney's 36th animated feature film, this parade is one of colorful floats, beautiful costumes, and wonderful music. It makes its way along Sunset and Hollywood Boulevards usually in midafternoon. During busier periods, this parade happens twice daily. Check your Studios guidemap, the "World Update," or the tip board at Hollywood Junction for times.

***VERY GOOD*, worth seeing**

Tip: Find a good viewing spot about 30 minutes before the parade.

 Disney's Toy Story Pizza Planet Arcade

Bring along some change (or better yet, some dollar bills) to this video arcade. If this is the kind of thing you really like, we suggest you save it for Downtown Disney's DisneyQuest, the last and final word in virtual entertainment.

The Restaurants at Disney–MGM Studios

Dining at Disney–MGM is better than at the Magic Kingdom. Here you will find the fine as well as the fun. There are four interesting table-service restaurants. The Hollywood Brown Derby ♥♥♥ is fine dining in a charming re-creation of the famous Hollywood eatery. The 50's Prime Time Cafe offers American food and fun, and Mama Melrose's Ristorante Italiano is Disney's neighborhood Italian eatery. The Sci-Fi Dine-In Theater will put you in the back (or front) seat of a car at the drive-in. For our reviews and more information, see Chapter 6. Reservations for these restaurants are strongly recommended.

The Studios has a large selection of counter-service restaurants. Hollywood & Vine Cafeteria of the Stars serves breakfast, lunch, and dinner. Meals are acceptable and inexpensive. The Soundstage Restaurant features a themed character buffet breakfast and lunch. The Commissary offers a modest variety of interesting sandwiches, including a half-pound burger in a fairly standard fast-food setting, and the new Toy Story Pizza Planet has a selection of not-so-great pizzas, salads, and pasta.

The Backlot Express, located near the Indiana Jones show, features good grilled chicken, burgers, and hot dogs in a pleasant outside sitting area, while Min and Bill's specializes in tacos, fruit, soft-serve, and snacks. Nearby, you'll find the Echo Park Fruit Stand. Studio Catering, located just off New York Street, features deli subs, barbecue sandwiches, and snacks. It also has a soft-serve ice cream counter.

On Sunset Boulevard, the Sunset Ranch Market is really a group of food outlets that are set in an outdoor farmer's market. From fresh fruits and salads to hot dogs and chili, there's a lot to choose from here. For snacks and desserts, you can go to Dinosaur Gertie's or Starring Rolls. Starring Rolls is a little bakery around the corner from the Brown Derby, and it offers hot cocoa and tea; it's a nice spot for a light breakfast. Ellen's Buy the Book is both a bookstore and coffee shop. It features espresso, cappuccino, and pastries.

NEW Opening in the spring of 1999 will be the Copperfield Magic Underground restaurant. Just outside the gates of the park but accessible from inside and outside the park, this restaurant will feature a magic dinner show of grand proportions. It will be an attraction in its own right. The 500-seat restaurant will seat guests in an atmosphere reflecting the history of magic and illusion. We can say with certainty that priority seating arrangements will be necessary.

Dining Tips for the Studios

- For good food and lots of fun, our choice is the 50's Prime Time Cafe. This is a place we love to bring people to.
- For an early lunch, try the Backlot Express. It is usually open by 11 A.M. The chicken sandwich here is pretty good.
- For fine dining, try the Brown Derby ♥♥♥. The Derby takes reservations for as late as 7:30 P.M. We highly recommend eating late and then walking out through the empty park.
- The best coffee here in the Studios is at the Joffrey coffee cart just inside the main gate. Espresso, cappuccino, and a variety of cold specialty coffee beverages are available.

The Lounges at Disney–MGM Studios

Because this theme park is geared more towards adults, there are lounges here at Disney–MGM Studios. So drop in for an afternoon cocktail or an evening sip of wine.

- The Catwalk Bar is located upstairs from the Soundstage Restaurant. It is very colorful and full of movie props. Seating is equally interesting. Beers, wines, specialty drinks, and a few sandwiches are offered in a quiet atmosphere away from the multitudes. This is a great escape, even if just for a couple of soft drinks.
- The Tune-In Lounge is part of the 50's Prime Time Cafe and has a good selection of beers and wines.
- Mama Melrose's Bar, located right alongside the kitchen, will give you a great view of the chefs at work as you quaff your beer or enjoy your wine. The selection here is small but interesting.

The Shops at Disney–MGM Studios

If you're into movie memorabilia, you've come to the right place. Sid Cahuenga's One-of-a-Kind is one of Disney's most unique shops. There are several other shops along the boulevards that feature movie stuff, from T-shirts to photo books. Much of it is quite good. You'll also find lots of Disney character merchandise. Keystone Clothiers even offers a mouse-ears umbrella. Cover Story will snap your photo and put it on the cover of a magazine. It's a goofy souvenir. For books and such, check out Ellen's Buy the Book, which is also a nice coffee shop. Other shops include Stage 1 Company Store's baby stuff, Twilight Zone Tower of Terror fashions, *Star Wars* memorabilia at Endor Vendors, and much more. The Studios provide interesting shopping, so set aside some time to browse. One of our favorites is the Animation Gallery. Books, Disney art, and collectibles are this shop's stock.

DISNEY–MGM ATTRACTIONS NOT TO MISS

- Disney–MGM Studios Backlot Tour
- Beauty and the Beast—Live on Stage
- The Great Movie Ride
- Indiana Jones Epic Stunt Spectacular
- The Magic of Disney Animation
- *Jim Henson's MuppetVision 4-D*
- Star Tours

- Twilight Zone Tower of Terror
- Voyage of The Little Mermaid
- The Hunchback of Notre Dame—A Musical Adventure
- NEW Fantasmic!

ROMANCE AT DISNEY–MGM STUDIOS

- Beauty and the Beast—Live on Stage: ♥♥
- Sorcery in the Sky fireworks (see Chapter 5): ♥♥
- The Hollywood Brown Derby Restaurant: ♥♥♥

NEW *Disney's Animal Kingdom*

They call it "the imagination of Disney gone wild," and to us, it's more than a theme park. Disney's Animal Kingdom is a botanical garden and wild animal habitat like no other in the world. It celebrates not only creatures that roam the earth today, but also those that once did and those that might have. From a prehistoric garden to the African savanna and from the jungles of Thailand to the rain forests of Indonesia, the Animal Kingdom takes theme parks to a whole new level.

The attractions, art, and architecture of the Animal Kingdom are an exuberant celebration of the world of creatures living, extinct, and imaginary. The Animal Kingdom is not so much a place of rides and exhibits as are the other Disney theme parks. Although you will find the expected theme park attractions, the Animal Kingdom is much more a world of sights, sounds, fragrances, and moods. It is a place of discovery and of creature encounters. From the whimsical fantasy of Safari Village to the stunning realism of Africa and Asia, the Animal Kingdom is a land of enchanting beauty and engaging details. It is a place that has been designed to provide an adventure around every corner. Intricately carved animal totems, reed-thatched roofs, the lilting melodies of Africa and Asia, and the majesty of the Tree of Life are only part of the magic of this, Disney's grandest adventure.

But don't come expecting to find animals in cages, for this is *their* kingdom and here the creatures roam "free" over hundreds of acres that have been transformed into an African savanna and tropical rain forests. To achieve this, Disney has planted more than four million trees, shrubs, and grasses and virtually redesigned the Central Florida landscape to create vistas that appear startlingly real. There are 110 species of trees and shrubs here that have never before been grown in North America.

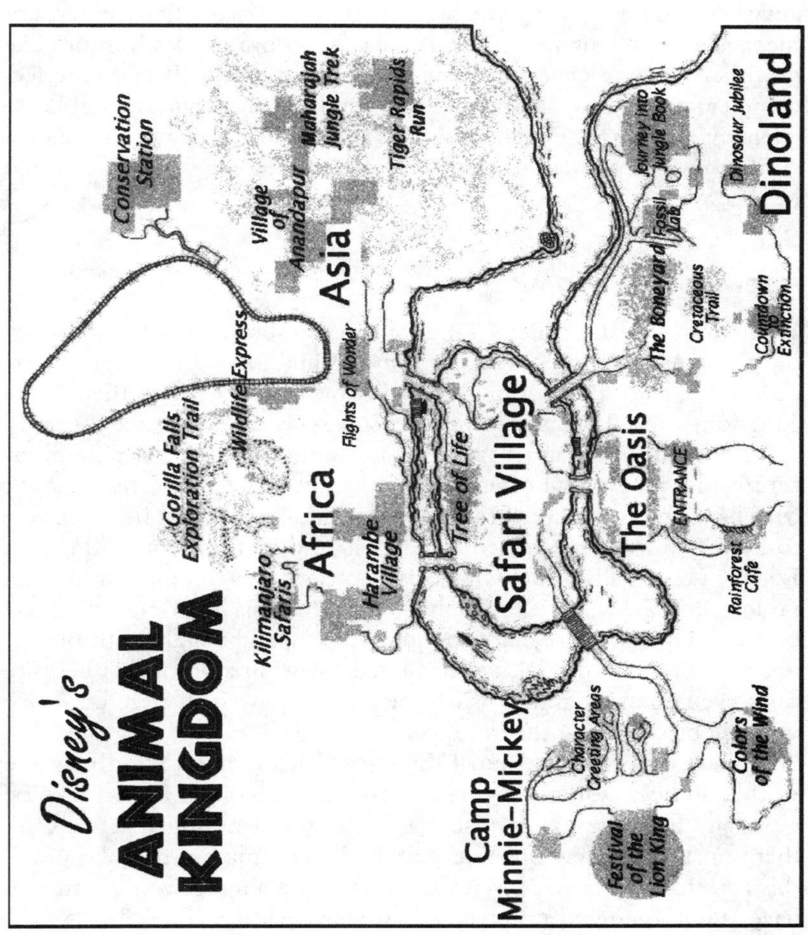
Disney's
ANIMAL
KINGDOM
Conservation Station
Gorilla Falls Exploration Trail
Wildlife Express
Kilimanjaro Safaris
Africa
Harambe Village
Flights of Wonder
Tree of Life
Village of Anandapur
Asia
Maharajah Jungle Trek
Tiger Rapids Run
Safari Village
The Oasis
ENTRANCE
Rainforest Cafe
Camp Minnie-Mickey
Character Greeting Areas
Colors of the Wind
Festival of the Lion King
The Boneyard
Fossil Lab
Cretaceous Trail
Countdown to Extinction
Journey into Jungle Book
Dinosaur Jubilee
Dinoland

Here at Disney's Animal Kingdom, you will encounter all kinds of creatures, from tiny insects to terrifying tyrannosaurs, and in the process, you'll be both entertained and educated. For here more than anywhere else at Disney, you will discover that truly great entertainment is also enlightening. The Animal Kingdom is an adventure like no other we have experienced at Walt Disney World. It is the perfect complement to the other theme parks, and it delivers unforgettable excitement and entertainment as well as a powerful message about global conservation. If we had to describe this place in a single word, it would be this: wow.

A Few Things to Consider

When you visit the Animal Kingdom, remember that it is a work-in-progress and that you are seeing it in its childhood. In the future, expect to see a lot of new things. At the time of this writing, the Animal Kingdom's Asia land is barely open. It is scheduled to arrive in spring of 1999 with the Asian village of Anandapur, a white-water raft adventure, and a jungle trail offering up-close encounters with tigers, giant fruit bats, and other creatures native to Asia. Restaurants here promise to be very interesting indeed. There will also be the Animal Kingdom Lodge, a resort adventure where every room looks out onto an African savanna and the wild creatures that live there. This luxurious resort will be a unique experience, allowing guests to "spend a night with the animals." What else the Disney Imagineers have in store for us here we can't even guess at, and as usual, they are keeping it all a secret. As for us, we'll be expecting the unexpected.

When you visit the Animal Kingdom, keep in mind that the whole world had been waiting for this amazing park to open. Expect it to be especially busy during its first year. It is worth noting that we were there on the first few opening days and were impressed by how well this park handles crowds. With some careful planning, you are sure to have as unforgettable a time here as we have had.

ANIMAL KINGDOM TIPS

- Park hours are early morning to near sunset. Check the "World Update" or your Animal Kingdom guidemap for the exact hours during your visit.
- Word is out that the animals on Kilimanjaro Safaris are most active in the early morning hours. While true to some degree, we found plenty of creatures throughout the day. This adventure can have a

two-hour wait in the early morning hours, so if you find yourselves there in the morning, we suggest that instead of going to Africa first, head over to Dinoland, catch Countdown to Extinction, then work your way back, through Safari Village, It's Tough to Be a Bug!, and Festival of the Lion King at Camp Minnie-Mickey. Later in the morning, when the crowds have moved on, it will be time for Africa.

- Our favorite time to visit this park is the four hours just before it closes: the crowds are down, the animals are active, and the lighting is picture-perfect. Be sure to stay until dark to catch some especially beautiful effects around the Tree of Life: ♥♥♥.
- There are nearly 100 cast members here at the Animal Kingdom who are from various African nations. Find them by their name tags and make an effort to talk about their homelands and their unique perspective on Disney's Animal Kingdom.
- Festival of the Lion King is one of the best live shows ever at Walt Disney World. Lines get so long here in the afternoon that you may not make it inside. Try to see it in the morning.
- For the live stage shows, arrive 30 minutes before performance time.
- Since this park already opens early, there are no Surprise Mornings.
- Don't forget your guidemap for this park. It's called the Adventurer's Guide and can be found at the front gate or from virtually any shop or vendor.
- Check one of the tip boards in Safari Village for show times, waits, closures, and special events.

The Lay of the Land

Before you even get through the gates, you'll see the Outpost gift shop. Here you'll find a small selection of Animal Kingdom logo merchandise. But save your money, there's much nicer stuff ahead.

As you come across the entrance plaza, you'll see a 65-foot waterfall. Hidden behind its vale of thundering water, towering cliffs, and clouds of mist is Disney World's second Rainforest Cafe. It's the perfect place to dine in this wild land.

The Rainforest Cafe at the Animal Kingdom is open for breakfast before the park opens and takes priority seating for all meals through the usual Disney channels. The food is very good, especially breakfast. If you wish to dine here, we strongly urge you to make plans ahead of time. Know that there is another entrance to it from within the park, at The Oasis. For our review of the Rainforest Cafe, see Chapter 6.

Once through the turnstiles, you'll find Garden Gate Gifts, with its assortment of the new Animal Kingdom merchandise as well as film and other sundry items. Adjacent to it is the rental center for wheelchairs, strollers, and electric convenience vehicles, an ATM, and rental lockers. Across the small plaza, there's guest services, rest rooms, and more lockers.

From here you'll enter The Oasis, and beyond that you'll cross the Discovery River. This winding jungle river surrounds the island of Safari Village, the hub of the Animal Kingdom. From here, further travel will take you "upcountry" to the four lands of the Animal Kingdom: Africa, Asia, Dinoland U.S.A., and Camp Minnie-Mickey.

The Oasis

This lush garden area is something of a foyer to the Animal Kingdom. Its dense greenery, flowering plants, gurgling waters, and multitude of small animals, reptiles, and winged creatures set the tone for the wild journey that lies ahead. Anteaters, spoonbills, and military macaws are just a few of the inhabitants here.

If you pause long enough to listen, you might hear a lion roar in the distance. There are delightful details everywhere, and although this is a place for exploration, we suggest you come back later, for ahead looms the Discovery River and your gateway to adventure.

Safari Village

As you come across the bridge to Safari Village, you'll see the Animal Kingdom's magnificent centerpiece: the towering Tree of Life. This 14-story creation celebrates Earth's amazing diversity of life. Beneath its leafy 175-foot-wide canopy and carved into its limbs, trunk, and roots are the intricate images of more than 300 creatures. It is a swirling tapestry of reptiles, mammals, birds, fish, and insects, and it is a dazzling sight. This is surely one of Disney's most majestic creations.

Surrounding the mighty tree are trails that meander through tropical glades and past falling waters. There are living creatures amidst the roots of the great Tree of Life, and if you keep your eyes open, you'll encounter river otters, ring-tailed lemurs, axis deer, flamingos, a cotton-topped Tamarin, macaws, and even red kangaroos.

Safari Village, which surrounds the tree, is a brightly colored fantasy land of playful creature imagery and equatorial architecture. It is home to many of the park's shops and restaurants and it features an amazing depth of details. From curious stone sculptures to ornate and whimsical paintings, this place is a delight to explore. It is a virtual art gallery of Balinese, Peruvian, African, and Polynesian folk art.

Buildings, benches, vendor carts, and street lamps are all festooned with a rainbow of fantastic creatures, and each building has its own animal theme. Island Mercantile features either migratory creatures or animals that work, such as bees, beavers, and camels. The theme of the Flame Tree Barbecue is predators and their prey. Even the island's bathrooms get into the show. We suggest that you take the time to simply wander around, taking in all the marvelous details. Don't miss the gecko tiles in Pizzafari's rest rooms.

Yes, there's entertainment everywhere here in Safari Village, in the art and in the architecture, on the walls, the roofs, and in the streets. There are several bands of street musicians, a storyteller, and even a mysterious "performing statue." Don't miss any of the fun.

The Animal Kingdom Tip Board

There are two tip boards in Safari Village. One is just over the bridge from The Oasis, in front of Disney Outfitters, and the other is at the footbridge to Africa. For wait times, closed attractions, and special events, these will help you map your Animal Kingdom explorations.

The Tree of Life

✓ A landmark display
✓ No time limit
✓ No real line

This simply has to be one of Disney's most awe-inspiring creations. It is thrilling from a distance and even more so up close. Look carefully too—not all the creatures are meant to be easily seen.

VERY GOOD, even breathtaking
Tip: **There are two perfect picture spots for the Tree of Life: one across the street from Island Mercantile and the other across the river, between Africa and Asia. Ask a cast member to take a photo of the two of you.**

It's Tough to Be a Bug!

✓ 3-D film and much, much more
✓ Lasts 8 minutes
✓ Line moves slowly to fill 460-seat theater

The theater that shows this 3-D movie is inside the Tree of Life, and while the theater alone seems worth the wait in line, the film is flat-out, over-the-top Disney fun. It features a whole new generation of outrageous 3-D and sensory entertainment, a la *Honey, I Shrunk the Audience*. Don't let anyone give away the many surprises and, whatever you do, *don't miss it.*

OUTSTANDING, Disney at its very best

Tip: Catch this one early while the crowds are at Africa. May be too intense for young children or people with bug phobias.

The Tree of Life Garden ♥♥

✓ Self-guided walking tour
✓ No set time
✓ No real line

Strolling along these beautiful paths is unforgettable. Besides the many exotic plants and creatures, you'll get a close-up look at the incredible Tree of Life.

OUTSTANDING, do not miss

Tip: Be sure to try this one just before the park closes, around sunset ♥♥♥.

Discovery River Boats at Safari Village

✓ One-way boat ride to Asia
✓ Lasts about 10 minutes
✓ Lines can be long but move quickly

These boats seem straight out of Africa, and the voyage to Upcountry Landing in Asia features a few interesting sights not easily seen from shore. You'll have to disembark before you can return to Safari Village, though. Each voyage also includes an animal encounter with a shipboard "animal presenter" and a variety of small creatures.

GOOD, a pleasant journey and an animal encounter too

March of the Animals Parade

This celebration of creatures includes music, floats, and people dressed as all creatures great and small. These stylized costumes are both works of art and masterpieces of ingenuity. Check your Animal Kingdom Adventurer's Guide (guidemap) for exact times during your visit and find a good viewing place before the parade starts.

Places to Eat at Safari Village

Eateries throughout the Animal Kingdom are counter-service. The good news is that the food is better than at their "counter" parts in the other theme parks.

The Flame Tree Barbecue is a good example. It features a small menu of tasty smoked meats, sandwiches, salad, steak fries, and a pleasant vegetarian wrap. Nearby are several shady and comfortable patios along the river where you can enjoy your meal amidst a profusion of brightly colored creature sculptures. Look for the anteater patio. It is one of the nicest eating places in all the Animal Kingdom.

Pizzafari offers a so-so Disney pizza, a salad, a not-so-good vegetable calzone, and a terrific hot deli sandwich. It has several large and colorful dining areas, each with its own unique creature theme. Both the Flame Tree and Pizzafari serve lunch and dinner.

Besides these eateries, you will find an assortment of vendors offering a variety of snacks and beverages at various places throughout the Village. Virtually all restaurants here in the Animal Kingdom offer wine and beer, including South African wines and a microbrewed Safari Amber.

The Shops of Safari Village

Team Disney has created a whole new herd of Animal Kingdom merchandise, and some of it is really entertaining. Island Mercantile features this park's logo merchandise, and from hats to toys there's a mammoth selection. If you're shopping for the kids, Creature Comforts is where you'll go for all things great but small. Beastly Bazaar features a monster assortment of tee-shirts and stuffed animals.

Africa

A few steps beyond Safari Village and over an old stone bridge, you'll discover Africa. Here in the village of Harambe, a crumbling old fort stands watch over a bend in the overgrown river. Traders ply their way past, heading upriver to other exotic ports of call. The main avenue of this bustling port town is dotted with reed-thatched roofs and shady verandahs. The buildings here are like nothing you've seen before: odd-shaped towers, gnarled stone faces, and weather-beaten stucco walls all bleached by a blazing equatorial sun. There are date palms, jacarandas, and yellow trumpet trees. At the far end of the street you'll see Mzee Mbuyu, "the old man Baobob." Harambe is a fascinating and exciting re-creation of a strange and exotic land. The village lies at the edge of the great Harambe Wildlife Reserve and it is your gateway to safari adventures.

Kilimanjaro Safaris

- ✓ Bumpy truck ride through the African savanna
- ✓ Lasts about 20 minutes
- ✓ Line moves fairly quickly to load 32-passenger trucks

This adventure is the very heart and soul of the Animal Kingdom's Africa. Passengers ride in a large, jeep-like, open-sided safari truck, which provides an outstanding view of the wildlife reserve. For as far as the eye can see, this looks like the African savanna and it is teeming with exotic wildlife. Even after half a dozen safaris, we have only just begun to really see it.

***OUTSTANDING*, not to be missed, and to do over and over**
Tips: There are plenty of animals to be seen throughout the day. Don't forget to bring plenty of film. One of our Disney favorites: the last safari of the day ♥.

Gorilla Falls Exploration Trail ♥♥

- ✓ 3/8-mile-long self-guided walking tour
- ✓ Lasts about 30 minutes or longer
- ✓ No real lines here

You'll begin your journey here along a shady footpath that tells a tale. Watch for the tracks of an antelope being stalked by a lion and the story's interesting conclusion. Further on, you'll catch a glimpse of the lives of researchers who spend their days in far-off jungle outposts. And of course, along the way you'll experience up-close encounters with animals too small or too shy to be seen from the safari trucks: giant African bullfrogs, dik diks, and meerkats. There's an underwater hippo viewing area, a stroll-through aviary, and naturally, several large gorilla habitats.

***OUTSTANDING*, one of our favorites, not to be missed**
Tips: Usually crowded early in the day; wait until later. Wheelchairs or electric convenience vehicles are easily accommodated along this trail, and there are numerous places to sit and rest. Take your time exploring this place—there's more to see than meets the eye. This is especially nice very late in the day.

Wildlife Express to Conservation Station

✓ 1.2-mile railroad loop with midway visit to a large exhibit
✓ Medium-length walk from train to Conservation Station
✓ Takes about 45 minutes or as long as you wish

The Eastern Star Railway features the replica of a British steam engine, the type designed for use in India around the turn of the century. The train carries 250 passengers and the journey is not as interesting as the train and the station, but it does furnish a brief peek backstage at the Safari. Once, late in the day, we were also able to see quite a few animals along the way. Conservation Station, however, provides a fascinating look behind the scenes here at the Animal Kingdom. It also delivers this park's powerful message about global conservation. Exhibits include the Affection Section, a domestic animal petting zoo, and some engaging interactive experiences. There's a food wagon and even a shop here. All in all, interesting and engaging. Don't miss the baby elephant hand-wash at the Affection Section.

***Good,* an interesting exhibit and a must for children**
Tips: Save this one for when the more popular attractions are crowded. Don't miss one of the *Song of the Rainforest* sound booths.

The Restaurants of Africa

At the Tusker House, the counter-service menu features a surprisingly good prime rib, rotisserie chicken, and a wonderful roasted vegetable sandwich. Meals are all under $10, and while it is a good food value it is not fine dining. The Tusker House features a charming indoor seating area and several delightful patios and serves both lunch and dinner.

Inside the restaurant is the Kusafiri Coffee Shop & Bakery with its selection of pastries and desserts, including a deadly cinnamon bun. Kusafiri opens when the park does and is a good spot for an early snack. Also available here are espresso, cappuccino, and soft drinks. There's also a walk-up window.

There are other places to grab a quick bite here in Africa, including Tamu Tamu Refreshments with its soft-serve sundaes and frozen yogurt. Look for a particularly beautiful patio inside the fort ♥♥. The Harambe Fruit Market features juices, beverages, ice cream bars, and a variety of fresh fruit.

Looking to cool off with an afternoon cocktail? The open-air African Lounge opens at 4 P.M. and offers a variety of refreshing tropical beverages served in Harambe's shady bazaar. Late in the afternoon, a wonderful group plays African pop music. It's a memorable place to recap your day of adventure in Africa.

The Shops of Africa

Harambe's Mombasa Marketplace and Ziwani Traders' assortment of "native African" Disney merchandise is quite entertaining. There's also a variety of real African curios, from masks and carved creatures to unusual jewelry. This place is most certainly worth a visit and prices are reasonable. This shop is also the best place in the park for safari-themed apparel, commemorative Animal Kingdom merchandise, and African decor. Across the street is Duka La Filimu, Harambe's place for film and photo accessories.

Out of the Wild is located at Conservation Station. Its selection of conservation-themed apparel, soaps and lotions, tagua nut sculptures, and stuffed animals make it worth the trip.

The "Secret" Path ♥♥

Tucked away somewhere in the park is this short but wonderful treat. Not appearing on any map (we've even left it for *you* to find) and not marked by any sign, it embodies this park's romance of discovery. It is this park's version of a hidden Mickey. Hints: It is not paved and you'll have to ford a small stream on stones.

Asia

Only a small part of this land is open as this book goes to press. This re-creation will feature the exotic plants, creatures, and architecture of the rain forests of India, Thailand, and Indonesia. It promises to be the Animal Kingdom's most unusual land and will deliver a truly exotic experience. Construction is well underway, and from the shores of Safari Village we watch with eager anticipation.

Discovery River Boats at Upcountry Landing

- ✓ One-way boat ride to Safari Village
- ✓ Lasts about 10 minutes
- ✓ Lines can be long but move along quickly

Of course, this is the other half of the voyage you took from Safari Village. On the way back, you'll get a pretty good look at what's to come in Asia as well as a few other surprises.

GOOD, along with the onboard animal encounter, this ride is a pleasant journey

Flights of Wonder

✓ Live bird show
✓ Lasts 25 minutes
✓ Lines move to fill 700-seat Caravan Stage

The setting for this engaging show is the ruins of a crumbling outpost deep in the jungles of Asia. The story has to do with a student's search for treasure, but these beautiful winged performers don't need much of a plot to keep you riveted. Performances by jungle fowl, cranes, hawks, and 20 other species of birds are often amazing.

OUTSTANDING, a "bird-brained" show that's worth seeing
Tips: Get here before show time so that you can be sure you'll get in. There's no shade here at the Caravan Stage. Bring a hat and something to drink with you. Check your Adventurer's Guide for show times.

The Village of Anandapur (opens spring 1999)

Once you leave Safari Village, headed across the ornate, red-brick Asia bridge, you'll suddenly find yourselves deep in the rain forests of India. Here, along the road to the rural village of Anandapur, the jungle works to reclaim the ruins of ancient stone temples that lie along the roadside. It is not hard to imagine that you are being watched by a tiger lurking in the deep forest. The rhythmic melodies of this exotic land surround you as you arrive in the bustling little town.

Here in Anandapur, you'll find rice paddies, grazing Banteng, and the ruins of an ancient tiger shrine. A pair of monument towers are home for two rival gangs of gibbons, and their screeches and hoots reverberate through the streets. Around you are Anandapur's temples, pagodas, and winding paths that lead through fragrant gardens of jasmine and bamboo. This is about as exotic a landscape as Disney has ever created and more unusual than many of us could even imagine.

Tiger Rapids Run (opens spring 1999)

✓ White-water raft adventure (somewhat rough and jerky)
✓ Lines are bound to be long here

This promises to be one of this park's most popular adventures and will feature a thrilling raft ride that will pit out-of-control loggers against the wild creatures of the threatened rain forest. The six-person rafts zoom down the raging Chakranadi River, through a bamboo tunnel and into the white-water rapids, past ruined temples and into a blazing inferno. Saving the imperiled rain forest is the theme of this attraction, and it is delivered with excitement and realism.

Maharaja Jungle Trek (opens spring 1999)

✓ Self-guided walking tour

✓ Set your own pace

When you disembark the river rafts, you'll be able to continue on this walk to come face-to-face with animals that appear to be roaming free. The trek will take you across a wooden footbridge and into the dense jungles and the ancient ruins of the Maharaja's palace. Along the way, you'll encounter Bengal tigers, giant komodo dragons, fruit bats, and Malayan tapirs.

Food in Asia

Along the shores of the Discovery River, you'll find Mr. Kamil's Burger Grill, featuring broiled burgers and drinks. Not far away is the exotic-looking Drinkwallah, where you can cool off with an ice-cold Coke. As for the other restaurants of this land, nothing has yet been announced, but we would be very surprised to find anything "usual" about the coming cuisine of Asia.

Dinoland U.S.A.

The gateway to this whimsical land is the Oldengate Bridge, a reconstruction of the bones of a 40-foot brachiosaurus. Beyond is a world that celebrates the era when these huge creatures roamed the earth. From a thrill ride and a stage show to a pleasant walk through an unusual garden, there's a lot going on here. See the actual bones of the world's most complete *T. rex,* help some wacky paleontologists excavate fossils, or journey back 65 million years to race a deadly meteor. This land definitely delivers its share of theme park entertainment.

Wandering the streets of Dinoland is a zany band of nutty professor types and wacky grad-student paleontologists with their bizarre fossil-hunting gear. These humorous street performers are ready to interact with you and simply love to provide some added "dinomosphere" for your Dinoland photos.

The Boneyard

- ✓ Playground and exhibit
- ✓ Take as long as you like
- ✓ Lines rarely get long

Billed as a playground for "children of all ages," we found it to be just mostly for children. Still, there are quite a few interesting sights, and if your kids want to play here, it will likely have enough to keep you absorbed too. For children, there are slides, nets, and a maze made from dinosaur remains. The whole area is rubberized for safety and there are also a number of educational exhibits.

PRETTY GOOD, try this one when it isn't busy

Journey into Jungle Book

- ✓ 30-minute musical stage show
- ✓ Line moves to fill 1,500-seat theater

The tent-like Theater in the Wild features a song-filled live production based on the Rudyard Kipling story of Mowgli, a boy raised in the jungle by animals. As you would expect, the sets and costumes are sheer Disney magic, and both song and dance are good. Young children are sure to like this.

GOOD, but not quite as marvelous as some other Disney musical productions

Tip: Check Adventurer's Guide for show times.

1998 Dinosaur Jubilee

- ✓ Walk-through exhibit
- ✓ Take as long as you wish
- ✓ Expect no lines here

We hear rumors that this exhibit will end in the near future. We hope not. Featured here are both real and recast skeletal remains of some incredible prehistoric creatures. Some are very large. Even if you think you have no interest in this sort of thing, we suggest you give it a look-see.

OUTSTANDING, a core experience here in Dinoland

Tip: See this exhibit when most others are crowded. If you are visiting this area with small children, please keep them nearby and out of the exhibits.

Fossil Preparations Lab

- ✓ Exhibit
- ✓ Linger as long as you like

This exhibits features the actual remains of a 59-foot *Tyrannosaurus rex* named "Sue" that is part of a find purchased by Disney, McDonald's, and the Field Museum of Chicago. You'll be able to watch real experts prepare some of the bones from this, the most complete set of *T. rex* remains ever unearthed.

Countdown to Extinction

- ✓ A vehicular adventure (a bit rough)
- ✓ 10-minute preshow, ride lasts 3 1/2 minutes
- ✓ Expect long lines that move slowly

This ride features the same type of cars used on the Indiana Jones ride at Disneyland. Hop aboard one, and you'll time-trip back to the age of dinosaurs to bring back a live iguanodon before a gigantic asteroid crashes to earth. This ride is exciting, loud, and frequently quite dark. If you like this sort of attraction, here's one not to miss.

***WILD AND EXCITING,* great special effects**
Tip: **Head here first thing in the morning for short lines. Too intense for very young children or people with motion sickness.**

Cretaceous Trail

- ✓ Walk through a garden area
- ✓ Takes a few minutes
- ✓ Expect no lines here

This short loop passes through a garden of plants and creatures that have survived since prehistoric times. There are monkey puzzle trees, Norfolk pines, Chinese alligators, magnolias, and a variety of unusual palms and ferns. It also features one of the world's largest collection of cycads. Some of the plant life here is so unusual that we'd like to know what it is.

***INTERESTING,* with some nice places to sit and listen to the birds**

Dino Dining

Restaurantosaurus is a joint food venture of both Disney and McDonald's. Mornings here feature a better-than-average character breakfast (we suggest priority seating arrangements) served in a comfortable and well-themed dining room. After breakfast, you'll find such McDonald's fare as Happy Meals, fries, and Chicken McNuggets, plus some Disney sandwiches and salads. Restaurantosaurus has been created to resemble the enclave of structures that make up a paleontological dig site. The dining area features dinosaur skeletons and mounted dino heads. It is all interesting and amusing.

There are also several fast-food stands here in Dinoland. Dinoland Diner is a small trailer near the entrance that features pastries, beverages, and turkey legs, and DinoLand Snacks is a McDonald's French fries kiosk.

Shopping in Dinoland U.S.A.

Before this park opened, a cast member told us that this shop would offer the tackiest dinosaur toys in the world. Wrong. Chester's & Hester's Dinosaur Treasures is a cheesy-looking shop filled with wacky dino stuff all right, but much of it, particularly the foam creatures, is really neat. Rick picked up a terrific embroidered "Tee-rex" (or was it a Rex tee?) and we saw lots of other nice gifts and souvenirs.

Camp Minnie-Mickey

Before you even cross the bridge to this area, you'll see it's a place teeming with Disney characters. This delightful woodland retreat is where Mickey and Minnie come to vacation with their friends. No jungle here but instead stone bridges, split-rail fences, and a landscape that is more typical of the Adirondacks than of darkest Africa.

Much of this whimsical land is dedicated to character encounters, and you'll find both Mickey and Minnie here, dressed in safari gear. It's a photo op not to be missed. Other characters are everywhere: Chip and Dale, Donald, Goofy, Timon and Rafiki from *The Lion King,* and Baloo and King Louie from *The Jungle Book.* Look for the trails that will take you into shady, wooded areas and to the gazebos where you'll meet even more characters.

There's more here than just characters. Camp Minnie-Mickey's two stage shows offer some major entertainment.

Tip: This is the perfect opportunity to get some great photos of yourselves with the Disney characters, especially Minnie and Mickey. This may seem silly now, but you will thank us later.

Festival of the Lion King

✓ Live, musical stage show
✓ Lasts 25 minutes
✓ Lines move to fill 1,000-seat theater

This great show features outstanding musical performances, giant floats, unforgettable costumes, song, dance, and acrobatics. The large, circular theater comes alive with this, one of the all-time greatest Disney stage productions.

OUTSTANDING, don't miss this great show
Tips: Check your guidemap for show times and get to an early one. Afternoon shows are hard to get into.

Colors of the Wind: Friends from the Animal Forest

✓ Live musical show
✓ Lasts 12 minutes
✓ Line moves slowly to fill 350-seat theater

The shady Grandmother Willow's Grove is the setting for this entertaining drama that stars Pocahontas, Grandmother Willow, and a forest of wild creatures. Real turtles, rabbits, skunks, an armadillo, and a boa constrictor all have roles in this story of the search for "the great protector," the animal who alone can save the forest.

QUITE GOOD, try to catch it
Tips: Shows are frequent and if you are here with your children, you won't want to miss this. Check the Adventurer's Guide for show times.

Snack Shops of Camp Minnie-Mickey

There's no restaurants here, but you'll find a couple of cute snack offerings at Chip and Dale's Cookie Cabin and the Funnel Cake Cart.

ANIMAL KINGDOM DINING TIPS

- The Rainforest Cafe here begins serving breakfast at 6:30 A.M. Try having an early meal and being ready for park opening, usually 7 A.M. Priority seating is recommended for meals at this restaurant.
- The Restaurantosaurus features a better-than-average character breakfast from park opening to 10:30 A.M.
- The Tusker House is a surprisingly good value. Both the roasted vegetable sandwich and prime rib are quite good. In good weather, eat on one of the patios behind the restaurant.

- Try taking your food from the Flame Tree Barbecue down to one of the patios overlooking Discovery River. Our favorite is the Anteater pavilion. Take a look at all of them.

THE ROMANCE OF THE ANIMAL KINGDOM

- Gorilla Falls Exploration Trail: ♥♥
- A sunset walk in the Tree of Life Garden: ♥♥
- A late-afternoon refreshment at the Tamu Tamu patio: ♥♥
- Finding the "secret" path: ♥♥
- The last safari of the day: ♥
- The African music at African Lounge after 4 P.M.: ♥♥

Downtown Disney

This incredible place brings a whole new level of entertainment to Walt Disney World. With 120 acres of shops, clubs, theaters, and restaurants, it is larger than Disneyland and more fun than most cities we know. The Downtown area is Team Disney's answer to such places as Underground Atlanta and San Antonio's River Walk. By day or night (and especially by night), it's a place you will not want to miss.

When Team Disney created the new West Side Esplanade, they renamed the entire area and included in it Pleasure Island and the Village Marketplace, now known as the Downtown Disney Marketplace. Of course, the change has brought lots of new faces everywhere throughout Downtown and created an area as big and as exciting as a theme park. From the House of Blues and the Wolfgang Puck Cafe to DisneyQuest and the AMC 24 Theater Complex, Downtown really packs a punch. Shopping, entertainment, great dining, and dancing: Downtown Disney has it all. It is nothing short of a fifth theme park.

Getting to Downtown Disney

Transportation from the Disney resorts is a simple matter, with buses running all day long and into the wee hours. There are three bus stops in the Downtown area, one each at the Marketplace, Pleasure Island, and the West Side. Resort buses stop at all three in that order. If you are in one of the hotels on the nearby Hotel Plaza Boulevard, it's just a stroll away, or after 6 P.M. you can take a bus. There are also double-decker shuttle buses that make the trip from one Downtown area to another.

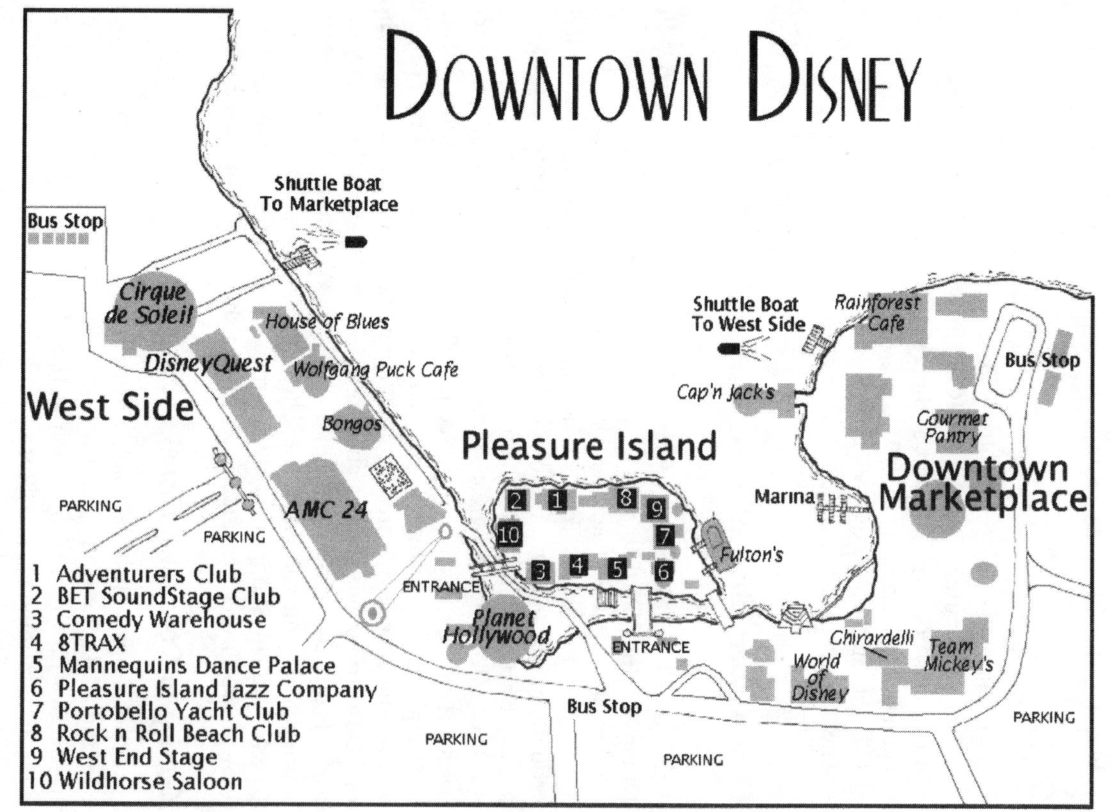
Downtown Disney
Shuttle Boat To Marketplace
Bus Stop
Cirque de Soleil
House of Blues
DisneyQuest
Wolfgang Puck Cafe
West Side
Bongos
AMC 24
PARKING
PARKING
Shuttle Boat To West Side
Rainforest Cafe
Bus Stop
Cap'n Jack's
Gourmet Pantry
Pleasure Island
Downtown Marketplace
Marina
Fulton's
ENTRANCE
Planet Hollywood
ENTRANCE
Chirardelli
World of Disney
Team Mickey's
Bus Stop
PARKING
PARKING
PARKING
1 Adventurers Club
2 BET SoundStage Club
3 Comedy Warehouse
4 8TRAX
5 Mannequins Dance Palace
6 Pleasure Island Jazz Company
7 Portobello Yacht Club
8 Rock n Roll Beach Club
9 West End Stage
10 Wildhorse Saloon

If you are driving in, there are large parking lots in all Downtown areas, but as the evening wears on, they become quite full and parking might become difficult. There is valet parking from 5:30 P.M. to 2 A.M. at both Pleasure Island and the West Side and costs $6 plus gratuity.

If you're staying at Old Key West, Port Orleans, or Dixie Landings, there's a boat that makes the trip along the beautiful Lake Buena Vista canals, 10:30 A.M. to 11:30 P.M. It is convenient and most pleasant.

The Areas of Downtown Disney

The Downtown Disney Marketplace, Pleasure Island, and the West Side Esplanade are the three lakeside areas of Downtown Disney. Only Pleasure Island charges admission (and only after 7 P.M.), and if you are enjoying an All-in-One Hopper or Length of Stay Pass, you're in. All three areas are connected by pleasant walkways and bridges and there is also a double-decker shuttle that makes the trip. There's even a water taxi that runs from Cap'n Jack's in the Marketplace to the House of Blues on the West Side (and back) from 6:30 P.M. to 12:30 A.M. It's a pleasant trip, but then again, so is the walk.

DOWNTOWN DISNEY TIPS

- Don't forget to pick up a Downtown Disney guidemap and read it over before you go. Like the theme park guidemaps, it will tell you about entertainment and special events for the times of your visit.
- There's lots going on during the day: shopping, restaurants, and movies; but if you're out for clubs and entertainment, make your Downtown Disney visit after dark. The shops at the Marketplace open at 9:30 A.M. and those on the West Side, 10:30 A.M.
- Tickets for House of Blues concerts can be purchased through the box office at HOB at (407) 934-2583. Shows with big names almost always sell out in advance. We suggest you call one month ahead to find out what's happening during your visit and to purchase tickets.
- Tickets for special Wildhorse Saloon concerts should be purchased in advance by calling (407) 827-WILD (9453).
- Priority seating arrangements for the restaurants of Downtown can be made through Disney Dining. Dial 55 on your resort phone or (407) WDW-DINE (939-3463).
- The restaurants of Downtown Disney can get very crowded in the evening hours. A good alternative is to enjoy them at lunch time or during the afternoon.

- If you're heading out for the nightlife and partying at Downtown Disney, use a designated driver: take the bus.

NEW *The West Side Esplanade*

This is the largest part of Downtown Disney and one of our favorite Disney destinations. There's no admission to this dazzling lakeside avenue of shops, theaters, fine dining, and nightclubs. And as if all that isn't enough, there's the high-tech, interactive entertainment of DisneyQuest and the avant-garde acrobatics of Cirque du Soleil (due to open in late 1998). The West Side leaves us wondering just how much better can Disney get?

For us, the West Side is Disney's premier evening destination. From dining and shopping to live entertainment, there's so much here that you might have to visit more than once to satisfy your curiosity. But there's a lot going on here during the day too, and if you are mostly interested in food and shopping, know that the restaurants here are infinitely less crowded in the afternoon. Expect lunch menus to be a bit more abbreviated and prices to be bit lower than in the evening, too. Shops here open at 10:30 A.M., and timing can be right for a few hours of browsing, a memorable lunch, and a matinee at the AMC cinemas. Or come early and spend the entire day playing at DisneyQuest. One thing is for sure about the West Side: by night or by day, you'll want to see it.

NEW DisneyQuest

Its creators call it a "theme park in a box," and it is so unique and so exciting that DisneyQuest has been given a completely new Mouse icon. It's called the "Hurricane Mickey," and this dynamic, swirling, mouse-in-motion makes the perfect symbol for this entirely original form of entertainment. DisneyQuest combines the storytelling of Disney with the latest in interactive, computer technologies. Our preview visit here allowed us to embark on adventures that actually let us become a part of the story and to determine its outcome. The real bottom line for us was that this place was incredibly fun—more fun than we would have thought possible. DisneyQuest is going to knock your socks off. One of the greatest things about it is that so much of it will have families and couples playing together. DisneyQuest will be a monster hit and the only question for us is: how are they going to handle all the people?

Yes, the five-story, 100,000-square-foot DisneyQuest really *is* a theme park in a box. A very large box.

Our DisneyQuest adventure began with a Cybrolator ride to the Ventureport, the hub of DisneyQuest. From here, we could enter any of its four adventure areas: the Create Zone, the Explore Zone, the Score Zone, and the Replay Zone. Our guide explained them all, and we headed off for an afternoon of excitement.

The **Create Zone** is an Imagineering studio where powerful computers provide the means for making the imaginary come true.

CyberSpace Mountain

✓ Design and ride your own roller coaster

✓ A super thrill ride: not for those with motion sickness!

This "attraction" provided a computer program that allowed us to design our own roller coaster, making it as wild and as fast as we wanted. After the creation phase, we were asked to empty our pockets before we boarded the 360-degree pitch-and-roll simulator to experience the ride we had created. It made Star Tours seem like Cinderella's Carousel. It's like nothing we've ever experienced.

***ON A 0–10 SCALE: GIVE THIS ONE A 15;* our favorite**

Tip: Skip the tamer coasters and go for the #5.

The Animation Academy

✓ A computer-aided animation experience

With the help of a live Disney artist, learn how to create an animated character.

***FUN BUT NOT EXCITIN;* save this one for later**

Magic Mirror

✓ Computer "morphing" station

Let the computer take a picture of your face, then make it into whatever you want. Afterwards, print it up and keep the picture.

DEFINITELY FUN

Living Easels

✓ Computer art program

Create your very own work of art, then take a full-color original home.

SOME FUN SPECIAL EFFECTS HERE but limited to preprogrammed art; kids will love it

Sid's Create-a-Toy

✓ Computer station creation

Gather up a handful of toy parts on-screen and design your own plaything. Drop by the counter to pick up the parts and assemble it at home later.

KIDS WILL LOVE THIS ONE

The **Explore Zone** is a place of virtual adventure where time knows no bounds and anything is possible.

Virtual Jungle Cruise

✓ A virtual, time-travel raft voyage (bumpy ride; takes some energy)
✓ Four-man raft ride, takes about 5 minutes

Hop aboard a real rubber raft and time-trip to the age of dinosaurs to navigate a complicate network of rivers, rapids, falls, beasts, and other "dangers." Paddling on this adventure will actually steer the boat. We did this one with some friends, and it was a riot.

GREAT, DON'T MISS THIS ONE-OF-A-KIND ADVENTURE

Treasures of the Incas

✓ Radio-controlled cars with video cameras
✓ A treasure hunt with prizes
✓ Lasts about 10 minutes

This hunt for hidden treasures in an Incan tomb goes on below a glass floor. It's interesting to watch and more fascinating to play.

FUN AND CHALLENGING and prize credits too

Aladdin's Magic Carpet Ride

✓ A virtual flight experience
✓ Lasts about 5 minutes

Put on the virtual reality helmet and take a flight on a magic carpet in search of gems and a genie's lamp. This is one of DisneyQuest's best.

AN AMAZING SIMULATION OF FLIGHT; don't miss this one

Hercules in the Underworld

✓ A 3-D interactive adventure

Become the friends of Hercules and battle Hades for thunderbolts in this riotous adventure.

FAST AND FURIOUS FUN; don't miss it

The **Score Zone** is the place to go for competition. Rack up the points against villains in the "attractions" or play one of the dozens of state-of-the-art arcade games in the Game Pit, the Sports Arena, or the Underground. From the Daytona USA Races to hand-to-hand combat, this place has it all. It would take days to play all the games here.

Ride the Comix!

✓ A space flight simulator and battle game
✓ Six players involved aboard a space vehicle

Go sword-to-sword against a world of 3-D comic book villains in a virtual space environment. The ultimate virtual combat experience.

MAKES HOME VIDEO GAMES OBSOLETE; literally and figuratively a blast

Mighty Ducks Pinball Slam

✓ A body action game

A pinball simulator: you're the ball! Play on life-size "joy sticks" and compete against each other to score goals. A work out.

MUCH MORE FUN THAN WE EXPECTED; another winner

Invasion! An Alien Encounter

✓ Cyber shoot-em-up in a space pod
✓ Four participants, lasts about 5 minutes

Board the planetary walker to rescue colonists and do battle on an alien landscape. One driver, three gunners. Cool.

NEAT, even better a second or third time

The **Replay Zone** brings back dozens of games of the past, and some of them feature a new attitude. The areas here are the Midway on the Moon and the Game Graveyard. There's enough stuff here to keep you busy for hours.

Buzz Lightyear's AstroBlaster

✓ Two-person bumper car game
✓ Lasts about 5 minutes

This is bumper cars with an attitude. The driver guides the car to suck up balls on the floor, and the gunner shoots them at other cars with hilarious results.

***WILD FUN;* don't miss this one either!**

The Cheesecake Factory Express at DisneyQuest

We've always loved the Cheesecake Factory and have always thought that it would really fit in here at Disney. Well, here it is. There will be two food areas at DisneyQuest, and both will be run by this wonderful restaurant company.

FoodQuest will feature a self-service offering of many of the most popular dishes from the Cheesecake Factory. From the famous signature salads such as the wonderful Chinese Chicken or Barbecue Ranch Salads to Tex-Mex egg rolls, we can promise you that this place will be good.

The Wonderland Cafe will showcase the company's 50 cheesecakes as well as espresso drinks, smoothies, gourmet coffees, and ice cream desserts. The Cafe will entertain guests with Wonderland Web Adventures while they eat. This will put diners right in front of live Internet terminals from which they can explore the Web or send postcards to friends back home.

TIPS FOR DISNEYQUEST

- This is not a video arcade. Most of the big "rides" here involve two or more people. This makes DisneyQuest an adventure that the whole family can do *together*. Attractions such as Buzz Lightyear's AstroBlaster, CyberSpace Mountain, and Virtual Jungle Cruise are only a few of the attractions that seem perfect for couples.
- Get there early. This place is going to be immensely popular.
- Many of the rides are fun, but they are even more fun the second or third time around, when you've learned the rules of the game and begin to get good at playing. This is especially true for the Score Zone games.
- There are a number of games that provide credits for winning. At the end of the day, turn in your credits for prizes.

DisneyQuest: How It Works

Admission to DisneyQuest is done on a "play for pay" basis, which is to say that each game or attraction has its own cost. The "adventures," such as Ride the Comix! or the Virtual Jungle Cruise, cost between 12 and 22 "play credits" each. For example, it costs 22 credits to both design and ride a coaster at CyberSpace Mountain. Games, such as those found in Replay Zone or Game Pit cost around five play credits each.

Guests purchase "stored value cards," each worth a certain number of play credits. There are four types of admission cards available: Quest 20, Quest 60, Quest 90, and the Ultimate Quest. For $7, Quest 20 provides 20 play credits. Quest 60 costs $15 and gives 60 credits, and Quest 90, at a cost of $20, supplies 90 play credits. The Ultimate Quest card cost $40 and provides three days of 100 credits per day. It is valid for 10 days from the date of purchase, and cardholders cannot use more than 100 credits on any of the three days. We have been told that more credits may be purchased inside of DisneyQuest.

AMC 24 Theaters

This cinema complex is state-of-the-art in every way, and with this many screens, there's bound to be something that interests you. There are 16 theaters here with comfortable, stadium-style seating and "love seats" with high backs and arm rests that lift up. Another eight auditoriums feature extra-wide theater rocker seats, and there's even two auditoriums with balconies. Every theater at the AMC has digital sound, and just about every recent release is on-screen here. For information and ticket reservation, call (407) 298-4488.

NEW Cirque de Soleil (opens late 1998)

Not quite a circus and not really a ballet, this mesmerizing performance is a little of both and a lot of acrobatics, original music, and special effects. We've heard it described as an "avant-garde circus," but after seeing a sample of this unique performance, we know now how impossible it is to describe.

The 1,650-seat Cirque de Soleil theater is itself a work of art, and this group is absolutely electrifying. Two times daily and five days a week, this 72-member troupe will take to the custom-designed stage to perform their magical 90-minute show. Shows take place Sundays at 2:30 and 5:30 P.M. and Wednesdays through Saturdays at 5:30 and 8:30 P.M. Prices are $56.50 general and $44.20 ages 3–9, tax not included. For tickets, call (407) 939-7600

Also located in this unique theater will be the Cirque du Soleil Boutique, which will feature clothing based on the exciting costumes of the performers.

Tip: This performance is something you'll not want to miss. Expect tickets to go quickly.

NEW Virgin Megastore

This giant store features 300 CD listening stations and the best collection of music we can remember seeing. We strolled in here one afternoon and after several hours of listening had to force ourselves to move on. There's also 20 video/laser viewing stations for previewing movies. The megastore sells books and software and occasionally even features big-name stars on a hydraulic stage over the store's main entrance. For a record store, this place sure has a lot of entertainment.

On the second floor, there's even a delightful espresso bar that features the coffee of Seattle's Torrefazione Italia and a selection of extravagant desserts and pastries.

Tip: The coffee beans are sold by the pound.

NEW House of Blues

Amidst all the glitz and glitter of Downtown Disney, this place looks pretty shabby. Its rusty old water tank towers over the ramshackle buildings, while inside, the House of Blues (HOB) more resembles a museum of African American folk art. Everything here is decorated, and we mean *everything*. More than just a club, HOB serves up both soulful blues and a mouthwatering Mississippi Delta cuisine. And it isn't just another theme restaurant. Behind the weathered, roadhouse exterior and beyond its tantalizing menu, HOB also manages to be a concert hall for all the big names in blues, R&B, and swing. There's even a store here that sells blues CDs and a line of House of Blues logo clothing and merchandise. (For our review of the House of Blues restaurant, see Chapter 6.)

One of our favorite places at Disney is right here at the House of Blues. We're talking about the Voodoo Garden ♥♥♥. This lovely area is behind the restaurant and overlooks the lake. At night, it is quiet, romantic, and a little slice of the Big Easy. The Voodoo Garden features both a porch where you can order food and a comfortable garden area for drinks and appetizers. We hope that this marvelous place remains as undiscovered as it is now. Look for it and look in the back of this book for our coupon, good for a free appetizer at the Voodoo Garden.

House of Blues Concert Hall Virtually every night there's a concert. More than just a few times a month, you're likely to find a performer of star magnitude. During one of our recent visits, one concert featured Aretha Franklin and another Ziggy Marley, and yet another John Mayall. The next week we managed to catch Big Bad Voodoo Daddy, our favorite swing band from the West Coast. Know that most concerts here get crowded, especially on weekends and especially with big-name performers. To avoid arriving at Disney only to discover that a concert you'd like to attend is sold out, we suggest that you call the House of Blues ticket office to find out who's playing during your visit. You can then purchase tickets over the phone. Try calling a month before your visit. The box office number is (407) 934-BLUE (2583).

The HOB Gospel Brunch Here's something not to miss. Each Sunday, HOB offers a down-home brunch buffet featuring jambalaya, boiled shrimp, grits, roast beef, ham, and a variety of breakfast dishes. It's all tasty home-style cookin'. Afterwards, roll up your sleeves for an hour of live gospel music. Now this is a buffet with character! It's also another one of HOB's popular events, and if you are interested (and we recommend it), call the box office at least a week in advance to book your tickets. There are three brunches each Sunday, at 10:45 A.M., 1 P.M., and 3 P.M. Cost is $23.99 per adult and $11.95 for children aged 4 to 12. Kids aged 3 and under are free.

NEW Bongos Cuban Cafe

Owned by superstar Gloria Estefan, this dazzling nightclub brings to Disney the excitement of Miami's Southbeach and the sizzle and spice of cuisine Cubano. The three-story Bongos pineapple has become the symbol for the excitement of the entire West Side. Inside, you will find a tropical decor that brings to mind the era of splashy nightspots, when the tango and cha-cha reigned supreme. Featured here Wednesdays through Sundays are the hot Latin rhythms of live bands, and besides being a supper club, this place is a dance club, too. This is a fun place to spend the evening eating, dancing, and romancing. For our review of the food at Bongos, see Chapter 6.

NEW Wolfgang Puck Cafe

This stylish place is really four restaurants in one. On the avenue is the sidewalk seating of the Wolfgang Puck Express. Drop in here to enjoy a quick bite of pizza, salad, or pasta. Inside, enjoy B's Bar (and some of the best sushi in town) or the downstairs cafe with its offerings of pizzas, salads, and pasta entrees. In the evening, take a trip upstairs to the elegant dining room for the California cuisine that has made Wolfgang Puck one of the world's most renowned chefs. Any of these "restaurants" is worth the trip. We have never been disappointed by a single thing we've eaten here. For our review and more information about the Wolfgang Puck Cafe, see Chapter 6.

Planet Hollywood

This well-known restaurant is really something to look at, both inside and out. Inside you'll find some of the world's most valuable movie and television memorabilia. The interesting menu features unusual pastas, pizzas, a variety of vegetarian offerings, and Arnold Schwarzenegger's mother's apple strudel. For our review, more information, and dining tips, see Chapter 6.

NEW Forty Thirst Street

This beverage "restaurant" is owned by the Joffrey Coffee Company, the same outfit that serves up great brew along the BoardWalk, at the Yacht and Beach Clubs, and at the entrances to both Epcot and Disney–MGM Studios. The coffee here is roasted daily and beans are available for purchase "within two minutes of roasting." Besides some terrific coffee and espresso drinks, both hot and cold, Forty Thirst Street has an outstanding selection of fat-free smoothies and juice chillers.

NEW Hoypoloi

This store seems more like an art gallery to us, probably because of the unusual nature of the stuff sold here. Much of it is created by artisans from around the U.S., and the rest includes unique furniture, light sculptures, and decorative accessories. The water, plants, incense, and the Zen-like feeling of this place makes it a shop you'll want to see.

NEW Starabilias

Here's another place not to miss. Starabilias features over 1,000 pieces of original memorabilia from film, music, and just about everything. Browsing among the autographed photos and real Hollywood costumes is fun, but what we like best is the large collection of restored coin-operated machines and antique furniture. There's much more, and all of it is ridiculously expensive but great to look at. Starabilias also features its own line of nostalgic gift and novelty items.

NEW Magnetron

This is heaven for refrigerator magnet lovers. The 20,000 magnets here sing, dance, light up, and glow in the dark. Why, they even sell themselves.

NEW The Guitar Gallery

This shop reminds us of the magnet store, only it's all guitars, and some of them are even famous. There's more here too, including guitar accessories, books, videos, and musically themed clothing. Guitar prices range from $199 to $25,000, but not to worry. If you're staying at a Disney resort, the Guitar Gallery will let you charge it to your room.

NEW Other Shops of the West Side

There are other shops here, and you might find some of them suit your interests. All Star Gear peddles the merchandise of its mother company, the All-Star Cafe. Ditto for the Wildhorse Store and the Planet Hollywood Store.

The Candy Cauldron features a show kitchen, more than 200 delectable sweets, and a dungeon atmosphere, while Sosa Family Cigars offers an assortment of premium cigars and humidors in a re-creation of the living room of founding father Don Juan Sosa Acosta. (Honest, we're not making this stuff up!)

Opening in late 1998 will be the Copperfield Magic Underground: The Store. It promises to offer a variety of amazing magic tricks for beginners and experienced magicians, plus signature clothing and "international oddities."

The Downtown Disney Marketplace

Whether you simply love to shop or are looking for a few gifts or souvenirs, you'll want to see this lovely lakeside village. With some 15 interesting shops, a variety of restaurants, and a marina of rental boats, a visit here during the day or in the evening is worth the trip.

Shopping at the Marketplace

Following are descriptions of some of our favorite shops here at the Downtown Disney Marketplace.

The World of Disney No trip to Walt Disney World would be complete without a visit to this, the largest and best Disney store on the planet. Besides an offering of decidedly upscale merchandise, this Disney department store itself is worth seeing. From toys and jewelry to sleepwear and sweatshirts, this place is full of great stuff.

The Art of Disney This gallery of one-of-a-kind Disney art features everything from animation cels to Mouse furniture. Don't miss it.

NEW **Disney at Home** This new shop features a collection of unique character items for bedroom and bath. Some of this is real "Hidden Mickey" kind of stuff and quite nice too. One of our favorites.

Team Mickey's Athletic Club The attraction here is sports clothing featuring the entire spectrum of Disney characters. From golf bags to soccer shirts, you're bound to find at least a few things here to bring home.

Gourmet Pantry This place is home to a bakery, deli, wine cellar, and a shop that's brimming with Disney character culinary gadgets, housewares, and cookbooks. It is also a good place to pick up a few basic grocery items such as milk, cereal, and bread or a picnic lunch.

Disney's Days of Christmas This wonderful shop features some really nice Christmas ornaments and decorations. This is not just character stuff; you'll also find some beautiful non-Disney Christmas things here as well.

2R's Reading and Riting A nice little book and card shop with some especially nice retro-Mickey cards. There's also Disney software and stationery.

There are other stores you'll want to browse as well. Summer Sands, Resortwear Unlimited (for women), and Harrington Bay Clothiers (for men) feature collections of stylish clothing and accessories. Disney toys can be found at the Captain's Tower, Pooh Corner, Toys Fantastic, and the amazing LEGO Imagination Center. Don't miss the full-size LEGO creations in and around the lake. We've never found Eurospain and its crystal collectibles to be our kind of store (but then again, this isn't the kind of stuff people who live on a boat should be collecting). Also featured here are glassblowing and custom engraving.

Food and Fun at the Marketplace

Whether you're here during the day or in the evening, you'll find lots of good places to eat or to snack. You'll also find some recreation here as well as live entertainment.

Rainforest Cafe This is a wild place to eat and offers a large menu of exciting dishes. The only downside is that it gets extremely busy and does not take reservations. Try an early or a midafternoon lunch. The cafe is open from 10:30 A.M. to 11 P.M.

Cap'n Jack's Oyster Bar This pleasant little restaurant is almost more of a bar than an eatery. It is right on the water here in the Marketplace and features a nautical ambience and small menu. Cap'n Jack's is open from 11:30 A.M. to 10:30 P.M.

NEW **Wolfgang Puck Express** Though a bit pricey for fast food, this counter-service cafe offers some really tasty items. The pizza and gazpacho are memorable. Probably the best fast food we've ever had. The Express is open from 11 A.M. to 11 P.M.

NEW **Ghirardelli Soda Fountain and Chocolate Shop** We'll admit it: it's tough for us to even walk by without stopping in for one of its wonderful ice cream creations. Our excuse for working our way through the entire menu is "research." Let yours be "vacation." Take your chocolate masterpiece over to the nice sitting area by the lake.

NEW **McDonald's: Ronald's Fun House** This is a showcase McDonald's, designed especially for Disney. Why, it's like being *inside* a great big Happy Meal! The cuisine here is the usual McDonald's fare. It's open from 8:30 A.M. to 3 A.M.

Gourmet Pantry The deli and bakery here offer a tasty selection of sandwiches, salads, and baked goods. There's even a pleasant outdoor patio with tables and chairs.

All around the Marketplace you'll also find a variety of vendor carts offering beverages and snacks. For our reviews of the Rainforest Cafe, Cap'n Jack's Oyster Bar, and Wolfgang Puck Express, see Chapter 6.

Studio M If you want to have a professional photo of yourselves with Mickey, he's right here for a $30 portfolio of prints. Other photo opportunities include having your picture computer-enhanced with Disney characters. There's also robot-decorated apparel. This one you'd better see for yourselves.

The Dock Stage Check the board here or the Marketplace Guest Services to see what performances and special events are happening here. During the holidays, this stage features a Christmas pageant.

Cap'n Jack's Marina Here you'll find rental "water mice," pontoon boats, and canopy boats. Also offered is a variety of fishing excursions; for more information, see Chapter 7 or call (407) 828-2204.

Pleasure Island

This island of nightclubs comes alive nightly from 7 P.M. to 2 A.M. and it is the drumbeat of Downtown Disney. It is also the only part of Downtown that charges admission, and visitors here must be 18 years of age or older or be accompanied by an adult. Besides seven exciting clubs, Pleasure Island (PI) features restaurants, shops, a zany carnival midway, street entertainment, and a New Year's Eve fireworks celebration every night of the year. It is nothing less than a small theme park, and its theme is adult, nighttime entertainment.

Admission

Admission is $19 and is included in both All-in-One Hopper and Length of Stay Passes as well as the Premium Annual Pass. There is also a Pleasure Island Annual Pass.

Warning

It is worth mentioning that this place is loud. There is music everywhere, in the clubs and in the streets, and most of it is at excessive volumes. For the life of us, we can't understand why Disney does sound in such a big way, but our theory is that the sound engineers have simply blown out their eardrums.

Several of the clubs offer entertainment that will not assault your ears, and we'll mark those with an ear-friendly ♫. If Pleasure Island doesn't sound like your cup of tea, you'll find lots to do in the other areas of Downtown Disney where there is no admission charge. If you are looking for an exciting evening out, one filled with bright lights, live bands, loud music, and rowdy fun, then Pleasure Island may well become a nightly part of your Disney vacation.

NEW Wildhorse Saloon

We love the motto of this, the newest club on Pleasure Island: "The most fun you can have with your boots on." The Wildhorse Saloon features live country music and dance, and even if this is not your favorite kind of entertainment, we'd suggest that you not write it off. The music is good and the line dancing, fun. There are resident dance instructors teaching the hottest steps. The saloon also features a good American barbecue dinner with such signature offerings as applewood-smoked ribs, barbecued salmon, and bourbon baked beans.

The Wildhorse has been built for Disney from the ground up, and it features a supper club atmosphere, themed bars, varnished wood dance floor, and a state-of-the-art performance stage. This is a small club, and it will feature outstanding country-and-western groups here each night as well as scheduled concerts by the biggest names in country music. For information regarding concerts during your vacation here at Disney or to purchase tickets, call (407) 827-9453. For our take on the eating side of this club, see Chapter 6.

Rock n Roll Beach Club

Before we discovered swing dancing, we used to come here to dance to the music of the '60s and '70s. With lights and special effects, the melodies here more reflects our times: the Beatles, the Rolling Stones, and other familiar sounds. Once the music gets cranked up, it won't take you long to get into dancing and singing along. The bands featured here always seem good, both instrumentally and vocally, and the songs they play really take us back. The full-service bar also offers pizza, subs, and a small selection of sandwiches.

Pleasure Island Jazz Company

This is a cozy club with small tables gathered around a stage that features good jazz. It's the best place here at PI if you are looking for good entertainment and a light meal or snack. Appetizer-size dishes, such as crab cakes, quesadillas, and salads, and a few rich desserts along with some good jazz makes this one of our favorite Pleasure Island destinations.

The Adventurer's Club

This is typically "Disney," which means it's unique and entertaining. We've never seen a club like this and we expect you haven't either. Masquerading as a stuffy, British gentleman's club of the 1920s, the Adventurer's Club offers instead a wacky troupe of actors who perform and interact with guests throughout the evening and throughout the zany rooms of this club. Be sure to pick up a schedule card when you enter so that you'll be able to keep up with all the entertainment as it moves from the Mask Room to the Library and so forth. There's a full-service bar and a small selection of light foods. This place is definitely worth a look, but be careful, we wandered in here on our first visit and stayed until 1:30 in the morning.

The Comedy Warehouse

This is one of the island's most popular clubs and features improvisational and stand-up comics. Of course, the humor is clean and harmless; vulgarities are not part of this or any other Disney show. Occasionally, a well-known comic may appear, in which case an additional admission may be charged. Five shows are offered here nightly, and long lines are a regular occurrence.

Tip: Try an early show.

NEW BET SoundStage Club

This stylish club is owned and operated by Black Entertainment Television. The two-story club includes a wraparound balcony, large dance floor, and state-of-the-art multimedia display. The club showcases the best of jazz, rhythm and blues, soul, and hip-hop with weekly live performances, an interactive deejay, BET dancers, and an "on-air" host. Offerings include Caribbean-style appetizers and exotic specialty drinks.

Mannequins Dance Palace

Mannequins is the only club on the island that requires patrons to be 21 years of age or older. The main dance floor is a huge turntable, and the decorative mannequins are all garbed in strange attire. All this and the contemporary music make this *the* place for the younger crowd.

8Trax

The deejay here plays the music of the '70s. We're not sure what we were listening to back then, but it wasn't this stuff. Still, the sound system is impressive, and the ambience, multilevel dance floor, and special effects are futuristic. Besides a full-service bar, you'll find burgers, fries, and sandwiches.

The Nightly New Year's Eve Party at the West End Stage

This stage features a nightly live band. The music is good and people are dancing in the street. This is the place to be for the countdown to the nightly New Year's Eve Celebration, which includes dancers, special effects, fireworks, and confetti cannons. It alone is nearly worth the price of admission to PI. Be sure to find out what time this will happen, because "midnight" here is not always at midnight.

Dining at Pleasure Island

As we've mentioned, you'll find something to eat at virtually every club. Much of it is little more than snack food, however. Our favorites for real food are the Jazz Club and the Wildhorse Saloon. There are also two very good restaurants here at Pleasure Island. We would recommend either the northern Italian cuisine of Portobello Yacht Club or Fulton's Crab House. For our reviews of both, see Chapter 6.

If you're looking for a quick bite or a pretty good sandwich, try the Missing Link Sausage Company. There is also a variety of snack and beverage vendors and D-Zertz, with its ice creams, frozen yogurt, and specialty coffees.

The Shops of Pleasure Island

The island offers a variety of stores, and there's some interesting stuff here. Check out Avigator's Supply and Changing Attitudes for men's and women's fashions, DTV and Island Depot for Disney merchandise, and Music Legends and Reel Finds for music and film memorabilia. Our favorite is Suspended Animation, which features an outstanding collection of Disney animation cels and limited-edition lithographs. Another amusing stop would be SuperStar Studios, where you can drop in to have your picture printed on the "cover" of the magazine of your choice. If only fame were this easy! It's a great souvenir.

The Other Walt Disney World Attractions

The Disney Institute

It's true that one of us wasn't very excited about this place. The very name "Institute" and such marketing catchphrases as "challenge," "self-discovery," "learning activity," and "program" were a turnoff. So, we both went (one of us reluctantly) and discovered what, oddly, is one of the Institute's best kept secrets: this place is fun. A lot of fun.

The Institute offers what it calls "Discovery Vacations." Guests select from a variety of programs (there's that word again!) that offer activities such as computer animation, sports, gardening, and culinary arts. A few days after we arrived, we began to see the Institute for what it really is: another theme park, one that allows guests to get their hands on the Disney magic, to play with it and to make a bit of it themselves.

If you visit the Institute, don't come expecting to sit in classrooms listening to lectures. We're talking hands-on stuff here, and everything has been Imagineered to get your creative juices flowing. Ready for a little golf? Prepare for play on a championship PGA course in a learning experience designed by Gary Player. Interested in computer animation? A powerful computer awaits you, loaded with the latest in 3-D software. Looking to try your hand at some of Disney's culinary wizardry? Join the famous chefs of the Institute in their state-of-the-art kitchens, and slice, stir, and sauté to your heart's delight. There's more: wine tasting, canoe adventures, and personal fitness. Let the Institute be your key to unlocking the mysteries and magic that have made Disney World the playground of the world.

Institute Special Events Programs

Throughout the year, the Institute also features special events programs that focus on popular interests, including the culinary arts, photography, animation, and gardening. These four-day, in-depth programs feature world-renowned experts and the usual Institute hands-on experiences. During a recent visit, the Institute was offering the Healthy Cooking and Lifestyle Event. It featured cooking workshops with Graham Kerr, wine and food tastings with cookbook author and restaurateur John Ash, and programs with Karen Voight, celebrity fitness guru. Another event on the horizon was a Disney photo safari with a panel of world-renowned photographers. These package programs are all four days in length and include accommodations and meals. Package prices begin at around $750, and a discount is offered for early booking. For information, call (800) 282-9282.

The Institute's Disney Day Camp for Kids

If you're wondering about coming here with a child, you'll want to know that the Institute provides a number of activities for children ages 7 through 15. These "discovery adventures" will bring your child right into all the Disney magic. All are included in your Institute package. For details and days of programs, see Chapter 1, Camp Disney Youth Discoveries.

The Seasons Dining Performance Package There are visiting artists in-residence at the Institute during the year, most frequently during special events. An evening performance or interaction is usually scheduled, and the Institute offers a dinner at Seasons Dining Room and the evening event in a package for around $33. This often means a concert or performing artist and is a particularly pleasant way to spend the evening. Call (407) WDW-DINE (939-3463) and ask for the Seasons Dining Performance Package.

The Spa at the Disney Institute

To balance all of this activity, there is the Spa at the Institute. With whirlpool tubs, steam rooms, and saunas, this luxurious and state-of-the-art spa offers an array of personal treatments and therapies that will get you both in a relaxed and sensual mood. Such temptations as aromatherapy and hydrotherapy, body wraps, facials, and massages of every sort are just a few of the spa's offerings. And the spa is not just for women. Our time here was sublime, and an afternoon of treatments left us *both* enjoying a sensuality that lasted our entire visit. For more information about the Spa at the Institute, see Chapter 7.

The Institute: Where and What

The Institute is located on 90 beautiful acres adjacent to the Buena Vista Golf Course and across the lake from Downtown Disney. Its studios, performance center, Amphitheater on the Green, cinema, and fitness center more resemble a small town than Disney World. Barns, mills, porches, and a town square all work to enhance this rural ambience. Dotted with lakes and landscaped in lush Disney fashion, the Institute offers a charm and sense of tranquillity simply not found elsewhere at Walt Disney World.

Besides atmosphere, the Institute features some impressive facilities. "State of the art" is pretty commonplace here and can describe any one of a dozen Institute areas: the performing arts or fitness centers, the closed-circuit television and radio stations, the 18-hole championship golf course, lighted hydro-grid tennis courts, six swimming pools, or full-service spa. All have been created to meet Team Disney's relentless pursuit of perfection.

The Institute is home to two eateries: Season's Dining Room and Reflections, a lakeside coffee and sandwich shop. Season's sunny and bright dining area is centrally located and features three meals daily. For more details about Season's, see Chapter 6. Reflections is located near the bungalows and features an interesting selection of gourmet coffees, quality baked goods and pastries, and sandwiches. The relaxing poolside patio is a place where you'll want to spend time.

Accommodations at the Disney Institute

As Institute guests, you'll stay in one of the accommodations of the Villas at the Disney Institute, either the bungalows or the townhouses. For more details and descriptions of these lodgings, see the Chapter 2.

How It All Works

So you like the Institute and want to be part of the fun. What next? There are two basic ways to participate. You can be either a day guest or an Institute guest. For $69 per person, day visitors get up to two programs, access to the Sports and Fitness Center, and an evening performance. Anyone can be a day guest, and reservations can be made up to two weeks in advance.

Institute guests stay at the Institute and can choose from the Basic or World Choice plans. The Basic plan includes accommodations at the Institute and Institute programs and entertainment for your length of stay as well as daily use of the Sports and Fitness Center. An additional $43 per night provides unlimited admission to all Disney attractions.

1999 Basic Plan Rates (three nights, per person/double occupancy)

Accommodation	Regular Season	Peak Season	Value Season
Bungalow	$570	$597	$529
One-bedroom townhouse	$614	$631	$590
Two-bedroom townhouse	$752	$777	$718
Additional person	$297	$297	$297
Additional nights:			
Bungalow	$179	$199	$190
One-bedroom townhouse	$196	$210	$204
Two-bedroom townhouse	$239	$259	$250
Additional guest	$ 99	$ 99	$ 99

- Regular season: April 25 to July 4
- Peak season: February 12 to April 24
- Value season: January 1 to February 11, July 5 to December 25
- Holiday season 1999: December 26 to December 31 (holiday season prices not available at press time)

For the World Choice plan, add $93 per person, per night to the Basic plan. This all-inclusive plan offers the features of the Basic plus unlimited admission to all Disney attractions for length of stay, $55 credit per guest each day at a wide variety of restaurants throughout Disney World, plus use of bicycles and nonmotorized recreation. A minimum three-night stay is required for all plans, and a deposit may be required.

When you've selected the dates for your Institute visit and made your reservations, a reservation kit will be mailed to you, detailing the programs available during your visit. After your deposit has been received, you may begin reserving programs, which can be done by telephone up to three months in advance. Institute reservationists are very knowledgeable and have actually participated in most of the activities. Once you have made these arrangements, you have only to arrive. Last-minute and day-to-day changes can be handled easily by the Institute's programming staff.

For Institute reservations, call (800) 282-9282.

OUR RECOMMENDATIONS FOR THE DISNEY INSTITUTE

- Give this place a chance. It's much more fun than you think.
- Make your arrangements as far ahead as possible in order to get the activities that most interest you both.
- Be sure to spend some time at the spa early in your visit. Book your treatments early.
- Rent or bring bikes for your Institute experience. It's the perfect mode of transportation for this lakeside enclave.
- During our visit, we particularly enjoyed both the Wine, Wonders, and Song and Romantic Dinners.

ROMANCE AT THE INSTITUTE

- We find this place to be quite romantic. Treatments at the spa, special activities together, and unforgettable evening entertainment all add up to a blissful and relaxed vacation. Remember, Pleasure Island and the rest of Walt Disney World await just around the corner ♥.

Discovery Island

This beautiful and densely tropical isle is Disney's own zoological park, certified and accredited by the American Association of Zoological Parks and Aquariums. A short boat ride from the Magic Kingdom, Discovery Island seems a world away. This overlooked Disney gem offers a unique getaway from the hustle and bustle of the other attractions.

Take a lazy stroll down a shady path. Watch hundreds of rare birds in one of America's largest walk-through aviaries. Come prepared to explore, and don't forget a picnic lunch from your favorite restaurant.

Discovery Island is an 11-acre sanctuary for more than 250 species of reptiles, mammals, and birds. While this may not be a place that you would wish to spend an entire day, you will find that there are plenty of things to fill a morning or afternoon. This is a small and quiet place, which is precisely what makes it so attractive. Not only is there no need to hurry here, but there is no temptation to.

What you will find are shady paths that wind lazily through bamboo thickets and under a dense canopy of trees. There are toucans, kookaburras, macaws, and dozens of other birds. In fact, there are whole flocks in natural aviaries. You may even be lucky enough to spy Discovery Island's resident bald eagle. The island also enjoys a small population of exotic mammals and reptiles. From the lumbering Galapagos tortoises to the miniature Asian muntjac deer, Discovery Island provides one delight after another. The two animal encounters here are small and intimate, like the rest of the island. The Thirsty Perch, the island's store, offers a selection of beverages, snacks, souvenirs, and rental binoculars. Storage lockers are available for rent. Several nice picnic areas are available.

One-day admission to Discovery Island is $12 for adults and $6.50 for children. Admission is included with the Length of Stay and All-in-One Hopper Passes.

OUR RECOMMENDATIONS FOR DISCOVERY ISLAND

- This place is especially nice and especially deserted during the fall months.
- Make arrangements with one of your favorite restaurants to prepare a picnic lunch ♥♥.
- Nesting season for the island's feathered inhabitants runs from February to early fall.
- This attraction is closed annually from mid-February to mid-March.

The Disney Water Parks

So far, Disney has built three water parks, and each one seems to get better. River Country was the first, followed by Typhoon Lagoon. Just when you thought they couldn't get much grander, along comes Blizzard Beach. Whether you're young or old, visiting with your family or as a couple, these parks will very likely provide a day's worth of excitement and entertainment. Each has kiddie pools, slides both tame and wild, raft rides, and wave pools.

Admission to all water parks is included in both the Length of Stay and the All-in-One Hopper Passes. One-day admission to either Typhoon Lagoon or Blizzard Beach is $26 for adults and $20.50 for children. A two-day pass is available for both parks for $39 ($31 for ages 3 to 9). Admission to River Country is $16 ($12.50 for children).

All three parks suffer from the same problem: too many people. At peak times, you will find yourselves spending more time in line than having fun. Here are a few ways to avoid the crowds:

- Arrive early. Get there 30 minutes before the park opens, and use the first few hours for the slides and raft runs. Save the lazy tubing, swimming, and surfing for later.
- Arrive late. During the summer months, the water parks stay open later. Arrive around 4 P.M., when the crowds are starting to thin out. In the summer, the late afternoon is cooler and the sun is kinder.
- Try a water park when the weather is "less than ideal." The water is heated to 80 degrees at each and, in inclement weather, it may be brisk, but the park will be all but empty.
- Arrive right after an afternoon thundershower. The rain will have driven the crowds away.

MORE WATER PARK TIPS

- The hours to the water parks vary with the seasons. Check with Guest Services or the "World Update" for the operating hours.
- During the hot and busy summer months, both Blizzard Beach and Typhoon Lagoon get so busy early in the day that they reach capacity in the first hour and close until later in the day, when guests begin to trickle out. Either get there before opening or go later in the day.
- Towels are available as rentals. Wear shoes or flip-flops. For women, one-piece bathing suits are best for the slides. There are changing rooms, but, if you like, you can wear your suit under your clothing to avoid having to change.
- Do not forget sunblock or sunscreen. The Florida sun is brutal, even on an overcast day. Besides being dangerous, a sunburn is uncomfortable. You don't want to spend your romantic Disney

vacation being too sore to be touched. We usually wear light T-shirts to protect ourselves from the sun.

- Leave jewelry and watches back in your room. This stuff tends to fall off while you're zooming down slides. No personal swim gear is allowed in any of the parks, including masks, fins, rafts, and floats. Life vests are available.
- As soon as the park opens, go stake out a place with lounge chairs. Some spots are in the shade, and some are not. Take your pick and deposit a few of your things on enough lounges to provide each of you with one. If you don't, someone else will.
- Rental lockers are available at all of the water parks. If you have valuables with you, such as a camera or a bag, you can't leave them lying around. This may be Disney World, but it is still planet Earth. Prices for the three different sizes are $7, $6, and $5.
- These places will make you thirsty. The water parks each offer a $9 thermal souvenir cup with free refills all day. It's a nice cup and a good deal.

River Country

The first of Disney's water recreation parks, River Country is also its smallest. This is the "ol' swimmin' hole" a la Huck Finn, and while it's not executed on the grand scale of Typhoon Lagoon or Blizzard Beach, it has its charm.

Not far from Discovery Island, River Country is set perfectly on the shore of Bay Lake. The cool breezes from the lake make it particularly nice. There is more emphasis here on landscaping and beauty than on exciting slides. Huge man-made boulders, waterfalls, and lots of trees make this place seem less of an attraction and more like a natural occurrence. River Country consists of several areas. Bay Cove is the large swimming area and the heart of the attraction. It is actually an area of the lake that has been walled off. The water here is kept clean and circulating, making it a large, sand-bottomed swimming pool. There is a lot of fun to be had here, though mostly for the younger set. Rope swings and a large boom are several ways to enter the cove. There are also two pretty decent water slides, Hoop 'n Holler Hollow, and a gentle raft ride, oddly misnamed White Water Rapids. If you are looking for excitement, this may not be the place for you.

River Country also has a large swimming pool. Upstream Plunge is not far from Bay Cove. It features two steep slides. Cypress Point Nature Trail is a short and scenic stroll through the wetland area along the lake.

There are two counter-service restaurants. Pop's Place is the larger of the two, offering burgers, hot dogs, salads, and a variety of snacks. The Waterin' Hole, a snack bar, opens only during the busier seasons. Picnicking is permitted at River Country.

River Country is located at Fort Wilderness. Buses make the trip from the Ticket and Transportation Center (TTC) throughout the day. The water park can also be reached by taking the Fort Wilderness boat from the Magic Kingdom dock.

Typhoon Lagoon

Typhoon Lagoon tells the story of a small fishing village hit by a typhoon. The storm has left the village in ruins—creating the perfect aquatic theme park. Mount Mayday is the most prominent feature of the crazy world of Typhoon Lagoon. Speared atop its peak is an old shrimp boat. Every half hour, a 50-foot geyser of water spews from its smoke stack. Look around, and you can't help but notice that things are way out-of-whack. The storm has left this place utterly askew. Buildings lean this way and that, seemingly about to topple.

These delightful effects are everywhere. Nothing has escaped the wrath of the typhoon or the notice of the Disney Imagineers. There is more here than just a cute story and some nifty props, though. Typhoon Lagoon's 56 acres is jammed with slides, creeks, raft rides, and a rumbling surf pool.

Of all the attractions here, Humunga Cowabunga is the only one that we would hesitate to recommend for everyone. This steep, 50-foot, high-speed water slide is a bit too vertical. If this kind of speed is your thing, you'll love it. Six other slides here range from mild to exciting. None approaches the speed or height of Humunga Cowabunga, and we think that you'll like them all. Three of them are raft runs of varying lengths. The remaining slides are body slides: Rudder Buster, Stern Burner, and Jib Jammer are each exciting and fairly fast.

Castaway Creek winds lazily around the park, and you can hop aboard a tube almost anywhere and float to your heart's content. This little river takes you through some amusing effects: a tunnel, a waterfall, and under a leaky bamboo pipe.

Ketchakiddie Creek is a miniversion of this park, and it is just for kids (adults admitted only when accompanied by a child). Shark Reef offers a snorkeling experience through a lagoon of live fish. The water in this pool is much cooler than the rest of Typhoon Lagoon.

Typhoon Lagoon offers two counter-service restaurants, the Leaning Palms and Typhoon Tilly's. There are also two "beach shacks" that serve snacks, soft drinks, beer, and wine coolers. And of course, no theme park would be complete without shopping. Here at Typhoon Lagoon, you have Singapore Sal's, which carries souvenirs, Typhoon Lagoon merchandise, and a variety of sundries.

Blizzard Beach

Disney Imagineers like to give every place a "spin," and this could be the tallest tale of all. Blizzard Beach, so the story goes, is the result of a freak winter storm that blasted this piece of Walt Disney World with snow and ice. It was too great an opportunity to pass up, so work was begun immediately on a ski resort. Before the resort was completed, however, the temperature returned to normal. Hopes for a Disney ski complex were dashed.

Ready to shut the whole thing down, the resort operators noticed an alligator frolicking in the water from the melting snow. The place would, they quickly realized, make for the perfect water adventure park. So, what had once been ski slopes, slalom courses, and bobsled runs were hastily converted into some of the wildest and tallest water slides anywhere. And so began Blizzard Beach.

We have told you more than once that Disney's creations continue to get better and better. Blizzard Beach is certainly proof of this. Words like wild, crazy, and zany only begin to describe it. The Disney Imagineers must have had a lot of fun thinking up this one.

The cluster of buildings at the entrance to Blizzard Beach resembles alpine lodges. Here and there are banks of melting "snow." Icicles hang from the eaves, and racks of skis sit useless in the sun. The centerpiece of the park is Mount Gushmore. A real chairlift runs to the small chalet on its snow-covered summit. From there, a steep staircase leads up to the nearly vertical ski jump/water slide. Other slides and chutes run down the mountain, twisting and turning in all directions. Ice and snow glitter realistically in the bright sun. Comic details are everywhere: the Avalunch snack bar, a lone ski sticking out of a snow bank, and a potbellied stove.

Summit Plummet is the high-speed water slide that claims to be the tallest and fastest in the world. Or jump aboard a large raft at Teamboat Springs and zoom down the mountain. The six-passenger raft twists and turns along 1,200 feet of splashing waterfalls.

Runoff Rapids is a tube ride down a choice of three flumes. Slush Gusher is a slide nearly as high as Summit Plummet but nowhere near as steep. Snow Stormers runs through a zigzag slalom course, complete with banks of snow and flag gates. Toboggan Racer is a rather tame eight-lane slide down one of the gentler slopes on Mount Gushmore.

If the slides of Blizzard Beach get too crowded, head off to explore. It won't be hard to find Melt-Away Bay, a one-acre swimming area with a sand beach. Here in the shadow of Mount Gushmore, waders and swimmers splash away the day. The Blizzard Beach Ski Patrol Training Camp, about halfway up the slope, is an area designed for preteens. Here, a series of events such as Mogul Mania and the Ice Flow Walk present comical challenges at this goofy training camp. Or, as an alternative, hours can be spent drifting lazily around the park in tubes along the wonderful Cross-Country Creek.

Blizzard Beach has two snack bars, Avalunch and the Warming Hut, and one rather large counter-service restaurant called the Lottawatta Lodge. With seating either inside or in a pleasant courtyard, this Caribbean-style ski lodge is the place to take your appetite. Pizza, hot dogs, hamburgers, and other fast Disney foods are available at the many counter windows. (Even with a large opening week crowd, the wait was minimal.) The Beach Haus offers a large selection of Blizzard Beach memorabilia, Disney character merchandise, and even some interesting apparel.

Tip: **Blizzard Beach now features a photo at Teamboat Springs. Have your picture taken on the raft and pick it up later near the front of the park. Cost is around $10, and it makes a very nice souvenir.**

CHAPTER 5

Live Entertainment and Nightlife

If we were to mention live Disney entertainment, you'd probably think of someone in a Pluto suit. But there's much more going on here than this. Walt Disney World is without a doubt the largest employer of musicians, singers, dancers, and actors in the world. Throughout the year, at least 2,000 regular cast members and 130,000 visiting entertainers perform in an astounding 150 shows, parades, street performances, and spectacles each *day*. Another 21,000 professional entertainers are involved in special events and holiday specials each year and another 1,000 nationally known singers and musicians perform here in limited engagements during the year.

You'll find the unusual, the unexpected, and the talented everywhere, from Harambe in the Animal Kingdom to the lobby of the Grand Floridian. There's so much going on around here that a lot of it is easy to miss. So, we have gathered it all together here in one convenient place. What follows is the live entertainment of Walt Disney World: where, when, and how to find this large variety of live performances.

Live Entertainment in the Theme Parks

There's a lot of live entertainment in the parks, and your ticket to finding it will be your theme park guidemaps. Updated weekly, these will tell you what you'll need to know to find parades, fireworks, character encounters, live performances, and other unique events: dates, times, and locations of performances. You can get one of these nearly anywhere in each of the parks or at your resort's Guest Services. You'll want to pick up all of the theme park guidemaps early in your visit and use them to help you find what interests you both.

Live Entertainment in the Magic Kingdom

Main Street USA The Walt Disney World Band performs every morning in Town Square on Main Street. During the busy summer months, they usually give several concerts.

One of our favorite Main Street groups is the Dapper Dans, Disney's tap-dancing barber shop quartet. They usually begin around 10 A.M. and wander Main Street, performing at unannounced times. Look for them in the barber shop.

Another group of musicians found here are the Rhythm Rascals, a zany washboard and banjo troupe that will have you laughing while you tap your feet. This gang reminds us of Spike Jones and his band (if you are old enough to remember them). At Casey's Corner, a ragtime pianist will bring the old days alive, and the Kids of the Kingdom offer musical shows at the Castle Forecourt Stage. They are particularly popular with children but are not among our favorite performers in the Magic Kingdom.

Adventureland J. P. and the Silver Stars ♥ is a steel band that performs authentic Caribbean music at the Caribbean Plaza, near Pirates of the Caribbean. Check out the unique instruments used by this rhythmic group as they offer up a touch of the islands.

Frontierland There's fun throughout the day at the Diamond Horseshoe Jamboree. This saloon show features singers, dancers, comedians, magicians, and lots more. See your Magic Kingdom guidemap for show times.

Fantasyland The Sword in the Stone Ceremony is scheduled throughout the day in the plaza near the castle. This reenactment of the King Arthur legend is performed with the participation of a young guest selected from the audience. It is cute and heartwarming, especially if the youngster is yours.

A variety of school bands from all over the U.S. perform each week at the Fantasy Faire Stage. On special occasions, you are likely to catch the Walt Disney World Band here as well.

Tomorrowland For out-of-this-world entertainment, try the Galaxy Palace in Tomorrowland. Imagineers have been beating the bushes for something a little, well, alien. Silly and largely for children.

Live Entertainment in Epcot

For us, live entertainment is one of the best things about Epcot. Each country in the World Showcase has its own offerings, and most of it is simply wonderful. Many performers seem to be permanent fixtures; others are guests. The guest artists come to Disney World for a year or two, usually performing in the "country" of their origin in the World Showcase. These are some of the most interesting performances at Walt Disney World, and we urge you to seek them out, not only to enjoy their performances but also to chat with the artists. It is a rare opportunity for cultural exchange.

Epcot also offers a variety of guest artisans that might include a Persian rugmaker or a French glassblower. Such craftspeople can be found in the countries around the World Showcase and are usually mentioned in the guidemap. Here and there around Epcot, you'll also find high school and college bands and choruses from all around the U.S. and the world.

First we'll discuss entertainment at Future World, then we'll cover the World Showcase.

Future Corps This drum and bugle group plays a variety of popular tunes. They are entertaining and, being professionals, are outstanding. Performances are usually at Innoventions Plaza.

The Anacomical Players This impromptu theater group performs in the Wonders of Life Pavilion. Their sketches about health often involve the audience. Look for the Anacomical Players stage area on the main floor of the pavilion.

The JaMMitors The JaMMitors are a wacky band of garbage can musicians. It looks like they should be using their "instruments" to clean the plaza instead of entertaining. Look for them daily in the Innoventions breezeway.

The Kristos The Kristos are android-like aliens that perform a hypnotic and acrobatic sort of dance at the Innoventions Logo Plaza. We think they are an act worth looking for.

Following are the live entertainment shows available at the World Showcase.

Showcase Plaza Featured here is the Junkanoo Bus. This great entertainment is a steel band from the Caribbean. Colorful and entertaining.

Mexico You're bound to find some good Mexican and Latin American musicians here each day. Try timing a performance to a snack at the sidewalk cantina ♥ and enjoy the melodies of Mariachi Cobre. Other performers include Huitzilin, a group of costumed Mexican musician-storytellers. Both are outstanding.

Norway Live entertainment here has been spotty of late, with none of the wonderful Norwegian folk music of previous years. Lately Norway has featured the World Class Brass band and Tzigantzi, a troupe of Gypsy musicians. What either has to do with Norway, we can't say, but both are good. Check your guidemap to see what's happening here; if they have Norwegian entertainment, don't miss it.

China The performances are typically a solo musical performer and a small group of Chinese acrobats. We suggest that you stroll by to see where they will be and then return for a later show, finding a bench nearby. Arrive early enough to sit and enjoy the courtyard. The piped-in music in China is particularly pleasant. If you take the time, you will see a lot that a walk-through would miss. By the time the performers arrive, you'll feel as though you're in China.

The Outpost Drop by to catch the African drum group Tam Tams, who play occasionally next to this shop.

Germany There's some fine German music here, with the Oktoberfest Musikanten playing daily in the courtyard and the lively Alpine Trio appearing in the Biergarten restaurant. Strolling around the pavilion while the live musicians play will provide the perfect mood for your "visit to Germany." Check the guidemap for times, and make your entrance accordingly.

Italy Several musical groups have been performing here lately. Singers I Cantanapoli, classical group Rondo Veneziano, and Gypsy band Tzigantzi are all worth the trip. Live entertainment is also part of dinner at L'Originale Alfredo di Roma Ristorante. This eatery is a little slice of Italy: gay, colorful, and noisy. It's a good choice for a fun and festive meal.

The American Adventure Inside the rotunda are the Voices of Liberty, an a cappella choral group performing medleys of traditional American ballads. Arrive a few minutes early. It is a good show, especially if you have a place to sit down. In front of the pavilion, check out the Spirit of America Fife and Drum Corps, complete with traditional costumes.

The America Gardens Theatre is one of the premier places for live shows here at Walt Disney World. During the course of a Disney week, the variety of entertainment here can be pretty impressive. From college bands to world-renowned performers, this theater is a place you'll want to check out. If someone well known is performing, give yourselves plenty of time to get a seat.

Japan With our favorite Epcot entertainer, the Fantasy DreamMaker, on a sabbatical, entertainment here in Japan now includes traditional Japanese drumming and Cirikli, a flock of performers on stilts in unusual bird and rider costumes. We think Cirikli features some of the best costumes we have ever seen and urge you to see them and to enjoy their mesmerizing performance.

Morocco There's almost always something exciting going on here: musicians, acrobats, dancers, and an exotic street show make Morocco one of Epcot's hottest showplaces. Check your Epcot guidemap for Festival Marrakesh and the Houzali acrobatics troupe.

Inside Marrakesh restaurant ♥♥ is a belly dance show during both lunch and dinner. In both cuisine and atmosphere, Marrakesh delivers a truly exotic restaurant experience.

France France is home to Bubble Nicolas, a mime who performs in a large plastic sphere. Don't miss him. Also here are the Living Statues. This performance is both astounding and humorous. Another winner.

The United Kingdom The music of the Beatles comes alive with British Invasion, a talented foursome of musicians who perform throughout the week. They are surprisingly good. Look here for a lively show by pianist Pam Brody in the Rose and Crown Pub.

Canada Nova Scotia's Caledonia Bagpipes are another of our favorites here at Epcot, and the folk singer–comedians, Off Kilter, are now performing on their own stage here in Canada. World Class Brass also plays here each day.

Live Entertainment at Disney–MGM Studios

The Boulevards' "Streetmosphere" Along both Hollywood and Sunset Boulevards, you'll find a wacky band of street performers, all in outrageous costumes. These zany "streetmosphere" characters almost always involve unwary onlookers in their comic routines. These are the denizens of Disney's 1930s Hollywood, and we urge you to catch their performances. It is easy to rush through the boulevards heading to rides and attractions elsewhere, never realizing what you're missing. Don't forget to come back here later to catch the shows.

The Studio's Soundstage Disney–MGM Studios is also a working studio. During the year, television programs are produced in its three large sound stages. Often, they involve audiences. Check at the Production Information Window just inside the front gate for ticket availability and show times.

Street Musicians A variety of bands play at various places throughout the park. The Tubafours Quartet, Toon Town Trio, and Hollywood Hitmen offer their own brand of musical entertainment and street comedy.

Beauty and the Beast—Live on Stage ♥♥ This lavish stage production takes place in a large theater on Sunset Boulevard. Beautifully costumed performers dance and sing to the memorable music of the animated Disney classic.

The Hunchback of Notre Dame—A Musical Adventure This amphitheater features live performances of one of Disney's animated feature films. The current offering is *The Hunchback of Notre Dame.* Sets, costumes, and performances are all memorable, and we advise that you not miss it.

NEW **Goosebumps Horrorland Fright Show** More entertaining for children, this sideshow-like performance features wacky magic and comedy spoofs. Cute.

NEW **Copperfield Magic Underground** This restaurant will have entrances both from inside and outside the park. It will feature a full menu of foods as well as a live show of illusions performed on a grand scale. Opens spring 1999.

NEW Live Entertainment at the Animal Kingdom

This place is literally teeming with herds of unusual live entertainment. After you've made it to the major attractions here, you'll want to take your own little safari in search of the Animal Kingdom's live performers.

Safari Village Take some time here to find the two marvelous musical groups that play at various times near the bridge from The Oasis, right in front of Disney Outfitters. Condor features the music of the Andes with drums, pan pipes, and stringed instruments. Incan music has long been a personal favorite of ours, and we find it to be transporting. Village Business is a much higher energy combo that plays a lively, African-Caribbean style. Look for them both. Also here in Safari

Village are "animal presenters" who ride the river launches with a variety of small creatures. Another "live" entertainer to be on the watch for is the "living statue." Look for this unusual entertainer near the Flame Tree Barbecue.

Africa Besides the live animals, there's a terrific African pop band that plays daily at the open-air African Lounge in Harambe. This is something you will not want to miss ♥♥. The music usually starts around 4 P.M. There are more animal presenters here too, and these creature encounters can be found just around the corner from Tamu Tamu and a few steps toward Asia.

Asia Flights of Wonder is this land's bird show, and it is entertaining and interesting. The birds in this show are not taught tricks but rather perform feats typical of their species. It's something of a "natural talent" show. Some of it will surprise you. Riverboats also depart nearby with more animal presenters.

Camp Minnie-Mickey There are two stage shows here, and one of them, Festival of the Lion King, could well be the best show of its type here at Walt Disney World. It features singing, dancing, acrobatics, and outstanding costumes. Don't miss this show. The other show, Colors of the Wind, is cute and engaging but more apt for the younger set. Still, you might want to see its animal performances.

Dinoland USA Remember the "streetmosphere" characters in Disney–MGM Studios? Well, here they're just as zany and entertaining, and besides having an act, these performers are always happy to pose with guests for photos with, well, real "dinomosphere." There's also a good stage production with singing and dancing, Journey into Jungle Book.

Romantic Live Entertainment

- Having a drink at Mexico's sidewalk cafe during a Mariachi performance: ♥
- The belly dance show during a meal at Morocco's Marrakesh restaurant: ♥♥
- Beauty and the Beast—Live on Stage at Disney–MGM Studios: ♥♥
- The African pop group in Harambe (after 4 P.M.): ♥♥

Nightlife at Walt Disney World

During your romantic getaway at Walt Disney World, you'll most certainly want to get out in the evening and have some fun. This is the

Vacation Capital of the World, and that means there'll be lots to do. During the busy times of years, the parks are all open late and Disney World is running at full-throttle. Finding something to do in the evening will be a matter of choice. Whether you want to follow dinner with SpectroMagic or the Twilight Zone Tower of Terror, or whether you wish to take a dip in the pool or go out dancing, you'll find plenty to do after dark.

During the off-season, the theme parks and attractions all close relatively early. The Magic Kingdom and Disney–MGM Studios usually close at 6 P.M. and the World Showcase at Epcot closes at 9 P.M. While Epcot features IllumiNations every night, the other parks stay open late with nighttime parades and fireworks only on weekends.

We like the off-season because it fits our pace. With fewer people in the parks during the days, we have plenty of time for theme park excitement. We then use the evening to ease back, spend some time together, and to get out in search of that something special. Whether it's the busy season or not, you'll both find lots of nightlife at Walt Disney World. Besides dining out, you will be able to enjoy Downtown Disney, the BoardWalk, dinner shows, the movies, great shopping, hot tubbing, special and seasonal events, and "resort hopping."

Fireworks and Other Evening Spectacles

Consult your attraction guidemaps for the dates, times, and locations of the following.

IllumiNations IllumiNations ♥♥ is a spectacular fireworks and laser light show staged each evening over the Epcot's World Showcase Lagoon. Featuring the perfect orchestration of music, blazing rockets, and colored fountains, this is an event simply too outstanding to miss. There are numerous spots along the lagoon from which to watch the show, and we suggest that you arrive early to get one. One of our favorites is from the bridge between the United Kingdom and France or in the garden area right below it. Other good spots are at the top of the stairs in Canada or shore side at the World Showcase Plaza. Be sure that you can see the large sphere in the center of the lagoon and do your best to avoid being downwind of the show, unless you enjoy the smell of sulfur.

Fantasy in the Sky Featured in the Magic Kingdom, Fantasy in the Sky ♥♥ is another great fireworks show set to music. The most symmetrical view of the show is from Main Street. A less-crowded view can be had from Mickey's Toontown Fair, where, at the end of the show, you can hop aboard the train waiting at the station and ride around to the Main Street Depot for an easy exit. Other viewing places include one of the swings along the beach at the Polynesian or at the California Grill, where the music from the show is piped in.

Sorcery in the Sky At MGM, Sorcery in the Sky ♥♥ is considered by many to be the finest pyrotechnic display at Disney. Set to the most memorable of Hollywood's film scores, this show occurs only when the park is open late, during the busier months, or on holidays. If it is scheduled during your visit, don't miss it. Viewing is best from Hollywood Boulevard.

Pleasure Island It's New Year's Eve every night at Pleasure Island, and the celebration includes a fireworks show, live band, dancers, and confetti cannons.

For dates and times of the above fireworks shows during your Disney visit, be sure to check your attraction guidemaps early in your stay. For details about the fireworks cruises of Walt Disney World, see Other Boating Adventures, Chapter 7.

The SpectroMagic Light Parade The SpectroMagic Light Parade ♥♥♥ is an event not to miss. This musical parade features floats and Disney characters all aglow with fiber-optics, lights, and special effects of every sort. After this show, parades will never be the same. We promise. Check the Magic Kingdom guidemap for dates and times.

The Electric Water Pageant on the Seven Seas Lagoon This floating parade ♥♥ features music and a continuously changing array of lighted barges towed around the lagoon, usually around 9 P.M. each evening. We like this a lot, not because it is so exciting but because of the viewing possibilities. A lagoon-view room at any of the resorts on the lake, including the Wilderness Lodge, should provide an outstanding view. Here are a few of our other favorite locations: from the beaches at the Grand Floridian, the Polynesian, or Fort Wilderness; from the beaches behind either garden wing at the Contemporary; from Sunset Point at the Poly; from Narcoossee's restaurant; and from almost anywhere along the Walk Around the World path on the lagoon.

NEW **Fantasmic! (begins spring 1999)** This after-dark spectacle of lasers, music, special effects, and dancing waters features 50 performers and is produced nightly in its own amphitheater at Disney–MGM Studios. It includes shooting comets, animated fountains, and swirling stars. For more details about this 25-minute show, see Chapter 4.

Disney's BoardWalk

More than a resort, Disney's BoardWalk features a 1930s "seaside" promenade of nighttime entertainment: shops, restaurants, clubs, amusements, a dance hall, and sidewalk entertainers. One of Disney's newest hot spots, we suggest you set aside an evening to spend here. Have dinner, catch some entertainment, take a stroll along the BoardWalk, and dance the night away. There is simply too much to do here to miss this exciting place. It is one of Disney's most engaging creations, and there is no ticket to buy or admission to pay.

Begin your evening at the BoardWalk with dinner reservations. For fine and innovative dining, the Flying Fish is one of our favorites. Spoodles Mediterranean cuisine is another fine choice, and both ESPN Club and the Big River Grille & Brewing Works feature good food. There are other fine restaurants at the nearby Yacht and Beach Clubs and the Swan and the Dolphin as well. For details about these restaurants, see Chapter 6.

After dinner, stroll the BoardWalk Promenade and nosh a dessert at BoardWalk Bakery or enjoy a soft-serve at Seashore Sweets. There are sidewalk vendors, too, offering a selection of treats that range from hot dogs and crepes to coffees and fried onion rings.

Then there's browsing along the Promenade. Wyland Gallery features the marine artistry of Peter Wyland as well as the work of other internationally renowned painters and sculptors. Thimbles and Threads offers shoppers a look at some of the latest Disney designer fashions, while the Screen Door General Store has an assortment of groceries, snacks, Disney stationery, and decorative items.

The BoardWalk's strong suit, though, is entertainment, and there's enough here to keep you busy into the wee hours: magicians, portrait artists, jugglers, face painters, a small arcade of carnival games, and the BoardWalk Buskers, a couple of juggler-musicians who joke and perform.

One of our favorite things to do to rent a "surrey" quadricycle. Riding around the lake on one of these four-wheel bicycle/carriages is more fun than we can describe.

Also along the BoardWalk are several of Disney's newest and most interesting nightspots.

Atlantic Dance This beautiful and stylish club offers live music and dancing throughout the week. Baby boomer hits of the '60s and '70s are featured here much of the week, but our favorite is Sunday's Sinatra Night ♥♥♥ and a live, swing orchestra playing the tunes of

Sinatra and other performers of his era. It is an unforgettable night of romance and slow dancing and is Disney's best alternative to Pleasure Island. The club features a full-service bar and a small assortment of appetizers.

Atlantic Dance is open from 8 P.M. to 2 A.M. nightly for those 21 and older. A cover charge might apply for some nights here. See the coupon in the back of this book for 20% off at Atlantic Dance.

Jellyroll's The main attraction at this neighborhood-style bar is the music and antics of its dueling pianists who match wits here each evening from 7 P.M. to 2 A.M. There's singing, playing, and lots of rowdy fun. Jelly's has a full bar, and we suggest that you give this place a try. It's a surprisingly good time.

ESPN Club Besides a good eatery and bar, this club is heaven for sports lovers. There are more than 70 video monitors here, with satellite feeds covering sporting events worldwide. Select what interests you with your own controls. There are scoreboards, live interviews, Internet terminals, state-of-the-art video games, pep rallies, and more than you can think of when it comes to sports input. There's also a theater-size video array featuring special sporting events. It is *the* place to go for the big game or championship boxing match (cover charges may apply to special events).

Big River Grille & Brewing Works Besides its pub menu, this place makes its own beers and ales. Drop in here and get a sampler of the day's brewing. The atmosphere is interesting, and the brews and food are quite good.

The BelleVue Room Located in the BoardWalk Inn, this quaint lounge ♥♥ features a full-service bar with variety "flights" of single-malt scotches, small-batch bourbons, and Grand Marniers. Furnishings here will take you back to the 1920s and '30s; vintage radios play old-time shows. It is a comfortable and quiet escape, and it even has a beautiful outside balcony overlooking the BoardWalk green.

Getting to the BoardWalk If you are staying in one of the Epcot resorts, you'll be a pleasant stroll away. If you are staying in one of the other Disney resorts, getting here will involve a trip to Downtown Disney and then hopping a bus to the BoardWalk. If you are driving in, know that there is a large self-parking lot across the street from the BoardWalk, and valet parking is also available after 6 P.M. for $6.

The BoardWalk is also a short walk from the World Showcase at Epcot. Simply exit through the International Gateway (between Great Britain and France) and take a left across the bridge.

Downtown Disney

There's enough going on here to make this area something of a fifth theme park, and the theme is nightlife and entertainment for adults. This exciting place is 120 acres large (bigger than Disneyland), and you just might find yourselves wanting to come here every night of your visit. From movies and shopping to a dozen nightclubs and fine dining, this place has a lot to offer. There are live concerts at the House of Blues and the Wildhorse Saloon and live Latino rhythms at Bongos Cuban Cafe. There's even the famous Gospel Brunch at the House of Blues each Sunday. In December of 1998, the world-renowned Cirque de Soleil theater opens its doors here at Downtown Disney. For details about this exciting area, see Downtown Disney in Chapter 4.

Live Entertainment at the Disney Institute

Many times throughout the year, the performing arts center at the Disney Institute features a guest artist. The Seasons Dining Performance Package features dinner at Season's followed by the evening's performance, for $33 per person. To see who is live and onstage during your visit, check the "World Update" or consult Guest Services at your resort.

Seasonal Nightlife

During the course of each year, Walt Disney World offers a variety of special events. Many of these happen during the evening hours, further spicing Disney nightlife. From the Jolly Holidays Dinner Show to the Epcot Food & Wine Festival, there's almost always something interesting going on. Other seasonal events include the Pleasure Island Mardi Gras Celebration, Mickey's Very Merry Christmas Party, Mickey's Not-So-Scary Halloween Party, the Annual Jazz Festival, Chinese New Year, and Epcot Swingin' Summer Nights. There are far too many to list here, and new events are being added constantly, so check to see what's going on during your visit by calling Disney information at (407) 824-4321, or after you arrive, look in the "World Update."

Resort Hopping

The resorts of Walt Disney World are entertaining enough to warrant a tour. We suggest a little "resort hopping" to visit some of the places you've never seen. Don't miss the award-winning lobby of the

Wilderness Lodge or the BoardWalk. Taking a monorail tour of the Magic Kingdom resorts is another engaging evening outing.

Resort hopping is especially fun during the weeks between Thanksgiving and Christmas, when the World is decked out in its Christmas finery. Nearly every resort has a beautifully decorated tree in its lobby, and there are tree-lighting ceremonies each night. Disney characters and free refreshments are almost always part of the entertainment. Once, we caught a chorus of bell ringers playing Christmas carols at the Wilderness Lodge.

Even if it's not the holiday season, many of Walt Disney World's lounges are quiet and romantic places and offer interesting selections of appetizers and hors d'oeuvres. Try skipping dinner and traveling around the World in search of tasty treats. Some of our favorite spots are the Crew's Cup at the Yacht Club, the Territory Lounge at the Wilderness Lodge, Scat Cat's at Port Orleans, and the California Grill Bar at the Contemporary. There are lots of others, and we'll leave them for you to discover.

There's lots of entertainment going on in the resorts too. Here's a rundown.

The Grand Floridian Lobby A harpist plays each day from 1 to 3 P.M. and from 3 to 6 P.M., a pianist. In the evenings, from 9 to 11 P.M., a small orchestra performs on the landing outside of Mizner's Lounge on the second floor. The music is pleasant and can be heard from anywhere below. Either entertainment is reason enough to drop by to enjoy this elegant place ♥.

The Polynesian Another form of live entertainment to consider is one of the three dinner shows at the Poly. The Luau ♥, Mickey's Tropical Revue, and 'Ohana each have something interesting to offer. For details, see Chapter 6. Both the Luau and the Tropical Revue are extremely popular. Be sure to make reserve your tickets at the same time you book your accommodations.

Fort Wilderness Both the Hoop-Dee-Doo Musical Revue and the All-American Backyard Barbecue are popular events here. Hoop-Dee-Doo is an old-fashioned saloon show, and the Barbecue features a good country band. Tickets for the Hoop-Dee-Doo can be purchased up to two years ahead of time, and we strongly suggest that you reserve yours when you book your accommodations. For more details, see Chapter 6.

While not exactly a performance, the Campfire Singalong is definitely entertainment. This nightly event is held near the Meadow

Trading Post and is free to all Disney resort guests. It features Disney movies on an outdoor screen, a marshmallow roast, a campfire sing-along, and a visit by Chip and Dale.

Port Orleans and Dixie Landings Both resorts feature entertainment in the lounges of their central areas. The Cotton Co-Op and Scat Cat's Club each usually have a singer/entertainer in the evenings. Performances usually beginning after 9 P.M. Drop in for a drink and enjoy.

Coronado Springs We've seen an entertaining marimba band here a few times, playing just outside the entrances to the Pepper Market and Maya Grill in the evening. This music is quite good.

THE ROMANCE OF DISNEY NIGHTLIFE

- A night of dancing on Sunday's Sinatra Night at Atlantic Dance: ♥♥♥
- Having a hot tub when you *come back* from an evening out: ♥♥♥
- SpectroMagic Light Parade at the Magic Kingdom: ♥♥♥
- Watching the Magic Kingdom fireworks or the Electric Water Pageant from one of the swings on the beach at the Grand Floridian or the Polynesian: ♥♥♥♥
- Dining at Portobello Yacht Club and having an evening out at Pleasure Island: ♥♥
- Dining on the outside patios of Wolfgang Puck Cafe or Bongos: ♥♥♥
- Fireworks from Wolfgang's dining room or Bongos upstairs patio: ♥♥♥
- A light dinner at Pleasure Island Jazz Company: ♥♥
- "Resort hopping" at Christmastime to see the decorations and tree-lighting ceremonies: ♥♥
- Watching IllumiNations from the second-floor outside balcony of Atlantic Dance: ♥♥
- The Voodoo Garden at House of Blues: ♥♥♥
- A wine flight at Hollywood Brown Derby just before park closing or a flight of Grand Marniers at BoardWalk's BelleVue Room: ♥♥
- Musical entertainment at the Grand Floridian: ♥
- The Polynesian Luau at the Polynesian Resort: ♥

CHAPTER 6

Dining at Walt Disney World

If you still think a Disney vacation means mediocre food, then you've been eating in all the wrong places. In the last few years, Walt Disney World has made the transition from a place renowned for lackluster cuisine to one of America's premier dining destinations. If you think we are exaggerating, we suggest that you check with the "experts." Lately, the restaurants of Disney have been winning awards by the plateful from food and travel experts alike. Recognition from *Wine Spectator, Esquire, Wine Enthusiast, The Zagat Guide, Travel Holiday,* AAA guidebooks, the *Mobile Travel Guide, Travel and Leisure,* and *Epicurean Rendezvous* are only a few of the kudos garnered by a whole new generation of Disney chefs and sommeliers. Such names as the California Grill, Victoria and Albert's, and the Flying Fish now enjoy international culinary recognition. And several of our favorites are stars on the rise: Narcoossee's and the Maya Grill. Open a food and wine magazine these days and you're likely to see the faces of Disney chefs Cliff Pleau, Scott Hunnel, Anette Grecchi, and John State. These are just a few of the superstars powering Disney's meteoric rise in cuisine.

While we really enjoy the fine dining, the really good news is that this transformation affects the rest of the spectrum of nearly 200 Disney eateries too. We used to tell our readers to avoid the food in the parks. No longer. From a grilled chicken sandwich at Disney–MGM Studios' Studio Express to the Spice-Encrusted Salmon at Cinderella's Royal Table, there's an improved taste for every palate and purse. The food at Walt Disney World just keeps getting better and better, and we keep enjoying it more and more. Staying current with the constant menu changes here is one of our favorite parts of keeping *Walt Disney World for Couples* up to date.

Making "Reservations"

Dinner reservations at Walt Disney World are now known as "priority seating arrangements." What this means is that you will make the usual "reservations." When you arrive at the restaurant, you will check in with the maitre d' and be given the next available table.

- We suggest that you do make priority arrangements and that you arrive 10 minutes early. Simply, there are places you just won't get into without them.
- Priority arrangements may be made up to 60 days in advance by phoning (407) WDW-DINE (939-3463).
- Same-day, theme park dining reservations by phone are available only to Disney resort guests. Touch 55 on your room phone.
- Guest Services at your resort has a variety of restaurant menus. Look them over, make your choice, and then let Guest Services make the call.
- Reservations are most necessary after 7 P.M., for character meals, dinner shows, and theme park table-service restaurants.
- For character breakfasts, Cinderella's Royal Table will take reservations only up to seven days ahead, and both Olivia's and the Soundstage at Disney–MGM Studios, 30 days ahead. All others will allow reservations up to 60 days in advance.
- Make arrangements for dinner shows when you reserve your room.
- Theme park eateries will take same-day reservations at the door beginning in the morning. Stroll by and make yours. At Epcot, you can make reservations at one of the three WorldKey terminals, and at Disney–MGM, at a booth near the tip board.
- If there are just two of you, know that your chances of walking in a busy restaurant and getting seated after only a short wait are much better than if you are a larger party.

Dining Tricks and Budget Tips

Over the years, we have learned to be imaginative with our approach to the pleasures of dining at Walt Disney World. Here are some of our ideas.

Our Tips for Breakfast

- Virtually all table-service restaurants and room services will fix anything that you desire. To get what you usually eat for breakfast, all you have to do is ask.
- For luxury and convenience, try room service and breakfast in bed: ♥♥♥♥. It's only a little more expensive and will leave you feeling as pampered as you should feel.
- Try sharing a breakfast. The portions at most table-service restaurants and room service are large enough for all but the hardiest of eaters.
- Enjoy a poolside breakfast: ♥. Pick up your breakfast at the food court and find a nice table on a shady patio or out by the pool.
- Fix your own breakfasts. Get a refrigerator from housekeeping ($5 a day or free, depending on your resort), and make a simple breakfast right in your room. Ingredients and supplies can be found either at the Gourmet Pantry at the Downtown Disney Marketplace or nearby at Gooding's at the Crossroads Plaza.
- Watch out for food courts if you are in a hurry for breakfast. The usual hours for breakfast are very crowded, and you can find yourself standing in line for pancakes instead of Splash Mountain. Try having breakfast earlier or later. Food courts usually open at 6 A.M.

Our Tips for Lunch

- Eat dinner for lunch. One bonus is that the same food served at dinner is cheaper at lunchtime.
- Have some appetizers for lunch. Pick a fancy, expensive restaurant and share a salad and an appetizer: ♥.
- Room service: ♥♥♥. Need we say more?
- Avoid the crowds and have an early lunch, as soon as places begin to serve, usually 11:30 A.M.
- Have a breakfast buffet for an early brunch. These are usually character meals and offer many foods appropriate for midday dining. Most usually serve until 11:30 A.M.
- Plan a picnic: ♥♥. Have your favorite restaurant pack a lunch and head off to Discovery Island, Typhoon Lagoon, or some other outdoor Disney attraction.
- Have a lunch in one of the restaurants at Downtown Disney's West Side Esplanade.

OUR TIPS FOR DINNER

- Share a meal at one of the pricier dining spots. Try sharing a salad, a couple of appetizers, an entree, and a dessert. We do this frequently.
- At most of the fine restaurants at Disney, the chefs or wine stewards have selected wines that are well-paired with the entrees of the evening, or ask your server what wine will go best with your meal.
- Pull out all the stops at least once during your vacation. Dress up and go someplace extravagant: ♥♥♥.
- At the deluxe resorts, try in-room dining: ♥♥♥. Hint: You can order anything from *any* restaurant at your resort, even if it's not on the room service menu.

Dining in a Lounge

Many of the lounges around Disney feature appetizers and finger foods from the restaurants adjacent to them. Lounges at Walt Disney World are not what you find in the outside world. Usually, they are quiet, comfortable, and often quite intimate. For a light meal, dining in a lounge will likely be quite pleasing. Some even feature live entertainment. The Matsu No Ma Lounge in Epcot, the Crew's Cup at the Yacht Club, the Territory Lounge at the Wilderness Lodge, and the California Grill bar are just a few of the many interesting choices.

Special Dietary Needs

In recent years, we have witnessed a "World"-wide change in menus all across the spectrum of Disney eating establishments. Menus have been revamped to include foods that more reflect what people are eating today. It is a simple matter to find low-fat meals and a host of healthier and lighter meals. Such foods can be found virtually everywhere, from counter-service eateries to the most elegant of gourmet dining spots. Fast-food outlets are even offering fruit as an option to French fries. Virtually every food outlet at Disney has at least one vegetarian item on the menu. Some offer many. Walt Disney World has become committed to satisfying the dietary needs of virtually every guest.

To test this commitment, we brought Aunt June and Uncle Jake to Walt Disney World. These folks are on a no fat, vegetarian diet. No fat, no nuts, no olives, no cheese, no fish. If you are wondering what that leaves, we can tell you how surprised even we were at what the chefs of Disney created. By notifying the kitchens when we made our reservations, Jake and June enjoyed dinners created especially for them. From cold melon soup to grilled vegetables and couscous, each entree was handcrafted. After a few meals, we were saying, "We'll have whatever they're having."

For kosher requirements, 24-hour notice is needed. Note that kosher foods arrive at Walt Disney World prepared and frozen.

Dining Out with Children

Eating out with children here at Disney is a breeze. Virtually every restaurant expects children on a regular basis. Except for Victoria and Albert's and Arthur's 27, there are kids' menus everywhere. And Team Disney really knows what kids like. Children's menus typically feature hamburgers, hot dogs, macaroni and cheese, and a variety of finger foods such as chicken nuggets. If you don't see what your child wants to eat, ask for it. The kitchen will only be too happy to fix it.

Buffets, though expensive, can be a good choice for dining with children. The variety of foods is so large that even the fussiest of eaters is likely to find something. Also, most buffets include "kids stations," which feature foods with plenty of kid appeal.

And of course, if you want to step out without the kids, there are plenty of options for providing the kids with their own Disney adventure while the two of you enjoy your night on the town. For child care options, see Chapter 1.

Disney Character Meals

These delightful experiences are usually buffets. Disney characters make the rounds during mealtime, visiting each table. Not just for kids, character meals can be fun and provide some great photo opportunities, too.

WHERE TO HAVE CHARACTER BREAKFASTS

- Artist Point, the Wilderness Lodge, with Winnie the Pooh and friends
- Baskerville's, the Grosvenor (Tuesday, Thursday, and Saturday)
- Cape May Cafe, the Beach Club, with Admiral Goofy and crew
- Chef Mickey's Buffet, the Contemporary, with Mickey and Minnie and friends
- Cinderella's Royal Table, Magic Kingdom, with Cinderella and friends

- County Fair, the Hilton (Sunday)
- Crystal Palace, Magic Kingdom, with Winnie the Pooh and friends
- Fulton's Crab House, Pleasure Island, with Mickey and crew
- Garden Grill, The Land, Epcot, with Farmer Mickey and Minnie
- Garden Grove Cafe, the Swan (weekends)
- Harry's Safari Bar and Grill, the Dolphin (Sunday brunch)
- 1900 Park Fare, the Grand Floridian, with Mary Poppins and friends
- 'Ohana, the Polynesian, with Minnie and friends
- Olivia's Cafe, Old Key West (Sunday, Monday, and Wednesday), with Winnie the Pooh and friends
- Restaurantosaurus, Animal Kingdom, with Mickey, Minnie, and gang
- Soundstage Restaurant, Disney–MGM Studios, with classic Disney film characters
- Watercress Cafe, Buena Vista Palace (Sunday)

WHERE TO HAVE CHARACTER LUNCHES

- Crystal Palace, Magic Kingdom, with Winnie the Pooh and friends
- Garden Grill, The Land, Epcot, with Farmer Mickey and Minnie
- Soundstage, Disney–MGM Studios, with classic Disney film characters

WHERE TO HAVE CHARACTER DINNERS

- Baskerville's, the Grosvenor (Wednesday)
- Chef Mickey's Buffet, the Contemporary, with Mickey and Minnie
- Crystal Palace, Magic Kingdom, with Winnie the Pooh and friends
- Garden Grill, The Land, Epcot, with Farmer Mickey and Minnie and friends
- Gulliver's Grill, the Swan (Sunday, Monday, Wednesday, Thursday, Friday)
- Liberty Tree Tavern, Magic Kingdom, with Minnie, Pluto, and Goofy
- 1900 Park Fare, the Grand Floridian, with Mickey, Minnie, and Goofy

Dinner Shows

For an evening of fun and food, try one of Disney's dinner shows. We suggest that you set aside some time for one and make a reservation when you book your room.

The Polynesian Luau

Unlike many of the cute and typical Disney productions, this one features authentic South Pacific entertainment. The colorful show features performers from a variety of South Sea islands. There is hula dancing, fire dancing, and the authentic music of the South Seas. This is just the kind of thing that we like best: authentic and exotic entertainment.

You'll be seated at long tables and fed endless amounts of Kahlua chicken, honey-roasted pork, and mahi-mahi. Tropical drinks (alcoholic or nonalcoholic) are included in the price. The food is good, though not memorable.

Adults, $38; children (ages 3 to 11), $20; children under 3, no charge. Gratuity is not included. There are two shows, at 6:45 and 9:30 P.M. A 10% discount is available with a Magic Kingdom Club or American Express card.

This show is a lot of fun. It's even romantic ♥♥.

Mickey's Tropical Revue

This is a late-afternoon children's version of the Polynesian Luau, featuring a mix of South Sea performers and Disney characters. It is fun if you have small children. At the end of the show, the performers bring the kids onto the stage to teach them Polynesian dancing. The food is the same as the Luau. Don't forget your camera.

Adults, $33; children (3–11), $16. Gratuity is not included. One show at 4:30 P.M. A 10% discount is available with Magic Kingdom Club or American Express card.

The Hoop-Dee-Doo Musical Revue

This saloon-style show has been a regular at Fort Wilderness for many years. It is very popular, and tickets to it do not come easily. Pioneer Hall, the setting for the Hoop-Dee-Doo, is an amusing re-creation of an Old West dance hall, complete with velvet curtains, rough-hewn beams, and saloon-like tables and chairs.

The cuisine is country cooking: barbecued ribs, fried chicken, salad, bread, corn on the cob, baked beans, and strawberry shortcake. Beverages include beer and wine. The show is memorable—a delight of song, dance, and corny laughs—and the food is good. The performers are obviously talented, and their timing is flawless. This is not sophisticated entertainment, mind you, but it is good, wholesome Disney fun.

Adults, $38; children (3–11), $20. 10% discount for American Express and Magic Kingdom Club.

Tip: Transportation to this show is tricky. Check with your Guest Services.

The All-American Backyard Barbecue

Offered from April to October, this picnic-table feast features live country music, Disney character fun, and a hearty selection of backyard favorites: chicken, burgers, hot dogs, ribs, corn bread, barbecue beans, and lots more. There's even beer and wine, and it's all surprisingly good. If you enjoy this kind of thing (or especially if you've never tried anything like it), we recommend you give it a go. Reservations are required and can be arranged through Disney dining reservations at (407) WDW-DINE (939-3463). Adults, $37; children (3–11), $25. Pricing includes tax and gratuity.

The Jolly Holidays Dinner Show

This seasonal show is one of our favorite Disney events. We rarely miss it. It is always offered during the weeks between Thanksgiving and Christmas. Part of a package including accommodations, tickets to this dinner show are usually available to the public. The feast is a traditional Christmas dinner of turkey, ham, and all of the accompaniments, and the food is fairly good.

The show features nearly 200 costumed performers in a Christmas tale. The music, song, and dance are all memorable, and the costumes are magnificent. Given that the Magical Holidays package also features some of the year's most outstanding resort discounts, this is one event not to miss.

The price is included in the package. If tickets are sold separately, the prices should be about $59 for adults and $35 for children.

NEW The House of Blues Gospel Brunch

One of our favorites, this brunch features a Bayou-inspired, home-cooked buffet of shrimp, roast beef, ham, jambalaya, and much more. Following the repast is an hour of live gospel music. For more details, see Downtown Disney, Chapter 4.

MurderWatch Mystery Theater

Presented on Saturday nights at the Grosvenor, this show features music and drama during a prime rib buffet. Guests participate in two nightly shows. Adults, $34; children, $19. For reservations, call (800) 624-4109.

A Bit of Dinner Entertainment

If you are looking for a bit of entertainment during dinner instead of a production, you can choose from among a number of restaurants that feature live dinner music.

- Gulliver's Grill at the Swan: magician/balloon artist on Tuesday, Saturday, and Sunday nights
- Hollywood Brown Derby at Disney–MGM ♥: a pianist
- House of Blues at Downtown Disney: blues performer after 11 P.M.
- L'Originale Alfredo di Roma Ristorante at Epcot: a group of musicians and singers
- Palio at the Swan ♥♥♥: strolling violinist or guitarist (or both), Tuesday through Saturday only
- Maya Grill at Coronado Springs ♥♥♥ : marimba band
- Marrakesh restaurant at Epcot ♥♥: Moroccan musicians and belly dancer, for lunch and dinner
- Victoria and Albert's at the Grand Floridian ♥♥♥♥: a harpist
- The Biergarten at Epcot: beer hall entertainment during lunch and dinner
- Bongos: live Latino rhythms after 10:30 P.M., Wednesday through Sunday
- Arthur's 27: a piano player

Not Your Unusual Dinner Shows

The following restaurants do not feature song or dance during dinner. What they do offer, however, are talented performing artists.

- Both the California Grill and the Flying Fish feature "performance kitchens" with counter seating. At either, chat with the chefs and enjoy watching them work. At the Grill, try our regular seats at Yoshi's sushi bar (if we're not there).
- Victoria and Albert's Chef's Table is much more than a fine show. Here in the kitchen of Chef Scott Hunnel, you will be wined and dined to *your* tastes and whims by a world-class culinary team. We promise you an unforgettable gastronomic event. With wine pairing, prix fixe dinner is $160 per person. Arrangements for this can be made six months in advance by calling Disney Group Dining at (407) 939-7707.

The Scoop on Coffee

For us, a day without a good cup of coffee is . . . well, a day we don't remember too well. If you enjoy your coffee like we do, strong, dark, and rich, then you'll likely find Disney coffee to be something of a disappointment. Most hotel and restaurant coffee at Walt Disney World is simply too bland for our tastes. The good news is that if you know where to look, you can find the type of coffee that Seattle has made famous. The best cup around is at the Swan's Lobby Court Lounge.

Joffrey Coffee Company also serves up some outstanding java, and they can be found at Downtown Disney's Forty Thirst Street, both on the BoardWalk and on the beach at the Yacht and Beach Clubs, and at the entrances to both Epcot and Disney–MGM Studios. Joffrey coffees are served hot, cold, and in specialty drinks such as granitas and mochaccinos. Just about every sit-down restaurant and food bar in Walt Disney World now serves espresso and cappuccino, so you can always have some of this if you are longing for something that tastes like real coffee.

Restaurants of Walt Disney World

The Ratings

$	Inexpensive, less than $15 per meal
$$	Moderately priced, $15 to $25 per meal
$$$	Expensive, more than $25 per meal
★	Acceptable means OK. This is our lowest rating.
★★	Good food means tasty but not memorable. This is the kind of meal that leaves you satisfied but that you won't go home talking about.
★★★	Quite good. Well prepared but not fine dining. You'd happily eat here again and bring friends, especially if the price was right.
★★★★	Very good food is well prepared, even creatively conceived. A find, indeed, if it is moderately priced.
★★★★★	Outstanding food; it's the stuff of memories: imaginative, perfectly prepared, and artfully presented, the creation of a world-class chef and a first-rate kitchen.

We didn't take any surveys to come up with the following reviews. We didn't poll other diners, and we didn't consult other restaurant reviews. Simply, we just ate everywhere—many places more than once, and some places many times. These are not all of Disney's eateries, simply those we felt were worthy of mention.

We expect that menus will change from time to time. Such is the way of good restaurants. Some of our favorite dishes may no longer be available. Quality and service may vary too, one of the unfortunate realities when it comes to restaurants. However, the following should give you a pretty good idea of what each restaurant is like and just how good the food is.

AKERSHUS

$$ ★★★

✓ Norway Pavilion, Epcot
✓ Table-service buffet, lunch and dinner
✓ Norwegian beer, wine, and full-service bar
✓ Priority seating advised
✓ Atmosphere is quaint and medieval. One of the best lunching places around the World Showcase Lagoon.

This is Norway's charming re-creation of a medieval fortress. It features a Norwegian "koldtbordt" buffet that includes the outstanding breads and cheeses of Norway and an assortment of hot and cold dishes. Herring, smoked salmon, stuffed pork loin, vegetable salad, and a daily chef's special are just a few of the 40 tasty items offered here. One of the more exotic eateries along the World Showcase, we think this is worth a meal. Akershus also serves Norway's Ringnes beer on draught. It's very good.

This restaurant is just what you'd expect if you were to dine in a castle: high, beamed ceilings; arched, cut-glass windows; and sturdy wooden furnishings. Cast members are young Norwegians dressed in traditional peasant garb. All in all, a good restaurant experience.

NEW ALL-STAR CAFE

$$ ★★

✓ Disney's Wide World of Sports
✓ Table service, lunch and dinner
✓ Atmosphere is noisy and busy: lots to look at

This theme restaurant is owned by a group that include Tiger Woods, Joe Montana, Wayne Gretzky, and other sports celebrities. Naturally, the theme here is sports, and you'll find different areas of the cafe featuring various sports. There are displays, awards, exhibits, and memorabilia everywhere from floor to ceiling. There are even a row of booths that look like huge baseball gloves. It's all entertaining and there is a lot to look at and even to discover. Fascinating sports facts are everywhere, and there are countless large-screen monitors displaying a variety of sporting events.

We had a small sampling of the menu and found our meal to be tasty and well-prepared. The menu features a variety of better-than-average burgers, fresh salads, sandwiches, and pastas. All in all, we'd say that the All-Star Cafe is pretty good, although a bit loud for our senses.

ARTHUR'S 27

$$$ ★★★★ ♥♥♥♥

✓ Buena Vista Palace Resort and Spa
✓ Table service, dinner only
✓ Full-service bar
✓ Reservations required
✓ Atmosphere is sublime and unforgettable
✓ Tips: Valet parking is complimentary for patrons of Arthur's. This restaurant is worth the trip. Evening attire is appropriate.

Without question, Arthur's features the most dramatic dining view to be had at Walt Disney World. Located high atop the 27-story Buena Vista Palace Resort and Spa, the panorama features all of Downtown Disney, Epcot, and as far as the Magic Kingdom. The elegant and comfortable dining room is exceptionally quiet, an oddity here at Disney. It is the perfect place for a romantic dinner, and considering both quality and price, Arthur's 27 is an outstanding alternative to the pricey Victoria and Albert's. The food is very good, and the service, faultless.

Our recent meal here included a sublime crab cake and a stunning squash and goat cheese ravioli. Both soups and salads were quite good. Like most menus, Arthur's has its standbys while other entrees offer what is seasonal and best. One of us enjoyed a blackened tuna with an unusually good Oriental sauce, while the other had a pan-seared Chilean sea bass with crimini mushrooms and red wine reduction. We suggest you ask your server what is recommended.

Arthur's features both a la carte and prix fixe dinners. For $49 per person, your choice of four courses; $55, five courses; and $60, six courses. Ambience, service, and cuisine combine to make Arthur's an appealing choice for a romantic dining experience.

Artist Point

$$ ★★★★ ♥♥

- ✓ Disney's Wilderness Lodge Resort
- ✓ Table service, breakfast and dinner
- ✓ Full-service bar, very good wine list from the Pacific Northwest
- ✓ Reservations suggested
- ✓ Atmosphere is woodsy and very pleasant
- ✓ Tips: This eatery excels at grilled fish. Ask which wine will best accompany your meal.

This handsome restaurant is set amidst the splendor of the Wilderness Lodge. Inlaid wooden tables and huge canvases of western vistas make this a very pleasant place. Large windows overlook the courtyard and geyser, immersing it in a high-timber ambience.

The Artist Point features the ever-changing fare of the Pacific Northwest. The emphasis here is on fresh and natural, and the Artist Point's menu changes with the seasons. Whether you are ordering from the seashore, the garden, from the pasture, or from the smoke house, the fare here is a virtual cornucopia of northwestern offerings. King salmon, Dungeness crab, Penn Cove mussels, buffalo, venison, quail, prime rib of beef: there's something for every taste.

Beaches and Cream Soda Shop

$ ★★

- ✓ Disney's Beach Club Resort
- ✓ Table service with take-out, breakfast, lunch, dinner, snacks
- ✓ Reservations not accepted

This fifties-style soda shop is one of our regular haunts when we are at the Beach or the Yacht. For us, a stay at either of these resorts is simply not complete without a swim and a great double-chocolate ice cream soda. Hamburgers and turkey burgers are very good, and the hot dogs are easily Disney's finest. Also a terrific assortment of soda-fountain concoctions. Beaches even has an egg cream. Nothing elaborate here, just good old American fare and someplace fun to enjoy it. Breakfasts here are fairly ordinary fast food or continental-style.

Biergarten

$$ ★★

- ✓ Germany Pavilion, Epcot
- ✓ Table-service buffet: lunch and dinner

- ✓ Beck's beer and German wines
- ✓ Priority seating advised
- ✓ Atmosphere is well themed, quaint, and fun

The inside of this restaurant feels like an Alpine village square, complete with building facades, waterwheel, and tree. Servers are costumed in Austrian peasant garb, and you'll find yourselves sitting beer hall–style at large tables with other guests. It's all quite pleasant, and the dinner show features a trio of musicians who will entertain you with music and zany antics. It is a fun taste of Germany.

The food here though, has suffered some since the Biergarten has become a buffet. Still, some of it is good. The large buffet includes sauerbraten, rotisserie chicken, sausages, wurst salad, and spaetzle, to mention just a few items. The apple strudel is memorable and the German beer comes in large steins. Overall, the restaurant is a pleasant experience. Note: We hear rumors that the Biergarten is slated for a "rehab," Disney terminology for a redesign.

Big River Grille & Brewing Works

$$ ★★★

- ✓ Disney's BoardWalk Promenade
- ✓ Table-service lunch and dinner
- ✓ Full-service bar and fresh-brewed beers and ales
- ✓ Priority seating not required
- ✓ Atmosphere is an eclectic blend of wood and metal; pleasant patio on the promenade

Yes, there's a microbrewery at Disney. This pub-style restaurant features such home brews as Rocket Red, Wowzer's Wheat, and Tilt Pale Ale. And good it is! Try a sample tray of small glasses of each, plus the day's special. The pub-style offerings include baby back ribs, N.Y. strips, Rocket Red Ale Chicken, Big River Salmon, and a selection of sandwiches and salads. Good food, good drink, and a nice place.

Boatwright's Dining Hall

$$ ★★★

- ✓ Disney's Dixie Landings Resort
- ✓ Table service, breakfast and dinner
- ✓ Bar features a variety of regional beers
- ✓ Reservations recommended only during peak mealtimes
- ✓ Atmosphere is themed but not unforgettable

This is Dixie Landings' only table-service eatery, and it is surprisingly good. This is not fine dining, but it is good, hearty fare for a reasonable price. The setting is a large, warehouse-like boat factory. The walls are covered with real antique shipwright tools, from giant augers to chisels and mallets. Overhead, you'll see a partially completed keel and framed-out vessel. Boatwright's is decorative and comfortable.

The cuisine has a definite bayou flair. Servings for both breakfast and dinner are large. If you are inclined to share an entree, this is a place to do it. Tin Pan Breakfasts are complete and hearty breakfasts served in a large pan. Dinners range from burgers and fried catfish to ribs and grilled pork loin. There are even more elaborately prepared Cajun specialties, such as Bayou Bouillabaisse and pirogue of pasta and seafood.

Bonfamille's Cafe

$$ ★★★ ♥♥

- ✓ Disney's Port Orleans Resort
- ✓ Table service, breakfast and dinner
- ✓ Full-service bar, regional specialty beers
- ✓ Reservations suggested during peak mealtimes
- ✓ Atmosphere near the garden is quite nice

The first time we visited Bonfamille's, it took us by surprise. The restaurant features a glassed-in garden area, and sitting by it was quite romantic. The menu features a mix of American and Creole entrees. Breakfasts include a wide array of standards plus Skillet Combos, which are large meals featuring eggs, potatoes, and ham, chicken, or Andouille sausage. Dinners run the gamut from Bourbon strip steak to Louisiana salmon. We loved the Shrimp Orleans, Dixie Blackened Voodoo lager, and Bourbon Street bread pudding. Not the finest dining at Disney, but good dining at a reasonable price.

NEW Bongos Cuban Cafe

$$$ ★★★★ ♥♥

- ✓ The West Side Esplanade, Downtown Disney
- ✓ Table service, lunch and dinner, open 11 A.M. to 2 A.M.
- ✓ Two full-service bars
- ✓ Priority seating suggested for dinner
- ✓ Atmosphere is tropical and beautiful
- ✓ Live Latino music 10:30 P.M. to 2 A.M., Wednesday through Sunday

We dined here recently with some friends from California. We ate late in the afternoon on the ground floor patio, overlooking Lake Buena Vista. It was beautiful and relaxing. Later, we reflected on our meal over some cafe Cubano and a few shared desserts.

Bongos is owned by singer Gloria Estefan and is operated by Lario's, a popular Miami South Beach supper club and one that was recently voted "Best Cuban Restaurant in the U.S." The cuisine is decidedly Latino, and the atmosphere recalls the days of splashy supper clubs and Latin rhythms. Inside and out, Bongos recalls Havana of the 1930s and '40s. Tile mosaics bring scenes of this old city to life, and art deco palms, bamboo curtains, and conga drum bar stools import all the exuberance and romance of Old Havana. Late in the evening, there is live music and dancing. Bongos is chic, stylish, nostalgic, and fun.

The large menu covers all the bases of Cuban cuisine with such standards as ropa vieja, bistec de Palomilla, churrasco, zarzuela de mariscos, and arroz con pollo. Seafood, steaks, poultry, and sandwiches: Bongos has it all. The menu is large and the food is interesting and well prepared. Dining here can be done downstairs or up, inside or on charming patios ♥♥ outside.

Bongos also brings to Downtown Disney a bit of Miami's Little Havana with its sidewalk cafe window. There are a thousand places like this in Miami, and they are as much a part of the Cuban culture as the Spanish language. The cafe features a variety of Cuban sandwiches and pastries and, of course, cafe Cubano. The small seating area is pleasant and right on the avenue.

California Grill

$$$ ★★★★★ ♥♥

- ✓ Disney's Contemporary Resort
- ✓ Table service, dinner only
- ✓ Full-service bar; outstanding California wine list
- ✓ Priority seating a must
- ✓ Atmosphere is stylish and modern with a stunning panorama
- ✓ Tips: Have dinner here during the Magic Kingdom's fireworks show or have late-night sushi in the bar. No reservation? Try getting here when it opens at 6 P.M.

The California Grill has the best food at Walt Disney World. There, we said it.

Our recent meal here has proved once again to us that Chef Cliff Pleau is out there on the leading edge of culinary creativity and that the kitchen staff of the Grill, in the face of large numbers of diners, somehow manages to maintain an unrelentingly high level of quality.

How do they do it? Cliff tells us that he frequently gets his best ideas when he is not even thinking about food. As for the staff, we have sat at Yoshi's sushi bar and watched with amazement. Everyone back there is *totally* into whatever they are doing, whether it's tossing a salad or plating a tuna steak. Even if you aren't watching, you will know as soon as your food arrives. These people *care.* It takes more than a great chef to make a great restaurant, and no one knows this better than Cliff Pleau. And no one appreciates it more than the hundreds who dine here nightly.

During our recent meal, we were able to sample a great many things on the Grill's continually changing menu. What is freshest and best in the marketplace is listed at the top of the menu and is repeated again throughout the descriptions of the evening's creations. During our visit, we applauded the smoked pompano sushi, black mussels with green garlic in Thai curry broth, and warm duck salad with Napa cabbage, organic beets, and blood orange vinaigrette. Hold on, this was just the first course. Later, we were thrilled with the chili dusted yellowfin tuna with angel hair pasta and spicy miso bouillon, spit roasted chicken with caramelized root vegetables and warm malt mustard vinaigrette, and barbecued grilled beef filet. We even managed small tastes of two of our longtime favorites, the bonsai tuna rolls and grilled pork tenderloin with polenta and balsamic smothered crimini mushrooms. While the Grill's menu will have likely moved on to new creations for your visit, we can promise an extraordinary dining experience. This may be a performance kitchen, but the real show here is the food.

A few suggestions are in order for this, Disney's most popular and most celebrated restaurant. First, be sure to go. This is a trip worth taking, so make your reservations and show up early. Next, the service staff here is extremely knowledgeable about both what comes out of the kitchen and what emerges from manager George Miliotes extraordinary wine cellar. Remember that every wine is served by the glass, so be sure to ask your server what is recommended for each course of your meal. And finally, leave enough room for dessert. This is a course you will surely not want to miss.

Cape May Cafe

$$ ★★

✓ Disney's Beach Club Resort
✓ Table-service buffet, breakfast and dinner
✓ Full-service bar
✓ Reservations suggested
✓ Atmosphere is pleasant, though hardly memorable
✓ Tip: To make the Clambake a memorable meal, add a lobster. It's the most reasonably priced one at Disney, too.

A character breakfast with Admiral Goofy and friends is featured here each morning. The spread is large, and the quality is quite good. If you can't find something here, they'll be glad to fix it for you.

We wish that the Clambake Dinner were as good as it sounds. Promising a buffet of New England–style seafood, Cape May delivers instead a large selection of food that is simply adequate. As good an idea as a seafood buffet may sound, this kind of delicate food just doesn't stand up well to large batches and steam tables. Still, while this is not seafood dining at its best, Cape May offers a moderately priced, all-you-can-eat buffet that includes chicken, shrimp, fish, clams, and much more.

Cap'n Jack's Oyster Bar

$ ★ ♥

✓ The Downtown Disney Marketplace
✓ Table service, lunch and dinner
✓ Full-service bar
✓ Reservations not accepted
✓ Atmosphere is charming, especially if you sit by a window overlooking the water

Cap'n Jack's is almost more of a bar than a restaurant. Almost. Overlooking the lake and Downtown Disney, this cozy little eatery is immersed in nautical decor. Fish nets, polished brass, and the usual seaside amenities make this place rather inviting.

This year though, we've noticed that Cap'n Jack's has made its menu a bit more upscale. Along with some of the old favorites, it now features prime rib and lobster tails. During our visit this year, we found the food to be not to our liking. If you are in the neighborhood looking for some seafood, we'd suggest that you walk over to Fulton's Crab House.

Captain's Tavern

$$ ★★

- ✓ Old Port Royale, Disney's Caribbean Beach Resort
- ✓ Table service, dinner only
- ✓ Beer, wine, and specialty drinks
- ✓ Priority seating suggested during peak hours
- ✓ Atmosphere is comfortable, woody, and nautical

The only table-service restaurant at the Caribbean Beach, Captain's Tavern offers a modest menu of seafood, poultry, and meats. Quality and value are both acceptable here. We particularly enjoyed the chicken wings and found our other choices to be tasty and competently prepared.

Chef Mickey's Buffet

$$ ★

- ✓ Disney's Contemporary Resort
- ✓ Table-service character buffet, breakfast and dinner
- ✓ Wine and beer
- ✓ Priority seating a must
- ✓ Atmosphere is noisy and fun

Both meals here are the usual Disney buffets. Breakfasts feature a spread of egg dishes, pancakes and French toast, breakfast meats, and fruits and cereals. Dinners offer an interesting selection of poultry, fish, pastas, and roast beef as well as numerous side dishes and desserts. The food is fair, but you'd be missing the point if you visited Chef Mickey's for that. This is a place for Disney character fun, and it is one of the most popular character meals in the land. A great place to eat with kids.

Chefs de France Restaurant

$$$ ★★★ ♥

- ✓ France Pavilion, Epcot
- ✓ Table service, lunch and dinner
- ✓ Full-service bar with French wines
- ✓ Reservations are a must, unless you arrive before 12:30 P.M. for lunch and 6 P.M. for dinner
- ✓ Atmosphere is pleasant, especially in the evening

The kitchen and menu at Chefs de France are supervised by three of France's most famous chefs: Roger Verdé, Paul Bocuse, and Gaston

LeNôtre. This large restaurant features paneled walls, exquisite fixtures, and works of French Impressionist art. Service is impeccable, and tables are dressed with white linens. It is a delightful re-creation of a Parisian restaurant and features a charming glassed-in porch dining room.

It is worth noting that Chefs has expanded into the areas that once belonged to the Bistro de Paris and Au Petit Cafe. We are sorry to report that these pleasant eateries no longer exist here at Disney's France. The romantic seating of the upstairs Bistro is now open only on the busiest of evenings. Ask to be seated there if you so desire.

As for the food at Chefs de France, it is imaginatively conceived and as well prepared as is possible for the large numbers of guests that are served here. The large and decidedly Gallic menu features classic French fare as well as the innovative cuisines of these three great chefs: Mediterranean seafood casserole, pot-au-feu, roast breast of duck in orange sauce, and grilled tenderloin of beef are only a few of the many good choices here. From appetizers to soups and salads, we are sure that you'll find something here to enjoy. The lunch menu at Chefs de France features many of the same entrees found at dinner, and we think this is a good place for an Epcot midday meal. Chefs de France features wines paired with each entree.

NEW CINDERELLA'S ROYAL TABLE

$$$ ★★★ ♥♥♥

✓ Fantasyland, Magic Kingdom
✓ Table service, breakfast, lunch, and dinner
✓ No alcohol (this is the Magic Kingdom!)
✓ Atmosphere is beautiful and memorable
✓ Tip: Priority seating is a must.

At last, Cinderella has a chef. After years of waiting, we are happy to report that the food here is finally worthy of the lovely surroundings.

This royal place is located inside the castle, and its ambience is just what you would wish for: a cavernous stone hall, "medieval" tapestries, stained glass windows, suits of armor, and great tables befit for lords and ladies. And of course, all the rest of the details are here too, and frequently, Cinderella herself greeting diners in the downstairs hall. Yes, this is a fantasy dining experience, one that is made all the finer by a chef and menu that live up to such a regal atmosphere.

The dinner menu here includes roasted prime rib, a shellfish risotto, herbed chicken with polenta, and a delicious spice-encrusted salmon. These and all accompaniments met with our approval. The lunch menu includes several of the dinner entrees as well as Major Domo's Pie and a few good sandwiches and salads. Mornings at the castle feature a Cinderella character buffet. Priority seating here is an absolute must, but if you are coming as a couple, you may well be able to get in after a short wait. Be sure to ask.

NEW CÍTRICOS

$$$ ★★★★★ ♥♥♥

✓ Disney's Grand Floridian Resort
✓ Table service, dinner only
✓ Full-service bar; outstanding wine list
✓ Priority seating advised
✓ Atmosphere is beautiful, elegant and romantic
✓ Tip: Try the Grand Wine Pairing for $20 per person and take advantage of manager/sommelier John Blazon's amazing knowledge of wine.

This stylish restaurant is the creation of the designer of the California Grill and the Flying Fish. From furnishings and wall sconces to plush carpets and table service, all things are uniquely original creations. Our waitress even wore a broach that was the restaurant's signature curl. Everything is pure Cítricos, and everything is serenely beautiful and more than just a bit romantic. But this restaurant isn't just another pretty face. In the open kitchen here at Cítricos is Chef Roland Muller, and it is his cuisine that is this restaurant's real focus.

Cítricos offerings are an intriguing melange of Mediterranean, French, and Caribbean sensibilities and are drawn from a palate of what is best in the marketplace each day. Our most recent meal here began with a veal and mushroom potato ravioli that was nothing short of stunning. Other openers followed as we oohed and aahed our way through the menu. Salmon tartare, lobster salad, and wild mushroom risotto were all exceptional. We hope that Chef Muller's grilled fresh foie gras with green lentil ragout will be there for your visit.

For entrees, one of us ordered the signature veal shank and the other had the Maine lobster and roasted loin of lamb with ratatouille. All were exceptional in every way. Yes, this was indeed a memorable meal, but it is worth noting that we have dined here more than twice and once ordered a steak and appetizer that were oddly less than the usual perfect. Still, we feel confident recommending Cítricos so highly.

If you are seeking a dining experience that will bring stylish presentations and rich creations together in a focus that is enchantingly beautiful, with service that is both knowledgeable and faultless, then you should set your sights on Cítricos.

Concourse Steakhouse

$$ (dinner $$$) ★★★

- ✓ Disney's Contemporary Resort
- ✓ Table service, breakfast, lunch, and dinner
- ✓ Full-service bar, good wine list
- ✓ Priority seating recommended for dinner
- ✓ Atmosphere is noisy and modern
- ✓ Tip: Get here early and beat the crowds.

For breakfast and lunch, the Concourse Steakhouse offers a well-prepared selection of a la carte standards. Lunches include salads, sandwiches, and a very good burger. While this would not be considered fine dining, it is most certainly good eating.

Dinners here enter yet another realm. With an upscale menu of seafood, poultry, and good cuts of meat, this restaurant features dishes that are well prepared, well conceived, and handsomely presented. The creamed spinach is memorable. But for the clamor of the Contemporary's noisy Concourse, we would not hesitate to recommend it.

Coral Cafe

$$ ★★

- ✓ The Walt Disney World Dolphin
- ✓ Table-service buffet, open 6 A.M. to 11 P.M.
- ✓ Beer and wine
- ✓ Reservations not required
- ✓ Atmosphere is not memorable

"All-day dining" is this restaurant's claim, and it offers both buffet and a la carte standards for breakfast, a salad bar and sandwiches for lunch, and a themed buffet each evening. Dinner entrees feature a Caribbean flair and include Jamaican Jerk Chicken, Cilantro Fettuccini, N.Y. Strip Steak West Indies, and Bahamian chicken and crab cakes. Also a variety of sandwiches, burgers, and salads. All in all, this is a pretty good "all-purpose" restaurant.

Coral Reef Restaurant

$$$ ★★★ ♥♥

✓ The Living Seas Pavilion, Future World, Epcot
✓ Table service, lunch and dinner
✓ Reservations required
✓ Atmosphere is especially nice by the aquarium

The Coral Reef is a beautiful and romantic place to dine. This is not the finest seafood at Disney, but the atmosphere more than makes up for it. The Reef is slated for a late 1998 total redesign, and it promises to be an major one. Designer Marty Dorff (Flying Fish, California Grill, and Cítricos) has come up with a plan that will make diners feel as though they are underwater. It will be stylish and memorable. As for menu changes, we would suggest that you expect pretty much the same kind of seafood from the Coral Reef: good but not Disney World's best.

Crystal Palace

$$ ★★★

✓ Main Street USA, Magic Kingdom
✓ Table-service character buffet, breakfast, lunch, and dinner
✓ Priority seating strongly suggested

We particularly enjoy the beautiful interior of this restaurant as well as its imaginative and tasty lunch and dinner buffets. We expect the menu will change over time, but during our meal we enjoyed a wonderful variety of quality fresh salads and both hot and cold entrees, including made-to-order fajitas and a variety of carved meats and fish filets. This is one of the best places to eat in the Magic Kingdom.

Dolphin Fountain

$ ★★

✓ The Walt Disney World Dolphin
✓ Table service, fifties soda shop, open 11 A.M. to 11 P.M.
✓ Atmosphere is loud, bright, and fun
✓ Tip: Good fries. Also serves espresso and cappuccino.

"The Golden Oldies" here refer more to the fried foods than to the fifties rock 'n roll background music. Hot dogs, hamburgers, grilled chicken sandwich, and BLT about sum it up. Toss in a salad, some nachos and fries, and a large selection of soda fountain sweets and ice creams, and you've pretty much described this fun place. This is the Beaches and Cream of the Dolphin. Every resort should have one!

ESPN Club

$$ ★★★

- ✓ Disney's BoardWalk Promenade
- ✓ Table service, lunch and dinner
- ✓ Full-service bar; Redhook beer on tap
- ✓ Atmosphere is noisy, like being at a sports event

This full-service restaurant is also a sports/entertainment club. With a 220-seat arena and wall of video monitors showing the most popular sporting events, this is definitely *the* place to go for the big fight or the playoff game. With more than 70 video monitors and tableside audio controls, a bank of Internet terminals, and state-of-the-art computer games, this is a sports lover's nirvana.

Not just the ultimate in sports entertainment, this place also has an interesting menu of well-prepared standards. Salads, pasta, and a selection of large and tasty sandwiches makes ESPN an eating place too: try the grilled chicken, BBQ pork, or the club sandwich. The burger here is outstanding (not to mention huge). Lots of good finger foods too, to go with the sporting events and drinks.

Evergreen's

$ ★★

- ✓ Poolside at Shades of Green
- ✓ Table service, lunch and dinner
- ✓ Full-service bar, including draught beer
- ✓ No reservations
- ✓ Atmosphere is pleasant
- ✓ Tip: Try the Angus Beef Burger.

This is basically a lunch place, but it is a good one. The menu is small, including pizza, rotisserie chicken, a very good hamburger, and a variety of sandwiches and salads. The atmosphere is pleasant and restaurant-like except for the upside-down tennis court (with players) on the ceiling. Antique golf and tennis equipment adorn the walls. This is a popular lunching place for golfers.

50's Prime Time Cafe

$$ ★★★

- ✓ Disney–MGM Studios
- ✓ Table service, lunch and dinner
- ✓ Full-service bar and lounge
- ✓ Reservations strongly suggested
- ✓ Atmosphere, though not romantic, is memorable and entertaining
- ✓ Tip: Don't leave without trying the shake of the day.

This is one *very* fun place to eat and a really good example of just how good Disney can get. The Prime Time looks just like your "average" American kitchen of the 1950s: Formica tables, knotty pine cupboards, and other authentic "antiques" of the period (our youth!). There's a TV at every table too and it shows clips from old '50s sitcoms: *I Love Lucy, My Little Margie, Our Miss Brooks*, and others. We took our mothers here once for one of our most memorable Disney experiences.

Servers at the Prime Time are brother or cousin, aunt or uncle, and you'd better keep your elbows off the table! There's lots of fun to be had here, but on our most recent visit, we discovered that something's been going on in Mom's kitchen, too. Chef Marianne Hunnel has been paying very close attention to the food, and what's coming out of the kitchen is as engaging as the entertainment. We managed to sample much of the menu and would recommend Cousin Eric's Cheese Steak Sandwich, the exceptional chicken salad croissant, and Granny's Pot Roast. There was more, and we enjoyed it all: Mom's Fried Chicken, a terrific chicken sandwich, and a wonderful grilled chicken Caesar salad. It was all good fun and good food. Oh yes, you'd better finish your meal if you want dessert!

Flying Fish Cafe

$$$ ★★★★★ ♥♥

- ✓ Disney's BoardWalk Promenade
- ✓ Table service, dinner only, from 6 P.M.
- ✓ Full-service bar, outstanding wine list
- ✓ Priority seating a must
- ✓ The atmosphere is 1930s and stylish; a beautiful restaurant with beautiful appointments
- ✓ Tip: For excitement, try the counter by the kitchen. There's a "back room" if you are in more of a quiet mood.

The Flying Fish features more than a dozen champagnes. It's a fitting specialty for our toast to a chef and restaurant that have never once let us down. Yes, the Flying Fish is one of our very favorites.

Because the menu here is "market driven" and forever changing, we aren't able to promise what you'll find on it except for the finest seafood, meats, poultry, and organic produce available. Chef John State's creations are so intriguing that you should prepare yourselves for some tough decisions. Among the Fish's "regulars" are a char-crusted New York strip steak that is the stuff of dreams and a finely seasoned potato-wrapped snapper with leek fondue and cabernet reduction. There's more of course, including the "Chef's Thunder," each evening's special offerings. Like the California Grill, this is one place where you'll leave wondering what delights you might have missed. From opening wine to after-dinner port, from starters to desserts, there is a lot to savor here. If you're like us, you'll be planning your next visit to the Flying Fish before you're even out the door.

Fulton's Crab House

$$$ ★★★★

✓ On the riverboat at Pleasure Island, Downtown Disney (admission not required)
✓ Buffet character breakfast; table-service lunch and dinner
✓ Full-service bar with a very good wine list
✓ Priority seating strongly suggested
✓ Atmosphere is fairly busy and noisy, with nice views from quarterdeck
✓ Tips: Shellfish is this restaurant's specialty. Try eating on the outside deck.

If you have an appetite for the freshest of shellfish and crabs without the fanfare of nouvelle cuisine, head over to Fulton's. Simply, this is an outstanding seafood eatery that specializes in seafood standards. What amazes us about this place is not just its incredible assortment of fish and shellfish but how it manages to get it here with that fresh-off-the-boat taste (check out the day's airfare receipts posted in the hallway for the answer). Fanny Bay oysters, Alaskan king crab, and Penn Cove mussels are but a few of the memorable offerings on Fulton's large menu. Be sure to ask the wine steward to suggest one of the fine West Coast vintages, something ideally suited to your entree. We heartily recommend one of the crab sampler platters. Mornings here at Fulton's feature a Disney character breakfast with Mickey and friends. During this year's visit, we noticed that Fulton's now serves lunch, which is good news for people who can't get in here for dinner.

Garden Grill Restaurant

$$ ★★

✓ The Land Pavilion, Future World, Epcot
✓ Table service, family-style, breakfast, lunch, and dinner
✓ Beer and wine
✓ Priority seating a must
✓ Atmosphere is pleasant, although part of the trip is noisy

Built on a revolving deck, this restaurant transports diners through a scenic part of this pavilion's attraction. Character meals are featured here throughout the day with Farmer Mickey and Minnie. Service is family-style, and the food will keep coming as long as you are willing. On a recent visit here, we found the food to be quite good. Hardly fine dining, the lunch and dinner menus included rotisserie chicken, steak, fried fish, and several side dishes. Breakfast is the usual Disney morning buffet. All in all, a very good value.

Garden Grove Cafe / Gulliver's Grill

$$ ★★ (lunch) / $$$ ★★★★ (dinner)

✓ The Walt Disney World Swan
✓ Table service, breakfast, lunch, and dinner
✓ Full-service bar with modest wine list
✓ Priority seating suggested for dinner
✓ Atmosphere tells a story; pleasant and comfortable

Not really two restaurants, this eatery changes its name for dinner to become Gulliver's Grill. As the Garden Grove Cafe, breakfast offerings include a large buffet of American standards as well as a large menu of morning standards. Lunches feature a la carte salads, sandwiches, and daily specials.

Dinner at Gulliver's Grill is much more upscale. Utilizing the story of *Gulliver's Travels,* dinner begins here with a bit of wine poured into cup-size thimbles. It's not long before you realize that the entire restaurant resembles a large birdcage and, like Gulliver, you are inside. The menu is fairly imaginative with a large selection of steaks, poultry, and seafood. Service is outstanding, the food is very well prepared, and all in all it's a very pleasant restaurant experience. The Caesar salad is the best we can remember having. Offerings include prime rib, lobster and filet mignon, baked shrimp stuffed with crab, and pecan crusted grouper. Disney characters appear here five nights a week.

Grand Floridian Cafe

$$ ★★★★ ♥

✓ Disney's Grand Floridian Resort
✓ Table service, breakfast, lunch, and dinner
✓ Full-service bar
✓ Reservations suggested during peak hours

This is the Grand Floridian's all-purpose restaurant, and as you might expect it is an outstanding place to eat. It is also a very good value. While the Grand Floridian Cafe is not fine dining, it is an excellent place to get a very good meal. Beautiful table service and a splendid view make this a good choice for any meal. The Grand Floridian Cafe is beautiful and pleasant.

Breakfasts include everything from a muffin to Mexican-style eggs served on a tortilla. Lunches include an impressive array of sandwiches, salads, and a few entrees. For dinner, the Cafe offers everything from an outstanding burger to prime rib. This is one of those restaurants that has something for everyone.

Harry's Safari Bar and Grill

$$$ ★★★★ ♥♥

- ✓ The Walt Disney World Dolphin
- ✓ Table service, dinner only
- ✓ Full-service bar, many imported beers
- ✓ Reservations recommended

Harry's is a fun place to dine, especially if you have your children with you. You and your kids will arrive at your table to find a giant stuffed gorilla already seated and waiting for you. The restaurant is safari-themed and memorable. Service is outstanding and the food is wonderful. In short, Harry's is worth the trip. Signature dishes here include venison osso buco, sesame seared tuna, and braised swordfish. Some of the other offerings are shrimp and crab cake, Harry's beef filet, and broiled achiote shrimp. Portions here are not overly large, but quality is quite good. Harry's is beautiful, well themed, and fun.

Hollywood Brown Derby

$$$ ★★★★ ♥♥

- ✓ Disney–MGM Studios
- ✓ Table service, lunch and dinner
- ✓ Full-service bar, good wine list
- ✓ Priority seating suggested
- ✓ Tip: In good weather, ask for a table on the patio.

The Derby is an elegant re-creation of the famous restaurant at Hollywood and Vine. It features the same sketches of 1930s and '40s celebrities, dark polished woodwork, and potted palms. In the evening, there's a grand pianist in the handsome sunken dining room. If you arrive early or late for lunch or for dinner, you're likely to find the Derby quiet and wonderfully romantic.

Our recent meal here convinced us that this is still an excellent choice for dining here at the Studios. For openers, we enjoyed both the crab and corn quesadilla and the chili barbecue scallops. One of us ordered the pork tenderloin and the other had the Tuna Oscar, a seared tuna loin topped with lump crab meat. The tuna was exceptional. For dessert, we split a slice of the grapefruit cake, a refreshing and delicious end to a satisfying dining experience.

NEW House of Blues

$$$ ★★★ ♥ (The Voodoo Garden ♥♥♥)

✓ Downtown Disney
✓ Table service, lunch and dinner
✓ Full-service bar, good wine list
✓ Priority seating suggested especially for weekends
✓ Tip: Try the Sunday Gospel Brunch (see Chapter 4, Downtown Disney).

This pleasing restaurant is a Mississippi roadhouse. Its tin roof and ramshackle exterior hide the unusual and eclectic works of art that virtually cover the interior. From inlaid bottle caps to garish portraits, House of Blues (HOB) features artwork the likes of which you've probably not seen.

The cuisine here is of the Bayou, and the large menu is more than just a bit interesting. Openers include a tasty seafood gumbo, blackened ahi tuna, New Orleans barbecue shrimp, and hickory smoked salmon. For entrees, you can make the trip from the famous Elwood sandwich to blackened prime rib. Other Delta offerings include shrimp and crawfish etouffee, southern fried chicken, Cajun meatloaf, and a good jambalaya. There's much more, even a mesquite-grilled veggie sandwich. Everything tastes fresh and well prepared, and the service is friendly and down-home.

One of our favorite things about HOB is the Voodoo Garden, behind the restaurant. This porch and garden area is exceptionally beautiful, and after dark, it's pure magic. Having a cocktail or dining here on the porch overlooking the lake is an experience we highly recommend. See the coupon in the back of our book for a free appetizer at the Voodoo Garden.

For more information about the House of Blues, its concerts, Gospel Brunch, and the HOB store, see Chapter 4, Downtown Disney.

Juan and Only's Cantina and Bar

$$ ★★★

- ✓ The Walt Disney World Dolphin
- ✓ Table service, dinner only, 6 to 11 P.M.
- ✓ Full-service bar
- ✓ Reservations not required
- ✓ Tip: Try a light meal of appetizers in the bar.

We think that Juan's offers some pretty good Mexican food. From fajitas, pork adobado, and poblano peppers stuffed with shrimp and scallops, to old favorites like burritos, chimichangas, enchiladas, and tacos, the offerings are competently prepared and the portions large. Juan's bar features sangria by the pitcher, a variety of specialty drinks, and a handful of Mexican beers. The atmosphere is cute and south-of-the-border. This place has a story, and the decor (the bar is actually a jail) and menu tell the tale. This is a nice, colorful place to eat.

Kimonos

$$$ ★★★ ♥♥

- ✓ The Walt Disney World Swan
- ✓ Table service and sushi bar, dinner only
- ✓ Full-service bar with good sakes
- ✓ Atmosphere is beautiful and romantic

If you are looking for a place to enjoy sushi and feel like something stunning, quiet, and out of the way, Kimonos is it. This handsome eatery features Japanese lanterns, black-enameled bamboo, plush leather chairs, and hanging kimonos. Offerings of sushi, sashimi, and tempura are quite good. The bar menu also features single-malt scotches, small-batch bourbons, and a variety of sakes. Karaoke is featured later in the evening, and we would suggest that you arrive and depart accordingly.

NEW Kona Cafe (opens late 1998)

$$

- ✓ Disney's Polynesian Resort
- ✓ Table-service: breakfast, lunch, and dinner

This used to be the Coral Isle Cafe but has now enjoyed this rebirth. Of course, we weren't able to actually see this restaurant, but from renderings we were able to see, it should be lively and modern. Brighter blues and purples and a central bakery area promise to make this quite a different place than the American coffee shop–like Coral Isle Cafe. We've been told that this place's signature will be the aroma of rich Kona coffee and the wonderful baked goods that will be turned out here. Expect the menu to be American favorites with a hint of the South Seas. This will continue to be the "all-purpose" restaurant here at the Polynesian.

L'Originale Alfredo di Roma Ristorante

$$ ★★

✓ Italy Pavilion, Epcot
✓ Table service, lunch and dinner
✓ Beer and Italian wines only
✓ Reservations suggested during mealtimes
✓ Restaurant is attractive but crowded and noisy

With a band of entertainers singing and playing during dinner, Alfredo's can be a fun place to eat if you don't mind the noise. Featured dishes here are the standards that have become known as Italian cuisine. Fettucini Alfredo, of course, is the signature dish. Pasta is made fresh.

NEW Le Cellier Steakhouse

$$ ★★★

✓ Canada Pavilion, Epcot
✓ Table service, lunch and dinner
✓ Beer and wine
✓ Priority seating suggested during peak seasons
✓ Atmosphere restful and quiet but not memorable

This is another restaurant that has enjoyed a rebirth of cuisine and one at which we recently enjoyed one of our most pleasant dining experiences here along the World Showcase. Compared to many of the other dining rooms here, Le Cellier is relatively small and able to create food that does not have the mass-produced feeling that is so common here in the countries of Epcot.

The menu features a roasted prime rib, a selection of grilled steaks, a wonderful steak salad, and a delicious glazed salmon. From outstanding salads to satisfying desserts, this is an entirely new restaurant. Not strong on ambience, Le Cellier is a comfortable and quiet retreat from the crowds and a very good choice for a meal here at Epcot.

Liberty Tree Tavern

$$ ★★

✓ Liberty Square, Magic Kingdom
✓ Table service, lunch and buffet dinner
✓ Reservations strongly suggested
✓ Atmosphere is pleasant and comfortable
✓ Tips: Try the Liberty Tree for lunch. If you are looking for a light meal, try splitting one of the large sandwiches.

Decor here is Colonial American and it is done quite well, down to the "hand-hewn" ceiling of the waiting area. The Liberty Tree Tavern is a pleasant and restful place to eat. The food is well prepared but not great. The lunch menu offers a variety of large sandwiches and such entrees as fresh fish, turkey dinner, pot roast, and shrimp and vegetable pasta. The strawberry vinaigrette salad dressing is quite good. The Liberty Tree Tavern is sponsored by Stouffers.

The Character dinner buffet features roasted chicken, flank steak, and several accompaniments.

Mama Melrose's Ristorante Italiano

$$ ★★★

✓ Disney–MGM Studios
✓ Table service, lunch and dinner
✓ Full-service bar
✓ Reservations strongly suggested
✓ Atmosphere is cute and interesting

Like many other restaurants here at Disney, Mama's has enjoyed an improved menu. Offerings these days include not only some Italian favorites such as veal scaloppini, seafood carbonara, and Caesar salad but also some more interesting dishes such as oak-grilled vegetables in pesto dressing, blackened New York strip steak, and pan seared ahi. Of course, Mama's still features its wonderful wood-fired pizzas. If it sounds a bit more upscale than you remember it to be, that's probably because it is.

Marrakesh

$$ ★★★ ♥♥

✓ Morocco Pavilion, Epcot
✓ Table service, lunch and dinner

- ✓ Full-service bar
- ✓ Reservations suggested
- ✓ The atmosphere here is exotic
- ✓ Tips: The Moroccan Diffa for Two provides a real assortment of tastes. There are other combination platters, too.

Marrakesh is one of Epcot's most exotic restaurants. Featuring a live belly dancer and musicians at both lunch and dinner, it is one of our favorites here. From a selection of couscous dishes to tagine of chicken, shish kebab, and Cornish Hen Emrouzia, Marrakesh delivers what so many other World Showcase restaurants merely promise: the exotic and the unique. If you are looking for a dining adventure beyond the usual, don't miss it.

NEW MAYA GRILL

$$$ ★★★★ ♥♥♥

- ✓ Disney's Coronado Springs Resort
- ✓ Table-service, dinner only
- ✓ Full-service bar, good wine list, a great margarita
- ✓ Priority seating strongly suggested
- ✓ Atmosphere is quiet and understated

One evening, we ran in to John State, chef of the Flying Fish. "Have you eaten at the Maya Grill?" he wanted to know.

He had and apparently had been very impressed by the food. It was somewhere on our list of new restaurants to try, but his recommendation gave us cause to get there sooner rather than later. We were not sorry. In fact, we can hardly find enough superlatives to describe our meal there. It was exciting, exotic, delicious, and perfectly prepared: just the kind of restaurant experience we look for.

Maya Grill purports to be "Nuevo Latino" and whatever *that* means, we found the menu here to be the perfect fusion of a dozen or so South and Central American cuisines. This is not a mix of foods redolent with chili peppers and it is definitely *not* tacos and enchiladas. No, Chef Beatriz Candelario takes the high road here, offering instead a painter's palate of extraordinary new tastes and combinations.

The atmosphere here at Maya Grill evokes the ancient Mayan world and its harmony with sun, fire, and water. Built to have the feel of a great stone Mayan temple, the decor is simple, almost spartan. An offering to the gods "burns" on a pedestal under the center of the pyramid-like interior.

Our journey at Maya Grill began with a basket of fresh bread and a chimichurri dipping sauce. Openers included Panuchos Yucatecos, an exciting sampler of pan fried corncakes with spiced pork, snapper, and roasted poblano peppers. The seafood ceviche was some of the best we can remember having, and the duck tamal was delicious. We were lucky enough to be able to sample almost every entree and, except for the Grilled Shrimp Pasta, everything was exceptional. We long for another taste of the extraordinary pumpkin seed encrusted snapper. Other memorable entrees were the Ropa Vieja and Grilled Tenderloin Churrasco. As we were leaving the Maya Grill, our only quandary was deciding who we'd like to bring with us on our next visit. It's our highest form of compliment.

NEW NARCOOSSEE'S

$$$ ★★★★★

- ✓ Disney's Grand Floridian Resort
- ✓ Table service, lunch and dinner
- ✓ Full-service bar, very good wine list
- ✓ Priority seating recommended for dinner
- ✓ Waterfront atmosphere with a pleasant view, but can be noisy
- ✓ Tip: If you can't make it for dinner, take the boat here from the Magic Kingdom for one of Disney's best lunch menus. See the back of this book for a valuable coupon good at this wonderful restaurant.

With the arrival of a new chef and a new cuisine, this restaurant has become one of our very favorite places to dine here at Disney (or anywhere else). Swiss Chef Anette Grecchi has come here from the kitchen of the California Grill and has managed to fuse her continental sensibilities with the excitement of West Coast cuisine. Her simple yet sophisticated touch shines brightly here at Narcoossee's, making this a dining experience rich in freshness and originality. We think that Chef Grecchi brings to Disney a new kind of cuisine, something of a synthesis of old, of new, and of what is yet to come. Less concerned with fancy plates of elaborate garnishes, Chef Grecchi's interest is more towards using the finest ingredients and towards preparations that allow their essential nature to shine through.

Each menu at Narcoossee's begins with the day's market cornucopia: what is freshest and best in the marketplace. These basic ingredients become the threads that run through the tapestry of each day's offerings, and Grecchi's ability to glorify them rather than to redefine them is what makes this such a memorable dining experience.

The perfection of Narcoossee's unforgettable Roasted Lamb Chops Provencale still haunts us. From asparagus soup and grilled tuna with couscous, to pasta with forest mushroom ragout, we haven't had a thing here that has not been exceptional. Chef Grecchi also offers several vegetarian dishes each day. Not simply entrees with the meat omitted, each is a carefully prepared original. From openers to the desserts, this place simply doesn't miss a beat.

Chef Grecchi is truly one of Disney's rising stars and Narcoossee's one of its most exciting dining destinations. Maybe we'll see you there.

See the back of this book for a coupon good for either a free appetizer sampler or two glasses of sparkling wine while dining at Narcoossee's.

NINE DRAGONS RESTAURANT

$$ ★★ ♥

- ✓ China Pavilion, Epcot
- ✓ Table service, lunch and dinner
- ✓ Full-service bar
- ✓ Reservations suggested
- ✓ A beautiful dining room; quiet and pleasant
- ✓ Tip: Try snacking here on dumplings, if you wish to enjoy the atmosphere. This restaurant is usually not too busy. If you can't get in elsewhere, it's a good choice.

With all of its carved furnishings and beautiful Chinese artwork, Nine Dragons is a lovely place to dine. The food is well prepared but just not quite exciting enough for our tastes. Offerings include Mu Shu Pork and Kung Pao Chicken. Still, if you enjoy Chinese food and are able to get yourselves over the expense of this elegant Chinese restaurant, we think you'll enjoy a meal here. Lately, Nine Dragons has been offering an evening noodle-making demonstration.

1900 PARK FARE

$$ ★★★

- ✓ Disney's Grand Floridian Resort
- ✓ Table service, character buffets, breakfast, and dinner
- ✓ Reservations recommended (this place is popular)
- ✓ Atmosphere is noisy and gay
- ✓ Tip: Bring your camera for some terrific pictures. Ask your server to snap a photo of the two of you with some of the Disney characters.

We think that this is Disney's best buffet. Offerings for both breakfast and dinner are large and the quality is surprisingly good. The only drawback is that Park Fare is noisy. First there's all of the children and characters and then there is the giant mechanical organ. If you are looking for peace and quiet, this isn't it. If you are looking for fun and a character meal, we doubt that you'll find a better one than this.

'Ohana

$$ ★★ ♥

✓ Great Ceremonial House, Disney's Polynesian Resort
✓ Table-service buffet, breakfast, and dinner
✓ Full-service bar, Polynesian specialty drinks
✓ Atmosphere is tropical, sometimes noisy

'Ohana is beautiful, and everything here is steeped in the flavor of the South Seas. From the "thatched roof" and stone floor to the fire-pit grill, 'Ohana has the feel of a Polynesian longhouse. Costumed servers bring you course after course of roasted meats and seafood on sword-like skewers. It is a South Seas feast, fit for a Polynesian king.

There is entertainment throughout the evening. Most of it is fun, and with games for kids, it can get quite noisy. The food here is pretty good. Grilled shrimp, chicken, and sausage as well as a vegetable lo mein make 'Ohana a good choice for fun dining.

Olivia's Cafe

$$ ★★

✓ Old Key West
✓ Table service, breakfast, lunch, and dinner
✓ Full-service bar; good wine list
✓ Reservations suggested for character breakfasts (Sunday, Monday, and Wednesday)

Key West is the theme here, and Olivia's manages to offer an airy and pleasant atmosphere. The menu here is fairly broad and although it purports to offer specialties of the Florida Keys, some of the local color, such as conch fritters, has disappeared from the menu in the last year. Still, it is an inviting menu, one that features a hearty selection of steaks, poultry, and seafood. There is also a nice offering of fresh salads and soups. In our experience here, the food has been a little unpredictable.

One drawback to Olivia's is getting there. You'll need a car or some fancy busing. Try busing from the Downtown Disney Marketplace or one of the theme parks back to Old Key West.

OUTBACK

$$ ★★★

- ✓ Buena Vista Palace Resort and Spa
- ✓ Table service, dinner only
- ✓ Full-service bar
- ✓ Reservations suggested

Don't confuse this place with the Outback Steakhouse chain. While both claim an Australian theme, this Outback really delivers. The open-hearth dining area enjoys such touches as a three-story waterfall and a fish pond. Specialties of the house include hearty grilled steaks and giant lobsters. If you can manage to devour one of these four-and-a-half-pound monsters, you'll get a plaque on the wall with your name on it. But one of the things that makes this place so "Aussie" is that the Outback serves both kangaroo and ostrich meat. We tried the ostrich and were pleasantly surprised. It was tender and tasty, and we found it to be a red meat that seemed lighter and more agreeable than beef.

The Outback menu is large and accommodates virtually any taste. From poultry to fish filets, this place has a lot to offer. We found both food and service to be quite good. We could see ourselves going back for the ostrich.

PALIO

$$ ★★★★ ♥♥♥

- ✓ The Walt Disney World Swan
- ✓ Table service, dinner only
- ✓ Full-service bar
- ✓ Reservations suggested
- ✓ Tips: If you want to make a budget meal out of it, order one pizza and one of the more moderately priced entrees. Drop by later in the evening for an espresso or cappuccino and your choice of desserts.

Your meal at Palio will begin with a Boccalino, the traditional "little jug" of wine. This restaurant is easily Disney World's finest in Italian cuisine and is, we think, one of the very best places to dine at Walt Disney World. If you are dining as a couple, let us suggest one of the comfortable booths where you may sit next to each other. Once the strolling violinist (or guitarist) begins, you'll begin to see why we rate this place as an outstanding romantic dining experience. Musicians play Tuesday through Saturday.

Palio is not a spaghetti-and-meatballs Italian restaurant. It is not difficult to eat here for about the same price as most of the Epcot restaurants. The food at Palio is incomparably superior. Entrees include seafood and spaghettini baked in parchment, ragout of lobster and tortellini, and pork alla Milanese. The osso buco was extraordinary, and we still long for the Risotto con Vongole. The specialty pizzas are small but exceptionally good. The dessert counter at Palio is Disney's finest, featuring about 20 incredible creations.

Planet Hollywood

$$ ★★

✓ Pleasure Island, Downtown Disney (admission not required)
✓ Table service, lunch and dinner
✓ Full-service bar
✓ No reservations accepted
✓ Atmosphere is very interesting, not at all romantic
✓ Tips: Ask for seating on the third floor. To avoid waiting in long lines at the door, try eating during the off-hours.

If this isn't the world's most outrageous Planet Hollywood, we would like to see the one that is. Built in a planet-shaped sphere, this restaurant is crammed full of real movie props and costumes. Loud and nightclub-like, it is also interesting and fun. Some of the food is quite good, but some is average. In our quest for the best burger of Disney, this one was a real disappointment. The Thai shrimp, however, was excellent.

Plaza Restaurant

$ ★★

✓ Main Street USA, Magic Kingdom
✓ Table service, lunch and dinner
✓ Priority seating suggested
✓ Atmosphere is quaint and a pleasant escape

This turn-of-the-century, art nouveau eatery offers a fairly standard menu of well-prepared sandwiches including a Reuben, double-decker roast beef, and grilled turkey. Other tasty offerings include a Southwest chicken salad and a variety of burgers. Most are under $10. This is a nice place for lunch.

Portobello Yacht Club

$$ ★★★★ ♥

✓ Pleasure Island, Downtown Disney (admission not required)
✓ Table service, lunch and dinner
✓ Full-service bar, good wine list
✓ No reservations accepted
✓ Atmosphere is casual; can be noisy at peak hours
✓ Tips: If the weather is pleasant, try sitting in the beautiful garden area outside.

Portobello is one of our favorite places to eat at Walt Disney World. The menu features a large array of Northern Italian foods, all elegantly prepared. We've never had anything here that we didn't like a lot. The gelato cappuccino is one of our very favorite desserts.

Don't miss eating here. For a moderately priced restaurant at Disney World, this place is one of the best. We like to share an entree along with several appetizers.

Rainforest Cafe

$$ ★★★

✓ The Downtown Disney Marketplace and the NEW Animal Kingdom
✓ Table service, breakfast (Animal Kingdom only), lunch, and dinner
✓ Full-service bar
✓ Atmosphere is fun, exciting, and very noisy
✓ Tips: Priority seating is available only at the Animal Kingdom. We advise it. At the Marketplace, avoid mealtimes; try eating before 11:30 A.M. or at 4:30 P.M.

This is one very busy but very fun place to eat. The smoldering volcano exterior of this restaurant towers above the rest of the Marketplace. At the Animal Kingdom, the Rainforest is hidden behind a 65-foot waterfall. Inside either is a dense "rain forest," complete with canopy of trees, periodic thunderstorms, and a host of robotic wildlife that all occasionally come to life. It has the detail and excitement of a theme park attraction. It's a wild place to eat!

Much of the food here is surprisingly good. Expecting the unremarkable cuisine common to theme-restaurants, we found instead a large and imaginative menu of well-prepared appetizers, entrees, sandwiches, and desserts. Even the collection of specialty drinks (alcoholic, if you like) was refreshing and delicious. We happily rate this place as a "not to miss" lunch or dinner. We'd suggest, however, that you steer away from the meat-type dishes, such as steak or pork chops. Everything else is simply wonderful. Don't miss the "Pieces of Ate" or the Coconut Bread Pudding.

The Rainforest Cafe at the Animal Kingdom serves breakfast, beginning each morning at 6:30. The menu features some interesting stuff: custom breakfast pizzas, jungle wraps, and our favorite, Tonga Toast. There's much more, and it's all unusual and unusually good. For the money, the Rainforest is a very good value.

Rose and Crown Pub & Dining Room

$$ ★★ ♥

✓ United Kingdom, Epcot
✓ Table service, lunch and dinner
✓ Full-service bar with English ales and beers
✓ Reservations suggested
✓ Atmosphere on the patio is memorable, especially during pleasant weather or during IllumiNations

A pleasant enough place to eat, especially if the weather is cool enough to dine on the patio overlooking the lagoon. The food here is well prepared and tasty, although nothing here seems particularly memorable (much like real British cuisine).

Fish and chips, roast lamb, steak and kidney pie, and a chicken and leek pie are among the many offerings. The restaurant is divided into three sections; each has a distinctly different decor, and each is comfortable and quiet.

San Angel Inn Restaurante

$$ ★★ ♥♥♥

✓ Mexico Pavilion, Epcot
✓ Table service, lunch and dinner
✓ Full-service bar with Mexican beer
✓ Reservations suggested during busy mealtimes
✓ Tip: Try having a cold Mexican beer and some nachos or other appetizer. This way, you'll get to enjoy the atmosphere without having to eat an entire meal.

What a beautiful place this is. It's always nighttime at the San Angel Inn, which is set amidst the facade of a quaint Mexican village. The restaurant overlooks the most scenic part of the pavilion's boat ride, where the River of Time passes through a dense and mountainous jungle. Enjoy your meal on the lovely plaza at the river's edge, while a volcano smolders in the distance. It is truly memorable; a charming and romantic spot.

The food here is good, though not memorable. It seems to be better if you manage to stay away from such standard items as enchiladas, burritos, and tacos and try something a bit more exotic. One of us particularly enjoyed the grilled tenderloin of beef here recently. Ask about the daily chef's special.

Sci-Fi Dine-In Theater

$$ ★★

- ✓ Disney–MGM Studios
- ✓ Table service, lunch and dinner
- ✓ Beer and wine
- ✓ Priority seating a must
- ✓ Atmosphere is cute and entertaining

At this popular restaurant, you'll eat in a "convertible" at a drive-in theater that shows nonstop 1950s sci-fi movie previews. Servers arrive on roller skates, and the menu features American standards jazzed up with such names as "Creature from the Pasta Lagoon" and "Attack of the Killer Sandwich." Sci-Fi's other offerings include a prime rib, Caesar salad, and marinated pork loin. It's all a lot of campy fun, and the food is fairly good.

Seasons Dining Room

$$ ★★

- ✓ The Disney Institute
- ✓ Table service, breakfast, lunch, and dinner
- ✓ Beer and good wine list
- ✓ Priority seating not required
- ✓ Atmosphere is sunny and pleasant
- ✓ Present your Annual Pass here for a 20% discount on food and beverage (does not include alcoholic beverages).

Being a bit off the beaten path has not helped Seasons make a name for itself. While the menu here certainly sounds inviting and the ingredients are fresh and in season, our recent meal here suggests that preparation is somewhat inconsistent. One of us ordered a marvelous portobello mushroom strudel. It was beautiful, imaginative, and delicious. Our other entree was a filet of fish, which was a bit dry and otherwise unremarkable. The menu here changes with what else but the seasons of the year. It is large and intriguing. We can only hope that in the future it lives up to its promise.

Spoodles

$$ ★★★★

- ✓ Disney's BoardWalk Promenade
- ✓ Table service, breakfast, lunch, and dinner
- ✓ Beer and large Mediterranean wine list
- ✓ Priority seating for dinner suggested
- ✓ Noisy, family-style atmosphere

We've always liked this restaurant and are happy to report that new chef Bart Hosmer and a new menu have made it even better. Spoodles features a lively Mediterranean cuisine that includes imaginative wood-fired pizzas, salads, and entrees ranging from a delicious scallops with white beans, lemon, fennel, and artichokes to osso buco. The real fun here though, is ordering a spread of appetizers and enjoying Spoodles "tapas-style." From caramelized onion and wild mushroom pizza to cinnamon lamb with cracked bulghur and mint yogurt, the great tastes just keep on coming. For lunches and dinners, kids can assemble their own Spoodles pizza and it will be baked by the cooks.

The breakfast buffet here features not only a tasty selection of usual favorites but also some interesting Mediterranean offerings. For us, it's the best breakfast menu at Disney. There's even a window on the BoardWalk that serves Spoodles' wonderful pizza.

Tempura Kiku

$$ ★★★ ♥♥

- ✓ Japan Pavilion, Epcot
- ✓ Table service, lunch and dinner
- ✓ Full-service bar
- ✓ Reservations suggested
- ✓ Atmosphere is exotic and quiet

If you're at Epcot and looking for an eating adventure, this is a good one. With fewer than 30 chairs, it is surely the smallest restaurant at Walt Disney World. It consists of three counters surrounding a compact cooking area. Chairs are comfortable, and watching the Japanese chefs practice their skillful art is engaging.

The menu includes a variety of good sushi and well-prepared tempura, a lightly battered and delicately fried variety of chicken, shrimp, or vegetables. Either may be ordered individually or in a variety of combinations. Other interesting items include Kabuki beef and a chestnut mousse dessert.

Teppanyaki Dining Room

$$ ★★★

✓ Japan Pavilion, Epcot
✓ Table service, lunch and dinner
✓ Full-service bar, Kirin beer and sake
✓ Reservations suggested during mealtimes
✓ Atmosphere is Japanese: pleasant and themed

If you have ever eaten at a Benihana's restaurant, then you will know what this experience is all about. Here at Teppanyaki, you sit at tables with other Disney guests. The center of each table is actually a cooking surface, where a Japanese chef will "perform." The chef's deft chopping and slicing skills and some knife-acrobatics are quite impressive. Entrees include shrimp, chicken, beef, and lobster, each sliced or cubed and grilled right in front of you. There are also grilled vegetables and several dipping sauces. The food is quite good, and the show is fairly entertaining.

Tony's Town Square Restaurant

$$ ★★★

✓ Main Street USA, Magic Kingdom
✓ Table service, breakfast, lunch, and dinner
✓ Reservations a must
✓ Atmosphere is pleasant, though noisy when crowded (nearly always)

The theme here is from *Lady and the Tramp,* Disney's classic animated film, and the cuisine is Italian. With the arrival of Chef Dee, Tony's has seen a sudden rebirth of cuisine, giving it some of the very best food in the Magic Kingdom. During our recent visit, we enjoyed the fried calamari, roasted goat cheese and fresh tomato dip, and the New York strip steak. We were particularly impressed by the eggplant panino. It certainly isn't the Tony's we used to avoid. Everything here is fresh and well seasoned, and we would happily return for lunch or dinner.

Breakfast is served here at Tony's, and the menu includes "Italian" toast, waffles, eggs, and several good frittatas.

NEW TUSKER HOUSE

$ ★★★

✓ Africa, the Animal Kingdom
✓ Counter service, lunch and dinner
✓ Beer and wine
✓ Atmosphere is exotic; very nice patio out back

Here's a counter-service place we thought worthy of coverage. The Tusker House features a small menu of well-prepared foods that is surprising both for its moderate price and because it is served up over the counter. Don't come here expecting fine dining but good food at moderate prices. This place has a lot going for it. It's beautiful and exotically themed. The quiet patio outside the back of the restaurant is one of our favorite places to eat at the Animal Kingdom.

The Tusker House menu includes a good prime rib with garlic mashed potatoes. Other entrees include a tasty rotisserie chicken, some fresh salads, and some outstanding sandwiches. It's easy to have a good meal here for around $10. We feel certain that the Tusker House will please you.

Located inside the restaurant is the Kusafiri Coffee Shop & Bakery. This is where you'll find dessert as well as a variety of specialty coffee drinks, both hot and cold.

VICTORIA AND ALBERT'S

$$$$ ★★★★★ ♥♥♥♥

✓ Disney's Grand Floridian Resort
✓ Table service, dinner only, two seatings: 6 P.M. and 9 P.M.
✓ Full-service bar, outstanding wine list
✓ Priority seating only: make them when you book your room
✓ Victorian charm and elegance come to life. A true romantic experience.

If you are celebrating something special at Walt Disney World, whether a honeymoon, an anniversary, or simply being in love, and you are looking for a romantic dining experience that you will remember for years to come, let us suggest the award-winning Victoria and Albert's. The ambience here is unforgettably romantic, the service is white-glove and impeccable, and the cuisine of chef Scott Hunnel is a carefully practiced art. Serving a limited number of guests each evening, Hunnel and his staff meticulously prepare imaginative and innovative dishes using only the finest of ingredients from the international marketplace. Hunnel himself picks herbs each day from his own garden on the grounds of the Grand Floridian. Each dish, which is served by "butler and maid" serving team Victoria and Albert, is an individually prepared work of art.

The menu changes daily to accommodate what is freshest and finest, and there are offerings enough to appeal to any sensibility. Victoria and Albert's features two menus: the Standard and the Elite. Royal Wine Pairing may be added to each and provides a variety of outstanding vintages carefully selected to enhance each of the six courses. Guests are served on Royal Doulton china, with Sambonet silver from Italy and Schott-Zwiesel crystal from Germany. During dinner, the live music of a harpist gently fills the air. Quite literally, we have experienced nothing like this restaurant. It is not your everyday *extraordinary* dining experience. We still gush about our experiences here.

If you are after something *really* special at Walt Disney World, and you are looking for a dining experience that you will *never* forget, let us suggest Victoria and Albert's "Chef's Table." This beautifully appointed table, located right in the kitchen, offers a unique gastronomic experience. The most sought-after dining table in Florida, the Chef's Table seats only once during the course of the evening, and it is a once-in-a-lifetime experience.

Make no mistake about it, Victoria and Albert's is an unforgettable and sublime experience. Expensive, no doubt, but worth the price. What better thing can lovers do than to gather such memories?

Whispering Canyon Cafe

$$ ★★

✓ Disney's Wilderness Lodge Resort
✓ Table service, buffet, and a la carte, breakfast, lunch, and dinner
✓ Full-service bar and specialty brews
✓ Priority seating recommended
✓ Wild West atmosphere is charming and entertaining
✓ Tip: There's a cozy little room in the back by the fireplace.

Whispering Canyon's real specialty is meals served family-style. Food arrives in large pans, and it's all-you-care-to-eat. "Sunrise Samplins'" include breakfast skillets of eggs, pan-fried potatoes, breakfast meats, biscuits, waffles, and more. A la carte offerings include fresh fruit platters or light continental fare. "Lunch Grub" is a barbecue served family-style: chicken, ribs, fried fish, baked beans, and corn on the cob. Other choices are available a la carte and include chili, salads, smoked prime rib, burgers, grilled chicken, and a sautéed vegetable platter. Whispering Canyon's fire-roasted dinner is a big spread, much of it smoked in the restaurant's outdoor smoker: ribs, beef, chicken, turkey leg, trail sausage, and a host of accompaniments too. Dinner a la carte offerings include a vegetable platter and a catch of the day. All in all, you get good hearty fare for a reasonable price.

NEW Wildhorse Saloon

$$

- ✓ Pleasure Island, Downtown Disney
- ✓ Table service, lunch and dinner
- ✓ Full-service bar
- ✓ Western-themed supper club

We were sorry to miss the opening of the Wildhorse by only a few weeks. This is a spin-off of the famous Nashville saloon, and it promises to provide both outstanding entertainment and good food, one of our favorite combinations. Inside the saloon, everything enjoys a western sensibility, and the small performance stage is the center of focus. You can belly up to long, wooden bars both upstairs and down or find a table and enjoy the live country-and-western music while you savor the barbecue cuisine. There are dining areas both downstairs around the large dance floor and on the upstairs balcony. As the night wears on, this supper club makes a slow transition towards nightclub as the tables and chairs make way for line dancing.

The Wildhorse Saloon is run by Levy Restaurants of Chicago, the same people who bring you Fulton's Crab House and the Portobello Yacht Club. We expect to find food here that is on par with both of these fine restaurants. Signature items include applewood-smoked ribs, barbecued salmon with charred tomato salsa, catfish, chocolate cherry cobbler, bourbon baked beans, sweet potato salad, fresh cream pie, and banana white chocolate bread pudding. Did we tell you how sorry we were to miss the opening?

For details regarding the Wildhorse Saloon concerts, see Downtown Disney, Chapter 4.

NEW Wolfgang Puck Cafe

$$–$$$ ★★★★

- ✓ The West Side Esplanade, Downtown Disney Marketplace
- ✓ Table service, lunch and dinner (upstairs: dinner only)
- ✓ Full-service bar, outstanding wine list
- ✓ Priority seating suggested for upstairs dining room
- ✓ Atmosphere is lively and artful

"Live, Love, Eat." It's the motto of the Wolfgang Puck Cafe, and it's just one of the things we like about this restaurant. That it is the creation of a husband and wife team naturally appeals to our sensibilities. The colorful, high-energy cafe has been designed by Mrs. Puck, Barbara Lazaroff, and while Chef Puck is not actually working in the kitchen here, the menu and recipes are his creations. But for us, there's even more to like about this place and of course it has to do with food.

One of the first things to know about the Wolfgang Puck Cafe is that it is really four restaurants in one stylish package. Along the avenue here at Downtown Disney, you'll find the counter-service cafe of the Wolfgang Puck Express (see our review of it, next). Inside and downstairs, you'll enjoy both The Cafe and B's Bar.

B's features some of the best sushi in town as well as a full-service bar. The Cafe menu includes many of the dishes that have made Puck so well known: a shrimp BLT, grilled vegetable sandwich, wild mushroom tortellini, Jerk chicken Caesar salad, and barbecue duck quesadillas are just a few. Pizzas are memorable and include spicy shrimp, four cheese, and smoked salmon. The Cafe has two pleasant outside dining areas; one overlooks the lake and the other is along the side of the cafe facing Bongos.

Upstairs at Wolf's is something different. The colorful cracked mosaics seen everywhere downstairs are but an accent here in this small and upscale bistro. Several tables here offer perfect views of the Pleasure Island New Year's Eve fireworks celebration and have even been requested for proposals of marriage. If you are like us, you may wish to be seated near the excitement of the performance kitchen.

Our meal here was memorable. From appetizers of lobster spring roll with papaya slaw to a salad of apples, radicchio, gorgonzola cheese, and caramelized pecans, our openers were sublime. Our entrees of steak and fish and all things on this market-driven menu were well conceived and well prepared. Puck's sense of marrying unlikely ingredients is what makes this food so fascinating. All things were fresh, imaginative, and perfectly prepared. We would not hesitate to return.

NEW WOLFGANG PUCK EXPRESS

$ ★★★

✓ The West Side Esplanade and the Downtown Disney Marketplace

✓ Counter service, lunch and dinner; West Side Esplanade: 11 A.M. to midnight; Marketplace: 11 A.M. to 11 P.M.

✓ A sidewalk cafe

This has got to be the best fast food we've ever had. You'll notice that there are two of these. Their large menus include many Puck favorite including such wood-fired pizzas as spicy chicken, four cheese, and our favorite, spinach, mushroom, and gorgonzola. Other offerings are Chinois chicken salad, tortilla soup, and a selection of signature sandwiches, and imaginative beverages. A bit pricey for counter-service food, but considering the quality, we are happy to stop in here any time.

Yacht Club Galley

$$ ★★★

✓ Disney's Yacht Club Resort
✓ Table service, breakfast, lunch, and dinner
✓ Full-service bar
✓ Reservations not required
✓ Atmosphere is themed and pleasant
✓ Tip: A nice place for lunch if you are over at Epcot. Simply stroll over from the International Gateway.

As we have mentioned, most of the premium resorts feature one all-purpose restaurant, which offers an assortment of dishes for each of the day's meals. We usually find ourselves comparing them all to the Yacht Club Galley. This is one of the best eating places around. Not a fine dining spot, the Galley serves food that is well prepared, tasty, and reasonably priced. Breakfasts are either a la carte or buffet. Lunches feature a large selection of soups, salads, and sandwiches, and dinner adds a number of New England–style entrees. In our many stays at the Yacht or the Beach, we have never been disappointed here.

Decor is yachty, with framed displays of knots and glass-encased models of the beautiful old J-Boats of last century's America's Cup races. Salt and pepper shakers resemble small lighthouses. This is a pleasant place to eat—not particularly memorable, but simply nice.

Yachtsman Steakhouse

$$$ ★★★★ ♥♥

✓ Disney's Yacht Club Resort
✓ Table service, dinner only
✓ Full-service bar
✓ Reservations suggested after 6:30 P.M.
✓ Atmosphere is warm and beautiful
✓ Tip: Try the Chateaubriand for Two.

When we go back to check on restaurants where we've dined in years past, it's nice to know that the great ones are staying great. A recent meal here for Rick's birthday showed us that some of the great ones are even getting better. After sampling a variety of cuts of beef in a variety of cuts of restaurants, we will repeat our claim for this restaurant: If you are looking for the best steak at Walt Disney World, look no further. The variety here is large, and you'll see the grain-fed beef aging in a glass case as you enter. From Kansas City strips to Chateaubriand, there is the perfect cut for every taste. And if steak is not your thing, the Yachtsman offers a full menu of lamb, pork, poultry, seafood, and pasta. All of it is exceptional.

Now to make this fine eatery even better, the Yachtsman has added a variety of more contemporary entrees to its well-established menu of traditional offerings. Ancho-dusted ahi tuna, bourbon charred steak, and even a vegetarian entree all enhance this outstanding experience. Rick's birthday steak was the chipotle rubbed beef filet, and it has become the standard by which all others are judged.

The Craftsman-style ambience of the Yachtsman Steakhouse makes it a charming place to dine. Like the menu, the decor here is simple yet elegant. We highly recommend this restaurant.

Yakitori House

$ ★★

- ✓ Japan Pavilion, Epcot
- ✓ Counter service, lunch and dinner
- ✓ Kirin beer
- ✓ No reservations
- ✓ Garden atmosphere is charming and restful

When we eat in a foreign country, we always like to find restaurants where the locals eat. We guess that this same principle applies to Disney World. The first time we peeked in the Yakitori House, we were surprised to see that nearly every patron was Japanese. That it attracts so many visitors from Japan attests to its authenticity.

The menu here includes teriyaki sandwiches and Kushi-Yaki: skewered chicken, shrimp, or beef that has been basted in soy sauce and sesame oil. Yakitori also features a selection of Japanese sweets and beverages.

The restaurant itself is a bamboo-like structure. In good weather, we suggest eating outside in the lovely garden area.

CHAPTER 7

Recreation and Other Pastimes

In the last few years, Disney has gotten into sports in a big way. Of course, Walt Disney World has always been a place of nearly unlimited recreation. Boating, biking, tennis, golf, horseback riding, fishing, and waterskiing are just a few of the possibilities when it comes to sports. There are spas, fitness centers, miniature golf, and personal training. Now, with the Walt Disney World Speedway and Disney's Wide World of Sports, both spectator and participation activities have been brought to an altogether new level. The real truth about Walt Disney World is that there is so much recreation that even *without* the theme parks, it would still be the Vacation Capital of the World.

Mixing your theme park adventures with this kind of fun and relaxation will make for a more leisurely and memorable holiday. These activities will get the two of you out of the mobs and into more intimate settings. So, open yourselves up to a delightfully different kind of Disney experience. Take a sail or a cruise. Ride a bike or ride a horse. Get massaged or go bass fishing. Watch a professional tennis match or catch the Harlem Globetrotters. Or be adventurous and take a few laps around the speedway at 145 miles an hour. Whatever you do, make your Disney vacation something more than just a theme park holiday. Get out and get in on all this fun.

Golf

No matter how you slice it, Walt Disney World is a golfer's paradise. With 99 holes of championship PGA-level golf and over 20,000 resort rooms, Disney World is the largest golf resort in the world. Disney's six courses each present unique challenges to both amateur and professional. There are five 18-hole championship courses and Oak Trail, a nine-hole executive course. All are open to the public and, as Disney resort guests, you'll get discounted green fees and preferential tee times.

Peak season at the Disney courses is November to April and green fees are $120 per round at either Osprey Ridge or Eagle Pines and $100 at either the Palm, Magnolia, or Lake Buena Vista Courses. Add $10 per round if you are not a Disney resort guest. Play during the May to October off-season is $90 for all courses, $100 for day guests. Green fees at Oak Trail are $35.

If this sounds a bit pricey, there are ways to make the extraordinary Disney courses more affordable. During the off-season, tee times after 10 A.M. are $65 for Osprey Ridge or Eagle Pines and $45 for the other courses. There are also a variety of attractive twilight rates that feature tee times of 3 P.M. during daylight savings and 2 P.M. during standard time.

If you are a Florida resident or a member of the Magic Kingdom Club, you might wish to pick up a Disney Golf Season Badge. This badge costs $50 and gives unlimited play after 10 A.M. on any of the five 18-hole Disney courses, for only $50 a round ($65 weekends). Good for a year and available at any of the Disney pro shops, this badge is a great deal if you plan to play even twice.

The six Disney courses are located at three different locations around Walt Disney World. Both Osprey Ridge and Eagle Pines can be found at the Bonnet Creek Golf Club, while the Palm, the Magnolia, and Oak Trail are located at Shades of Green. The Lake Buena Vista course is near the Disney Institute. Here are the links, rated in order of difficulty by pros of the PGA:

- Osprey Ridge (6,680 yards, designed by Tom Fazio): Rated by the pros as the toughest course here at Disney, this course has elevations that are not at all typical of central Florida. Osprey Ridge does not double-back on itself. It just takes off into the woods. Tom Fazio himself considers this one of his best courses.
- The Palm (6,461 yards, designed by Joe Lee): The eighteenth hole here has been rated the fourth toughest on the PGA Tour.
- The Magnolia (6,642 yards, designed by Joe Lee): This course has the Disney signature "Mousetrap" on its sixth hole. The final round of the Oldsmobile Classic is played here.
- Eagle Pines (6,309 yards, designed by Pete Dye): This low-profile course features dished instead of crowned fairways. Relatively flat, this course has no grass for rough.
- Lake Buena Vista (6,268 yards, designed by Joe Lee): This is a fairly short, wide-open course. Hole 16 is called the "Intimidator."

- Oak Trail (executive course, 2,913 yards, designed by Joe Lee): No electric carts are allowed on this course, and golfers are allowed to carry their own bags.

Logistics

Tee times may be reserved up to 60 days in advance by Disney resort guests and 30 days ahead by day guests. These courses are busy during the peak seasons, and we strongly suggest that you arrange your tee times if you want to play early in the day. For tee times and information about any of the six courses, call (407) 939-4653.

Club and shoe rentals are available at all six courses and are $35 per round for men's or women's clubs and $6 a round for shoes. Rental clubs here are Calloway.

Transportation

Complimentary transportation to any of the Disney golf courses is furnished at any of the Disney resorts. This does not include the Swan, the Dolphin, and the hotels on Hotel Plaza Boulevard. To arrange your transportation at a Disney resort, notify Bell Services of your tee times. Try to give them a day's notice.

Fantasia Gardens and Fantasia Fairways

These are Disney's entry into the mini-golf arena, and as you might expect, they are fanciful and fun. The theme of Fantasia Gardens is the animated classic *Fantasia*. With an amusing mix of music, dancing hippos, waterfalls, pirouetting alligators, and other such "hazards," this course specializes in the quirky and the absurd. Fantasia Fairways is something else altogether. This innovative putting course is designed to challenge even the advanced golfer. Sand traps, water hazards, and diabolically terraced greens make this both fun and good practice.

Both courses are located next door to the Swan. Open from 10 A.M. to midnight every day, green fees are around $9 for adults and $8 for children. The Starter Shack features a snack bar and video arcade.

OUR RECOMMENDATIONS FOR GOLF

- The Disney/Oldsmobile Classic takes place in October. Guests are advised not to schedule play during this week.
- Shirts with collars are required at all Disney courses.

- We suggest that you arrange tee times 60 days in advance, especially from November to April.
- The Disney Institute features outstanding golf clinics.

Tennis

There are so many tennis courts around Walt Disney World that you might think it's a tennis resort. Located in a variety of places, you'll have little trouble finding a convenient court. Most feature full-service pro shops.

- Tennis at the Contemporary, the Grand Floridian, and the Institute are now managed by Peter Burwash International and feature experienced tennis pros, clinics, lessons, racquet rentals, and play on a variety of courts. The Contemporary features six lighted, hydrogrid clay courts; the Grand Floridian two clay courts; and the Institute, four hydrogrid courts. Hours are from 8 A.M. to 8 P.M. and are subject to change. Featured in all locations are "Tennis Non-Stop" aerobic clinics, the Pro-Drill, and Hit with a Pro. Play and clinics cost $15 per hour. Hit With a Pro is $40 per hour. For information and reservations, call (407) WDW-PLAY (939-7529).
- The Yacht and the Beach Clubs have two lighted courts, use of which is complimentary to all guests of these resorts. The courts are adjacent to the Beach Club. Open 7 A.M. to 10 P.M. No pro shop, no reservations. Equipment is available at the resort's health club at no charge.
- Fort Wilderness has two lighted courts. Open 8 A.M. to 6 P.M., there is no charge for their use. Open to all Disney resort guests. Rental racquets are available at the Bike Barn. No reservations.
- Old Key West has two lighted courts, open 7 A.M. to 11 P.M. Use is complimentary for registered guests of Old Key West on a first-come, first-serve basis. Rental equipment is available at Hank's.
- The Swan and the Dolphin share four lighted tennis courts. Open from 8 A.M. to 11 P.M., and use is complimentary.
- Shades of Green has two lighted tennis courts. Open from dawn until 10 P.M., use is complimentary for guests of the resort. No reservations.
- The BoardWalk has two lighted, clay courts. Use is free to all BoardWalk guests. Equipment rentals are available at Community Hall.

Our Recommendations for Tennis

- Play or lessons at the Contemporary, the Grand Floridian, and the Institute are all open to the public at no additional cost.
- Tennis attire is required at all courts. Rental equipment is available everywhere.

Boating Around the World

One of our favorite things to do at Walt Disney World is to go boating. Despite the fact that we live on our own sailboat and have our own little fleet, we simply love floating around Disney. It is fun and gives an interesting perspective on this fabulous place.

A variety of craft are available nearly anywhere there's a body of water. Most marina rental areas open at 10 A.M. and stay open until dusk.

Marina rental locations are listed following.

- The Seven Seas Lagoon and Bay Lake
  - The Contemporary
  - The Polynesian
  - The Grand Floridian
  - The Wilderness Lodge
  - Fort Wilderness
- Lake Buena Vista and its connecting waterways
  - Cap'n Jack's Marina at Downtown Disney Marketplace
  - Old Key West
  - Port Orleans
  - Dixie Landings
- Crescent Lake
  - The Yacht and the Beach Clubs
  - The Swan and Dolphin
  - Disney's BoardWalk
- Barefoot Bay at the Caribbean Beach
- Lago Dorado at Disney's Coronado Springs

Watercraft

All boats are not available at all locations. While prices and hourly minimums vary a little from marina to marina, the following should give you a good idea of what you will spend to rent a watercraft:

- Pedal boats, rowboats, and canoes: about $6 per half-hour
- Sailboats: most about $7 per half-hour

- Sunfish: $12 hourly
- Capri sailboats: $14 hourly
- Hobie Cats (for experienced sailors only): $16 hourly
- Aqua Cats, Aqua Fins: $14 hourly
- Water Mouse (two-person mini "speed" boat): $19 per half-hour
- Canopy boats: $22 per half-hour
- Pontoon boats (Flote boats), 20 or 24 feet: $44 or $50 hourly
  20-foot pontoon boats can accommodate a maximum of 10 people.
  24-foot pontoon boats come with a driver.
- SeaRayder speedboats (the Contemporary only): $37 per half-hour

OUR RECOMMENDATIONS FOR BOAT RENTALS

- The Seven Seas Lagoon and Bay Lake are the best places to rent a boat. Since these two bodies of water connect, this makes for the largest area to explore. There is more to see, as well. If you are not staying in one of the resorts here, simply go and rent the boat of your choice at any of the marinas listed at the Seven Seas Lagoon or Bay Lake.
- Charging your boating adventures to American Express will give you a 10% discount.

Other Boating Adventures

There are a few really special things that you can do on the waters of Disney. The most enchanting is to take a ride aboard *Breathless,* the Yacht Club's replica 1934 Chris Craft speedboat. With perfect varnish-work and shiny chrome fittings, *Breathless* is every yachtsman's dream. A half-hour cruise with driver will cost $65 with up to five passengers. For a shorter trip, $23 will get you a 10 minute "*Breathless* Burst." *Breathless* cruises begin at 3 P.M. See the back of this book for a coupon good for a 10% discount on a *Breathless* Burst. The most memorable *Breathless* cruise, however, is the fireworks cruise. For $140, this elegant yacht ♥♥♥♥ will take you over to Epcot to watch IllumiNations. Truly romantic and unforgettable, this is the perfect experience for a special occasion.

There are other fireworks cruises too, for both the Magic Kingdom's Fantasy in the Sky and for Epcot's IllumiNations. Magic Kingdom Cruises leave from both the Contemporary and the Grand Floridian 30 minutes prior to the fireworks show. At the Contemporary, the trip includes complimentary champagne and costs $33 per adult and $17 per child. This is booked by the person and is not necessarily a private cruise. The Grand's fireworks cruise is private, and booking is for the whole boat for $85. The pontoon boats can accommodate up to eight guests, 10 with children, and catering is available.

Another offering at the Grand Floridian is this resort's 44-foot luxury motor yacht, *The Grand One*. Available for crewed charters during the day, for dinner cruises, and for evening fireworks voyages, this unforgettable experience costs around $275 per hour. It is the perfect setting for a romantic dinner. We've even heard stories of this boat being used for proposals of marriage.

IllumiNations pontoon boat cruises leave around 8:30 P.M. from both the Yacht Club and the BoardWalk marinas. Both cost $85 and can take up to 10 guests at the Yacht and 12 at the BoardWalk. The BoardWalk also features a party boat fireworks cruise for $200 that includes themed decoration, a cake, beverages, and party favors. It can handle a party of 12.

Dixie Landings is now offering a moonlight cruise for $150 per couple. This includes dinner for two at either Bonfamille's or Boatwright's followed by a one-hour champagne voyage. No children are allowed on this trip, and there may also be other couples aboard.

Cancellations for all fireworks cruises must be made at least 24 hours prior to cruise time. For reservations and further information about these cruises, call (407) WDW-PLAY (939-7529).

Biking

Rentals can be found at Fort Wilderness, the Wilderness Lodge, Old Key West, Dixie Landings, Port Orleans, the BoardWalk, Caribbean Beach, the Villas at the Institute, and Coronado Springs. Rates are pretty much the same everywhere, around $5 per hour or $12 a day, and the variety includes men's, women's, children's, tandems, and bikes with child carriers. Most rental shops open around 10 A.M. and close around sunset.

The BoardWalk, Caribbean Beach, Port Orleans and Dixie Landings, and Old Key West offer some really unique biking with their "surrey" quadricycles. These four-wheeled, carriage-like cycles are some of the most fun we've ever had pedaling. Available for two, four, or six persons, rentals start at $14 per half hour. Surrey rentals at the BoardWalk continue late into the evening.

Our Recommendations for Cycling

- Try one of the surrey quadricycles. They're simply too much fun!
- Rent your bikes at the Wilderness Lodge and ride around the lake to Fort Wilderness. Continue on to the Fort Wilderness Swamp Trail Nature Path for some real scenery.
- The best biking areas: Old Key West and Wilderness Lodge/Fort Wilderness

Fishing Excursions

Over the years, the lakes and waterways of Walt Disney World have been stocked with thousands of fingerling bass. Fishing throughout central Florida is world famous, and guided fishing trips are available in a number of places at Disney World. Trips on Bay Lake, Lake Buena Vista, and on Crescent Lake all last two hours, accommodate up to five persons, and cost around $150. Trips include guide, gear, and refreshments. Live bait is an additional $10. Reservations must be made in advance; trips may be canceled due to inclement weather. For reservations at Bay Lake and the Epcot Resorts, call (407) WDW-PLAY (939-7529); for Cap'n Jack's Marina at the Downtown Disney Marketplace and Lake Buena Vista, call (407) 828-2204. All fishing excursions are catch-and-release only.

For something less extravagant, there's the Dixie Landings two-hour fishing adventure along the Sassagoula Waterway, for $50 per person. The boat can take up to five people; guide, equipment, bait, and soft drinks are included. Reservations for the 6:30 A.M. departure should be made in advance by calling (407) WDW-PLAY (939-7529). During the summer months, there's another trip at 6:30 P.M. For something even simpler, try the Ol' Fishin' Hole at Dixie Landings for $3.50 per hour or head out to the Fort Wilderness Bike Barn, rent a pole for about $4 a day, and fish the many waterways there. You can even rent a canoe and make a day of it.

Jogging and Walking

Nearly every resort offers a jogging or walking path. Check with the Guest Services at your resort for a map. Some of our favorite paths include the ones at the Yacht and the Beach/Swan and the Dolphin area, the Wilderness Lodge to Fort Wilderness area, Dixie Landings and Port Orleans, and a long circuit around the Polynesian and the Grand Floridian. There are also especially nice paths at Old Key West,

Coronado Springs, the Villas at the Institute, and the Caribbean Beach as well. Walking and jogging have become national pastimes, and the folks at Disney have been paying attention.

Nature Walks

There are two pleasant nature walks at Walt Disney World. One is Discovery Island, Disney's own wildlife preserve. Admission is charged, but there is much more here than simply a walk. There are also exhibits and wild animals encounters. See Chapter 4 for details. The other walk is on the north end of Fort Wilderness, which is open to anyone interested. The Wilderness Swamp trail runs for nearly two miles along the shores of Bay Lake and through some heavily forested areas. It is beautiful and quiet. This trail can be most easily reached by taking a boat to Fort Wilderness from the dock at the front of the Magic Kingdom. Pick up a map of the trail at Guest Services in nearby Pioneer Hall.

Horseback Riding

The Fort Wilderness Trail Ride departs daily from the Tri-Circle-D Ranch Livery and Trail Blaze Corral, located near the parking area to Fort Wilderness. The horses are Arabians and Appaloosas but the pace is very slow. It is more of a horseback walk. No galloping is allowed. If you are not an experienced rider, you may find this to be something special. It is scenic and fun.

Cost is about $23 per person. Children under 9 years of age are not permitted, and there is a 250-pound weight limit. Reservations are a good idea here, as this is a popular pursuit. For reservations up to five days in advance, call (407) WDW-PLAY (939-7529).

HORSEBACK RIDING TIPS

- Wear long pants and don't bring along a lot of stuff such as cameras and pocketbooks. Horses don't have back seats or glove compartments.
- Trips begin at 9 A.M., 10:30 A.M., 12 P.M., and 2 P.M. The ride lasts about 45 minutes.
- For experienced riders, this isn't much of a ride. But novices will enjoy it, perhaps even catching a glimpse of the Fort Wilderness wildlife population: deer, wild birds, and maybe even a gator.

The Walt Disney World Speedway

Most raceways merely offer races for people to come and watch. Of course, this isn't *most* race tracks. This is the Walt Disney World Speedway, and it gives spectators not only a chance to watch one of NASCAR's premier events but also a chance to get out of the grandstands and into a race car. Besides the January Indy 200, this speedway also features the Richard Petty Driving Experience every day (except during January).

Located next to the parking lot of the Magic Kingdom, this one-mile oval track features seating capacity for 50,000 plus infield hospitality suites. Tickets for the Indy 200 may be purchased by telephone at (800) 822-4639. We recommend booking as far in advance as possible.

NEW The Richard Petty Driving Experience

This could well be Disney's ultimate thrill ride. Participants have a choice of four different programs: three driving and one riding. Riders must be at least 16 years old and drivers at least 18 years old. A Magic Kingdom Club card or Annual Pass will give a 10% discount, and for other specials and discounts, check at the Richard Petty show car display in the Magic Kingdom at Tomorrowland's Grand Prix Raceway. The three driving programs involve time in the classroom as well as on the track. Plan on spending three to four hours. Reservations are necessary for the driving programs and may be made by calling (800) 237-3889.

Ride-Along Program Take a three-lap, 145 mph spin in a two-seater stock car. No reservation necessary, and rides begin at 9 A.M. daily, seven days a week. Cost is $90. A second ride is discounted nearly $20.

Rookie Experience Take the wheel for eight laps around the track at 125 mph. Cost is $330.

Winston Experience This is a 16-lap, two-session program at 125 mph. Cost is $742.

Experience of a Lifetime This 30-lap program includes three 10-lap sessions. Cost is $1,100. Speeds reached are in excess of 130 mph.

The Richard Petty Driving Experience also has a merchandise shop with logo hats, polo shirts, and T-shirts as well as an assortment of model race cars and novelties. Chips and sodas are available at the track, but if you plan on being there all day, we would suggest having your resort prepare box lunches for you.

NEW Disney's Wide World of Sports

The first time we visited this 200-acre sports complex, we felt like we were going back in time. The mission-style architecture and Florida landscaping made us feel like we were in 1950s Southern California. We had expected throngs of people crowded onto noisy fields and into packed stadiums. What we found was nothing like this at all.

The pale yellow, tile-roofed buildings of Disney's Wide World of Sports are perfectly placed amidst acres of lush green playing fields. Footpaths lined with tall palms crisscross in perfect symmetry from field house to stadium to playing areas. This may be one of the world's state-of-the-art sports facilities, but it's also a place of quiet beauty.

Of course, we would tell you to come out here, but there's much more going on than simply an interesting place to look at. The Wide World of Sports features a huge variety of spectator sports as well as a training facility for amateur and professional athletes. There are even programs for Disney guests such as the NFL Experience and the Doyle Baseball School.

Disney's Wide World of Sports includes a 7,000-seat baseball stadium, a six-court basketball field house, four soccer fields, a softball quadriplex, four youth baseball fields, a track and field complex, a velodrome, 11 ISP clay courts, three major league baseball fields, and locker and training facilities for all regimens. Besides the sports facilities, there are two sports shops, the All-Star Cafe, and arriving in 1999, a Foot Locker megastore.

The Wide World of Sports is the spring training home of the Atlanta Braves and the practice site for the Harlem Globetrotters. Of course, this means a baseball-packed month of March and a December Holiday Globetrotter's series. This facility also hosts so many other athletic events each year that it would take pages to list them all. Just to mention a few: the annual WDW Marathon (January), the U.S. Men's Clay Court Tennis Championship (April), Cincinnati Bengals Mini-Camp (April), ACC Men and Women's Track and Field Championships, the NFL Quarterback Challenge (May), major league soccer all-stars (July), and the Senior Olympics (October 1999). There are championship events in nearly every sport for both amateur and collegiate athletics on just about any given day. It would be pretty tough to come out here and not find something of interest.

Getting to the Wide World of Sports

If you're driving, you'll need a map to find this place, which is located right off of the Osceola Parkway in the south-central part of Disney World. If you are a guest in one of the Disney resorts, all you'll have to do is take a couple of bus rides. From 10 A.M. to 6 P.M., Wide World of Sports buses arrive and depart from Disney–MGM Studios. From 6 P.M. to 11 P.M., you'll have to come and go from Downtown Disney.

Admission to Disney's Wide World of Sports

General admission to Disney Wide World of Sports costs $8 ($6.75 for children) and is included in both Length of Stay and 5-Day Park Hopper passes. This covers admission to all but the premier events here at Wide World of Sports.

Each day, at 11 A.M. and 2 and 4 P.M., there are tours of the entire complex, and we would highly recommend one. For information about the events during your visit and tickets to premier events, call the Sports Line at (407) 363-6600. For Atlanta Braves and Harlem Globetrotters games, advance ticketing is strongly recommended.

NEW The NFL Experience

Originally invented as a road show for super bowls, this NFL Experience is the only permanent one in existence and it is designed to be both a football mini-training camp as well as a taste of what it is like to be in the NFL. Fans here participate in a variety of activities such as the Quarterback Challenge; Punt, Pass, and Kick; Look Like a Pro; and Quick Release. It is designed to be both fun and a learning experience. The NFL Experience is open daily from 10 A.M. to 5 P.M. and is included in general admission.

NEW The Doyle Baseball School

This baseball school is run by three brothers who were all in the big leagues. Classes run from Monday through Friday and cover all aspects of the game. This school has 30 graduates in "the bigs." The school offers both a package that includes accommodations, admission to the Disney theme parks, breakfasts, lunches, and one dinner and a "commuter package" without accommodations. Prices begin around $540 for the five-day course.

During March, Doyle's offers three-hour training sessions following Atlanta Braves' spring training games. For information about these and the package programs, call Doyle Baseball School at (941) 439-1000.

Disney Institute Activities

The Institute offers an exciting variety of recreation that also involves hands-on learning experiences. Wilderness canoeing, rock climbing, golf, and tennis clinics are just a few. For more details, see the Disney Institute, Chapter 4.

NEW *The Typhoon Lagoon Learn-to-Surf Program*

Learn to surf the big ones when the waves are turned up at Typhoon Lagoon. This class includes both dry land and big wave instruction before this water park opens. Available to Disney resort guests only, this course is offered on Wednesdays from 7 A.M. to 9:30 A.M. and costs $125 per person. Classes are limited to 14 people. For reservations, call (407) WDW-PLAY (939-7529).

Miscellaneous Sports

Some of the Disney resorts feature special sports that are not found elsewhere. Here is a brief list of them.

- Basketball: Old Key West
- Croquet: the Yacht and Beach Clubs, the BoardWalk, Port Orleans
- Volleyball: the Beach Club, the Contemporary, Coronado Springs
- Bocci ball (lawn bowling): the Yacht and Beach Clubs
- Horseshoes and "yolf": Fort Wilderness

Disney Adult Discoveries

Disney offers an interesting variety of tours and programs that are simply not widely known or heavily promoted. Some will have you exploring behind the scenes and others, the tunnels under the Magic Kingdom. All are entertaining and enlightening. Some are simply unique Disney experiences. If this is starting to sound good, take a look at the possibilities here. For more details and to arrange your special Disney experiences, call (407) WDW-TOUR (939-8687).

Tips: **Reservations should be made at least six weeks in advance, except those for Backstage Magic, which should be made two months in advance.**

American Express cardholders are entitled to a discount on these programs (usually 10%), and 10 to 15% discounts are given to Annual or Seasonal Pass holders.

Backstage Safari

Get behind the scenes at Disney's newest theme park and learn how it's all done. $60 per person plus theme park admission; Monday, Wednesday, and Friday; three-hour tour.

Backstage Magic

Take a good look behind the scenes at Disney's theme parks. See the Utilidor tunnels system under the Magic Kingdom, examine the backstage control systems of Body Wars at Epcot, and get inside the animator's studio at Disney–MGM Studios. There's more in this seven-hour program. Monday through Saturday, $185 per person. Reservations must be made at least two months in advance.

Inside Animation

During this two-and-a-half-hour program you'll get an exciting look at the history of Disney feature animation to learn how the classics were created. You'll even get into the animator's studio and create your own "cel." $45 per person. Theme park admission not required.

Hidden Treasures

This assortment of programs feature discovery tours of Epcot in search of this park's many hidden features, architecture, and art.

Hidden Treasures East is a two-hour program that explores Mexico, Norway, China, Germany, Italy, and the American Adventure. Offered on Tuesdays only. $35 per person plus theme park admission.

Hidden Treasures West is a two-hour Saturday exploration of Canada, the United Kingdom, France, Morocco, Japan, and the American Adventure. $35 per person plus theme park admission.

Hidden Treasures is a journey that will take you to all 11 lands of Epcot and includes a lunch in Morocco. Offered on Wednesdays only, this five-hour program costs $75 per person and no theme park admission is required.

Gardens of the World

Offered on Tuesdays and Thursdays, this three-hour program is an in-depth study of the landscaping and gardens of Epcot. The perfect experience for gardening enthusiasts. $45 per person plus theme park admission.

Disney's Architecture

If you find yourselves wondering about the amazing architecture here at Disney, this is the course for you. Learn the hows and whys behind some of Disney most eye-opening creations. Three and a half hours, on Mondays, Wednesdays, and Fridays. $69 per person, theme park admission not required.

Keys to the Kingdom

Learn the lore, the magic, and the trivia of the Magic Kingdom on this four-and-a-half-hour daily tour. Go backstage and even visit the tunnel system. $45 per person, plus theme park admission.

Epcot Divequest

This daily diving experience will take you into the Living Seas' six-million-gallon aquarium. Swim with turtles, tropical fish, and sharks. $140 per person. Theme park admission not required, but proof of current open water SCUBA certification is necessary.

Family Magic Tour

This daily tour takes place in the Magic Kingdom and admission is required. This family activity includes a scavenger hunt and lasts from 9:30 to 11:30 A.M. Cost is $25 ($15 for children 3 to 9 years of age).

Disney's Dolphins In Depth

This three-and-a-half-hour program is available Monday through Friday and is conducted at the Living Seas Pavilion at Epcot. It includes a hands-on encounter with a dolphin. $140 per person plus theme park admission. Guests under 18 years of age must be accompanied by an adult.

The Spas of Walt Disney World

Spas are like sushi. If you've never eaten it, you might be a bit reluctant to try it ("What do I order? Will I like it? How do I eat it?"). These are not too different than the questions most people have when considering their first spa visit. As a couple that loves spas, let us set your minds at ease. Spa treatments are soothing and sublime. Whether partaking in aroma hydrotherapy or a facial, a seaweed wrap or a sports massage, we have discovered that these pampering treatments not only *feel* great but they leave us both with an enhanced sense of relaxation and sensuality. Spa treatments are all about relieving stress, and we simply can't think of a better way to spend the first afternoon of a vacation than in a spa. From our own experience, we can tell you that just a few treatments will get you both in the perfect mood for your romantic escape and we urge you to consider indulging yourselves, even if for just a short treatment ♥♥.

Walt Disney World is home to three spas, and each has its specialties and character. All are designed to enrapture guests with a soothing blend of colors, music, and mood, and all three feature steam rooms, whirlpool baths, plush locker rooms, and comfortable lounges. Spa treatments fall loosely into several categories: massage therapies, skin and body treatments, and water therapies. There are many massage techniques: Swedish, Shiatsu, reflexology, and sports massage are the most common. Water therapies might mean a hydrotherapy massage, a mineral bath, or an exotic soak. Skin treatments include facials, body masques, seaweed wraps, aromatherapies, and body polishing. There's even hand and foot treatments. These things sound unusual, we know, but any of them will relieve tension, leave you feeling utterly pampered, and will bring your senses wonderfully to life. Spa treatments are *not* just for women. All of the Disney World spas feature treatments designed for men and we must tell you that *both* of us have really enjoyed these sensual experiences.

Another feature of spas is that they are expensive. Treatments usually cost from $30 to about $80, depending on choice and length. We think this kind of pampering is what vacations are all about. More than merely self-indulgent, the spa experience is about relieving stress, soothing sore muscles, and promoting well-being. We warn you: once you start, you won't want to stop. This stuff is deliciously habit-forming.

Each of the spas also has a health and fitness center with the latest in equipment. Also, all three feature a "spa cuisine" of fresh juices, soups, sandwiches, smoothies, and salads. Each of the spas offers a variety of a la carte treatments and day or half-day packages. Each also features gift certificates, and all have knowledgeable staffs of reservationists waiting to help you plan your spa experiences.

The Grand Floridian Spa and Health Club

Florida is the theme of this elegant place, and simply walking in the door will immerse you in the heavenly smells of its custom-formulated, citrus-based spa and skin products. We are already hooked on the ruby-red grapefruit bath gel. Comfortable treatment rooms and spacious and luxurious lounges, complete with plush robes and slippers, herbal teas, and world-class amenities, make this the perfect addition to the exquisite Grand Floridian resort. Facilities and service here are first-class, and the ambience is exceptionally intimate and personal. This spa is run by Niki Bryan Spas.

Offerings include a couple's massage room ♥♥♥, "My First Facial" for young guests, a gentleman's facial, a Secret Garden Bath, soothing tired-legs treatment, a post-sports package, an antistress collection, and "For the Bride." There's even a soothing aloe wrap for sunburns. We could spend a whole vacation here.

This spa is so popular that we recommend making your plans here before you arrive at Walt Disney World, especially from Thanksgiving through April. To reserve your grand, Grand Floridian spa experience, call (407) 824-2332.

The Spa at the Disney Institute

No expenses were spared in creating this place. From aerobics pool, gymnasium, and Cybex fitness center to the well-appointed and spacious lounges and treatment rooms, this spa is the very definition of "state of the art." Offering Phytomer beauty products, Sothys skin treatments, and the Judith Jackson line of aromatherapies, the Spa at the Disney Institute knows what it takes to please.

The wonderful "menu" here has such treatments as a half-day men's program, deluxe seaweed program, after-sports body therapy, European facials, French body polish, and aromatherapy hydromassage.

To get the treatment that you desire, we suggest reserving well in advance. For arrangements, call the Spa at the Disney Institute at (407) 827-4455.

For a free length-of-stay pass at the Health and Fitness Center, see the back of this book for details.

The Spa and Fitness Center at the Buena Vista Palace

It only follows that this elegant and luxurious hotel, located across the street from Downtown Disney, would offer a full-service spa to its guests. This spa offers not only a line of extraordinary treatments and a modern fitness center but also a first-class hair salon. This whole package is located in a separate part of the resort and features a private lap pool, outdoor whirlpools, specialized treatment rooms, and a wonderful spa cuisine.

Whether you are looking for herbal body wraps, relaxing massages, soothing aromatherapies, or rejuvenating facials, you'll find it all here. With an emphasis on the natural, the Spa at the Buena Vista Palace offers the full line of luxurious and natural Pevonia Botanical® and EcoCare® products. To arrange your blissful time here, call (800) 981-1472.

OUR RECOMMENDATIONS FOR THE SPAS OF DISNEY

- Be sure to arrive at least 30 minutes early to relax yourselves in the spa's steam rooms and whirlpool baths.
- A single treatment will give you the whole day's use of the spa's fitness center.
- Get "His and Hers" massages ♥♥♥ together in the couple's treatment room at the Grand Floridian Spa.
- The aromatherapy massage and seaweed facial at the Spa at the Disney Institute are particularly outstanding.
- The Spa at the Buena Vista Palace offers some very well-priced packages. Check them out.
- Guys: this is *not* just for women!
- Call to ask for a brochure from each spa to see full array of treatments.
- By the way, if you've never tried sushi, it *is* like a spa treatment: once you try it, you'll be hooked.

Health and Fitness Clubs

- The Health and Fitness Center at the Disney Institute is in a class by itself. Along with the luxurious facilities of the spa, guests here are treated to Cybex equipment that is still being developed: video exercise games, computerized training gear, and lots of other neat stuff. There's also a weight room and aerobics pool. The Health and Fitness Center at the Disney Institute is available without additional cost to Institute guests. Day guests and Disney resort guests pay $15 per visit, and there's a bargain length of stay pass for Disney resort guests only. For information, call (407) 827-4455.

  For a free length-of-stay pass at the Health and Fitness Center at the Disney Institute, see the coupon at the back of this book.

- The Buena Vista Palace Spa and Fitness Center is another superb facility. Life Fitness and Reebok equipment, one-on-one training, a full range of cardiovascular equipment, and the spa's private lap pool, steam room, sauna, and outdoor whirlpool tub are this club's offerings. Afterwards, enjoy a soak or a massage. Highlights here are Reebok Sky Walkers and Life Fitness Entertainment Cycles. Palace guests may use the facilities for $10 per day. Non-Palace guests pay $20 daily. For details, call (407) 827-3222.
- The Grand Floridian Spa and Health Club offers the very latest in Cybex equipment and the superb facilities of the spa: sauna, steam room, whirlpool tub, and luxurious lounges and locker rooms. When you're finished exercising, enjoy one of the spa's treatments. Spa guests are entitled to use of these facilities and they are available for $12 per day for individuals, $8 per day family rate, for Disney resort guests. A length of stay rate is $32 per person. For information, call (407) 824-2332.
- The four health centers at the Yacht and Beach Clubs, the BoardWalk, the Contemporary, and NEW Coronado Springs are all operated by Niki Bryan Spas. At the Yacht and Beach you'll find the Ship Shape Health Club; at BoardWalk it's Muscles and Bustles; at the Contemporary, it's the Olympiad Health Club; and there's the La Vida Health Club at Coronado. These clubs are available to all Disney resort guests at a cost of $8 per day, $20 for individual length of stay, and $35 for family length of stay. Massages are available by appointment only, and these clubs all have the latest in Nautilus and LifeCycle equipment. Personal training is by appointment, and tanning beds are available at BoardWalk, Coronado Springs, and the Contemporary. Only the Ship Shape Health Club features its own indoor hot tub and sauna. For more information, call (407) 934-3256 (Ship Shape Health Club); (407) 939-2370 (Muscles and Bustles); (407) 824-3410 (Olympiad Health Club); and (407) 939-3030 (La Vida Health Club).
- Body by Jake is the Dolphin's health club. With a complete selection of Polaris equipment, a coed Jacuzzi, saunas, an array of personal training, massages, and water-aerobics, Jake's is a complete fitness center. Jake's is available for $5 per day per room for all guests of the Dolphin (this also includes a daily newspaper, coffee, and free local calls); for other Disney resort guests, it's $10 per day. Hours vary seasonally.
- The Health Club at the Swan is a modern facility with exercise equipment, Sprint weight systems, and a sauna. Use of this facility is complimentary with a stay at the Swan.

- R.E.S.T. Fitness Center at Old Key West offers a fairly complete exercise room, and use of it is complimentary to guests and club members. Facilities include a coed steam room, whirlpool bath, and Nautilus equipment.
- Shades of Green and all of the hotels along Hotel Plaza (except the Travelodge) have fitness rooms with exercise equipment. All are available to resort guests of each hotel.

Bargain Hunting for Character Merchandise

This is not exactly sports or recreation, but if you have access to a car, you might be interested in the Character Warehouse and Character Premier. These stores are located in Belz Outlet Center in Orlando and sell last year's Disney character merchandise at bargain prices. Items that sold last year for $36 might be found here for $15. You never know what you'll find, but at these prices you're certain to see something.

To get there, take I-4 East (to Orlando) to International Drive. Take a left at the light and follow International Drive to the end. Look for Mall #2, with two towers, for the Character Warehouse. Character Premier is in the building next door, Mall #1. Happy shopping.

PART 3

The Ultimate Romance at Walt Disney World

CHAPTER 8

Disney Fairy Tale Weddings

If you wonder who would ever want to get married at Walt Disney World, consider this: Disney Fairy Tale Weddings has already celebrated its 10,000th ceremony. If you've been a part of one of them, you'll know, as we do, why so many couples are celebrating their weddings here at Walt Disney World. Besides the union of husband and wife, marriages are meant to be memorable. For Disney, "memorable" is just everyday stuff. Disney Fairy Tale Weddings specializes in *exceeding* expectations.

A wedding is something of a mix of celebration and theater. Guest accommodations, rehearsal dinner, ceremony, reception, entertainment, and honeymoon are all possibilities that seem to have no limit here at Walt Disney World. In fact, Walt Disney World seems the perfect place to have such a celebration of life and family.

Enjoy your ceremony at the wedding gazebo in the garden at the Yacht Club or in the Magic Kingdom after closing. Or have a traditional celebration in the beautiful Disney Wedding Pavilion overlooking the Seven Seas Lagoon. Arrive in a horse-drawn coach and depart with the wedding party aboard a Mississippi riverboat for your reception at the Grand Floridian. Guests can stay in any of the Disney resorts, and for them, your wedding will also mean a Disney vacation.

From Old West–style rehearsal barbecues at Fort Wilderness to elegant receptions at the California Grill, weddings here at Walt Disney World can be as themed or as traditional as you desire. Calypso beach parties, Hollywood extravaganzas, or ceremonies in the courtyard of Cinderella Castle: all the fantastic possibilities Walt Disney World has to offer.

That a Disney wedding will be fantastic and fun should be making some sense. But who besides the rich and famous can afford such an extravagant event? If you are thinking that a Disney Fairy Tale Wedding is beyond your reach, know that there are two types of Disney weddings and that prices begin around $3,300. Of course, the sky's the limit here, but we're getting ahead of ourselves.

Types of Fairy Tale Weddings

There are two basic varieties of Disney Fairy Tale Weddings: Intimate Weddings and Customized Weddings. Intimate Weddings are small. With a maximum of six guests, these lovely affairs are beautiful and private. Larger weddings fall into the next category. Facilities, reception, and accommodations all become factors in an affair that includes more people and more planning. Of course, the bigger and grander the wedding, the greater the cost. And for the really spectacular, a Customized Wedding can be a Theme Park Wedding. This would take the event into yet another area altogether and include after-hours use of one of the Disney theme parks. Of course, this would mean a significantly greater expense.

With an Intimate Wedding beginning at around $3,300, fabulous honeymoon included, we hope that you are beginning to see the possibilities in a new light. If price is no object, then you may be viewing all of this with great interest. The potential for your Disney wedding and honeymoon will be without limit.

Most weddings do have a budget, though, and reality will very likely demand something more down-to-earth than a Cinderella fantasy in the Magic Kingdom. Between the intimate and the extravagant lies a great deal of territory. Somewhere in this area lies the special Disney wedding for you.

Disney Intimate Weddings

If you are planning a wedding with only a small handful of guests, the Intimate Wedding may be just the thing. For one price, you get a lovely ceremony at one of the beautiful and romantic Disney wedding locations and an unforgettable Disney honeymoon. The Intimate Wedding ceremony includes an officiant to perform the service, a bouquet for the bride and boutonniere for the groom, and a two-tiered wedding cake and champagne toast. For live music, you'll have your choice of a solo flautist or violinist during ceremony and reception. If you choose an Intimate Wedding, you'll have your own wedding consultant, who not only will help you make all the decisions but will also make all of the arrangements.

And with the bride and groom already here at Walt Disney World, the honeymoon begins at once. You'll both be the pampered guests of either the Grand Floridian, the Contemporary, the Yacht or Beach Clubs, the Polynesian, the BoardWalk, or the Wilderness Lodge. Any one of these luxurious resorts is guaranteed to provide an exciting and unforgettably romantic atmosphere. You'll also have, for the length of your stay, unlimited admission to all of the Disney attractions. From the Animal Kingdom to Blizzard Beach, you'll get in on all the fun. Also included in this package is an elegant dinner for two at one of Disney's finest restaurants, a chartered limousine, $100 gift certificate at the Grand Floridian Spa, and one Disney flex feature for each of you (for details, see Chapter 1, Vacation Packages: Are They for You?). You'll even receive a Romance Basket filled with special treats such as bubble bath, chocolates, champagne, and souvenir wine glasses. The World will be yours.

The marvelous locations for the Intimate Weddings are varied. One would be the beautiful and peaceful gazebo at the Yacht Club. Set in a lovely rose garden on Crescent Lake, it has been designed especially for Disney Fairy Tale Weddings. The stately elegance of this setting provides much more than simply a touch of romance.

You will approach along the cobbled path that leads through the garden and up to the Victorian gazebo. With its carved wooden hearts and Cupid weathervane, this beautiful creation is the quintessential setting for love. Wedding planners have been hard at work before your arrival and champagne and wedding cake await. This is a white-glove affair. Guests are seated in the rose garden and the flutist begins to play. After the ceremony, everyone enjoys a champagne toast, all set to the music that you have selected. The cake is cut, the magic begins.

Variations of this theme are what Disney Fairy Tale Wedding specialists do best. We stayed at the Yacht Club and watched as several of these memorable events unfolded. Believe us when we tell you that, time after time, we were moved. These charming affairs are most definitely not performed on an assembly line. Each reflected careful planning as well as the personal touches of both bride and groom. In two days, we witnessed five of these touching ceremonies. Each was unique. All were enchanting.

One ceremony was in the morning, three were in the afternoon, and another was late in the day, near sunset. One couple arrived by horse-drawn coach, another in Disney's vintage white Cadillac motorcar. Others simply arrived on foot. One wedding had a handful of guests, three others had six, and one simply involved the bride and groom, an officiant, and several attendants.

Music at one wedding featured a flautist; at the others, a violinist performed. Tunes varied from "Wish upon a Star" to the more traditional. Mickey, in top hat and tails, and Minnie, in a sparkling evening gown, appeared at several ceremonies. Some were videotaped, and each was well photographed. The guests were thrilled at the perfection of the event, and so were we.

Each of these wedding ceremonies was definitely traditional. Dress ranged from formal to casually elegant. Even the presence of Disney characters during the champagne toast and cake cutting brought only a touch of Disney to the affairs. There are other beautiful locations available for Intimate Weddings, and each offers a special and romantic vista of Walt Disney World. Among them are either the Rose Courtyard or Sea Breeze Point at the BoardWalk, Sunset Point on the beach at the Polynesian, or the lovely Disney Wedding Pavilion on its own tropical island in the Seven Seas Lagoon.

There are two types of Intimate Weddings, the Deluxe and the Premium. The Deluxe package includes a variety of outdoor locations, and packages begin at $3,300 per couple for accommodations at the Wilderness Lodge. The Premium package means a ceremony at Disney's Wedding Pavilion with an organist and cake and champagne on the terrace at the Grand Floridian, overlooking the lagoon. Weddings must take place on Mondays through Thursdays, and these packages begin at $4,100 per couple. The most important thing to remember about the Intimate Weddings is that they are limited to six guests. Extra guests may be invited, but this will increase the cost of your wedding. Consult with your wedding coordinator for details.

To either of these packages you can add either the Disney Dining Style Plan or the World of Recreation Plan. One would provide a 10% discount on meals, the other, use of Walt Disney World recreation such as golf, tennis, and watercraft. For details, see Chapter 1, Vacation Packages: Are They for You?

Planning Your Intimate Wedding

Your Intimate Wedding will begin with a phone call: Walt Disney Fairy Tale Weddings at (407) 828-3400.

You will be asked for your name and address, and a packet of information will be mailed to you explaining the most current details about the Intimate Wedding packages. The information will include a telephone number, which you will be able to call to schedule your Intimate Wedding or simply to ask for more information.

If you have read what we have written here and are calling to schedule your ceremony, you'll need to tell the person you speak with, and a wedding coordinator will return your call as soon as possible. Disney Fairy Tale Weddings requires a minimum 10-day notice.

Customized Weddings

One of the most important things to know when it comes to a Customized Wedding is that it is not a product. You will not be shown Package A, Package B, and Package C. Far from it. Disney Fairy Tale Weddings is a service, one that has been created to help you design your very own and very special wedding.

Since a Customized Wedding involves more people, there will be many more elements to consider. Even a modest wedding will entail such considerations as catering, guest accommodations, floral arrangements, and dozens of other important details. Overseeing, organizing, and orchestrating your entire Disney wedding will be your very own wedding specialist. Throughout the entire process, this specialist will be there to answer your questions, to find solutions to your problems, and to make your every dream come true.

Each Fairy Tale Wedding is a unique interpretation of your wishes. You can decide whether to have your traditional ceremony with Walt Disney World as the backdrop or to make your wedding a celebration complete with Disney characters and themed decorations. The choice will also be yours whether to have your wedding at the beautiful Disney Wedding Pavilion or in one of the many other unforgettable Disney locations. Choose the romantic and Victorian elegance of the Grand Floridian, or enjoy the casual, seaside splendor of the Beach Club. Whatever location you select, you will be free to make your wedding as "Disney" as you want it to be.

The use of characters is only one way to make your wedding a themed affair. Props, scenery, landscaping, and special effects can also be used to fashion the ultimate fantasy for any or all of your wedding plans. Such motifs as Beauty and the Beast, Cinderella's Ball, and Aladdin are but a few of the hundreds of themes that can be created. Have a Wild West Wedding at Fort Wilderness, a moonlight wedding cruise on the *General Joe Potter* stern-wheeler, or let Disney create a storybook Alice in Wonderland setting. There are no limits to the magic at hand.

Of the Customized Weddings, Theme Park Weddings are the grandest of all. Each of these is staged after-hours at either Epcot,

Disney–MGM Studios, or the Magic Kingdom. These weddings tend towards the spectacular, with prices to match.

A fantasy wedding at Disney–MGM Studios might be the perfect marriage for two film buffs. It begins with the bride's arrival by motorcade down Hollywood Boulevard. Vintage vehicles, fireworks, and cheering crowds set the scene. The wedding ceremony takes place in the courtyard of the Chinese Theater, finalized with the traditional Hollywood handprint in cement. The wedding party then boards the Great Movie Ride for a trip through the most memorable cinematic scenes of all time. The ride ends as the wedding party arrives in the soundstage, where a glittering and lavish sit-down dinner and dance await. Potted palms, sparkling lights, and a champagne toast begin the evening's festivities. The movie screen backdrop of silent film clips and a small orchestra craft the magical atmosphere for this unforgettable event.

This is but one of countless such scenarios. Have an Under the Sea Wedding at the Living Seas Lounge in Epcot or enjoy something more traditional in the formal English garden of the United Kingdom Pavilion. For something a bit offbeat, there's always the unusual atmosphere of the Twilight Zone Tower of Terror courtyard. The possibilities for Theme Park Weddings are limited only by your imagination.

Planning Your Customized Wedding

Having compared Disney weddings to those that can be arranged outside of Walt Disney World, we must tell you that these weddings are, indeed, expensive. We are talking Disney World here, and, for such a setting and such quality, you must expect to pay more. Exactly how much more will depend on your choices and just how large a wedding you are planning. We suggest that you shop around wherever you live in order to give yourselves an idea of just how much a wedding will cost in your home town. Take into consideration the difference between having your reception at a local restaurant or country club and having it in the Grand Floridian Ballroom.

The Guidelines

Because Disney Fairy Tale Weddings does not charge for the use of private banquet rooms, a $10,000 minimum expenditure applies to all wedding groups that exceed 10 persons. This minimum applies only to what is spent on the actual day of your wedding. It includes food and beverages, entertainment, flowers, transportation, and, if you wish to use it, the cost of the Wedding Pavilion. It does not include guest accommodations or anything that occurs on previous days, such as the rehearsal dinner. It also does not include extras such as the officiant and photographic services.

Minimum food and beverage expenditures are $75 per person for functions held before 2 P.M. and $100 per person for luncheons and dinners held later. All include service staff in tuxedo attire with white glove service, head table, white linen, elegant place settings, tables for gifts, cake, and guest book, and, of course, all include the traditional cake and champagne toast. Sales tax, 19% service charge, and alcoholic beverages are additional.

Of course, the menu will be of your choosing. A typical wedding dinner would include a seven-course banquet created by Disney's award-winning culinary staff. Your wedding cake will be a custom-designed, multitiered masterpiece.

Are you still with us? There is more. Both you and your guests will be expected to stay in Disney resorts. A minimum number of resort nights must be guaranteed based upon the size of your wedding party. It is a simple formula, one that you should have no difficulty satisfying. Know too that rooms are available for all wedding guests, with prices beginning at $74 per night. Having your entire wedding group along with you at Disney will enhance the affair, making it even more memorable for everyone. Transportation for your guests will be simpler, and they will be having their own Disney vacations.

A Sample Customized Wedding for Fifty People

Set at the enchanting Wedding Pavilion, this unforgettable ceremony begins with the bride's arrival in the glittering, horse-drawn Cinderella's glass coach. Floral decorations, two bridesmaids, maid of honor, organist, and a full wedding ensemble make this both a charming and a traditional affair. The bride and groom take their vows before the backdrop of Cinderella Castle. Following the ceremony, doves are released and the now-married couple depart for the reception in the glass coach.

The reception takes place at the Grand Floridian Ballroom, where a musical trio furnishes the atmosphere for this white-glove affair. The dazzling menu features platters of fresh fruits and assortments of cheese, and hot and cold hors d'oeuvres. A champagne toast and open bar begin the festive occasion.

Following this, an elegant and formal dinner is prepared by the master chefs of Disney. Table settings feature chair covers with bows, floral centerpieces, crisp linens, and crystal glassware. A typical menu might include poached filet of salmon pasta, Whitehall salad, roasted potatoes, seasonal vegetables, a choice of either of two entrees, and for dessert a banana and white chocolate pate laced with dark chocolate and Frangelica sauce. Afterwards, everyone enjoys the wedding cake, a champagne toast to bride and groom, and a memorable evening of dancing and cocktails in the lovely ballroom. Special guests, Mickey and Minnie, drop by to wish the newlyweds happiness.

Such a lavish wedding would cost about $14,400, with tax and gratuities. This includes limousine transportation for the wedding party, floral arrangements for the ceremony and reception, a four-hour open bar, three hours of entertainment with a musical trio or disc jockey, and a complimentary wedding night at the Grand Floridian for bride and groom. Not included are photography, wedding invitations, and favors. Considering that the average wedding in the U.S. costs $18,000, this affair, modest by Disney standards, seems reasonable. Keep in mind that the average Disney Fairy Tale Wedding costs $19,000 for 100 guests.

If these figures seems out of reach and your heart is set on a Disney Fairy Tale Wedding, we suggest that you inquire about a ceremony that might better suit your needs. Sometimes, special arrangements can be made for dates and times that are not so busy. You can save money simply by having a brunch or tea reception.

Customized Theme Park Weddings

A Magic Kingdom wedding could take place in the lovely rose garden at the Swan Boat Landing near Cinderella Castle. Guests arrive by horse-drawn trolleys down Main Street. The bride arrives in Cinderella's glass carriage, drawn by six white ponies and driven by two costumed footmen. Following the ceremony is a fantasy reception in the castle courtyard, after which guests ride on Cinderella's Golden Carousel. The new husband and wife appear on the castle parapet, heralded by costumed trumpeters, and guests dine in the castle at Cinderella's Royal Table for a specially prepared meal and a magical evening of dancing.

This storybook wedding includes round-trip transportation for all guests to the Magic Kingdom entrance and private use of the theme park for the duration of the wedding. All setup services for landscaping, dance, reception, and ceremony would be included, as would the sound system, lighting, and a special bridal dressing area.

The food and beverage package would include a one-hour reception with a variety of hors d'oeuvres and a four-hour unlimited open bar. Dinner would feature a seven-course meal, the menu to be arranged with Disney catering services. Cake and a champagne toast cap off the dinner. Floral arrangements, photography, wedding officiant, invitations, and wedding favors are not included. The total cost for this would begin around $45,000. For a wedding at Epcot, expect to pay at least $16,000 and for Disney–MGM Studios no less than $20,000.

The Customized or Theme Park Wedding Process

A Customized Wedding or a Customized Theme Park Wedding takes a great deal of planning. On average, couples make their initial contact with Disney about one year before the anticipated day. Tentative reservations may be made one year in advance and plans may be finalized up to eight months in advance. Again, the process begins with a phone call to Disney Fairy Tale Weddings. Request a full information kit and look it over carefully.

Once you have decided upon a date, you are ready to make your second call to Disney Fairy Tale Weddings. A sales manager will happily provide you with any information. This person will be knowledgeable in helping you to sort out the many possibilities and to limit the selections to something that reflects your own unique personalities and expectations.

When the magical date arrives to make your reservations, you will both be prepared. This will be the real beginning of your Disney wedding adventure. You will receive a letter of agreement and be asked to make a deposit to secure your banquet hall and special hotel rates. This deposit will apply to your minimum expenditures. At this time, you will also meet your wedding event manager. This knowledgeable and dedicated specialist will be with you throughout the entire process of your Fairy Tale Wedding. Once you have locked in your locations and date, you will be asked to make an on-site inspection to ensure that everything meets your expectations. If you are unable to do this, your wedding event manager will see that you receive the proper information and photographs.

Now that the basics are out of the way, the real fun begins. You will need to make a lot of important decisions, and your wedding event manager will know the ins and outs of the entire process. Your specialist will work within the parameters of your budget to orchestrate every element of your wedding. Invitations, menus, china and place settings, floral designs, entertainment, photographic services, and guest accommodations are just a few of the considerations. Simply looking over locations, inspecting fabric swatches, and tasting sample menus will be a pleasure. Disney's famous and meticulous attention to detail will focus on every phase of your storybook wedding. Due to the numerous wedding events each weekend, planning sessions can only be accommodated Monday through Friday.

Once you have made the decisions, you will be free to enjoy yourselves right up until the traditional preceremonial jitters. All of the work and worry, all of the organization and implementation, will have been done by your wedding event manager and a team of dedicated experts. Disney Fairy Tales Weddings is dedicated to making the reality of your wedding *exceed* your expectations.

The Particulars

You have many options when it comes to Disney Fairy Tale Weddings. The following sections cover this information. Remember, though, that prices are subject to change and can only be guaranteed six months ahead of your wedding date.

The Walt Disney World Wedding Pavilion

Built on its own special island in the Seven Seas Lagoon, this marvelous creation's only purpose is to be the perfect location for your storybook wedding. Like a Victorian summer house, the charming glass-enclosed building sets the perfect stage. Gabled roofs and sloped turrets, intricate gingerbread of carved hearts and cupids, and arched windows and panoramic vistas of the lagoon create an atmosphere that is enchanting and unforgettable.

The location, the elegant pavilion itself, and Disney's unfaltering sense of landscaping come together in an island masterpiece. Quaint yet lavish, the Wedding Pavilion is yet another success for the Disney Imagineers.

The spacious chapel is large enough to accommodate 250 guests. Attention has been focused on every detail, from the vaulted ceilings to state-of-the-art sound and video systems. Nothing has been overlooked. Behind the altar, a stained-glass window perfectly frames Cinderella Castle. Sound, lighting, and every possible camera angle have been calculated into this formula for the perfect wedding.

The Pavilion's on-site florist ensures the freshest of wedding flowers. Outside, Picture Point has been placed to provide a picturesque backdrop both for the wedding and for the bridal portraits. Picture Point's ornate trellis is set amidst a formal rose garden, overlooking the Seven Seas Lagoon and Cinderella Castle.

The Wedding Pavilion also features Franck's Wedding Salon, borrowed from the Disney film *Father of the Bride*. It is in this elegant French Provincial setting that the two of you will meet with your wedding specialist to make your plans. Besides its ideal location and captivating charm, Disney's Wedding Pavilion offers every conceivable amenity for a memorable celebration.

The fee for use of the Wedding Pavilion is $1,500 for 10 to 250 guests and includes an organist.

Beverage Options

For a four-hour, hosted open bar, expect to spend about $34 per person. For beer and wine, four hours per person costs about $22. Other options are host-sponsored per drink or cash.

Special Transportation

Whether you are arriving in Cinderella's glass coach or departing in a vintage white automobile, Disney offers an assortment of memorable transportation. A horse and carriage costs around $1,000, and the charming glass coach, complete with four horses and three costumed footmen is $2,200. The chauffeured classic car costs $350 and a Flote boat, with driver, only $85.

Entertainment

Single performers such as harpist, vocalist, or violinist are available from $275. For a duo, prices begin at $450 and for a trio of musicians, such as a jazz or calypso group, from $600. Rock bands, orchestras, and country and western bands all start around $2,000. A disc jockey is from $850. All prices are based on three-hour minimums.

Disney Character Entertainers

For one Disney character, the cost is $450. For two, $650; for three, $850. A herald trumpeter in full regalia is $300, and the Dapper Dans barbershop quartet is $875.

Theme Park Wedding Add-Ons

- Merlin the Magician and the Sorcery and the Stone show in Fantasyland: $600
- Magic Kingdom attractions: from $1,000
- Fantasy in the Sky fireworks show: $15,000

The Rehearsal Dinner

While it is not mandatory to have a rehearsal dinner, it is common. There is nothing common, however, about the possibilities of a rehearsal dinner at Walt Disney World. From a dinner in the library of the Adventurer's Club at Pleasure Island to a sumptuous meal in your own private room at the California Grill, the options are many. Have a cookout on the beach with a calypso band or a nostalgic seaside dinner at BoardWalk's "Attic." You can choose from any of the fine dining places, the clubs at Pleasure Island, or have a catered rehearsal dinner at nearly any Disney location.

A Fort Wilderness cookout with all the fixings would cost around $25 per person. Something a bit more upscale but still casual, such as a Grand Floridian Summerhouse cookout with grilled chicken and a more gourmet selection of accompaniments, would cost a bit more than $35 per person. Pull out all the stops at the California Grill for a truly sumptuous dinner, and the cost would be about $50 per person.

Other Weddings at Walt Disney World

There are a few options to a Disney Fairy Tale Wedding, but of course none of them are able to offer anything like that of Disney. Arrangements can be made for weddings at the following places: the Lake Buena Vista Resort and Spa, both the Swan and the Dolphin, Shades of Green, the Hotel Royal Plaza, and Fulton's Crab House. For more information, contact any of these facilities.

CHAPTER 9

Honeymoon Packages

Honeymooning used to mean a trip to Niagara Falls. Then a cruise to the Caribbean became the rage. Nowadays, newlyweds are in search of honeymoon adventures. Disney World combines nearly every element desired for a honeymoon: warm weather, luxurious and romantic resorts, great nightlife, and first-class dining. In a single visit, a couple can boat, swim, golf, play tennis, dance, go horseback riding, enjoy gourmet dining, and go out for a night on the town, *and* they can also enjoy the Disney attractions. It is easy to see why Walt Disney World has become the number one honeymoon destination in the world.

Newlyweds also look for all-inclusive packages. These include everything from resort accommodations and recreation to meals. With all the money paid up front, a packaged honeymoon allows the bride and groom to enjoy their time together without worrying about overspending. With an all-inclusive package, the only concern will be what to do next.

Of course, there is nothing that says you must get a package. If you are careful spenders, we know that you will be able to enjoy your Disney honeymoon with resort reservations and some planning. But you will do this at a cost, and that cost is the carefree and pampered feeling that you get from a package. Without a package, all of the possibilities remain, but you'll have to be careful. We'll give you some ideas later on getting the most out of your own honeymoon "package."

Walt Disney World Fairy Tale Honeymoon Packages

Disney offers two vacation packages for newlyweds. Each includes resort accommodations and admission to all of the Disney attractions.

The Romance Escape is the most basic. The Grand Honeymoon is an all-inclusive package, which means that it provides virtually everything from fine dining to fireworks cruises, virtually whatever you wish to do. For details or to book your Disney Fairy Tale Honeymoons, call (800) 370-6009.

The Romance Escape

Prices begin at $970 and include:

- A minimum four-night stay in your choice of Walt Disney World resorts
- Unlimited admission to all Disney attractions (includes the Magic Kingdom, Epcot, Disney–MGM Studios, the Animal Kingdom, Pleasure Island, Blizzard Beach, Typhoon Lagoon, River Country, Discovery Island, and the Wide World of Sports)
- A Romance Basket of special treats such as champagne, bath soaps, and chocolates
- Disney's "flex feature" with a choice of one (per person) of the following: admission to DisneyQuest with 30 play, a Fantasmic! Cap, golf or tennis lessons, an Animal Kingdom collector's box, Mickey 'n You Photo Session, a character breakfast, choice of Disney Tour, golf at Oak Trail executive course, or choice of T-shirts.
- Choice of 1999 Guest Choice features, one per person, from the following: dinner in a choice of select Disney restaurants, one spa treatment, 30-minute golf or tennis lesson, 30-minute theme park photo session, or admission to Cirque de Soleil.

The price of $970 is for the All-Star Resorts, which would not be our choice for a honeymoon destination. You can upgrade to any other Disney resort, but it will cost more. For example, a four-night Romance Escape at one of the moderate resorts, such as Port Orleans, is about $1,261, while a four-night Romance Escape at a deluxe resort such as the Wilderness Lodge is about $1,530.

If four nights doesn't sound like much of a honeymoon to you (it doesn't to us), then you could easily add more nights to this package. A seven-night Romance Escape at one of the moderate resorts is about $1,900.

To make the Romance Escape more "all inclusive," the Disney Dining Style Plan can be added for $110 per couple. This provides a daily food allowance of $120 in most Disney restaurants.

The Grand Honeymoon

The Grand Honeymoon ♥♥♥♥ is an exceptionally elegant package. Expensive, most certainly, but it will have you feeling like Cinderella and Prince Charming. Four-night, three-day minimums begin at around $2,700 per couple, and your every wish will be granted with:

- Three-night accommodations at your choice of deluxe Disney resorts
- Unlimited admission to all Disney attractions (includes the Magic Kingdom, Epcot, Disney–MGM Studios, the Animal Kingdom, Pleasure Island, Blizzard Beach, Typhoon Lagoon, River Country, Discovery Island, and the Wide World of Sports)
- Breakfast, lunch, and dinner each day in your choice of Disney dining locations, including Victoria and Albert's ♥♥♥♥; also includes snacks and all gratuities
- One golf or tennis lesson per person
- One 15-minute spa treatment at the Grand Floridian Spa
- Admission nightly to Atlantic Dance at the BoardWalk
- Unlimited Disney Institute day programs
- Mickey 'n You photo session
- IllumiNations fireworks cruise
- Use of health club
- Nightly turndown service
- One special in-room gift
- Use of two robes during your visit

Upgrading to a More Expensive Resort

The prices quoted for these packages are for the least expensive deluxe resort. Upgrading to a more expensive one adds to the cost. A three-night Grand Honeymoon at the Yacht or Beach Club would cost $3,089.

Adding Nights

Adding extra nights to the four-night package is easy. For seven nights of bliss and eight days of fun at the Grand Floridian, the price would be $5,934.

Upgrading Your Package to a Suite

It is also possible to upgrade any of the honeymoon packages to either a suite or to concierge service. This must be done through Central Reservations (407-939-7639).

Upgrading to a suite will be an expensive affair. Most suites begin at around $500 per night, and some cost considerably more. We recommend three honeymoon "rooms" that are relatively affordable. Two are at the Grand Floridian and enjoy concierge service: either the honeymoon room on the private Clarendon level or the Turret room, each costing about $525 nightly. The other honeymoon room is at the Wilderness Lodge and costs about $230 per night. (For more information about these rooms, see Chapter 2.) Here is an example of honeymoon package upgrades to these rooms:

- Seven-night Grand Honeymoon at the Grand Floridian, in either of the honeymoon rooms: about $6,323

The Disney Cruise Line Honeymoons

For a really special honeymoon, you might be interested in Disney's Land & Sea Odyssey package. This includes both a resort vacation at Walt Disney World and a cruise aboard the brand new *Disney Magic* cruise ship. Prices for these seven-day vacations begin around $3,300 per couple during regular season. Land & Sea Odyssey packages include:

- Round-trip airfare from select gateway cities to and from Walt Disney World, Port Canaveral, and a Central Florida Airport
- Three- or four-day accommodations at Walt Disney World
- Unlimited admission to all Disney attractions during resort stay
- Three- or four-day Disney Cruise Line cruise to the Bahamas
- Honeymoon gift amenity delivered to your stateroom (includes champagne, truffles, fresh fruit, cheese, crackers, and silk rose)
- Priority seating for two at Palo, the adult-only restaurant, during your cruise

The basic price includes a Disney stay at either Port Orleans or Dixie Landings and an inside stateroom aboard ship. Upgrading means both a more expensive resort and a fancier stateroom. Naturally, this would add to the cost of the package. A Land & Sea Odyssey at the Beach Club and in an outside cabin with veranda would cost $4,300 per couple. To make your Land & Sea Odyssey honeymoon something even more special, you could enhance the above package with one of the following packages:

The Romantic Indulgence Package

This enhancement costs about $200 extra, and added amenities include a Romance Basket delivered to your resort room, which includes champagne, bath crystals, loofah sponge, votive and candle, massage oil, and rosewood shaving kit with Crabtree and Evelyn® shaving soap in a heart-shaped basket; choice of one Disney flex feature per person (see Chapter 1); and one half-hour aromatherapy massage for two aboard ship at the Vista Spa and Salon.

The Romantic Adventure Package

This package includes the Romance Basket, the Disney World of Recreation Plan, and free snorkeling for two all day on Castaway Cay. Add about $370 for this enhancement.

Tips

- Please note that all prices above are good through August of 1999 only. Pricing for dates after this has not yet been announced.
- Prices reflect value season rates; expect to pay a little more during regular, peak, or holiday seasons.
- Remember that the rates quoted include airfare from select cities. Subtract $500 for approximate price without air.
- Booking early will provide a savings of $400 to $700 per stateroom. Magic Kingdom Club discount is approximately the same (early booking not required) but cannot be used in conjunction with the early booking savings.

Disney's Vero Beach Resort

Disney's Vero Beach Resort's Seaside Romance Package provides the perfect way to end your honeymoon. For around $265, relax for another day in a luxurious Vacation Villa overlooking the ocean. Enjoy your own whirlpool tub, breakfast at Shutter's Restaurant, and a special wedding celebration gift. Additional days may be added.

Creating Your Own Honeymoon "Package"

Not all couples can afford the Grand Plan. You can easily arrange your own honeymoon and still have a marvelous and carefree time. Here are some tips for getting the most out of your own honeymoon package:

- Make full use of all resort discounts: Magic Kingdom Club, Florida Resident Specials, Annual or Florida Resident's Seasonal Pass, AAA, or whatever you are able to get. Check out all of the sources for the best resort deal.

- Take advantage of value season. You'll save money, and you'll find Walt Disney World a more pleasant and romantic place without mobs of people.
- When you make your reservation, be sure to have them note that it is your honeymoon. Most resorts will deliver a small gift to your room. Free upgrades to nicer rooms are not unheard of, especially during value season, when those rooms may be vacant. Try asking at check-in.
- The Length of Stay Pass is a good deal and will give you the freedom to hop parks and see whatever you'd like, whenever you want to see it.
- Have your own Romance Basket ($75 plus tax) delivered right to your room. Call Walt Disney World Florists at (407) 827-3505 to make arrangements.
- Some reasonably priced and romantic rooms (prices are for value season):

  A Honeymoon room at the Wilderness Lodge, about $230 per night: ♥♥♥

  King bed with courtyard view at Port Orleans or the Caribbean Beach, about $139 per night: ♥

  One-bedroom Villa at the BoardWalk, about $315 nightly: ♥♥♥
- Concierge rooms are expensive, but they still cost less than the all-inclusive packages. They include upgraded room amenities, continental breakfasts, day-long snacking, and afternoon-to-evening wines and cordials. This is a level of pampering that you will truly appreciate. Disney World concierge services are offered at the following resorts (prices are for value season):

  The Polynesian concierge, from $345 nightly

  The Yacht Club concierge, from $395 nightly

  The Grand Floridian concierge, from $510 nightly

  The BoardWalk Inn, Innkeepers Club, from $395 nightly

OUR HONEYMOON RECOMMENDATIONS

- If you can afford the Grand Honeymoon, go for it. It will make a special and romantic experience that you will remember always. It's expensive, but remember this is your honeymoon. If you can't spoil yourselves now, when can you?
- For honeymoon package reservations, call (800) 370-6009 or the Walt Disney World Travel Company at (800) 828-0228.
- See the back of this book for our coupon for a free room upgrade on a romance package at the Swan or Dolphin resorts.

- Most of the prices we have quoted are for standard-view rooms. Since this is your honeymoon, we urge you to get the best view that you can. The truth is that standard-view rooms just don't provide the magic of looking at Cinderella Castle or even a beautiful garden. There is a time for a standard room, and there is a time for something special.
- Prices quoted here are for value season.
- Don't forget to request a king-size bed when you make your reservations.
- For honeymooners, we especially recommend these romantic resorts:
  - The Grand Floridian
  - The Yacht and the Beach Clubs
  - Port Orleans
  - The Polynesian
  - The Caribbean Beach Resort
  - The Wilderness Lodge
  - Disney's BoardWalk Inn
- Here are some of our favorite romantic resort rooms:
  - Lagoon-view rooms at the Grand Floridian or the Polynesian
  - Any concierge service room
  - One of the four honeymoon rooms at the Wilderness Lodge
  - The honeymoon Turret suite at the Grand Floridian
  - The Premier King View room at the Dolphin
  - Upper-floor Epcot-view room at the Beach Club
  - One-bedroom Villa at the BoardWalk Villas or Old Key West
  - The suite at Shades of Green
  - A Rose Garden Suite at the BoardWalk Inn
- If money is no object, the following are absolutely lavish suites:
  - The Yellowstone, Wilderness Lodge
  - The Commodore, the Yacht Club
  - Garden King suite, Bali Hai, the Polynesian
  - The Steeplechase at the BoardWalk

APPENDIX A 

Romantic Adventures

Here are a few romantic things that you'll find waiting for you at Walt Disney World, although we're sure you won't have much trouble coming up with some of your own ideas.

- A private IllumiNations cruise for two on *Breathless,* the Yacht Club's vintage 1934 speedboat: ♥♥♥♥
- High tea at the Garden View Lounge of the Grand Floridian: ♥♥
- A Grand Marnier flight at BoardWalk's BelleVue Room: ♥♥
- A picnic lunch from a favorite restaurant on Discovery Island after a relaxing morning: ♥♥
- His and hers in-room massages: ♥♥♥
- The free Sassagoula River launch up to Port Orleans and dinner at Bonfamille's Cafe: ♥♥
- An evening on the BoardWalk Promenade: ♥♥
- A special and unforgettable dinner at Victoria and Albert's: ♥♥♥♥
- Quiet, romantic moments for just the two of you: ♥♥♥
- Tree of Life Garden at the Animal Kingdom at dusk: ♥♥
- Fantasy in the Sky or the Electric Water Pageant from the beach swings at the Polynesian resort: ♥♥♥♥
- Breakfast in bed: ♥♥♥♥
- Private dining in your room or on your balcony: ♥♥♥
- A romantic cruise on the *Disney Magic*: ♥♥♥♥
- A torchlit stroll on the Polynesian grounds: ♥♥
- The last safari of the day at the Animal Kingdom: ♥
- A sketch of yourselves at Epcot's France: ♥♥
- The view from the fifteenth-floor observation deck at the Contemporary, or a nightcap at the California Grill Bar: ♥♥
- Send someone you love a rose—Disney Florist, (407) 827-3505: ♥♥♥
- A massage at Serenity Cove on the Cruise Line's Castaway Cay: ♥♥♥

- An evening stroll along Coronado Springs' lakeside esplanade: ♥♥
- A light dinner at the Pleasure Island Jazz Club while you enjoy the music: ♥♥
- One of the Magic Kingdom fireworks cruises from the Grand Floridian, the Polynesian, or the Contemporary: ♥♥♥
- Dinner on the upstairs patio at Bongos Cuban Cafe: ♥♥
- Drinks and hors d'oeuvres during IllumiNations at Japan's Matsu No Ma Lounge at Epcot: ♥♥♥
- A late-night hot tub: ♥♥♥
- Sushi at the California Grill lounge at night overlooking the Magic Kingdom: ♥♥♥
- Sinatra Night (Sundays) at Atlantic Dance on the Board-Walk: ♥♥♥
- Stroll the beach behind the Contemporary's north Garden Wing at night and watch the Electric Water Pageant: ♥♥♥♥
- Massages for two in the Grand Floridian Spa Couple's Room: ♥♥
- Moonlight stroll on the Seven Seas Lagoon's Walk Around the World: ♥♥
- IllumiNations from the second floor outside balcony at Atlantic Dance: ♥♥
- A Grand Plan vacation: ♥♥♥♥
- Late night at Hemingway Cove at the Grand Floridian: ♥♥♥
- A hammock-for-two under the stars at Caribbean Beach or the Swan: ♥♥♥
- A romantic vacation in the Grand Floridian's Turret Honeymoon Suite: ♥♥♥♥
- Wine tasting at the California Grill lounge, Fridays 6 P.M.: ♥
- Rent a surrey for two at the BoardWalk and ride around the lake: ♥♥♥
- A hot tub after your evening out: ♥♥♥

APPENDIX B

The Disney Phone Directory

Automotive Service

Disney Car Care Center: (407) 824-0976

Barber and Beauty Shops

Casa de Belleza, Coronado Springs: (407) 939-3965

Contemporary Hair Styling Salon: (407) 824-3411

Ivy Trellis Barber and Beauty Shop, the Grand Floridian: (407) 824-3000, ext. 2581

Niki Bryan Hair Salon, the Dolphin: (407) 934-4250

Periwigs Hair Salon, the Yacht and the Beach Clubs: (407) 934-3260

Birthday Parties

Cub's Den, the Wilderness Lodge: (407) 824-1083

Lil' Toots Harbor Club, the BoardWalk: (407) 939-6301

Theme park: (407) 934-6411

Child Care

Cub's Den, the Wilderness Lodge: (407) 824-1083

Harbor Club, the BoardWalk: (407) 939-6301

KinderCare: (407) 827-5444

Mouseketeer Clubhouse, the Contemporary: (407) 824-1000 ext. 3038

Mouseketeer Clubhouse, the Grand Floridian: (407) 824-1666

Neverland Club, the Polynesian: (407) 824-2000 ext. 2170

Sandcastle Club, the Yacht and the Beach Clubs: (407) 934-3750

Dining

Disney Dinning Experience: (407) 828-5792

Reservations, Buena Vista Palace, Arthur's 27: (407) 827-3450

Reservations, the Dolphin restaurants: (407) 934-4025

Reservations, the Swan restaurants: (407) 934-3000 ext. 2181

Reservations, theme park and Disney resort restaurants (includes Victoria and Albert's regular dining room), dinner shows, and special-request meals: (407) WDW-DINE (939-3463)

Victoria and Albert's "Chef's Table" reservations: (407) 939-7707

Florist

Walt Disney World Florist: (407) 827-3505

Foreign Language Services

Foreign Language Center: (407) 824-7900

Health Clubs

Body by Jake, the Dolphin: (407) 934-4264
Buena Vista Palace Fitness Center: (407) 827-3222
Grand Floridian Spa and Health Club: (407) 824-2332
The Health and Fitness Center at the Disney Institute: (407) 827-4455
La Vida Health Club, the Coronado: (407) 939-3030
Muscles and Bustles, the BoardWalk: (407) 939-2370
Olympiad Health Club, the Contemporary: (407) 824-3410
Ship Shape Health Club, the Yacht and the Beach Clubs: (407) 934-3256
Swan Health Club: (407) 934-1360

Information

Disney's Walk Around the World: (407) 272-6201
General WDW Information: (407) 824-4321
Guided Tour Information: (407) WDW-TOUR (939-8687)
Hearing-Impaired Guest Information: (407) 827-5141
Magic Kingdom Club: (407) 824-2600
Magic Kingdom Club Gold Card: (800) 466-5365

Kennels

Fort Wilderness Kennel and general kennel information: (407) 824-2735

Lost and Found

Same day: Magic Kingdom: (407) 824-4521
Epcot: (407) 560-6105
MGM: (407) 560-4668
Animal Kingdom: (407) 938-2265
Central Lost and Found, TTC: (407) 824-4245

Medical Facilities

Buena Vista Medical Center Pharmacy: (407) 828-8125 (free delivery for WDW resort guests)
Buena Vista Walk-in Medical Center: (407) 828-3434
First Aid and Emergency Dental Referral: (407) 648-9234 or 846-2093
Gooding's Pharmacy: (407) 827-1207
HouseMed/Mediclinic: (407) 396-1195
Sand Lake Hospital: (407) 351-8500

Recreation

Disney Speedway Events: (800) 822-4639
Disney's Wide World of Sports: (407) 363-6600
Fishing excursions: (407) WDW-PLAY (939-7529)
Fishing, Lake Buena Vista, Downtown Disney Marketplace: (407) 828-2204

Golf, advance tee times: (407) 939-4653
Horseback riding: WDW-PLAY (939-7529)
Richard Petty Driving Experience: (800) 237-3889
Tennis reservations, the Contemporary, Grand Floridian, Institute: (407) WDW-PLAY (939-7529)
Trail ride, Fort Wilderness: (407) WDW-PLAY (939-7529)
Waterskiing: (407) WDW-PLAY (939-7529)

Resort Reservations

Buena Vista Palace Resort and Spa: (800) 327-2990
Central Reservations Office (CRO): (407) W-DISNEY (934-7639)
Courtyard by Marriot: (800) 223-9930
Disney Cruise Line: (800) 511-1333
Disney Institute: (800) 4-WONDER (496-6337)
DoubleTree Guest Suites: (800) 222-TREE (222-8733)
The Grosvenor: (800) 624-4109
The Hilton: (800) 782-4414
Hotel Royal Plaza: (800) 248-7890
Magic Kingdom Club: (407) 824-2600
Shades of Green: (407) 824-3600
Travelodge Hotel: (800) 348-3765
WDW Travel Company: (800) 828-0228

Resort Reservations, Hotel Plaza

Buena Vista Palace Resort and Spa: (800) 327-2990
Courtyard by Marriot: (800) 223-9930
DoubleTree Guest Suites: (800) 222-TREE (8733)
The Grosvenor: (800) 624-4109
The Hilton: (800) 782-4414
Hotel Royal Plaza: (800) 248-7890
Travelodge Hotel: (800) 348-3765

Spas

Buena Vista Palace Spa: (800) 981-1472
Grand Floridian Spa: (407) 824-2332
Spa at the Disney Institute: (407) 827-4455

Theaters and Clubs

AMC, Pleasure Island: (407) 298-4488
House of Blues concert tickets: (407) 934-BLUE (2583)
Wildhorse Saloon events: (407) 827-WILD (9453)

Transportation

Florida Town Cars: (800) 525-7246, (407) 277-5466
Mears: (800) 759-5219, (407) 423-5566
Taxi services at WDW: (407) 824-3360

Travel Services

AAA Disney Travel Center in Orlando: (407) 854-0770

American Express Office, Epcot: (407) 827-7500
Delta Travel, Delta Airlines Orlando: (800) 221-1212, (407) 849-6400

Weddings

Disney Fairy Tale Weddings: (407) 828-3400
Romance Photos: (407) 827-5029

Index

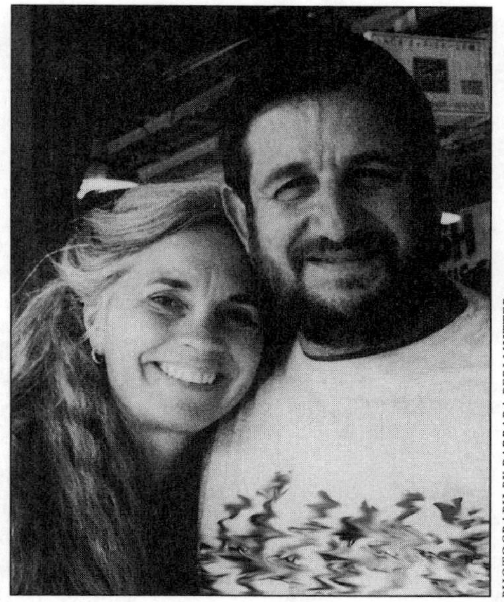

PHOTOGRAPH BY BARBARA PERLMUTTER

The Perlmutters arrived at travel writing via a number of other careers. Both have educational backgrounds in writing, Gayle in English and Rick in journalism, and both have worked as registered nurses, Gayle in neonatal ICU and Rick in the operating room. Rick has also been a chef, pastry chef, and baker, and has taught gourmet cooking at a Florida community college (very helpful experience when it comes to restaurant reviews).

Walt Disney World for Couples is the product of the authors' love of travel and adventure, as well as their continuing quest for great Florida romantic getaways. Having lived for over 20 years aboard their sailboat, *Big Otter,* the Perlmutters have traveled extensively in the U.S. and abroad. Other interests include boating, diving, biking, cooking, and wines. The Perlmutters retreat regularly to their lakeside camp in Maine to enjoy hiking, exploring, and "life as it ought to be."

The authors have three grown children. Brian owns and operates a chimney sweep business, and Jennifer is a registered nurse. Both live in North Carolina. Tyra lives in California and does costume work in the movies. The Perlmutters particularly enjoy taking their three grandchildren, Guin, Ben, and Noah to Walt Disney World.

in the WALT DISNEY WORLD® Resort

Stay five nights at the award-winning *Buena Vista Palace Resort & Spa* in the Walt Disney World Resort at Downtown Disney at the published rate, and receive the sixth night **FREE!**

Offer valid with six-night consecutive stay only. Not valid with any other discounts, offers, or special hotel promotions. Offer is subject to availability. We suggest you make your reservations at least 30 days in advance by calling 1 (800) 327-2990, (407) 827-2727, or visit the resort's web site at www.bvp-resort.com. Please inform the reservationist of this special offer at the time of booking, and present this coupon upon check-in at the resort.

DISNEY INSTITUTE

Present this coupon for a
FREE Length-of-Stay Admission for two (2) at the Disney Institute Sports and Fitness Center with the purchase of a 50-minute Disney Institute Spa treatment.

Guests must be staying at a Walt Disney World resort.
Must be 16 years of age or older.
Must present a valid Walt Disney World Resort ID card.
Coupon valid through October 1999.

Present this coupon for a 10% DISCOUNT on a *Breathless* Burst, A 10-minute spin aboard a vintage 1934 speedboat!

Coupon good through September 1999

ENJOY A COMPLIMENTARY ROOM UPGRADE

Turn your romantic getaway into a honeymoon you'll treasure.

The WALT DISNEY WORLD SWAN and DOLPHIN

"Remember the Romance" all-inclusive honeymoon package *includes:* **Walt Disney World®** tickets, full breakfast each day, dinner one night in any of the resort's 17 restaurants and lounges, champagne and keepsake flutes, gourmet chocolates, souvenir basket and tablecloth and more!

Packages available from 4–6 nights.

Just call **1-800-227-1500** and ask for the ***Walt Disney World for Couples*** offer through 4/30/99
Subject to rate plan availability
www.swandolphin.com

Offer valid only with purchase of "Remember the Romance" Package

Join **HOUSE OF BLUES** for lakefront dining under the stars in the *Voodoo Garden.*

FREE APPETIZER
(with the purchase of an appetizer)

(407) 934-BLUE

Please present coupon to your server prior to ordering.
Valid from 5 PM to 2 AM any evening. One coupon per party. Expires 12/30/98
(In the event of inclement weather, coupon will be honored inside the main restaurant. House of Blues restaurant periodically closes for special events—please call ahead to ensure dining availability.)

Come and experience a one-of-a-kind waterfront night spot at

ATLANTIC DANCE

20% OFF YOUR ENTIRE CHECK!

when you present your *Walt Disney World for Couples* Special Coupon

NARCOOSSEE'S

ENJOY a *free* **APPETIZER SAMPLER** or *two free glasses* of **SPARKLING WINE** when you order 2 entrees at NARCOOSSEE'S at *Disney's Grand Floridian Resort and Spa*

Coupon must be presented to server